EAST ASIA

HISTORY, POLITICS, SOCIOLOGY, CULTURE

Edited by
Edward Beauchamp
UNIVERSITY OF HAWAII

A ROUTLEDGE SERIES

EAST ASIA
HISTORY, POLITICS, SOCIOLOGY, CULTURE
EDWARD BEAUCHAMP, *General Editor*

AN AMERICAN EDITOR IN EARLY REVOLUTIONARY CHINA

John William Powell and the
China Weekly/Monthly Review

Neil L. O'Brien

ROUTLEDGE
NEW YORK & LONDON

Published in 2003 by
Routledge
29 West 35th Street
New York, NY 10001
www.routledge-ny.com

Published in Great Britain by
Routledge
11 New Fetter Lane
London EC4P 4EE
www.routledge.co.uk

Routledge is an imprint of the Taylor & Francis Group.
Copyright © 2003 by Taylor & Francis Books, Inc.

10 9 8 7 6 5 4 3 2 1

Library of Congress Cataloging-in-Publication Data

O'Brien, Neil, L.
    An American editor in early revolutionary China : John William Powell and the China weekly/monthly review / by Neil L. O'Brien.
        p. cm.
    Includes bibliographical references (p.).
    ISBN 0-415-94424-4
        1. United States—Foreign relations—China—Press coverage. 2. China—Foreign relations—United States—Press coverage. 3. United States—Foreign relations—1945–1953—Press coverage. 4. China—History—Civil War, 1945–1949—Press coverage. 5. Powell, John William. 6. Newspaper editors—United Staes—Biography. 7. Newspaper editors—China—Shanghai—Biography. 8. China weekly review. 9. China monthly review. I. Title.

E183.8.C502/2003
327.73051'09'044–dc21

                                                2002038173

Printed on acid-free, 250 year-life paper
Manufactured in the United States of America

Dedication

Kevin T. O'Brien, Leonard H. O'Brien,

Hasegawa Tamio,

J.V. Soucy and Bridget Soucy

CONTENTS

Acknowledgements

I wish to thank my committee chair, Dr. Thomas L. Kennedy for his patience and perseverance. Without his guidance and support this project would certainly never have been finished. I would also like to thank the members of my committee, Dr. Noriko Kawamura and Dr. Richard L. Hume, who along with Dr. Kennedy, put in many hours reading and suggesting improvements to the text. I owe you all a debt of gratitude and will never forget your assistance. As for my wife, Yoko, and my three sons, Joseph, Kevin, and Daniel, I thank them for being there, and for their endurance.

PREFACE

This is a study of the editorial policy of the *China Weekly Review* / *China Monthly Review*, published in Shanghai by John William Powell during the Chinese Civil War and the Korean War. It is based principally on primary materials from that journal. The *Review* supported U.S. attempts to avert Civil War in early 1946 through creation of a coalition government. By 1947, it reflected increasing disillusionment with Guomindang policies, and growing sympathy for the demands of impoverished students and faculty for multi-party democracy and peace. The *Review* publicized Nationalist repression of the student peace movement, and of the 1947 Taiwan Revolt.

As the Civil War shifted in favor of the Chinese Communists in late 1948, Powell and the *Review* counselled U.S. businessmen to remain in Shanghai and urged the U.S. government to establish working relations with the Communists, and later, to recognize the new regime. Staying in Shanghai to report changes engendered by the Revolution, the *Review*'s staff accommodated themselves to the new orthodoxy, and to the regime's coordination of the press.

During the Korean War, the *Review* opposed the expanding U.S. air war, becoming the foremost American purveyor of Chinese and North Korean allegations of American use of bacteriological weapons. The *Review* was also utilized by the Chinese People's Volunteers for political indoctrination of U.S. prisoners of war.

After closing the *Review* for financial reasons in July, 1953, and returning to the United States, Powell, his wife Sylvia Campbell, and assistant editor Julian Schuman, were put on trial for sedition. As the government narrowed its focus to the bacteriological warfare issue, Powell and his lawyers countered by trying to prove the veracity of the charges, and seeking witnesses in China and North Korea. Adverse publicity led to a mistrial in January, 1959. Limitations in both the sedition, and treason statutes ended plans to renew prosecution.

Powell and the *Review* had insisted that positive diplomatic and economic relations between China and the United States were both possible, and desirable. Dramatic events since the 1970's, the normalization of relations, and of trade and investment, seem to validate this belief.

Neil L. O'Brien, Ph.D.
Washington State University
May 2001

JOHN WILLIAM POWELL AND THE *CHINA WEEKLY/MONTHLY REVIEW*, AN AMERICAN EDITOR IN EARLY REVOLUTIONARY CHINA

John William Powell was the editor of the *China Weekly Review*, an English language journal published in Shanghai from December 1945 to July 1953. When Powell came to China as a journalist for the U.S. Office of War Information (OWI) in 1943, his views were not unlike those of other American correspondents in wartime Chongqing. As the Nationalist government and the ruling Guomindang (GMD) Party began to falter during the Chinese Civil War of 1945–1949, Powell's *China Weekly Review* became more critical of the corruption and ineptitude of the Guomindang and more insistent on the importance of reform.

The *Review* wanted an American foreign policy which welcomed the emergence of new democratic nations in South and Southeast Asia and rejected recolonization. After the defeat of Nationalist forces in 1949, Sino-American relations entered a state of limbo. The United States had clearly identified itself with the Nationalist cause and was having difficulty breaking the connection largely because of the influence of the pro-GMD "China Lobby" and the developing anti-communist crusade at home.

Some journalists, State Department officials, and Foreign Service personnel believed it was in the national interest of the United States to continue Sino-American relations on the basis of mutual benefit and recognition of the new Chinese Communist government. John W. Powell was one of these. During the period before the Communist takeover, he urged American businessmen to remain in Shanghai and searched for ways to ease the transition from GMD to Chinese Communist Party (CCP) rule.

Determined to make whatever accommodations were necessary, Powell stayed after China fell to the Communists and continued publishing his journal until financial difficulties forced it to close in 1953. During this period, the *Review*'s main thrust became explaining the changes occurring as a result of the Revolution with an eye toward eventual American recognition of the Communist Regime and trade with mainland China.

Powell's criticism of U.S. policy became strident after the Korean War broke out. Allegations of bacteriological warfare made by China and North Korea echoed through the pages of his journal, which in the course of reporting news from Chinese sources became perhaps the most persistent American-owned expositor of germ warfare charges. His journal was used, along with other English language materials, by the Chinese military in Korea for the forced political reeducation of American prisoners of war.

Having publicized germ warfare allegations and other charges against the U.S. during the war, and his journal having been used to indoctrinate U.S. POW's, Powell was called before the Senate Judiciary Sub-Committee on Interlocking Subversion in Government upon his return to the United States. He was subsequently charged with sedition and brought to trial.

This study will seek to explain Powell's editorial stewardship of the *China Weekly/Monthly Review* and the major issues in which the Review became involved. How did a promising journalism student from the American Mid-West with views much like those of his peers, and values well within the American mainstream, wind-up on trial for sedition?

*

BACKGROUND INFORMATION ON JOHN W. POWELL

John William Powell was born in Shanghai, China, July 3, 1919 to Martha Hinton Powell and John Benjamin Powell. His father was a graduate of the University of Missouri School of Journalism who would win renown as the chief editor and eventually the owner of Thomas Franklin Fairfax Millard's *Review of the Far East*. John Benjamin Powell and Millard used Herbert Croly's and Walter Lippman's *New Republic* and Oswald Garrison Villard's *The Nation* as models for their publication, which had a forward-looking orientation and soon became a strong supporter of Sun Yatsen and the Nationalist cause in China. In 1922, J. B. Powell bought out Millard's share of the publication, and changed the name first to *The Weekly Review of the Far East*, and the following year to *The China Weekly Review*.

In 1920, J. B. Powell sent his son back to the United States to live with his wife's family in Hannibal, Missouri. Here the younger Powell attended grammar school from 1926 to 1934, except for a year spent with his parents in 1927 attending the American School in Shanghai. John William graduated from Hickman High School in Columbia, Missouri. During the sixth year (1938) of Franklin Roosevelt's New Deal, he entered the University of Missouri, where he divided his course work almost evenly between Journalism, which was his major, and History (22 hours in Journalism and 27 Hours in History).

In 1937, full scale war broke out between China and Japan, which had been expanding its control over Manchuria and Northeast China since 1931. Taking a year off from his studies in 1940, the younger Powell journeyed to Shanghai, where he joined his surprised father. According to Randall Gould, managing editor of the *Shanghai Evening Post and Mercury*, the younger Powell arrived unannounced and much to his father's chagrin. Nevertheless, the elder Powell put his son to work under Wu Giadang (Woo Kya-tang), managing editor of the pro-Guomindang *China Press*. Wu, also a graduate of the University of Missouri School of Journalism and a close friend of J. B. Powell, entrusted the younger Powell with general reporting, rewriting articles by the Chinese staff, copyreading and proofreading from October, 1940 to July, 1941. In the evenings, John William worked on his father's *China Weekly Review*, composing stories out of news service and press bulletins. By late summer, Japanese forces had gained control of most of the important ocean and river port cities of Eastern China.

According to J. B. Powell, his son left China on one of the last American ships which the Japanese allowed out of Shanghai in 1941, along with Randall Gould, editor of the *Shanghai Evening Post and Mercury*, and a number of other foreign newspapermen. The younger Powell never forgot his father's heroic decision to stay on in Shanghai to report the Japanese occupation of the city, and to try and protect his Chinese employees.[1]

The elder Powell, a longtime foe of Japanese aggression and staunch supporter of Chiang Kai-shek, was arrested and imprisoned by the Japanese, who sealed the *China Weekly Review* offices along with those of the *China Press*, on December 8, 1941. Malnourished, mistreated, and suffering from beriberi, J. B. Powell's feet became infected and finally gangrenous. Parts of them had to be removed. After State Department intervention, the elder Powell, weak and in constant pain, was repatriated as part of a prisoner exchange in 1943. On arriving in New York harbor, he was met aboard ship by his son, John William.[2]

In the United States, J. B. Powell endured numerous operations to try and repair the damage to his feet, but would never fully recover. Not well enough to return to Shanghai and resume control of the *Review*, the elder Powell testified at the Tokyo War Crimes Tribunal in 1946, fell ill, and returned to the United States for further treatment. In spite of failing health, he campaigned vigorously for a strong American presence in the Pacific, and supported the Nationalist cause against the Chinese Communists. He died after delivering a speech to the University of Missouri Alumni Association in early March, 1947.[3]

The younger Powell, back in the United States by September, 1941, resumed his studies at the University of Missouri through April, 1942, working as a student assistant for the dean of the Journalism School, grading term papers and exams.[4] After America's entry into World War II, as the early Japanese juggernaut swept on to victory after victory, Powell, who had failed his induction physical, sought to play a part in the war effort through government journalism. He began working in the Foreign Broadcast Monitoring Service of the Federal Communications Commission in Washington D.C. in April, 1942.

After seven months in Washington, Powell applied for a transfer to the Office of War Information (OWI) hoping to get overseas field work in China. His transfer accepted, he spent a short apprenticeship in New York learning to select, process and cable news items from the wire services and various Washington and New York papers to China. Soon afterward he was sent to the Office of War Information Overseas Operations Branch which stationed him in Chongqing, Guilin, and Kunming respectively, as a field representative (news editor), sending out stories he received from the New York office to numerous Chinese newspapers. In the wartime capital Chongqing, Powell and other correspondents with OWI studied rudimentary Chinese[5], experienced repeated Japanese bombing, and witnessed the gradual worsening of conditions in Nationalist China due to inflation, corruption, and malfeasance by governing officials.

Among the significant persons Powell met at this time was Liu Zunqi (Liu Tsun Ch'i), who was head of OWI Chinese staff. According to Powell, Liu, who had been a member of the Chinese Communist Party since the 1930's, worked for OWI until the war's end, studied in the U.S. on a scholarship, and returned to China to work for the United States Information Service. After the Communist takeover of China, Liu became an important information official in the new government and an advocate of journalistic reform.[6]

In 1982, Powell used the story of Liu Zunqi and his American counterpart in OWI, McCracken Fisher, to restate essentially the "lost chance" hypothesis: the notion that America had an opportunity to improve relations with Communist China during the late 1940's, but let it slip away. In the mid 1950's, Fisher had been the subject of an anti-communist inquisition, while Liu Zunqi in China had been labeled disloyal, a "rightist", and consigned to twenty years in labor camps, first after the "Hundred Flowers" campaign of 1956, and again during the Great Proletarian Cultural Revolution. According to Powell:

> The tragedy goes beyond the ruined careers of Mac Fisher, an American who understood China, and Liu Tsun Ch'i, a Chinese who understood America.
>
> If irrationality had not prevailed, they, and many others like them on both sides, might have succeeded in lessening the hostility between China and America and the estrangement would not have lasted for twenty-five years. If this had been the case, we might have avoided two costly and futile wars on the Asian Mainland.[7]

In many ways, Powell was summarizing the purpose and intent of his own stay in China, from 1943 to 1953.

As World War II drew towards its conclusion in China, Powell was transferred to the Psychological Warfare Section where he did liaison work, involving the dropping of propaganda leaflets, with General Claire Chennault's Fourteenth Air Force. After the war ended, Powell remained with OWI until December 1, 1945, receiving regular promotions and good service evaluations. When he left the Office of War Information, it was to resume publication of his father's *China Weekly Review*, defunct since December 6, 1941.

*

THE "LOST CHANCE" LITERATURE

Powell and the *China Weekly Review* were staunch advocates of better Sino-American relations. The *Review* supported both the Marshall mission and the Political Consultative Conference Agreements it produced, and hoped in 1949 that the talks between Huang Hua, CCP Foreign Resident Affairs Office Director for Nanjing, and U.S. Ambassador John Leighton Stuart would result in normalized relations and trade between China and the United States. In a sense, Powell tried to help push America's "lost chances" into some kind of positive development. Consequently, a brief consideration of recent scholarship on the "lost chance" theme is appropriate.

In 1944–1945, the United States, faced with the possibility of landing U.S. troops in China to fight the Japanese, was interested in exploring possible cooperation with Chinese Communist forces. Toward this end, the United States sent the U.S. Army Observation Group, or "Dixie Mission" to the Communist capital of Yan'an. The mission proceeded in spite of the opposition of Chiang Kai-shek, who had tried to block it.

American military personnel found the Communists eager to cooperate and desirous of establishing further contact with the U.S. government. Impressed by the competence and vigor of Communist forces and administration, in contrast to the ineptitude, corruption and lassitude of Nationalist military forces and administration, mission members warned Washington that China's future would likely belong to the CCP rather than the GMD.

The U.S. Joint Chiefs of Staff, by the summer of 1944, determined to stop the deteriorating military situation in China by bringing all Chinese forces and resources to bear against the Japanese, including Nationalist divisions blockading Communist base areas. President Roosevelt asked Chiang Kai-shek to allow General Joseph Stilwell to assume a unified command of all Chinese troops, both Nationalist and Communist. Roosevelt sent General Patrick Hurley to negotiate Chinese political as well as military unification.[8] Hurley signed a five point agreement with Communist leaders in Yan'an for their participation in a coalition government and the CCP's legalization. But when Chiang Kai-shek refused to accept its provisions, Hurley reneged on the agreement in favor of exclusive, unconditional support of Chiang and the Nationalist government,

During this period Mao Zedong and Zhou Enlai expressed a desire to visit Washington D.C. to personally present their case to President Roosevelt. Although the successful testing of the atomic bomb and the Soviet Union's promise to enter the war in Manchuria precluded further American interest in working with the CCP, this period of contact has come to be seen as the first of three possible "lost chances" for improved relations between the United States government and the Chinese Communist Party.

The second "lost chance" revolved around the Marshall Mission of 1945–1946 to avoid all-out civil war between the GMD and CCP through creation of a coalition government that would include both the Communists and the Nationalists. This would require Chiang Kai-shek to give up his one-party dictatorship and embrace a multi-party democratization of the Chinese government. It would also have required the CCP to amalgamate its forces into the Nationalist army, and to open political participation in local Communist base area governments to other political parties.

Under General Marshall's guidance, a Political Consultative Conference of all parties was held between December, 1945 and January, 1946. It resulted in agreements on all major points of contention. Believing that he had prevented civil war and set in motion agreements which would lead to a multi-party coalition government and a unified China, Marshall returned to the United States only to see the agreements abrogated and full-scale civil war raging by mid-summer, 1946.[9] Although historians have generally been cynical about Marshall's efforts, recent documentary evidence seems to indicate that the CCP was in earnest.[10]

The third and final "lost chance" involved talks between U.S. ambassador John Leighton Stuart and Communist foreign affairs representative Huang Hua during the spring and summer of 1949. By that time the GMD had been defeated and Communist victory throughout China was assured. While establishing closer ties with Stalin and the Soviet Union, the Chinese Communist leadership needed to resume trade in newly conquered port cities as soon as possible to relieve economic distress in these centers. They believed that Britain and the United States would soon cut their ties to the losing party (the GMD) and were desirous of establishing trade and normalized relations with the new government of China.

The high point of the Huang-Stuart talks was an invitation to Stuart to visit Beijing for talks with Mao Zedong and Zhou Enlai, which the American government rejected out of hand. Up to that point the policies of both governments appeared ambiguous and uncertain. Both were trying to decipher the intentions of the other; both were under considerable pressure not to come to terms, in spite of the advantages it might offer to both nations. Ultimately, pressure from the Soviet Union in China's case, and political pressure from domestic anti-communist ferment in the case of the United

States, precluded positive conclusion of the talks and determined the hostile paths which both nations would pursue.

In 1971, John S. Service, who had been in Yan'an as part of the "Dixie Mission" of 1944–45 and was later singled out for attack by anticommunist Congressmen for his views on the CCP and GMD, published a selective account of the first "lost chance" in his book, *The Amerasia Papers: Some Problems in the History of US-China Relations*. While this was primarily a defense against the charges of disloyalty which Hurley leveled at his Foreign Service advisors after the failure of mediation efforts, Service also made a well-documented case that Mao Zedong and the Communist leaders in 1944 desired American aid and good will both during the war and afterward to help with China's reconstruction. In the book, Service produced written records of several long conversations with Mao Zedong which unequivocally supported his assertions.

A few years latter, Joseph Esherick augmented the same theme by publishing the wartime dispatches of John Service: *Lost Chance in China: The World War II Despatches of John S. Service*.[11] While acknowledging that a victorious CCP would establish close ties with the Soviet Union, Service said that Mao expected independence and freedom of action in regard to Moscow, not a satellite relationship. He believed Mao wanted to avoid an "isolated" reliance on the USSR through access to American aid. According to Service, Mao hoped to avoid civil war through CCP participation in a coalition government, but it would have to recognize CCP local governments in areas already under Communist control and would have to allow the CCP to continue control over its own military forces. Recognizing the weakness of such a coalition, Service nevertheless concluded that two Chinas not at war would be better than a civil war with the U.S. committed to the losing side.[12]

As early as 1946, John King Fairbank, a future Harvard University professor,[13] and former director of the Office of War Information and then the United States Information Service in China, wrote an article for the *Atlantic Monthly* which pursued a similar theme. He decried the American tendency to profess liberal beliefs while upholding a government in China (the Nationalists) which had become thoroughly totalitarian. Fairbank warned that no amount of American military aid could arrest the Guomindang's decline. He feared that blind opposition to the Revolution would result in the United States being "eventually expelled from Asia by a mass movement." To avoid this, he advocated "developing and maintaining contact with Communist China as fully as with the rest of China".[14] These views were later incorporated into one of Fairbank's many books, *China Perceived, Images and Policies in Chinese-American Relations* in 1971, just about the time the "lost chance" school was taking shape.

In 1980, Dorothy Borg and Waldo Heinrichs edited the first important volume of essays by prominent Asian scholars on the "lost chance" theme, *Uncertain Years: Chinese-American Relations, 1947–1950*.[15] This volume contained several landmark essays. In one of them, Steven Levine noted Mao Zedong's mistrust of Stalin and verified that Chinese Communist leaders initially hoped for diplomatic contact and trade with the United States as well as with the Soviet Union. However, the Cold War and increasing American animosity pushed the CCP into a close alliance with the USSR.[16] In another essay, Warren I. Cohen found that Secretary of State Dean Acheson was aware the Nationalist government was losing the civil war, and was moving toward accommodation with the Communist regime to avoid pushing China completely into the Soviet camp.[17] Another contributor, Michael Hunt portrayed Mao Zedong as able to transcend ideology in the interests of pragmatic concerns, and argued that the degree to which China would "lean" toward the Soviet Union depended on the American response.[18] Steven Goldstein, on the other hand, felt that ideological considerations were paramount and rendered any real accommodation with the United States impossible.[19]

In 1983, Nancy Bernkopf Tucker's detailed study of Sino-American diplomatic relations from the American side was published: *Patterns in the Dust, Chinese-American Relations and the Recognition Controversy, 1949–1950.* Tucker especially focused on 1949, when the prospect of Communist takeover was imminent and the period of early Communist rule before the outbreak of the Korean War. She found American businessmen and missionaries intent on remaining in China in the belief that the Chinese Communists had moderated their socialist goals, and wanted them to stay. This dissertation agrees with Tucker's perception of the interim period.

In spite of what Tucker saw as State Department efforts to gradually disengage with the Guomindang and seek closer relations with the new Communist government, efforts by a small partisan group in Congress, the "China Bloc", in alliance with other GOP opposition groups, effectively blocked this course. Government attempts to utilize China scholars as useful allies were lost on the mass of American voters who were largely ignorant on the subject of China. Ultimately, the outbreak of the Korean War ended any lingering prospect for normalized Sino-American relations.[20]

In 1989, thanks to improved Sino-American relations, a joint conference of American and Chinese scholars led to the publication of essays reassessing the "lost chance" hypothesis from both the American and Chinese Communist points of view: *Sino-American Relations, 1945–1955, A Joint Reassessment of a Critical Decade.* Intended as more than just a scholarly exercise, these pre-Tiananmen joint efforts aimed at avoiding further impediments to healthy Sino-American relations by developing a better understanding of the elements leading to the failure of U.S.-China policy in the late 1940's. Especially enlightening were the essays by scholars from the People's Republic.

He Di, of the Institute of American Studies of the Chinese Academy of Social Sciences, traced the entire "lost chance" series of sequences, from the "Dixie Mission, the recall of Stilwell and Hurley's mediation in 1944–45, through the Marshall Mission of 1945–47, and the talks between John Leighton Stuart and Huang Hua in 1949. In He's view, the United States really did have a chance to develop better relations with the CCP, but "U.S. decision makers did not fully understand the political reality of Chinese society and treated their relations with the CCP merely as an expediency."

According to He, Mao was furious in December 1944 when General Patrick Hurley disregarded the Five Point Draft Agreement he had signed with the CCP, in favor of collaborating with the GMD right wing in their efforts to induce the CCP to give up its military forces and abandon its base areas. Yet Mao informed Hurley that the CCP had no intentions of breaking relations with the U.S. and apart from basic principles, everything was negotiable. He Di noted that CCP leaders sent a letter to Washington stating their wish for continued cooperation with the U.S. and indicating that if necessary, Mao Zedong and Zhou Enlai would personally go to the White House to meet with President Roosevelt.

When Hurley announced that the administration would exclusively uphold the government of Chiang Kai-shek and would not support any "warlords" or "armed political parties", the CCP decided that reactionaries had gotten the upper hand in Washington. In He's view, Hurley's actions increased the likelihood of civil war by reinforcing Chiang's determination to fight. Opposition to Hurley in the State Department led to his resignation in November, 1945.

After President Truman issued a statement calling for a peaceful settlement between the GMD and CCP, and sent General George C. Marshall to mediate, the CCP again decided to cooperate since American policy seemed to benefit the CCP's own struggle for peace and its version of "democracy". In He's judgement, the fact that Stalin approved of the Marshall Mission and that Marshall demonstrated fairness in deciding a number of early issues confirmed the Party's confidence in his efforts.

With the successful adjournment of the Political Consultative Conference, which under Marshall's direction had reached agreement on most major issues, Mao, addressing United Press journalists on February 9, 1946, praised Marshall lavishly for his role in promoting peace, unity and democracy in China. He Di noted that CCP Central Committee Member Liu Shaoqi issued directives to all cadres on the new stage of peaceful construction that China would soon be entering.

But Marshall's Mission was unable to prevent the outbreak of hostilities and proved unable to stop the war's escalation as well. When Marshall negotiated the withdrawal of Communist troops from Siping and Changchun in May, 1946, which resulted in GMD forces pouring into the vacuum with American assistance, Communist leaders felt they had been tricked. Yet, the CCP Central Committee instructed Zhou Enlai that, although he was free to criticize Chiang and the United States, he was not to criticize either Marshall or the new U.S. Ambassador, John Leighton Stuart.[21]

In talks between Stuart and Huang Hua on the eve of Communist victory in May, 1949, the CCP informed the U.S. ambassador that it was willing to establish diplomatic relations and hoped that the United States would recognize China's new government. President Truman's decision to veto an invitation for Stuart to visit Beijing for talks with Mao and Zhou, confirmed CCP suspicions of American hostility. According to He, the sudden increase of military activity by the U.S. Army in Qingdao in April, 1949 was misinterpreted by the CCP as a prelude to direct intervention by the United States military in the Chinese Revolution. He Di confirmed that strong ideological considerations predisposed the CCP to its "Lean to One Side" policy of close alliance with the Soviet Union. U.S. Secretary of State Dean Acheson's policy of "waiting for the dust to settle", in He's view, only created the Taiwan problem, "making it impossible for the CCP to develop normal diplomatic relations with the United States."[22]

Rao Geping, from Beijing University, argued that Chiang was convinced that the United States, out of its own interests, would never abandon the GMD government, even in its darkest hour. This idea, Rao insists, guided Chiang and his inner circle of supporters throughout the civil war of 1946–1949. Under pressure from U.S. ambassador John Leighton Stuart to democratize and liberalize his government, Chiang, while actually strengthening his "fascist dictatorship", produced various cosmetic "reforms" for the consumption of American politicians, often timed to coincide with important votes in the U.S. Congress for additional China funds. According to Rao, the Nationalist government routinely utilized the fortunes of the Chiang, Soong, Kung, and Chen families to bribe Americans involved in policy formation.[23]

Steven M.Goldstein contributed an essay reaffirming the same opposition to the "lost chance" thesis that he had outlined earlier (1980) in *Uncertain Years*. In his essay, "Sino-American Relations, 1948–1950: Lost Chance or No Chance?", Goldstein agreed that in 1949, most American businessmen were indeed willing to stay put after Communist takeover, a position with which the State Department concurred. The CCP for its part reassured law-abiding Westerners that their property and persons would be respected. Yet within two years, there was only acrimony and war in Korea.

According to Goldstein, the ideological world view of the Communists, with its built-in constraints on policy, made it no more likely that the CCP could have chosen better relations with the U.S. ". . . than at lunch a hungry rabbi can "choose" to eat a ham sandwich." Goldstein presented the specter of two nations locked in a confrontation that neither of them particularly wanted, in which ideological considerations had removed the ability of either to avoid.[24]

A more recent reexamination of the "lost chance" thesis was published in 1997 in the journal *Diplomatic History*. The results of a symposium entitled "Rethinking the Lost Chance in China", all of the essays concerned, except for the Introductory one by Warren I. Cohen, were revisionist approaches to the "lost chance" scenario, which denied that there ever was an opportunity for better relations between the United States and Communist China. While Cohen remained unconvinced by the revisionist antithesis, which was engendered by the release of new documentary evidence from Moscow and China, one revisionist essay by Chen Jian was important because it may indicate the limits of potential cooperation, and because the author is one of the two editors of an important new source of collected documents from the Chinese Communist Party Central Committee: *Chinese Communist Foreign Policy and the Cold War in Asia, New Documentary Evidence, 1944–1950.*

In the essay "The Myth of America's 'Lost Chance' in China", Chen says that in 1949–1950, Mao and the CCP didn't want Western recognition or diplomatic relations with the West. Rather, the CCP acted to "squeeze" Western diplomats out of Shenyang (Mukden) in November 1948. According to Chen, Mao Zedong and Zhou Enlai worried that American diplomats would use consulate radio transmitters to relay military information to the GMD, and for this reason approved the house detainment of U.S. Consul Angus Ward and his staff after they refused to turn their transmitter over to Communist military authorities.

According to Chen, the CCP wanted to make a "fresh start" in China's external relations, and had to "clean the house before entertaining guests". Although Chen conceded "It is true that for a short time in the spring of 1949, Mao and the CCP leadership showed some interest in having contacts with the United States", yet the CCP intended to treat U.S. and Soviet diplomats differently. Chinese Communist policy toward "democratic" socialist countries would be different from policy toward capitalist countries.

In regard to the Stuart-Huang Hua talks in 1949, Chen concluded that the two pre-conditions indicated by the CCP for the establishment of diplomatic relations — cutting off connections with the GMD and a willingness to treat China on a basis of equality — were "impossible" for the U.S. to meet. According to Chen, "Fulfilling the first condition, cutting off connections with the GMD, would require the complete turnover of America's China policy since the end of World War II."[25]

This is hardly a convincing argument since Chiang's own weakness and defeat by 1949 had already overthrown U.S. China policy. Moreover, Chiang had never supported the American desire to see the central government transformed into a multi-party democracy, which was also part of U.S. China policy. In the last two years of the decade (1948–9), American policy planners turned to Japan as a potential stabilizing force in East Asia after they realized China would be unable to fulfill that role.

Chen presented a series of telegrams between Mao and Stalin, wherein Mao informed Stalin that China would soon be making some adjustments to its foreign policy by initiating contacts with the United States. Stalin not only approved, but indicated to Mao that it would also be proper for China to accept foreign loans and do business with the capitalist countries. Chen intended the telegrams to demonstrate the growing closeness between the CCP and the USSR, and consequently the unlikelihood of improved Sino-American relations. Yet the contents of the documents do indicate a readiness on the part of the CCP, with Russian approval, to enter into a closer relationship with the United States.[26]

In a similar fashion, the documents which Chen and his fellow editor Shuguang Zhang present in *Chinese Communist Foreign Policy and the Cold War in Asia, New Documentary Evidence, 1944–1950*, by no means put an end to the "lost chance" hypothesis. These items are essentially ambiguous and one of the strengths of this volume is that the editors simply present the documents without trying to draw conclusions. Many of the items in this collection strongly support the notion that the Marshall Mission and the Political Consultative Conference agreements of January 1946 which it produced, had they been carried out, really did represent a "lost chance" for better relations between the Chinese Communist Party and the United States.[27]

John W. Garver, speaking of the critical year 1949 in his essay "Little Chance," claimed: "The United States, as it turned out, had followed essentially the policy lost chance theorists would have had it follow." Consequently, CCP leaders understood that the U.S. was offering them a chance at accommodation which they refused to consider.[28]

Anyone familiar with the events in question knows that this was not at all the case. The most important requirement for a rapprochement was for the United States to stop supporting the GMD and this it did not do. When Stuart received his invitation to talk with Mao and Zhou in Beijing, the U.S. government absolutely forbade him to go. Instead he was ordered to visit Chiang Kai-shek in Taipei. It should also be noted that at the time the Huang-Stuart talks were reaching a conclusion, the Nationalists were blockading the port of Shanghai with naval vessels supplied by the United States, and bombing the city with American-supplied bombs and bombers. No, the United States was not following essentially the policy lost chance theorists would have it pursue.

Michael Sheng informed his readers in his essay "The Triumph of Internationalism" that: "There was never a chance for the United States to win over the CCP as a potential ally against Moscow" and conversely that ". . . the CCP's friendly overtures toward the United States were never indications of a genuine desire to form an alliance with Washington against Moscow." For decades, Sheng said, the CCP had been downplaying its relationship with the Soviet Union and intentionally feeding Americans misleading information so as to project the image of nationalists who were independent of Moscow. In reality, however, Mao and the CCP were ardent internationalists eager to throw their weight into the world-wide struggle of socialism against capitalism, Sheng concluded.[29]

But what "lost chance" proponent ever said that the U.S. might have been able to recruit the CCP as an ally against the Soviet Union? And did any U.S. diplomat ever think the CCP was trying to recruit the U.S. as an ally against the Soviet Union? The real question for "lost chance" proponents was whether less hostile relations, or perhaps even normal relations, might have been possible at some juncture. Except for Chen Jian, all of the anti-lost chance partisans in the *Diplomatic History* Symposium advanced an argument based primarily on ideological concerns. Steven Goldstein, who had been one of the earliest to advance this line of reasoning was also the first to recognize the danger of historical reductionism inherent in it.[30]

The final essay in the Symposium, by Odd Arne Westad, underscored the fragility and difficulty involved in the CCP's attempts to form a closer understanding with Stalin and the Soviet Union. She too sought to undermine the "lost chance" hypothesis by emphasizing emerging Sino-Soviet relations. Yet her study demonstrated that "mutual rancor" between Stalin and Mao had permeated the alliance from the start. Westad felt that during the Marshall Mediation mission,

> Had the Truman administration ceased its military assistance to the GMD in the spring of 1946 and been able to force Jiang to shelve his plans for attacks on the CCP, then it is possible that the United States could have exploited the already existing frictions between the CCP and Moscow to improve its own relations with the Chinese Communists.[31]

U.S. relations with China remained paralyzed after the Communist takeover, retaining freedom of action only to distance itself even further from the People's Republic. By 1950, the United States found itself at war with China in Korea, followed by 30 years of hostility without any diplomatic relations, an abnormal situation to say the least. Given the cost, to write-off the notion that the U.S. might have done better in Sino-American relations, or to dismiss attempts to discern opportunities that might have led to an easing of tensions, seems less than responsible.

Powell's *China Weekly Review*, during the period of 1946–1950 tried to guide U.S. China policy toward pressuring the Nationalist government to respect human rights, to end its one-party dictatorship, and to enter a coalition government with the Communists. After China fell to the CCP, the *Review* urged the United States to pursue positive relations and recognition of the new government. These were not subversive goals, and were for a time in line with the views of the United States government and of President Truman.

When Professor Wen Yido, an important member of the Democratic League, was assassinated in Kunming (chapter one) in July, 1946, John

King Fairbank, Director of the United States Information Service, protested in an article published by the *Atlantic Monthly*:

> Professor Wen was American trained, a graduate of the University of Chicago, and a symbol of the American interest in China. He was killed by agents of those who hold the real power in the Chinese Nationalist Government, which the United States recognizes and has been supporting. . .[32]

President Truman also protested Wen's murder in a letter to Chinese Nationalist President Chiang Kai-shek, warning him :

> The assassinations of distinguished Chinese liberals at Kunming recently have not been ignored. Regardless of where responsibility may lie for these cruel murders, the result has been to cause American attention to focus on the China situation, and there is increasing belief that an attempt is being made to resort to force, military or secret police rather than democratic processes to settle major social issues.[33]

The Marshall Mission to negotiate peace and an end to one-party rule in China had by this time ended in failure. Civil war had broken out in earnest and the agreements of the Political Consultative Conference, which was supposed to usher in a multi-party coalition government, had been abrogated. Truman complained to Chiang that:

> . . . the hopes of the people of China are being thwarted by militarists and a small group of political reactionaries who are obstructing the advancement of the general good of the nation by failing to understand the liberal trend of the times.[34]

These sentiments were virtually the same as those of Powell and the *China Weekly Review*. Yet, from this time on, the editorial policy of the *Review* and U.S. China policy began to diverge, slowly at first, then more rapidly as the Cold War progressed and the United States developed the policy of containment of Communism abroad.

CHAPTER NOTES

1. John B. Powell, *My Twenty-Five Years in China*. (New York: Macmillian, 1945.) p.341.

2. J.B. Powell, *My Twenty-Five Years in China*. p.417.

3. Powell, ed. "'J.B.' Powell Passes", CWR, 8 March 1947, p.33.

4. John W. Powell, *Personal History Statement*, United States Civil Service Commission, 11 December 1942, Washington, D.C., p.3–4, as found in: United States Senate, Subcommittee to Investigate the Administration of the Internal Security Act and Other Internal Security Laws of the Committee on the Judiciary, *Hearings: Interlocking Subversion in Government Departments*, Washington D.C., 27 September 1954, p.1858–9.

5. MacKinnon and Friesen, *China Reporting*, p.59.

6. Stephen R. MacKinnon and Oris Friesen, *China Reporting, An Oral History of American Journalism in the 1930's and 1940's.*(Berkeley: University of California Press, 1987.)p.196–9.

7. MacKinnon and Friesen, *China Reporting*. p.197–9.

8. Paul A. Varg, *The Closing of the Door, Sino-American Relations 1936–1946*. (East Lansing: Michigan State University Press, 1973.) p.137–147.

9. Varg, *The Closing of the Door*. p.264–274. After the PCC agreements broke down and fighting resumed, Marshall continued trying to negotiate an end to hostilities. According to Varg, Marshall ultimately came to feel that he and American negotiators "were being used as a 'stooges' by the [Nationalist] government, which was only pretending to negotiate while in reality making war."

10. Instruction, CCP Central Committee, "On Current Situation and Our Tasks," 1 February 1946, in: Shuguang Zhang and Jian Chen, eds. *Chinese Communist Foreign Policy and the Cold War in Asia, New Documentary Evidence, 1944–1950*. (Chicago: Imprint Publications, 1996) p.58–62.

11. Joseph W. Esherick, ed. *Lost Chance in China: The World War II Despatches of John S. Service*.(New York: Random House, 1974.).

12. John S. Service, *The Amerasia Papers: Some Problems in the History of US-China Relations*.(Berkeley: Center for Chinese Studies China Research Monographs, 1971.)p.182–189.

13. Stephen R. MacKinnon and Oris Friesen, *China Reporting, An Oral History of American Journalism in the 1930s and 1940s*. (Berkeley: University of California Press, 1987).p.xviii. Fairbank's long productive career at Harvard University stretched all the way back to the 1940's, according to MacKinnon and Friesen.

14. John King Fairbank, "Our Chances in China", *Atlantic Monthly*, September 1946; John King Fairbank, *China Perceived, Images and Policies in Chinese-American Relations*.(New York: Vintage Books, 1976.)p.18.

15. Dorothy Borg and Waldo Heinrichs, eds. *Uncertain Years: Chinese-American Relations, 1947–1950*.(New York: Columbia University Press, 1980.)

16. Steven I. Levine, "Notes on Soviet Policy in China and Chinese Communist Perceptions, 1945–1950", in: *Uncertain Years: Chinese-American Relations, 1947–1950*, eds. Dorothy Borg and Waldo Heinrichs, p.293–303.

17. Warren I. Cohen,"Acheson, His Advisers, and China, 1949–1950," in: *Uncertain Years*, eds. Borg and Heinrich, p.13–52.

18. Michael H. Hunt,"Mao Tse-tung and the Issue of Accommodation with the United States, 1948–1950," in: *Uncertain Years*, eds. Borg and Heinrich, p.185–233.

19. Steven M. Goldstein,"Chinese Communist Policy toward the United States: Opportunities and Constraints, 1944–1950," in: *Uncertain Years*, eds. Borg and Heinrich, p.235–278.

20. Nancy Bernkopf Tucker, *Patterns in the Dust, Chinese-American Relations and the Recognition Controversy, 1949–1950*. New York: Columbia University Press, 1983.) p.113–133; 161–168;195.

21. He Di, "The Evolution of the Communist Party's Policy toward the United States, 1944–1949", in: *Sino-American Relations, 1945–1955, A Joint Reassessment of a Critical Decade*, eds. Harry Harding and Yuan Ming (Wilmington: Scholarly Resources Books, 1989.) p.31–50.

22. *Ibid*, p.44–45.

23. Rao Geping, "The Kuomintang Government's Policy toward the United States, 1945–1949," in: *Sino-American Relations, 1945–1955, A Joint Reassessment of a Critical Decade*. eds. Harding and Yuan, p.51–77.

24. Steven M. Goldstein, "Sino-American Relations, 1948–1950: Lost Chance or No Chance?" in: *Sino-American Relations, 1945–1955, A Joint Reassessment of a Critical Decade*, eds. Harding and Yuan, p.119–142.

25. Chen Jian, "The Myth of America's 'Lost Chance' in China", *Diplomatic History*, 21, no.1 (Winter 1997), p.71–86.

26. *Ibid*, p.84.

27. Shuguang Zhang and Jian Chen, eds. *Chinese Communist Foreign Policy and the Cold War in Asia, New Documentary Evidence, 1944–1950.*(Chicago: Imprint Publications, 1996.)

28. John W. Garver, "Little Chance", *Diplomatic History*, 21, no.1 (Winter 1997) p. 92.

29. Michael Sheng,"The Triumph of Internationalism: CCP-Moscow Relations before 1949", *Diplomatic History*, 21, no.1 (Winter 1997) p.95.

30. Steven M.Goldstein, "Sino-American Relations, 1948–1950: Lost Chance or No Chance?", in: *Sino-American Relations, 1945–1955, A Joint Reassessment of a Critical Decade*, eds. Harding and Ming, p.138.

31. Odd Arne Westad, "Losses, Chances, and Myths: The United States and the Creation of the Sino-Soviet Alliance, 1945–1950", *Diplomatic History*, 21, no.1 (Winter 1997)p.107.

32. John King Fairbank, "Our Chances in China", *Atlantic Monthly*, September 1946; John King Fairbank, *China Perceived, Images and Policies in Chinese-American Relations*. (New York: Vintage Books, 1976.)p.3–4.

33. *Letter*, President Truman to President Chiang Kai-shek, Washington, D.C.,10 August 1946, United States Department of State, *United States Relations with China, with Special Reference to the Period 1944–1949*. (Washington, D.C.: Government Printing Office, 1949.) p.652.

34. *Ibid*.

CHAPTER TWO

THE STRANDS OF DISILLUSIONMENT, A THREE YEAR OVERVIEW OF *THE CHINA WEEKLY REVIEW*, 1946–1948: PART I

With the surrender of Japan, Bill Powell's propaganda work with General Clair Chenault's Fourteenth Airforce was over. Still in the employ of the Office of War Information, Powell was flown from Kunming just two weeks after VJ-Day, to Shanghai and the former offices of his father's *China Weekly Review*, defunct since 1941.[1] He found the premises in disarray, the library looted, even the light switches and wiring ripped from the walls.[2] Gathering about him new and former staff members, Powell resumed publication on December 1, 1945. His father, too ill to return to China, remained in the United States and had little to do with the resurrected *Review*.

By the end of 1945, American policy in China had shifted toward preventing a renewed outbreak of civil war by promoting the formation of a coalition government of the two armed rivals, the Guomindang and the Chinese Communist Party. Consequently, smaller minority liberal parties such as the China Democratic League, the Young China Party, and the Democratic Socialist Party assumed new importance as a bridge between the two major hostile camps.

Blessed with an abundance of foreign advertisers, Powell's *Review* supported American mediation efforts and provided a rallying point and voice for many independent foreign-educated Chinese liberals who supported the American position. The *Review* advocated a multi-party solution to the problem of war and peace, and backed Chinese groups such as the Democratic League, which wanted to transplant Western liberal institutions and democracy to China.

As hopes for a coalition faded in 1946 and civil strife intensified, Powell and the *Review* defended student anti-war demonstrators and educators, and shared their goal of getting both sides back to the negotiating table. When both the Democratic League and the Communist Party refused to participate in the National Assembly convened by the Nationalist government in November, 1946, Powell was dismayed. He nonetheless counseled the remaining representatives to resist rubber-stamping the 1936 Constitution and to win the people's confidence through adopting a truly democratic charter with guarantees of civil liberties. But, as Powell came to realize, the draft Constitution and government reorganization that followed amounted to little more than window dressing for continued one-party rule by the Guomindang.

In March, 1947, Powell slipped illegally into Taiwan, where he gathered first hand evidence of the brutal, island-wide suppression of the Taiwanese Revolt; a revolt brought on by eighteen months of misrule and oppression by the newly installed GMD government. The series of articles he wrote defying the government's news blackout alerted the world to the Taiwan debacle and caught the eyes of the *Washington Post*, the *New York Times*, and other prominent journals.[3]

Returning to Shanghai, Powell found the city in turmoil due to spiralling inflation and the deteriorating standard of living, the result of the government's issuance of unbacked currency to finance the civil war. Against a backdrop of rice riots and widespread strikes, a new wave of student mass demonstrations in most cities under Guomindang control, the "Anti-Civil War, Anti-Hunger" movement, reached a crescendo by May, 1947. Powell and the *Review* followed the movement sympathetically, lending it support and fighting its battles in a stream of articles and editorials. The *Review*'s "Letters From the People" section provided an open forum to students, faculty, and parents whose sons and daughters were sometimes held incommunicado by the police.

The Nationalist government used the military and the police to suppress student discontent ruthlessly. During this period, Powell drew the fire of the Shanghai District Court for criticizing flawed judicial proceedings and the squalid conditions of China's prisons. He was equally strident in objecting to the interruption of court proceedings and intimidation of the court by the military.

As the government moved to suppress the voices of discontent on college campuses, on the streets, and in the press, it decided to move against other critics as well. In October, 1947, the Nationalist government banned the Democratic League. Powell lamented:"The twilight of liberalism has come to China: Henceforth a Chinese is either a reactionary or a radical."[4]

The repression in Taiwan, the May Anti-Civil War, Anti-Hunger demonstrations and the government's full scale repressive response, hastened the alienation of Chinese liberals and the intellectual community. Powell and the *Review* staff had been close to these elements and shared their disillusionment.

By spring 1947 drastic changes were occurring in the U.S. as well. President Truman and the Democrats sought to deflect G.O.P. attacks on Democratic foreign and domestic policy, and the charge that they were "soft on communism," by instituting the federal loyalty review program at home.

In the international sphere, Communist insurgency in Greece and Soviet pressure on Turkey, combined with hardening Soviet control over Eastern Europe seemed to portend an expansionist policy by the USSR. Truman saw little difference between Nazi totalitarianism and Soviet totalitarianism. He believed both were bent on world conquest and that any display of weakness or appeasement, as with Hitler at Munich, would only encourage further Communist aggression. Therefore, the president and his advisors devised a tough, new foreign policy designed to commit the United States to containing communism world-wide: the Truman Doctrine.

With the end of World War II, Powell anticipated with approval the end of Dutch, French, and British colonial control in South and Southeast Asia. He believed the emergence of newly independent countries in the region would open up new markets and investment opportunities for American businessmen throughout Asia. Attempts by the three European powers to reestablish colonial control threatened to upset this vision. Powell feared that the Truman Doctrine would be used by former colonial powers to involve the United States in helping them to reimpose colonial authority. Throughout the spring of 1947 and into 1948, Powell opposed the new direction of U.S. policy, pointing out that it would commit America to propping up weak, unpopular, reactionary regimes the world over simply because they professed to be combatting communism.

The *Review* closely followed national independence movements all over Asia. Powell moved from support for moderate, negotiated solutions in 1946, to strong opposition to any U.S. aid for recolonization and sympathy for national liberation movements. He feared that the United States, which he felt should be a beacon of democracy and freedom, was in danger of becoming the bastion of reaction. He urged America to use its economic power to force France and the Netherlands out of Southeast Asia.

*

Powell and the *China Weekly Review* depended heavily on liberal, often Western-educated Chinese intellectuals for much of their information. By 1946, Urban, Western educated journalists, technocrats, civil servants, and college professors comprised a large part of the *Review*'s staff and contributors. A close reading of the *Review* between 1946–1948 suggests that their influence was considerable. Powell depended on them for all of his translations of Chinese newspapers and magazines (a weekly service of the *Review*), for half of his feature articles, and for their opinions in general.

Doak Barnett, who had come to China in 1947 as a journalist for the *Chicago Daily News*, recalled that:

> In Shanghai, Nanking, and Peking too, people like those in the Democratic League were among the main sources that shaped the environment in which foreign correspondents were operating. People interviewed Kuomintang officials, and they tried to have contact with the Communists, but the people whom correspondents had most contact with were

the university people, intellectuals and the like, most of whom were connected with the Democratic League. If you looked at that group and its in-
teraction with the press, you will find a very major influence on foreign
reporting in China at that time.[5]

Powell, speaking at a gathering of former journalists in 1982, said essentially the same thing:

> Most of us found, very early on, that whatever information you got from
> the Kuomintang was not very good, and we began looking for other
> sources..I think the main source of information were Chinese intellectuals
> who were dissatisfied. I never met Chou En-lai or went to any of his press
> conferences. That wasn't where we got our information. We got it from a
> rather large group of people we met during the war. Some of them I knew
> in Shanghai - newspapermen, Chinese newspapermen before the war, pro-
> fessors, and others. You have to remember that most of the intellectuals
> were disenchanted with the Kuomintang. These were the people you re-
> lied on.[6]

For educated Chinese, the *China Weekly Review* served as a relatively
safe haven for the expression of protest and outrage against unpopular
policies of the central government, in the relative security of a foreign language. The *Review*, because it was American-owned, by the son of a well
known journalist, J.B. Powell, who had been an heroic opponent of Japanese expansionism, could not simply be shut down as independent Chinese
journals sometimes were. It was a vehicle of expression which was partly
insulated from the full arm of official censure.

While the central government did withhold newsprint subsidies from
the *Review*, forcing it to buy newsprint on the black market at several
times the government rate, it could not just send in the local military garrison to close it down or otherwise harass its American editor. Similarly,
while Chinese newsmen critical of the government risked arrest and occa-
sional death in detention[7], U.S. journalists were relatively untouchable due
to the potential danger of upsetting relations with the country on which
the Nationalist government depended for financial and military support.

A survey of the *Review's* readership by occupations indicated a large
number of teachers and college professors (Twenty-two percent), profes-
sionals (thirteen percent), government employees (eighteen percent), businessmen (twenty-eight percent), as well as students, whose numbers were
difficult to determine since they tended to share or circulate copies.[8] By
1947, these groups included those hardest hit by inflation: teachers and
government employees whose salaries were not pegged to the cost of living
index, and students, whose pitiful living allowances fell far below subsis-
tence level. It also included businessmen, who were the objects of Chiang's
son, Jiang Jingguo's draconian suppression of merchant speculators in
Shanghai during the Gold Yuan Reform of August-October, 1948.[9]

Through his Chinese staff and their connections, and through his readership, Powell became involved in and was moved by the momentous events of 1946–1948: the Nationalist government's mismanagement of the economy, mishandling of the Taiwan crisis, mismanagement of protests by students and their liberal supporters, and its cynical disdain for "democratization". Through his staff and readers Powell aligned himself with the student movement and the Democratic League. He published photos of the fallen and letters of the distraught. Their enemies became his enemies. And though he tried to maintain a modicum of professional detachment, in the end, their struggle became his struggle, their exasperation became his exasperation. This experience moved him beyond the limits of his toleration for the Guomindang's illiberal, callous one-party rule, and prepared him for the transition of 1949. This chapter will consider the first three threads in this process: the failure of a middle path to democratization which Chinese liberals and the United States had supported, the *Review*'s early support for the student peace movement, and Powell's expose on the 1947 Taiwan Revolt and its suppression.

*

CHINA WEEKLY REVIEW AND THE CHINA DEMOCRATIC LEAGUE

Throughout summer and early fall, 1945, at American insistence, the Chinese Communist Party and the Guomindang conducted negotiations. The object of their talks was to avoid a renewal of the 1930's Civil War through creation of a multi-party coalition government. Although unable to agree on specifics concerning the control of territory, and unification of Communist and Nationalist armed forces, Mao Zedong and Chiang Kai-shek did arrange to call a nationwide Political Consultative Conference (PCC) of delegates from all parties, which was to resolve these issues and to create a multi-party coalition government that would include the Communists.

Powell and the staff of the *Review* supported the China Democratic League, a loose coalition of small opposition parties and Chinese liberals affiliated with no party, formed during World War II. Comprised largely of intellectuals, especially from academic and professional circles,[10] the League lacked the cohesion and discipline of an actual political party. Of all groups in China, the League was the most familiar with the Western liberal political tradition. The testimony of Powell and Doak Barnett indicated that most American newspapermen relied for news and opinion on Chinese liberals, who were often associated with the Democratic League.[11] The perception of a shared community of beliefs in the efficacy of Western liberal political institutions, led Powell and his staff to endorse the League.

The *Review* disapproved of the authoritarian nature of both the Guomindang and the Communists. It looked to the Democratic League and the Political Consultative Conference of January 11–31, 1946, to introduce liberal political and legal institutions and practices to China. Powell and his staff (like U.S. mediator General George C.Marshall) expected the League to provide leadership and to play an important mediating role between the two armed antagonists, the GMD and the CCP.

After parliamentary multi-party government and political rights were in place, Powell and the *Review* hoped the League would develop into the leading force shaping the reconstruction of China. They envisioned it uniting all minority parties into a third force, pragmatically incorporating dynamic economic and social policies in a European-style blend of socialism and capitalism, within a framework of liberal political institutions.[12]

But these expectations were not met. After the PCC agreements had resolved most issues and raised hopes for peace, the Guomindang, bowing to pressure from its right-wing, unilaterally abrogated the PCC agreement to create a coalition government before attempting Constitutional revision. It resumed military actions against the CCP and announced that it would convene the National Assembly under its own auspices, rather than under the supervision of a multi-party coalition government as the PCC agreements had stipulated.

Powell, although disappointed, invested his hope in the attempt to create a "third Party" coalition of minority parties under Democratic League leadership, as a liberalizing force in the coming National Assembly. When the League refused to participate in the November 1946 National Assembly, which was to revise the 1936 Constitution[13] Powell's hopes were again dashed. Even so, he was initially inclined to accept the amended Constitution which the National Assembly produced ("Half a loaf is better than none"), and to hope for its implementation while pointing out its flaws.

The year 1947 would prove pivotal. The death of J.B.Powell, Bill's father, in the early spring, removed one of the *Review*'s lingering bonds of attachment to the GMD, while his marriage the same year to Sylvia Campbell, a U.N. relief worker in China, seemed to forecast a deeper concern for Chinese political developments.[14] Bill Powell's on the spot coverage of the Nationalist Government's bloody repression of the Taiwanese revolt in February and March of that year demonstrated to him the regime's callous contempt for the lives of its own people. The *Review*'s increasing involvement and sympathy for the Anti-Civil War movement led Powell to document assiduously the government's brutal repression of student anti-war protesters and their academic supporters, and to battle judicial improprieties on their behalf. As the Nationalist government prepared to convene the People's Political Council[15], a multi-party advisory body, in May, 1947, Powell urged the Democratic League, which would attend the PPC, and other minority parties to coordinate their efforts to produce a peace plan, with the wave of demonstrations then shaking the country.

With the government intent on crushing all opposition by force, and manipulating the abrogated PCC agreements to present the illusion of democratization, Powell and the *Review* shared the sense of alienation that most Chinese liberals felt toward the central government. In late May 1947, the Guomindang, which had already crushed the Taiwan Revolt and was busy suppressing the student Anti-Hunger, Anti-Civil War demonstrations, banned the Democratic League altogether. This seemed to mark the end of any hope for democratic reform, and confirmed Powell and his staff's complete disillusionment with the Nationalist Government.

*

Just before the opening of the Political Consultative Conference (PCC) in early January 1946, the *Review* endorsed the Democratic League and explicated its history, personnel, and political program. It also noted the congruence of President Truman's China policy and the overall policy of the League.

> President Truman, in his recent clarification of United States Policy toward China, not only expressed the views of the American people, but also the majority of the Chinese people. It is interesting to note that the American president advocated the very things the Chinese people have been demanding through a small and progressive third party: The Chinese Democratic League.
>
> Truman said a broadening of the Chungking government to include all other political parties was necessary, that the Kuomintang and the Communists must stop the fratricidal war immediately, that the existence of autonomous armies within a state is illegal and that all political parties should jointly convoke a national assembly at the earliest date. These very same recommendations were the major portion of the League's platform which was made public last October when the party held its provisional congress in Chungking.[16]

Contributing editor C.Y.W.Meng summarized parts of the *Political Report of the China Democratic League* prepared at that body's October 1946 Congress, along with its forty-nine point political program, and its four point peace proposal.[17] In the League's view, the PCC's first task was to create a coalition government, end one party rule, unify the nation politically and militarily, and create an elected National Assembly truly representative of the Chinese People. The general platform of the League called for political and economic democracy to equalize the distribution of wealth and raise the peoples' living standards. The League envisioned a mixed economy of private and public ownership, and planned production and distribution by the state to ensure systematic economic development. Progressive taxation, and nationalization of banks, communications industries, utilities, and extractive industries rounded out its economic program.[18]

A large part of the GMD's and CCP's political power was based on their possession of massive armed force. Their reliance on force undermined the emergence of democratic processes. The League therefore called for an end to the militarizing of political parties, and hoped to prevent military men from holding public office in an effort to demilitarize the national government.[19]

The Political Consultative Conference opened January 11, 1946, and represented all major political parties and groups in China. Although the largest number of delegates among individual parties belonged to the GMD and CCP, the aggregate from the smaller parties together with independent delegates outnumbered these. Under the guidance of U.S. Presidential Ambassador General George C.Marshall, the PCC delegates laid the foundation for a coalition government with a multi-party state council holding both legislative and executive powers, which was to be the supreme governing body of the state. The PCC produced agreements on reorganizing the structure of the national government, providing for revision of the 1936 Constitution, ending the long period of GMD tutelage, providing for an elected National Assembly, and establishing ratios for the consolidation of GMD and CCP armies.[20]

According to the PCC agreements, the Coalition government was to be set up first, and afterwards, elections would be held for a National Constitutional Assembly which would institute the Constitutional revisions mandated by the PCC. The Coalition government would oversee governmental reorganization, and call elections for the Executive and Legislative Yuans, or branches, and a new National Assembly. This would have safeguarded the new political system, since any changes to the PCC agreement would have required a two-thirds vote of the State Council, which could have been easily blocked by a CCP-Democratic League combined opposition vote. The last items agreed upon by the Political Consultative Conference were GMD-CCP troop strength ratios and local control of former base areas.

With the successful conclusion of the Political Consultative Conference in February, the CCP looked forward to the legalization "of our party, our army and the liberated areas." The Central Committee informed cadres of impending changes:

> At present the major form of the Chinese revolution has changed from military struggle to non-military mass work and to struggle in the parliament. Domestic problems will be solved through political means. The entire agenda of our party should be adjusted to fit this new situation.
>
> (3) Our party will soon join the government. Other parties will conduct a variety of social activities in the liberated areas, and even join the governments there. Our troops will soon be reorganized as part of the formal national army and the local guards or self-defense corps. In the reorganized troops, political commissars, Party branches, and Party committees will be eliminated; our Party will stop its direct leadership over the troops (this will be carried out in a few months), and our Party will no longer give direct orders to the troops. . .
>
> (4) It is still possible that the GMD might assault us in some places, and we should thus maintain high vigilance, but generally speaking, the military struggle has ceased.[21]

As the CCP began preparing drafts of a constitution and platform to present at the PCC, they sought closer cooperation and friendship with the urban liberals of the Democratic League. In early December the CCP Central Committee sent word to "our friends in the Democratic League" that the Communist Party was ready to solve all problems "through democratic channels", and that it hoped League members would be ". . . well prepared on such issues as the platform, the coalition government, the National Assembly, and [the drafting of] the Constitution."[22] In February, 1946, the Chinese Communist Party fully expected to take its place in the new coalition government of China[23], and peace seemed possible. But this was not to be.

*

While the PCC was still in session, and in spite of Guomindang statements guaranteeing freedom of the press, free and open debate, and the inviolability of PCC delegates, Nationalist police raided the home of Huang Yebei, a Democratic League delegate to the Political Consultative Conference. Simultaneously police also ransacked Democratic League headquarters and the offices of the CCP. When the League protested by staging a one-day walkout from the PCC, Powell and the *China Weekly Review* condemned the police raid and upheld the League's response.

The *Review* castigated the government for breaking its promise to respect the inviolability of delegates and to allow free and open debate. Instead, the administration had employed "gestapo" tactics by sending the secret police to despoil a delegate's home. Legislative power was supreme in a democracy, the *Review* remonstrated; there should be no police power superior to the legislature. The secret police must not have the authority to terrorize and punish legislators at will, the journal insisted.[24]

When the Democratic League's official organ in Kunming, the *Democratic Weekly*, and two other opposition papers, the student paper *Xio Sheng Bao* and *Time Review*, edited by Dr. Fei Xiaodong[25] were closed by the government, the *Review* pointed out that this contradicted numerous government statements guaranteeing press freedom. In his opening address to the Political Consultative Conference, Chiang Kai-shek himself had specifically promised freedom of the press, the *Review* pointed out.[26]

After the PCC adjourned and Marshall returned to The United States to secure economic aid for China, the Guomindang right wing moved to revoke the PCC agreements in a number of areas. It nullified the power of opposition parties in the State Council, eliminated the cabinet's responsibility to the legislature, and revoked the agreements on provincial autonomy. The current Nationalist government was to continue rather than the coalition government previously agreed to, and the National Assembly was to be held under its auspices, rather than that of the planned coalition government.[27]

At the same time, the cease fire in effect since January began to break down as both GMD and CCP military forces fought for control of outlying areas. As civil war intensified, opposition took the form of student demonstrations, which were often supported by outspoken faculty members. In one of the early centers of anti-war protest, Kunming, the Yunnan Military Command took action to silence the government's critics.

In Kunming, on July 11, 1946, lower level officers assassinated Li Gongpu, a Yunnan University professor and prominent member of the Democratic League's Central Committee. Li had been shot through the abdomen as he left a theater with his wife. Immediately, newspapers began speculating that this was the start of a series of planned political assassinations.[28]

Four days later, a second important League member, Wen Yiduo, a popular university literature professor and well known poet, was gunned down as he returned from a memorial service for Li Gongpu. Wen and his son had just finished listening to Li's wife deliver a eulogy for her murdered husband when they were hit by a fusillade of bullets outside the memorial meeting. Wen was shot three times in the face and once in the chest. His son was hit five times. Both Li Gongpu and Wen Yiduo had been outspoken critics of the government who often spoke at student anti-war gatherings. Stunned by the double murders and fearing for their lives, ten other leading members of the Democratic League sought refuge in the U.S.Consulate in Kunming.[29]

In his lead editorial, Powell angrily condemned the terrorist assassinations of these two prominent League members by the "fascist right wing" of the Guomindang. A feature article in the same issue covered the assassination story in more detail and included photographs of the widow of Li Gongpu grieving over his body. According to the *Review*, since both professors had spoken out against the civil war, right wing elements within the GMD reputedly held them responsible for the burgeoning student peace movement in Kunming. Powell's journal had been covering the Anti-Civil War Movement in Kunming, and it placed the assassinations within this context.[30]

To place the *Review*'s response in perspective, both the Chinese Communist Party and President Truman of the United States responded to the murders of Li Gongpu and Wen Yiduo. Truman sent a personal letter protesting the assassinations to President Chiang Kai-shek on August 10, 1946, warning him that

> The assassination of distinguished Chinese liberals at Kunming recently have not been ignored. Regardless of where responsibility may lie for these cruel murders . . . there is an increasing belief that an attempt is being made to resort to force, military or secret police rather than democratic processes to settle major social issues. . . The hopes of the people of China are being thwarted by militarists and a small group of political reactionaries who are obstructing the advancement of the general good of the nation

by failing to understand the liberal trend of the times. The people of the United States view with violent repugnance this state of affairs.[31]

A statement by the Chinese Communist Party Central Committee six months after the assassinations, on January 29, 1947, blamed the murders of Li and Wen on Chiang Kai-shek himself.[32]

Shortly after Wen's assassination, concerned Democratic League members decided to create an organization to enlist the aid of foreign liberals in protecting the lives of opposition figures: the League for the Protection of Human Rights in China. In August, 1946, they asked Paul Yen, James Endicott, Talitha Gerlach, Y.T. Wu and others to write a constitution for the organization. The organization's founders evoked President Franklin Roosevelt's Four Freedoms, and set as its main task the investigation and publication of facts concerning violations of human rights in China. *China Weekly Review* editor John W. Powell was elected, along with ten other founding members, to serve on the organization's executive Committee, which would oversee International League affairs.[33] Events were drawing Powell into a deeper involvement in China's political turmoil.

Just after the assassinations, the *Review* ran biographies of prominent members of the Democratic League. In July, it sketched the life of Liang Shuming, social reformer and a founding member of the League. Shortly afterward, it featured a brief biography of Ma Yinzhu, economist, professor at Shanghai Commercial College, and another League founding member.[34] Powell watched the growth of the Democratic League with satisfaction throughout the summer and early fall of 1946. As the time set by the GMD for the meeting of the National Assembly approached and civil war continued unabated, he remained optimistic:

> For, a new thing in China, the Democratic League continues to exist, indeed to grow, despite the fact that it has neither an army, a group of political bodyguards-cum storm troopers or a few influential warlords. In other words, here is a party that exists only because certain masses of the people will not see it suppressed or bludgeoned into extinction. That such a party can exist at all is another proof of the gradual turn of the tide of Chinese affairs.
>
> That is why, despite the roar of guns and the shedding of blood in all the four corners of China today, we can still see hope.[35]

The *Review*'s editor-in-chief was pleased when in mid-1946, China's three leading minority parties: the Democratic League, the Young China Party, and the Democratic Socialist Party united in a common front. He felt that the "Third Party" had already become "a potent force in the negotiations between China's two major parties."[36] Interestingly, *Review* senior contributing editor C.Y.W. Meng, a staunch supporter of the Democratic League, and prominent Western-trained economist, journeyed to Yan'an for talks with the Communists in October, 1946.[37]

Powell was therefore disappointed when, just before China's National Assembly was scheduled to open, the two major parties, the GMD and the CCP, angling to win over the new third party with concessions, succeed in splitting it apart. The Young China Party and the Democratic Socialist Party joined the government's side while the Democratic League adopted a policy "characterized by its willingness to join local assemblies and administrations in both zones (GMD and CCP) of China." To Powell, "this implied tacit recognition of both regimes as the authorized government of China", and made little sense.[38]

Powell was dismayed at the "disunity, suspicion, and party conflict" among Chinese liberals. In his view, "The people-the vast majority of them-have indicated time and time again that they are willing, ready, to back a truly democratic party intent only on establishing a democratic government for the masses."[39] Though discouraged, he continued to call for "a concerted coordinated, common struggle by the third parties to gain power-not for themselves but-for the people."[40]

The National Assembly adjourned after sanctioning changes in the 1936 Constitution. Chiang Kai-shek signed the document and decreed by executive order that it should go into effect in 1948. Quoting *Da Gong Bao*, the *Review* noted that although the revised Constitution contained provisions for greater local democracy than the 1936 version had, it was marred by the fact that neither the CCP nor the Democratic League had participated in the process.[41] Powell raised the question of whether the GMD would stop funding itself out of public revenues once the new Constitution went into effect, and the period of GMD tutelage and one-party rule officially ended.[42]

With the resumption of full scale civil war (a cease fire had been in effect while the National Assembly met), Zhou Enlai was flown back to Yan'an by General Marshall. The U.S. Mediation Mission had ended in failure. All CCP property left behind in Nationalist-controlled areas was commended to the safe keeping of the Democratic League by Zhou Enlai.

In February and March, 1947, the Central Government ruthlessly crushed a large scale revolt by Taiwanese residents against what they judged to be Guomindang misrule. As noted previously, Powell evaded the government news blackout by slipping into Taiwan and covering the story. By early spring, the government stepped up its repression in Shanghai and other cities as rice riots, strikes, and renewed student unrest followed in the wake of a failed government attempt at economic retrenchment.[43] The National Government used the opportunity to arrest prominent Democratic League supporters. The *Review* reported the attempts by League leaders Luo Longji, Zhang Pozhun and the League Standing Central Committee to negotiate the release of incarcerated League proponents.[44]

Against a background of the mounting Anti-Hunger, Anti-Civil War Movement in all major GMD-held cities and escalating government repression, the *Review* was skeptical about government claims, in March 1947, that a document had been found that proved the Democratic League, the Democratic National Reconstruction Association, the Union of People's Principles, and the Democracy Protection Association were all fronts for Communist subversion. The Government claimed that the League in particular was completely dominated by Communists.

Rejecting the government's charge, the *Review* pointed out that this included ". . . all those parties and groups which remain in opposition to the 'reorganized' government in Guomindang areas." It quoted Democratic League leader Luo Longji's characterization of the government's statements as ". . . signals impending a well planned suppression of the League and all other democratic organizations."[45] The *Review* reminded its readers in closing that Luo Longji had been one of the strongest supporters of the People's Consultative Conference.

Luo proved to be correct. The government officially banned the Democratic League on October 27, 1947. Powell castigated nationalist repression of the student movement and of the Democratic League. He accused the Nationalist Government of failing to observe human rights guaranteed by the Constitution. "As things stand today", he wrote,

> The concept of human rights is dictated by officials, this perception being their personal understanding of human freedom, and not the universally accepted interpretation. First we have the announcement that human rights will be safeguarded, freedom of assembly and speech guaranteed. Then we see that only officially approved demonstrations have freedom of assembly, only officially approved opinions have full freedom of being expressed. Arrests of students and workers followed charges of Communist affiliation and instigation, for now it transpires that those belonging to the 'treacherous' party have no right to enjoy the human rights granted under the Constitution, which has yet to come to life. The Democratic League itself - an organization which has as its members some of the very liberals General Marshall proposed for leadership in this country's affairs - is to be eradicated. The *Ho Ping Jih Pao*, for example, on October 3, suggested that the Democratic League be 'drastically liquidated', while the *Lih Pao* - the workers' paper - wants to 'eliminate the appendage of the Communist bandits'. . . It seems that all those criticizing the government ipso facto belong to the 'treacherous party'. This is paying too high a tribute to the Chinese Communists, who undoubtedly do not enjoy the support which the Kuomintang attributes to them.[46]

Powell complained that the only criterion the government used to determine whether one was a Communist was "opposition to actions of Government officials and policies." Summing up the current situation in China, Powell declared that "With the all out attack on the Democratic League, the twilight of liberalism has come to China; henceforth a Chinese is either a reactionary or a radical."[47]

Five days after the League was officially banned, Powell expressed his disappointment and exasperation at the government's refusal to end one party rule and embrace democracy:

> The National Government this week outlawed the Democratic League, thus ending the organized political life of the last group in Kuomintang dominated China which might be called an opposition party. From now on the KMT will be the undisputed master of the political arena having only to contend with the so-called minor parties, the Democratic Socialists and the Young China Party, which actually amount to nothing more than mere appendages scrambling among themselves to gobble up the precious few crumbs left after the Kuomintang has finished feeding.[48]

Powell questioned the alleged proof of the League's Communist connections that the government had announced, but refused to allow the press and public to scrutinize. He underscored the government's "increasingly hostile attitude toward anyone who refuses to bow down in abject, submissive agreement, let alone anyone who dares to question the infallible wisdom of Nanking's bureaucrats."[49] In retrospect, Powell believed that the League's "most heinous crimes" in the eyes of the Guomindang had been its insistence on a coalition government rather than a war of extermination, and its refusal to participate in the "reorganized" Nationalist government.

Since the Chinese Communist Party had taken a similar position, Powell realized that this might be construed by some as following the Communist line. Both the CCP and the Democratic League considered the National Assembly and the Constitution it drafted as nothing more than a farce, staged by the GMD to convince the world that China was now democratic. Yet the important point, he felt, was that both the League and the CCP were still willing to join a coalition government.

Powell worried that "the chance for compromise apparently grows more distant everyday as the GMD attempts to tighten its control over the country and . . . its own membership." No longer a party of the bourgeoisie, the Guomindang was simply a group ". . . anxious to stay in power at all costs", which if successful might develop into a "corporate state", by which he meant a fascist state. "If it fails", he prophesied, "we will probably see a totalitarian Communist regime come to power within the foreseeable future." Still, the only solution Powell could forsee in the fall of 1947 was compromise, but, he complained, ". . . the mere mention of the word 'compromise' is almost a crime today."[50]

٭

THE *REVIEW* AND THE STUDENT MOVEMENT, 1945–1947

The curtailment of the *Review*'s hopes for the Democratic League, for an open multi-party democracy and for a compromise solution to China's Civil War occurred against a larger backdrop of the growing student anti-civil war movement. From the start, the *Review* shared the students' opposition to the war, and their desire for an open, democratic coalition government. From the beginning the *Review* acted as interpreter of the movement, sympathized with its goals, publicized its struggles and exposed its repression by the government to the full light of public scrutiny. It became a forum for the student movement; its columns resonated with editorials, articles and letters to the editor by impoverished students and professors.

As the Government brutally suppressed the swelling Anti-Hunger, Anti-Civil War demonstrations that had engulfed most major cities by the summer of 1947, Powell and the *Review* staff shared the alienation of students and faculty from the Nationalist government. Taken together with the Guomindang's bloody suppression of the Taiwan revolt and its banning of the Democratic League and failure to end one party rule, this marked the final step in the disillusionment of Powell and the editorial policies of the *Review* with the Nationalist regime.

*

There were four main concentrations of student protests between 1945–1948. The smallest, the "December First Movement", December-January, 1945–6, began in Kunming, where Powell had been stationed with the U.S. Office of War Information. The second, lasting from December 1946 to early 1947, was precipitated by the rape of a Peking University co-ed by two American marines. The third and largest of the student protests, the "Anti-Hunger, Anti-Civil War Movement" (May-June 1947) involved universities and middle schools in most cities under Guomindang control. The final protest movement (April-June 1948) developed mainly out of opposition to potential American rearmament of Japan.[51]

In late Fall, 1945, although the CCP and GMD had agreed upon the general outlines of a coalition government, they were still far apart on specifics. Clashes between the two armies continued in Manchuria as both sides maneuvered to control disputed areas.[52] In response, thirty thousand students from over thirty universities and middle schools[53] in Kunming staged a three day boycott of classes starting November 27, 1945. The students called for an end to civil war, formation of a coalition government, democracy, freedom of the press, assembly, and speech.[54]

Powell had been stationed in Kunming before he returned to Shanghai to resurrect the *China Weekly Review*. Still in his twenties, and recently a student himself, he was doubtless aware of the opposition to renewed civil war among students in Kunming. Most of the urban Chinese intellectuals affiliated with the *Review* shared this view, as did Powell himself. Moreover, U.S. China policy at this time converged with the students' demands: it also sought to avert civil war through creation of a multi-party democratic coalition government. Not surprisingly, the *Review* followed developments in the movement sympathetically from its inception.

On November 25, government soldiers used gunfire to disperse a student rally at Yunnan University. As student agitation continued to grow, on December 1, 1945, elements of the GMD Fifth Army and local plainclothes police attacked students at a number of university campuses in Kunming, including Yunnan University, Southwest Associated University, Teachers' Training College, and Gunhua Technical School. Three students and one teacher were killed and over thirty more injured.[55] A wave of sympathetic demonstrations for the Kunming martyrs erupted at universities in urban centers throughout Nationalist China. The government was quick to blame both the protests and the killings on the CCP.[56]

In Shanghai, on January 12, 1946, students from a number of colleges and middle schools attended a protest march and memorial service for those killed in Kunming. The *Review* characterized the protests as "an exhibition of healthy, progressive student spirit . . . an orderly affair, well conducted and well led."[57] In other articles, the *Review* covered all aspects of the marches, and publicized student demands, complete with photographs of the crowd and speakers. Above all, the demonstrators opposed Civil War. Students called for the formation of a democratic coalition government, elections of delegates to a People's Congress, freedom of thought and assembly, an increase in the pay of teachers and workers, release of arrested students in Nanjing and Beijing, and punishment of those officials responsible for the killings in Kunming.[58]

Powell refuted the notion that the demonstrations had been Communist led. They were depicted as spontaneous and idealistic.[59] Staff writer Charles J.Canning visited Kunming, where he spoke with dozens of students and professors. Although they attacked corruption, one party rule, suppression of civil liberties, and government by decree, Canning noted, they did not call for the overthrow of the government. Rather, student strikers advocated the creation of a coalition government as per the Political Consultative Conference Agreements, civil liberties and an end to civil war and one party rule.[60]

When Shanghai held local elections a short while later, Powell protested the fact that students were specifically disqualified from running as candidates, pointing out that students were usually better informed than most of the population.[61] He called on the Nationalist government to extend financial help to students who were returning with their universities from wartime locations in the interior.[62]

Powell told of a flood of letters to the *Review* from students and teachers "describing almost intolerable conditions", wherein "the teachers receive little or no pay, both students and teachers receive scanty rations of poorest quality" and housing was "pitifully inadequate". He complained that

> nearly every move made by educational authorities is a hostile one, calculated to aggravate rather than to improve. While the government an-

nounces improved conditions for civil servants, soldiers, and others, the only announcements regarding schools and colleges are statements 'explaining' why aid cannot be given or why new repressive measures have been instituted. China's schools are being neglected and allowed to deteriorate rapidly.[63]

The *Review* publicized cases of government repression of students. In May, C.Y.W. Meng prepared a list of seven different instances where troops, or plain-clothes police had fired on demonstrators. He called on the government to recognize the seriousness of the situation and to take constructive measures to correct it:

> When such a situation is permitted to go on, and incidents occur one after another, in the wartime national capital and leading cities, the matter is certainly serious.[64]

On June 25, 1946, after an angry argument with Hsuchow Middle School students, Nationalist army commander Fang Jingxing set up three machine guns just outside the school gates and opened fire. Ten students were killed and twenty wounded. Initially, only the liberal Chinese journal *Wen Wei Bao* and the *China Weekly Review* reported the story. Belatedly the government-sponsored *Central News Agency* issued a brief statement admitting the occurrence.[65] Powell warned U.S. officials that since these troops had been American-trained and supplied, their commander riding in an American jeep, in Chinese eyes, the United States shared in the responsibility. He urged U.S. and Chinese authorities to investigate.[66]

As the Civil War intensified in the early summer, student protests continued. The *Review*'s Frank L. Zao reported that after the demonstrations of June 23, 1946, hundreds of students at the Utopia Middle School and the Shanghai Middle School for Girls were dismissed for taking part, while liberal teachers were fired. Other students active in anti-Civil War protests received anonymous letters threatening bodily harm unless they ceased their activities.[67]

Only a half year after resuming publication, the *China Weekly Review* was well on its way to becoming what Jack Belden called "a kind of wailing wall where the people howled out their anguish".[68] By May,1946, Powell observed:

> We have always been pretty close to student movements and activities, since students and teachers have formed a large section of our reading audience. Each week we receive dozens of letters from educational institutions throughout the country in which the writers describe local conditions, express agreement with us or take issue.[69]

Chinese publications were subject to reprisals for reporting stories detrimental to the government. The *Review*, however, because it was American owned, and run by the son of a well-known GMD supporter, enjoyed a relatively privileged position in this regard.

Powell railed at the government for the lack of civil liberties which the Chinese suffered. In spite of Chiang Kai-shek removing restrictions on the press, on the rights of free speech and assembly, Nationalist authorities throughout the country continued to ignore these directives, ". . . secure in the knowledge that unless they become involved in something really serious, such as the Kunming assassinations, the long arm of Nanking will not reach out for them."[70] He highlighted cases of abusive behavior by both the police and the military in Shanghai toward unoffending citizens.[71]

By the end of November, worsening economic conditions, the rising cost of living,[72] and police repression resulted in two days of rioting by Shanghai's street vendors. The *Review*'s editor rejected the government's contention that the riots were chiefly the work of Communist agitators, and noted that other sectors of the population had been involved as well. For Powell, "The essential reason for the regrettable disturbances is the poor economic situation in which a larger and larger section of Shanghai's population finds itself each week." He warned that the city would see more rioting and civil disturbances as the weather got colder unless the government took effective measures to lessen unemployment and lower the price of basic commodities.[73]

Students were adversely effected by the deteriorating economic situation. "One of the main reasons why the Chinese students are more easily inclined to the left is due to their constant poverty and the constant economic struggle", contributing editor Frank L.Zao observed. According to Zao, students worried that rising commodity prices would prevent them from being able to pay tuition or support themselves. Factory closures could easily end college for many students if family members were thrown out of work. Not only had the government failed to set aside sufficient funds for student stipends due to the demands of the civil war, but now acted to prevent the traditional cooperative activities of "Student Aid Movements" to raise the funds themselves.[74]

The second round of nation-wide student protests occurred in late December, 1946 and early 1947. It was precipitated by the rape of a female Beijing University student by two American marines.[75] Resentment of America's positive contribution to Chiang's military operations against the CCP had been growing throughout the summer of 1946. American agreements to transfer military supplies to the Nationalists only fed the resentment. During this period the *Review* brimmed with irate letters to the editor about the rape incident.[76] Powell explained that students believed U.S. support for the government's war effort only served to prolong the Civil War and to prevent both sides from coming back to the negotiating table.

> The average Chinese is convinced that only America's support to the Nationalist government has kept China's Civil War going. Students, almost always liberal-minded, are thoroughly dissatisfied with their treatment and with the war in general. They heap all the blame- whether it is de-

served or not-upon Nanking and since America obviously is Nanking's chief foreign friend and certainly has been giving support to this regime, the United States is also blamed.[77]

The incident had placed Nanjing in a difficult position: if it silenced the unrest, it would be seen as a U.S. puppet, and if it did not, it might lose American good will. The rape case had also hurt American prestige, and in Powell's opinion, was a good argument for withdrawing the remaining U.S. troops from China.[78]

As mass rallies, student strikes, and demonstrations swept most of China's large cities, Charles Canning pointed out that a strong anti-American undercurrent had been growing for some time before the rape case brought it to a head. Chinese liberals and democrats felt American support was one reason for the continuation of one party rule and civil war, and the growth of what they perceived as "fascism".[79] By contrast, supporters of the government's harsh policies were irritated by the American influence in China's internal affairs. These attitudes nurtured resentment against the United States which the Beijing Rape Case released in a torrent of anti-U.S. agitation, Canning explained.[80]

Frank L. Zao defended anti-American demonstrators, comparing them to the May Fourth Movement of 1919, and asking how Americans would respond if Chinese troops had been stationed in the U.S. and a similar incident had occurred? Zao felt the demand for the withdrawal of U.S.troops was reasonable.[81]

Powell, in spite of his general support for student demonstrators' goals, resented the anti-American tone of the demonstrations, and suspected that xenophobia played an important part. Recalling the widespread outrage in the Chinese press over the Beijing Rape Incident, Powell called attention to the curious silence in journals and on campuses after the rape and murder of Zhou Yueyi, a female elementary school teacher in Wuxi by four Nationalist soldiers in June, 1947.[82]

When he thought it necessary, Powell was not above scolding student activists. A Texas Oil Company truck struck and killed a Jiaotong University student in Shanghai on April fourth. Irate students ignored the Chinese driver and seized two American lawyers who had arrived to negotiate a settlement, and demanded an exorbitant indemnity for their release. Powell questioned the students' motives, criticized their exorbitant demands, and urged them to demonstrate for political reform, not extortion.[83] "It is especially important that students make every effort to avoid pitfalls which may discredit them in the public eye," he counseled.[84]

When Communist Radio broadcasts tried to fuel student discontent by charging American military personnel in China with responsibility for 3,800 cases of rape, murder and robbery of Chinese civilians over a fifteen month period, Powell called them liars, and challenged the CCP to provide proof to back its claims.

. . . in an effort to be eminently fair to our Communist friends, we wish to offer them a chance to prove their statements. If they will provide us with a detailed list of these 'atrocities', we will attempt to check them against Army and Navy records and will print a complete expose of our findings, listing all 3,800 incidents if necessary. . . To be perfectly frank, we think the Communists are lying. However, we are always willing to change our minds when proven wrong and, if we are, will be the first to admit it and apologize. The whole matter is now up to Yenan and we suggest the that the boys in the north get busy and dig up a little proof or admit that their recent broadcasts have been outright prevarications designed as political propaganda rather than information.[85]

At the same time, Powell published counter charges of Communist atrocities involving "the naked mutilated bodies of hundreds of non-combatants wantonly slain and left in the burning compound of a Catholic Church, among them the bodies of several priests." The article recounted other instances of slaughtered civilians and concluded that: "The trail of the Chinese Communists is long, bloody, and unmistakably marked."[86]

Throughout February and March, university campuses were relatively quiet. During this lull, Powell slipped into Taiwan to cover the Nationalist repression of the Taiwanese revolt. The coverage he provided broke the story of the brutal suppression to a shocked world. Upon his return to Shanghai, Powell and the *Review* would become involved in the massive Anti-Civil War, Anti-Hunger demonstrations. When the government used the army to put down the movement in June, 1947, the *Review* documented the repression, opened its pages to the persecuted, called judicial proceedings into question, and protested conditions in government jails. These events,taken together with the failure of GMD democratization and the banning of the Democratic League doubtless precipitated the final alienation of Powell from the Guomindang.

*

THE *REVIEW* AND GMD REPRESSION OF THE TAIWANESE REVOLT

John King Fairbank and Merle Goldman in their text *China, A New History* (1998) introduced the Nationalist reoccupation of Taiwan following World War II with the following summary:

As in the coastal cities of the mainland, the Nationalist occupation of Taiwan after 1945 turned out to be a first class disaster. Instead of being "liberated," the Taiwanese Chinese were treated as enemy collaborators; their goods were seized and the economy despoiled by Nationalist military and politicians seeking personal loot. In February 1947, when unarmed demonstrators protested the corruption of the Nationalist occupation, the military government shot many of them down, sent for mainland reinforcements, and then for several days pursued a pogrom of murdering Taiwanese citizens. A somber estimate is that 8,000 to 10,000 were killed, including much of the potential leadership of the community. This was a triumph for China's backwardness, posited on the assumption of uninhibited autocracy as the primal law of the Chinese political order: policy opponents are disloyal and should be killed.[87]

This massacre established the political dominance of the mainland Chinese minority and the exclusion of the Taiwanese majority from self-government, an effect that would last, along with martial law, well into the 1980's on the island. It was only during the 1990's that the first cautious accounts of the Insurrection by resident Taiwanese historians began to appear.[88]

*

Powell first became alarmed at Nationalist government mismanagement in its takeover of Taiwan from Japanese control as early as April, 1946. During fifty years of colonial rule, he editorialized, Japan, although exploiting the island, had built up a modern infrastructure, educational and communications structures, and a healthy, diversified economy. But now, Powell stated, Guomindang mismanagement in a relatively short time had set the island back ten years. Factories were idle, corruption permeated all levels of the government, and the people were on the verge of revolt. If Taiwan's administration were not reconstructed from the ground up, he warned, Taiwan could become another Ireland, a seething hotbed of rebellion against exploitative metropolitan rule.[89]

In January, an article by Joshua W. Liao intoned a similar warning, charging that Governor General Chen Yi had set up his own personal fiefdom on Taiwan, dismissing native factory managers in favor of incompetent favorites, and installing the worst kind of carpetbag rule.[90] Therefore, when large scale rioting broke out in Taipei in February, Powell was not surprised.

Only eighteen months before, he noted, the Taiwanese had welcomed the mainland government, believing their long colonial experience was over. But after a year and a half of deteriorating administration and destruction of the economy, the disillusioned Taiwanese fought back out of desperation. Powell worried there would be ". . . a magnificent job of covering up the Taipei Revolt", which would probably be blamed on the Communists. He again urged the immediate reorganization of the government in Taipei.[91]

The following week, Powell began an editorial campaign to expose the situation in Taiwan to the light of day. He was pleased to see Generalissimo Chiang Kai-shek taking over direct control of the government's Taiwan policy, and advised that Governor General Chen Yi be removed and a massive shakeup of the Taiwan government undertaken. Powell also urged the establishment of a system of laws written by jurists, reduction of government monopolies to a bare minimum, restoration of freedom of speech and the press, and increasing Taiwanese participation in their government.[92]

Taiwanese grievances reinforcing these suggestions were publicized: demands for local self-government, demands for abolition of the Sales Monopoly Office and of the government monopoly on trade.[93]

As the crisis on Taiwan deepened, the government enforced martial law and a complete news blackout[94] in the wake of spreading rebellion and violence.[95] Not content to report from afar, Powell slipped into Taiwan for nine days in March while the military was still quelling the rebellion. Traveling from Taipei to other parts of the island, he gathered material for a series of eye-witness accounts; the first of these, "An Exclusive Account of Taiwan's Bloodbath" appeared March 29, just after he returned.[96]

"Governor General Chen Yi, coupling trickery with a reign of terror probably not equaled in China in the history of the Kuomintang, has virtually suppressed the Taiwan Rebellion,"[97] Powell wrote. Estimating the death toll at 5000, he told of the mutilated bodies of executed youths washing up daily on beaches, of soldiers machine-gunning a hapless crowd at a railway station, and of continuous chaos as truckloads of troops with automatic weapons rampaged through Taipei from March 8 through 13.

Powell collected eyewitness accounts of the murder of twenty youths in a village between Taipei and Keelung; they had been castrated, their ears cut off and noses split before being bayoneted. He spoke of economic disintegration in the midst of factories and plants capable of fueling vast reconstruction projects, of a government rotten with corruption, nepotism, and gross mismanagement. The Taiwanese were fed up with Chinese control, he reported, and now preferred to be placed under United Nations mandate.[98]

In a second exclusive account, Powell sketched the chronology of events. Rioting began on February 28 and grew in intensity until most of the island was in native hands. A series of demands were given to Chen Yi, who, not having enough troops on hand at the time, temporized by agreeing to settle the original incident that had sparked the riots. He also promised reforms, including elections for a new provisional government to replace his own regime. Once reinforcements arrived, however, Chen Yi went back on his agreements, and ruthless repression followed.[99]

For Powell, the Taiwan revolt was just the worst of a whole series of riots and minor rebellions current all over Nationalist China. According to the *Wen Wei Bao*, uprisings had occurred throughout March in Sichuan, Shaanxi, Sikang, Guizhou, Hunan, Guangxi, Guangdong, Zhejiang, and in the Jiangsu-Zhejiang border area. In Powell's view, these underscored the widespread discontent across large areas under government control.[100]

By mid-April, news of the Taiwan repression, first publicized by Powell and the *Review*, had been picked up by journals all over the world. In the United States, the *Washington Post*, the *New York Times*, the *Washington Star* and the *San Francisco Chronicle* all drew from Powell's Taiwan reports. The *Washington Post* underscored the importance of Powell's efforts:

People stopped referring to Bill as J.B.'s son when he ducked into Taiwan (Formosa) in March this year and returned with an account of the 'blood bath' massacre imposed by the deposed governor, Gen. Chen Yi.[101]

In so doing, Powell was able to "Pierce the temporary news blackout over Formosa- torn by revolt and virtually sealed off from the outside world."[102] In spite of denials by the government in Nanjing, his account was confirmed by United Nations Relief and Rehabilitation Administration workers who had been stationed in Taiwan, by numerous foreign residents who had fled the violence, and by U.S.Consulate accounts that included unreleased photographs taken by Foreign Service personnel.[103]

In its coverage of the Taiwan Revolt, the *New York Times* included portions of Powell's reporting in its March 30, and April 5, 1947, news stories. On March 30, it announced:

> An American weekly magazine, The *China Weekly Review*, today was the first publication in the country to give a full story of the recent tragic events on the island. The *Review* carries a detailed account, written by John W. Powell, the publisher, who has just returned from a week's visit to the island.[104]

On April 4, the *Times* quoted Powell again as it summarized the first complete chronology of events from an article which would appear the following day in the *China Weekly Review*.[105]

The details of Powell's articles were mirrored by similar eyewitness accounts included in the *New York Times* articles of Tillman Durdin. These, together with the reports emanating from the U.S.Consulate at Taipei, and letters collected by U.S.Vice Consul Kerr from UNRRA workers in Taiwan, all verified the truth of Powell's assertions.[106]

The *Times*, which had previously estimated 10,000 deaths during the Nationalist suppression of the revolt, noted that Powell ventured a more conservative figure of 5000 killed.[107] A comparison of Powell's estimated mortality figures to those of more recent historical accounts of the Revolt yields a further measure of the accuracy of his reporting. Peng Ming-min, a former victim of the repression who left Taiwan to study at Harvard University under Henry Kissinger, stated in his account of the revolt, "Nobody knows how many Formosans died in the following weeks, but the estimates ranged from ten to twenty thousand."[108] American Vice Consul George H. Kerr, an eyewitness to the revolt, noted in his monograph *Formosa Betrayed* that

> Formosan leaders in exile charge that more than 10,000 people were slaughtered in the month of March. I must assume that there could not have been less than 5000 and I am inclined to accept the higher figure. If we add to this the thousands who have been seized and done away with since March, 1947, on the pretext that they were involved in the affair, the number may reach the 20,000 figure often given by Formosan writers.[109]

Steven Phillips (*Taiwan, A New History*) commented that

> . . . estimates of the number killed range from the ridiculously low (500) to high (100,000). . . . One common estimate is 10,000 killed and 30,000 wounded. The most detailed English language account of the incident provides a figure of 8000 dead.[110]

A recent study of the Taiwan uprising by Lai Tse-Han, Ramon H. Meyers, and Wei Wou, published by Stanford University, was sympathetic to the Nationalists and to governor Chen Yi, yet accepted the general accuracy of Powell's reporting.[111] After reviewing all of the mortality estimates, from revolt leaders' figures of more than 100,000, to Nationalist estimates of only a few thousand, Lai, Wei and Meyers settled on a figure of about 8000 persons killed.[112] In retrospect, Powell's estimate of 5000 deaths was an understated, restrained figure, well within the bounds of all the accounts above.

Apprised of the situation in Taiwan by U.S. Consulate reports from Taipei, U.S. Ambassador John Leighton Stuart on April 18, 1947, sent a long account of the uprising and its repression, directly to Generalissimo Chiang Kai-shek, who professed to not be aware of conditions on the island.[113] The United States pressured Chiang to remove General Chen Yi from his governorship.[114]

*

In mid-April, 1947, with a whirlwind of criticism breaking all around the GMD, Powell prodded Chiang Kai-shek to stop procrastinating and take rapid action: "There is no longer any valid reason for inaction, the greatest atrocity of the postwar world can no longer be covered up, or ignored."[115]

When Chiang appointed former Chinese Ambassador to the United States Dr. Wei Daoming as the new governor of Taiwan, and the Nationalist government announced a series of economic and political reforms he was to undertake, Powell was satisfied. He felt it was due to the pressure of public opinion and two months of agitation that General Chen Yi's administration was finally brought down. He was proud of the role he and the *Review* had performed in keeping the public informed.[116]

But the government of Chen Yi lingered on even after a new governor had been appointed. Censorship was tightened. All publications on Taiwan were closed down after the riots, and those from the mainland had to be submitted to the Taipei Garrison Headquarters before distributors could put them on the news stands. The *Review* was yanked off the news stands and lost its distributor in Taiwan. Chen Yi's staff wrote and circulated a pamphlet, *A Taiwanese Scholar Assails Powell's Riot Write-Up*, attacking Powell and his journal, claiming the atrocities in Taiwan had never occurred.[117]

Within a year, Powell felt, with certain reservations, that Wei Daoming's reforms, better administration, and the granting of a greater voice in local government to the Taiwanese had led to the end of any real separatist movement on the island.[118] In retrospect, Powell analyzed the uprising of February-March, 1947: fifty years of Japanese control had built up the island's industry and economy, improved the peoples' health and education. When China stepped in, Taiwan became a highly developed colony of a backward country. Chinese engineers and managers were inferior to the native Taiwanese they replaced. Their revolt had been crushed with great brutality and no doubt left a residue of hatred. Although Wei Daoming's reforms had improved things somewhat, Powell reminded the government that much remained to be done.[119]

If Powell thought that he had seen the worst with the suppression of the Taiwan insurrection in February and March, and that the situation in China would improve somewhat, he was mistaken. The blood of murdered Taiwanese, the Kunming assassinations, and his defense of student demonstrators were beginning to draw Powell deeper into China's turmoil. There would be no breathing spell. Soon the greatest wave of student demonstrations in China's history, and the Guomindang's blatant disregard for human rights as it struggled to suppress that unrest, would engulf the *Review* and constitute the final strand of Powell's and the Chinese intellectual community's loss of faith in the Nationalist government of Chiang Kai-shek.

CHAPTER NOTES

1. United States Civil Service Commission, Service Record Division, Washington D.C., 6 August 1954. *Statement of Federal Service, Powell, John W.*,(prepared by A.M.Deem, Chief, Audit Section). ; Office of War Information, Overseas Branch, China, Kunming, *Report of Efficiency Rating, Powell,John W., Senior Field Representative*, A-1-7 (William L.Holland, Deputy Director, China Division, 22 June 1945). Both documents in: United States Senate, Subcommittee to Investigate the Administration of the Internal Security Act and Other Internal Security Laws of the Committee on the Judiciary, *Hearings: Interlocking Subversion in Government Departments*, 83 Congress,2 Session, 27 September 1954, p.1851,1884; See also: John W.Powell, Testimony, United States Senate, Subcommittee to Investigate the Administration of the Internal Security Act and Other Internal Security Laws of the Committee on the Judiciary, *Hearings: Interlocking Subversion in Government Departments*. 27 September 1954, p.1887.

2. "J.B.'s Boy", *Time*, 24 March 1947, p.72–5; Roy Essoyan,"China Editor's Son Has Own Rapier Pen", *Washington Post*, 6 July 1947,p.B3.

3. John W. Powell, "An Exclusive Account of Taiwan's Bloodbath As Detailed by Eyewitnesses", *CWR*, 29 March 1947, p.115–117; John W. Powell,"Good Government, Common Sense Needed in Administering Taiwan", *CWR*, 5 April 1947, p.142–144.

4. Powell, ed. "Efforts of Thirty-Six Years", *CWR*, 11 October 1947, p.163–5.

5. Stephen R. MacKinnon and Oris Friesen, *China Reporting, An Oral History of American Journalism in the 1930's and 1940's.* (Berkeley: University of California Press, 1987.), p.94. Doak Barnett Interview.

6 MacKinnon and Friesen, *China Reporting*, p.92–3. Powell Interview.

7. Powell, ed. "Death of a Journalist", *CWR*, 19 January 1946, p.129.

8. Powell, ed. "What Our Readers Think", *CWR*, 10 May 1947, p.286–7. Results of questionnaire to readers.

9. Suzanne Pepper, *Civil War in China, The Political Struggle, 1945–1949.* (Berkeley: University of California Press, 1978.) p.121–125. Inundated by hyperinflation of its own making, the government decided to abandon the old currency, the *fapi* or "Chinese National Currency" (CNC), for new "Gold Yuan" notes at the rate of GY 1 = CNC 3,000,000. All gold, silver and foreign currency was to be turned over to the government in return for Gold Yuan notes. But this too failed. In spite of extreme efforts by Chiang's son in Shanghai to curb speculation, within four months prices had risen to ten times their August rates.

10. John K.Fairbank and Albert Feuerwerker, eds. *The Cambridge History of China, Volume 13, Republican China 1912–1949, Part 2.* (Cambridge, U.K.: Cambridge University Press, 1986) p.417, 707.

11. MacKinnon and Friesen, "*China Reporting.* p.92–94.

12. C.Y.W.Meng, "Chinese Democratic League Works for Unity and Peace", *CWR*, 5 January 1946,p.92–3; Powell, ed. "Legacy of Dr. Sun", *CWR*, 12 October 1946,p.160; Arnold Chao, "Democratic League Mirrors Views of Middle Classes", *CWR*, 19 October 1946, p.202.

13. Fairbank and Feuerwerker, eds. *The Cambridge History of China, Volume 13.* p.731.

14. Powell, ed. "J.B.Powell Passes", *CWR*, 8 March 1947, p.33–4. Powell married Sylvia Campbell, of Pendleton, Or. on December 27, 1947. Sylvia was a graduate of Reed College, in Portland, Or, and worked for the United Nations Relief and Rehabilitation Administration. Her experience doubtless helped broaden her husband's compassion for the suffering of the Chinese people.

15. Not to be confused with the People's Consultative Conference of January, 1946.

16. C.Y.W.Meng, "Chinese Democratic League Works for Unity and Peace", *CWR*, 5 January 1946, p.92–93.

17. Meng, "Chinese Democratic League", p.93.

18. *Ibid.*

19. *Ibid.*

20. Pepper, *Civil War in China*, p.137–8; Immanuel C.Y.Hsu, *The Rise of Modern China.* (New York: Oxford University Press, 2000) p.624–27; Fairbank and Feuerwerker, eds. *The Cambridge History of China, Volume 13*, p.730–1.

21. Instruction, Chinese Communist Party Central Committee, "On the Current Situation and Our Tasks", 1 February 1946, in Shuguang Zhang and Jian Chen, eds. *Chinese Communist Foreign Policy and the Cold War in Asia, New Documentary Evidence, 1944-1950.* (Chicago: Imprint Publications, 1996)p.58–62. Hereafter cited as *CCFPCWA.*

22. Telegram, CCP Central Committee to Dong Biwu and Wang Ruofei, 9 December 1945, *CCFPCWA*, p.56.

23. Instruction, CCP Central Committee, "On Current Situation and Our Tasks", 1 February 1946, *CCFPCWA*, p.58–62.

24. Powell, ed. "Democratic League's Protest", *CWR*, 2 February 1946, p.164–5. The delegate concerned was Huang Yeh-pei.

25. For more on the American trained and published sociologist specializing in rural China, Dr.Fei Hsiao-tung, and his role in the CCP's thought reform move-

ment during 1949–1950, see Chapters 6 and 7 of this dissertation. It may be worth noting that Powell mentioned Fei at the 1982 Scottsdale conference of former China journalists: "A better way to find out what life was like in the countryside was to read Fei Hsiao-tung's books on peasant life and then spend long hours talking with him and other knowledgeable Chinese." MacKinnon and Friesen, *China Reporting*, p.99.

26. Charles J.Canning, "Settlement of Kunming Student Strike Does Not End Struggle", *CWR*, 23 February 1946, p.215. Canning refers to the name of the student paper as: *Hsioh Sheng Pao* (student paper).

27. Pepper, *Civil War in China*, p.137–8; Fairbank and Feuerwerker,eds. *The Cambridge History of China, Volume 13*, p.731; Carsun Chang, *The Third Force in China*. (New York: Bookman, 1952) p.142–222; John F.Melby, *The Mandate of Heaven*. (Toronto: University of Toronto Press, 1968), p.88–9.

28. Peter S. Wang, "Kunming Killings May Herald Reign of Terror in China", *CWR*, 27 July 1946, p.200.

29. Powell, ed. "Political Assassinations", *CWR*, 27 July 1946, p.191–2; Peter S.Wang, "Kunming Killings May Herald Reign of Terror In China", *CWR*, 27 July 1946, p.200–201; Fairbank and Feuerwerker, eds, *The Cambridge History of China, Volume 13*, p.418; Pepper, *Civil War in China*, p.143–4. Pepper has the dates reversed and says that Wen Yiduo(Wen I-to) was shot first, then Li Gongpu(Li Kung-p'u) four days later.

30. Powell, ed. "Political Assassination", *CWR*, 27 July 1946, p.191–2; Peter S.Wang, "Kunming Killings May Herald Reign of Terror In China", *CWR*, 27 July 1946,p.200–1.

31. *Letter*, President Truman to President Chiang Kai-shek, Washington, 10 August 1946, United States Department of State, *United States Relations with China, With Special Reference to the Period 1944–1949*.(Washington, D.C.: Government Printing Office, 1949; reprint, Stanford: Stanford University Press, 1967.) p.652.

32. "Statement by Lu Ting-yi, Chief of the Department of Information, Central Committee, Chinese Communist Party", 29 January 1947, United States Department of State, *United States Relations With China, With Special Reference to the Period 1944–1949*,p.702.

33. Arthur C.P.Kwei, "Liberals Form League To Protect Basic Human Rights, Freedoms", *CWR*, 18 January 1947, p.195.

34. "Who's Who in China: Liang Shu-ming", *CWR*, 13 July 1946, p.155; "Who's Who in China: Ma Yin-chu", *CWR*, 7 September 1946, p.25.

35. Powell, ed. "The Legacy of Dr.Sun", *CWR*, 12 October 1946, p.159–60.

36. Powell, ed. "Common Front or Eclipse?", *CWR*, 1 February 1947, p.240–1.

37. Sidney Rittenberg and Amanda Bennett, *The Man Who Stayed Behind*.(New York: Simon and Schuster, 1993.)p. 72. Rittenberg had studied Chinese at Stanford University while in the Army, had been stationed in Kunming at the same time Powell was there, had joined the UNRRA after his tour of duty was over, and accompanied C.W.Y.Meng, "a distinguished economist and newspaper man," during his journey to Yan'an in Mid-October, 1946.

38. Powell, ed. "Common Front or Eclipse?", *CWR*, 1 February 1947, p.240–1; Tseng Yu-hao, Ph.D., "Kuomintang's Efforts to Win Over Social Democrats Reviewed", *CWR*, 1 February 1947,p.244. The Democratic League and the Communist Party both refused to take part in the November National Assembly, citing the GMD's failure to first create the coalition government as mandated by the PCC

agreements. Afterward, however, the League partially reversed itself by participating in local assemblies in Nationalist China. When the People's Political Council convened in May, 1947 (under GMD auspices), the Democratic League delegates participated.

39. Powell, ed. "Common Front or Eclipse", *CWR*, 1 February 1947, p.240–1.

40. *Ibid.*

41. "Chiang Signs New Constitution; Mao Exhorts Against Reaction", News of the Week, *CWR*, 4 January 1947, p.146; "What Chinese Papers Say, Constitution", *CWR*, 4 January 1947, p.151.

42. Powell, ed. "The Kuomintang's Future", *CWR*, 18 January 1947,p.187–8.

43. Fairbank and Feuerwerker, eds. *The Cambridge History of China, Volume 13*, p.742–6.

44. "Democrats Arrested", *CWR*, 26 April 1947, p.246.

45. "Pressure on Democrats", *CWR*, 10 May 1947, p.299–300.

46. Powell, ed. "Efforts of Thirty-Six Years", *CWR*, 11 October 1947, p.163–5.

47. *Ibid.*

48. Powell, ed. "One More Step", *CWR*, 1 November 1947, p.283–4.

49. *Ibid.*

50. *Ibid.*

51. Suzanne Pepper, *Civil War in China*, p.42; Jeffrey N. Wasserstrom, *Student Protests in Twentieth-Century China, the View from Shanghai*. (Stanford: Stanford University Press, 1991) p.242–276.

52. Suzanne Pepper, *Civil War in China*, p.45.

53. high schools.

54. Pepper, *Civil War in China*. p.47–50.

55. *Ibid.*; Wasserstrom, *Student Protests in Twentieth-Century China*. pp.242–250.

56. Pepper, *Civil War in China*. p.49, 51.

57. Powell, ed. "Student Demonstrators", *CWR*, 19 January 1946, p.129.

58. Y.F.Chao, "Shanghai Students Stage Demonstration", *CWR*, 19 January 1946, p.136–7.

59. Powell, ed. "Students' Detractors", *CWR*, 26 January 1946, p.145 ; Powell, ed. "Voice of Reaction Again", *CWR*, 4 May 1946, p.203.

60. Charles J.Canning, "Settlement of Kunming Student Strike Does Not End Struggle", *CWR*, 23 February 1946, p.215.

61. Powell, ed. "Democratic Elections?", *CWR*, 16 March 1946, p.48–9.

62. Powell, ed. "China's Universities", *CWR*, 13 April 1946, p.138–9. During the war against Japan, the faculty and students of most universities withdrew into the interior with Nationalist forces and the government. After the war, these universities in exile had to make the long trek back to their original campuses without any government help.

63. Powell, ed. "Educational Reform", *CWR*, 18 May 1946, p.247–248.

64. C.Y.W.Meng, "Constructive Efforts, Government Needed to Put China's House in Order at Once", *CWR*, 25 May 1946,p.272–3. These incidents were: the Kunming Tragedy, the Zhong Beidang (Chung Pei Tang) Incident, the Jiao Zhenggao (Chiao Cheng Kow) Incident, the Fudan (Fuh Tan) University Incident, the Central University Girls' College Incident, the College of Fine Arts Incident, and the Nandong (Nantung) Tragedy.

65. Powell, ed. "Student Slaughter", *CWR*, 6 July 1946, p.117.

66. Powell, ed. "Student Slaughter", *CWR*, 6 July 1946, p.117; Powell, ed. "Hsuchow Incident", *CWR*, 14 September 1946, p.37–8.

67. Frank L.Tsao, "Hundreds of Students Expelled For'We Demand Peace' Parades", *CWR*, 16 November 1946, p.332–3.

68. Jack Belden, *China Shakes the World*.(Beijing: New World Press, 1989) p.407. "The letter columns of the *China Weekly Review* became a kind of wailing wall where the people howled out their anguish."

69. Powell, ed. "Educational Reforms", *CWR*, 18 May 1946, p.247–8.

70. Powell, ed. "Personal Liberties", *CWR*, 31 August 1946, p.325–6.

71. *Ibid*.p.327.

72.Chang Kia-Ngau, *The Inflationary Spiral, The Experience in China, 1939–1950*.(New York: Massachusetts Institute of Technology and John Wiley and Sons, 1958.)p.71–73. Chang indicated that, especially after November, 1946, "prices in Shanghai were almost doubling every two or three months." Inflationary pressure was mainly generated by huge increases in government civil war military spending against totally inadequate revenues.

73. Powell, ed. "Shanghai's Riots", *CWR*, 7 December 1946,p.7–8.

74. Frank L.Tsao, "Hundreds Of Students Expelled for 'We Demand Peace' Parades", *CWR*, 16 November 1946, p.332–3.

75. Pepper. *Civil War in China*,p.42; 52–3.

76. *Letter*, Chen Tse-kiang to ed.,Peiping, 25 December 1946, "Protest from Peiping", *CWR*, 11 January 1947, p.155 ; *Letter*, Richard Ma, et al.to ed., Shanghai, 31 December 1946, "Alleged Rape", *CWR*, 11 January 1947,p.155; *Letter*, Committee for Protesting Against Misconduct by U.S. Troops, Chiaotung Middle School, Shanghai, 1 January 1947, "Letter to Dr.Stuart", *CWR*, 11 January 1947, p.155–6; *Letter*, 'Third Person' to ed., Shanghai 5 January 1947, "Up to U.S.A.?", *CWR*, 11 January 1947,p.156; *Letter*,Chang Pei-lin to ed., Shanghai, 27 December 1946, "How Chinese Feel", *CWR*, 11 January 1947,p.157.

77. Powell, ed. "The Peiping Rape Case", *CWR*, 11 January 1947,p.163–4.

78. *Ibid*.p.163.

79. Fairbank and Feuerwerker, eds. *The Cambridge History of China, Volume 13, Republican China 1912–1949*, p.142–147; John King Fairbank and Merle Goldman, *China, A New History*. (Cambridge, Mass.: The Belknap Press of Harvard University Press, 1998.) p.291; Lloyd E.Eastman, "Fascism in Kuomintang China: The Blue Shirts", *CQ*,Volume 49 (January-March 1972) p.1–31. From 1932–1937, Chiang admired and wished to duplicate Nazi Germany and Fascist Italy's militaristic organization of government and society in China. He helped found the fascist Blue Shirt organization within the GMD, which was responsible for numerous assassinations; he believed that fascism could regenerate Chinese society and he incorporated its ideology into his New Life movement. By 1937, Nationalist China had steadily increased its economic and military relations with Nazi Germany. Although war with Japan meant that Chiang's relationship with the U.S. suddenly became more important, he was never strongly committed to democratic ideals, and continued to trust the military above all else.

80. Charles J.Canning, "Peiping Rape Case Has Deep Social, Political Background", *CWR*, 11 January 1947,p.166–7.

81. Frank L.Tsao, "A Review and Study of the Student Demonstrations", *CWR*, 18 January 1947,p.194.

82. *Ta Kung Pao*, 6 June 1947; *Letter*, Fei Liang to ed.,Wusih,Kiangsu, 9 June 1947, "Rape-Murder", *CWR*, 28 June 1947,p.95; Powell, ed. "Rape Cases and Rape Cases", *CWR*, 28 June 1947,p.103. The teacher's name was written Chou Yueh-e in Fei's letter.

83. Powell, ed. "Student Behavior", *CWR*, 19 April 1947,p.206.

84. *Ibid*.

85. Powell, ed. "American 'Atrocities'", *CWR*, 25 January 1947,p.213.

86. Lam On-pong, "Communists Scored For Blocking Peace Move; Patriotism Queried", *CWR*, 1 February 1947, p.246.

87.John King Fairbank and Merle Goldman, *China, A New History*.(Cambridge, Mass.: The Belknap Press of Harvard University Press, 1998.) p.339.

88. Steven Phillips, "Between Assimilation and Independence, Taiwanese Political Aspirations Under Nationalist Chinese Rule, 1945–1948", in: *Taiwan, A New History*, ed. Murray A.Rubinstein (Armonk,N.Y.: M.E. Sharpe, 1999.) p.302–3. see also n.2.

89. Powell, ed. "Taiwan Travesty", *CWR*, 6 April 1946,p.113.

90. Joshua W.K.Liao, "Imperialism vs. Nationalism in Formosa", *CWR*, 18 January 1947,p.191–3. The *Review* was by no means the only journal to draw attention to the deteriorating quality of Nationalist rule on Taiwan. The *Washington Post* on March 29, 1946 and the *Washington News* on March 21, 22, and 28, 1946 both ran stories on the "Formosa Scandal". Also, U.S.Consulate officials at Taipei tried to warn the U.S.Embassy and the State Department throughout late 1946 and early 1947 about Nationalist abuses and growing Taiwanese discontent. See (former U.S.Vice Consul at Taipei) George H.Kerr, *Formosa Betrayed*.(Boston: Houghton Mifflin Company, The Riverside Press Cambridge, 1965.) p.149.

91. Powell,ed. "Rioting in Taiwan", *CWR*, 8 March 1947,p.34–5.

92. Powell,ed. "Reforms in Taiwan",*CWR*, 15 March 1947,p.59–60.

93. L.E.F., "The Formosan Crisis", *CWR*, 15 March 1947,p.70.

94. Lai Tse-Han, Ramon H.Myers, and Wei Wou, *A Tragic Beginning, The Taiwan Uprising of February 28, 1947*.(Stanford: Stanford University Press, 1991.)p.100, 182; Tillman Durbin, "Nanking Censures Formosa Governor", *New York Times*, 23 March 1947,p.16; George H. Kerr, *Formosa Betrayed*.(Boston: Houghton Mifflin Company, The Riverside Press Cambridge, 1965.) p.267. Martial law, and with it a blackout of all independent foreign news gathering, was initiated on February 28, and remained in de-facto effect through May 17, although ship and telegraph communications with the outside world were restored by March 22. Lai, Myers, and Wei noted that the mainland Chinese press reported very little about the uprising or its suppression. General Chen Yi's government controlled the radio stations and cable services on Taiwan and, according to U.S.Vice Consul at Taipei George H.Kerr (an eyewitness to the tragedy), used them to "manipulate rumor, plant stories, and twist facts."

95. "Constitutional Rights Demanded In Taiwan; Rebellion Spreads", *CWR*, 15 March 1947, p.74–5.

96. John W. Powell, "An Exclusive Account of Taiwan's Bloodbath As Detailed by Eyewitnesses", *CWR*, 29 March 1947, p.115–117.

97. *Ibid*.

98. *Ibid*.

99. John W. Powell, "Good Government, Common Sense Needed in Administering Taiwan", *CWR*, 5 April 1947,p.142–144.

100. Powell, ed. "Armed Riots Spread", *CWR*, 5 April 1947,p.138–9. Sikang Province is now part of Xizang Autonomous Region, and is called Chamdo.
101. Roy Essoyan, "China Editor's Son Has Own Rapier Pen", *Washington Post*, 6 July 1947.
102. *Ibid.*
103. Memorandum by the Vice Consul at Taipei (Kerr) to the Ambassador in China (Stuart), Nanking, 10 April 1947, United States Department of State, *Foreign Relations of the United States, Diplomatic Papers, 1947, Volume 7,the Far East: China.* (Washington D.C.: Government Printing Office.) p.426–455. Hereafter cited as *FRUS 1947, Vol.7* ; Powell, ed. "Nanking Should Act", *CWR*, 12 April 1947,p.165; Powell, ed. "Dust in the Eyes", *CWR*, 9 October 1948,p.133–4. Powell said two American Vice Councils toured the city, at considerable danger to themselves, taking photographs of the atrocities.
104.Tillman Durdin, "Formosans' Plea for Red Aid Seen, Harsh Repression of Revolt Is Expected to Increase Efforts to Escape Rule by China", *New York Times*, 30 March 1947, p.27.
105. "Story of Repression in Formosa Detailed", *New York Times*, 5 April 1947,p.8; John W.Powell, "Good Government, Common Sense Needed in Administering Taiwan", *CWR*, 5 April 1947, p.142–144. The *New York Times* story was written on April 4. "The story of how governor Chen Yi halted the demonstrations on Formosa last month 'sounds as if it had occurred several centuries ago', American journalist John W. Powell says in an article that will appear tomorrow in his China Weekly Review."
106. Tillman Durdin, "Nanking Censures Formosa Governor", *New York Times*, 23 March 1947, p.16; Tillman Durdin, "Formosa Killings Are Put at 10,000", *New York Times*, 29 March 1947, p.6; Tillman Durdin, "Formosans' Plea for Red Aid Seen", *New York Times*, 30 March 1947,p.27; *Letter*, Louise Tomsett (UNRRA, New Zealand) to Kerr, 7 June 1947, in Kerr, *Formosa Betrayed*, p.301–2; *Letter*, Ira D.Herschy,M.D.(Chief Medical Officer, UNRRA, Taiwan) to E.E.Paine(UNRRA Reports Officer), n.d.,*Ibid.* p.305–6; *Letter*, Hans Johansen (UNRRA, Norway) to E.E.Paine, 17 April 1947, *Ibid.* p.335–6.
107. Tillman Durdin, "Formosa Killings Are Put at 10,000", *New York Times*, 29 March 1947, p.6; Tillman Durdin, "Formosans' Plea for Red Aid Seen", *New York Times*, 30 March 1947, p.27.
108. Peng Ming-min, *A Taste of Freedom, Memoirs of a Formosan Independence Leader.*(New York: Holt, Rinehart and Winston, 1972.) p.70.
109.George H. Kerr, *Formosa Betrayed.*(Boston: Houghton Mifflin Company, The Riverside Press, 1965.) p.310.
110. Steven Phillips, "Between Assimilation and Independence", in: *Taiwan, A New History*, ed.Murray A.Rubinstein, p.295–6.
111. Lai Tse-Han, Ramon H. Meyers and Wei Wou, *A Tragic Beginning, The Taiwan Uprising of February 28, 1947.*(Stanford: Stanford University Press, 1991.) p.156.
112. *Ibid.*p.160.
113. The U.S.Ambassador to China (Stuart) to President Chiang Kai-shek, 18 April 1947, "Memorandum on the Situation in Taiwan", United States Department of State, *United States Relations with China with Special Reference to the Period 1944–1949.* (Washington,D.C.:United States Government Printing Office, 1949.)

p.923–938; *Ibid.* p.308. "The Generalissimo . . . professed to be unaware of conditions as they were reported to him by the Ambassador. . ."

114. *Ibid.*

115. Powell, ed. "Nanking Should Act", *CWR*, 12 April 1947, p.165–6.

116. Powell, ed. "Taiwan's New Deal", *CWR*, 26 April 1947,p.233; Fred W. Riggs, *Formosa Under Chinese Nationalist Rule.*(New York: Octagon Books, 1972.) p.47. Riggs tends to confirm Powell's assumptions about the role played by the press. Riggs said that Nanjing, with American reaction in mind, announced it would recall Chen Yi and replace him with Wei Tao-ming.

117. Powell, ed. "Censorship in Taiwan", *CWR*, 10 May 1947, p.285–6; Lee Yu-chi. *A Taiwanese Scholar Assails Powell's Write-Up.*(Taipei: The Taiwan News Service, 1947.)

118. Powell, ed. "Taiwan in Trouble", *CWR*, 13 December 1947, p.44–5; Powell, ed."An Independent Taiwan?", *CWR*, 18 September 1948, p.56–7.

119. *Ibid.*; Powell, ed. "Dust in the Eyes", *CWR*, 9 October 1948,p.133–4; Powell, ed. "Taiwan Travel Restrictions", *CWR*, 23 October 1948, p.200.

CHAPTER THREE

THE STRANDS OF DISILLUSIONMENT, PART II: FINAL LOSS OF FAITH

By late spring, 1947, Powell had seen the prospects for a coalition government and Constitutional democracy fall by the wayside, due in his view to the intransigence of the GMD right wing. The *Review*'s hopes that a liberal third party under Democratic League auspices would lead China into a new age of Western liberal democratic political institutions had been dashed by all-out Civil War.

From its reopening in 1945, the *Review* had sympathized with and defended student and faculty demonstrators calling for an end to the Civil War and a return to the agreements of the Political Consultative Conference of January, 1946. The *Review* had protested whenever student, faculty, or Democratic League proponents of peace and democracy had been gunned down or arrested without due process of law. Powell had alerted the world to the brutal repression of the Taiwan Revolt of February-March, 1947, winning for himself the undying enmity of the Nationalist government. Now, as spring came to China, a new wave of student anti-war demonstrations, by far the largest of their kind, spawned by scarce commodities, shrinking salaries, hyperinflation and the voracious demands of the Civil War, broke out. These brought Powell and the *Review* to a final loss of faith in the Nationalist government.

His disillusionment with the Nationalist cause in China was reflected in the evolution of his views on decolonization in South and Southeast Asia. Powell went from espousal of a moderate, compromise solution in 1946, to eventual support for national liberation struggles and opposition to American efforts to bolster neo-colonial regimes in the name of containing communism abroad.

By 1948, the *Review* and its liberal Chinese supporters had lost all confidence in the Guomindang's ability to reform the political system and the economy, or even to remain in power much longer. These were the strands, then, that prepared Powell and his journal to expect the demise of Chiang's government and to hope for better rule under China's new masters.

*

THE ANTI-CIVIL WAR, ANTI-HUNGER MOVEMENT AND THE *REVIEW*

Throughout most of February-March, 1947, when Powell was focusing on the Taiwan repression, mainland university and middle school campuses were relatively quiet.[1] The American Mediation Mission had been withdrawn in January and full civil war raged in China. Economic collapse accelerated at a bewildering pace. No longer could students and liberals hope for a postwar recovery.

There were 2,538 strikes in Shanghai during 1947— twice the number of the previous year.[2] The average rate of commodity price increase was 33.7% per month in Shanghai, but from February 8–15, 1947, there was a sudden sharp jump in prices. Panic followed. Violent hunger riots broke out. Factories, unable to get raw materials, closed and unemployment grew. Among the hardest hit by hyperinflation was the urban middle class: teachers, civil servants, public-sector workers, and students who lived on a meager government allowance, the very groups from which the bulk of the Review's Chinese readers were drawn.[3]

The cause of this spiraling inflation was the government's irrepressible issuance of currency, the fapi, or Chinese National Currency (CNC) 40 billion per day, to fill the huge gap between revenues collected and expenditures on the Civil War.[4] The government reacted to the crisis by instituting partial wage and price controls in Shanghai and other major cities in its Emergency Regulations of February 1947.[5] In rural areas however, the price of rice was not fixed.

Another sudden upsurge in prices in April left workers unable to afford basic commodities. The urban price ceiling on rice forced prices higher outside the cities and in rice-producing regions, consequently urban rice dealers were unable to replenish their stock. As shelves grew bare, the poor ransacked rice shops and many people were near starvation.[6] The Central Government abandoned its price ceilings and wage subsidies in early May. The disruption of the flow of commodities into the cities, which the partial regulations had caused, ultimately accelerated inflation and further damaged the government's already low prestige.[7]

During this time, as a direct result of these economic hardships, a massive Anti-Hunger, Anti-Civil War Movement developed. Students lacked food, clothing, and tuition, and faced unemployment upon graduation. The salaries of college professors and middle school teachers, along with government employees and others, had shrunk to a small fraction of their pre-war levels. They lived in deepening poverty and humiliation. Students and teachers were dismayed that educational spending in the national budget had been squeezed to only 4% by the huge expenditures on the Civil War.[8]

The Anti-Hunger, Anti-Civil War Movement started in April when professors at National Central University in Nanjing, Shandong University in Qingdao, Henan University in Kaifeng, and Northeastern University in Shenyang went on strike for an increase of the national budget for education, from 4.5 to 15% of the total. They were joined by students in most major cities.[9] Demonstrations and strikes erupted nation-wide as students in Shanghai, Nanjing, Hangzhou, Hangkou, Chongqing, Chengdu, Kunming, Guangzhou, Xiamen, Fuzhou, Kaifeng, Qingdao, Tianjin, Beijing and Shenyang all took to the streets in support of their professors.[10]

Recognizing the seriousness of the teachers' plight from the many letters which the *Review* received, Powell called on the government to raise teacher salaries to prevent starvation.

> How can China look for salvation to her educated citizens if they are suffering from malnutrition and must strain every faculty to keep body and soul together? . . . In China today the starving student or professor is far from an exception. He is the rule.[11]

C. Y. W. Meng pinned the cause of hyper-inflation squarely on the Civil War and the government's policy of printing up its revenue needs. As long as the war continued, there would be no way to stop inflation or to regulate prices.[12] To rectify the deficiencies in education, contributor C.C. Liu advocated the immediate cessation of the Civil War, economic security for professors, and an increase in the building of schools.[13]

Since his visit to Taiwan, Powell had become more aware of government repression. He feared that the "forces of reaction" were gaining strength and that the Chinese people were in danger of losing the few liberties they had. He noted the increasing numbers of people picked up by plain clothes police and never seen again. He pointed to the temporary closure of *Xin Min Wan Bao* on March 4, the *Da Gong Bao* on March 14, and the threatened closure of *Wen Wei Bao*, all for publishing comments critical of the government. He publicized the case of Chang Lien-hua, a teacher in the Shanghai YMCA night school, who was snatched off the street by police and held in prison under great pressure to admit falsely to being a communist.[14]

Frank L. Tsao maintained that the government had tried to arrest potential agitators "before they had time to brew dissatisfaction among the public." In February, three thousand persons had been detained in Beijing and another three thousand, in Qingdao, for this reason. The *Shanghai Evening Post and Mercury* reported more than eighty local citizens were picked up in March never to be seen again. *Wen Wei Bao* recorded the number of missing in Shanghai at more than 200.[15]

With urban economic discontent so pervasive, preventative measures had little effect except to excite further indignation. By May, the Anti-Hunger, Anti-Civil War demonstrations had become a massive nationwide phenomenon, eliciting widespread popular sympathy. With the movement assuming such widespread proportions, Powell urged China's small third parties, about to take part in the People's Political Council (PPC), a multi-party, parliament-like advisory body first established in 1938, to revive their flagging political fortunes by synchronizing their demands with those of the protestors:

> The nation is crying for peace, for peace at almost any price. That is the consensus of liberal officials, the press, educators, intellectuals- in fact everybody who is not directly implicated in the Civil War.[16]

Powell called on the participants in the People's Political Council to forget party dogmas and rivalry, and to join together with liberal elements in the government, minority parties, and independent statesmen to push through measures aimed at ending the Civil War. The minority parties had lost ground over the past seven months ". . . because they have drifted further and further from the people." But here was a chance to regain some of their former support by championing the cause of peace.[17]

Neither side had been able to defeat the other decisively in the Civil War, and as it continued, "the people have less to eat, more men are mercilessly slaughtered, and more miseries are piled on the Chinese people." Powell called on the Communists to announce what their reaction would be to a proposal that peace negotiations be re-opened.[18]

Mid-May witnessed a continuing series of demonstrations and strikes at most universities in Nationalist China. On May eighteenth members of the government's 208th Division of the Youth Army attacked students passing out leaflets in Beijing, injuring eight. This incident led students to plan co-ordinated demonstrations all over the country for May twentieth. The government moved to prevent that planned action by promulgating the Provisional Measures for the Maintenance of Public Order. All strikes, parades and petitions were banned and local authorities, police and military garrisons were empowered to use as much force as necessary to enforce the ban.[19]

Powell charged that the government, by issuing orders banning public demonstrations and authorizing troops and police to break up protests

> showed a distinct lack of understanding of the basic issues involved. . .
> The student unrest, like the labor and agrarian unrest, is a product of the times, a result of civil war and the breakdown of the economy.[20]

The students were displeased over the political, military and economic conditions in China and in Powell's view, had ". . . a right to be displeased as does every other citizen who sees his livelihood worsening virtually every day."[21] As long as expenditures for the Civil War rose each month, there would be that much less for the needs of the populace.

Powell advised the government to adopt a policy of conciliation and explanation together with concrete attempts to raise students' and teachers' living standards. "Student demonstrations have a habit of spreading from city to city and involving workers and other sectors of the general population", he warned Nanjing.

> With all the efforts concentrated on the war front, it is quite possible that the government's small contingent of troops and police in the rear might not be able to handle the situation if first class riots broke out simultaneously in Shanghai and a few other major cities.[22]

As the People's Political Council opened its session on May 19, 1947, Nanjing students defied the government ban and marched through the streets urging the PPC to support a plan calling for a negotiated peace.[23] The following day, demonstrations occurred as scheduled in many large cities, including Beijing. In spite of the ban on demonstrations, which had Chiang's full backing, military authorities at first adopted a lenient attitude toward demonstrators and did not intervene to stop them. Nevertheless, as demonstrations continued, incidents of violence by plain-clothes police multiplied, gaining sympathy from other sectors of the population. By May twenty-seventh, military authorities had decided to use all the force necessary to stop new large-scale demonstrations being planned for June second, the day when the People's Political Council would adjourn.[24]

In Shanghai, Frank L. Tsao catalogued the demands of the May 20th student general strike: protection of human rights, increase of educational funds to 15% of the national budget, a government allowance for all university and middle school students, an end to requisition of cereals[25], confiscation of the property of bureaucratic capitalists[26] to solve the economic crisis, restoration the Political Consultative Conference and the realization of real peace and democracy.[27]

Powell urged his readers to make their voices heard. Now was the time for all to put aside party labels and for the whole nation to back those in the PPC who supported peace negotiations, and to shout down those who would continue the war, he exclaimed. A Majority of the people supported neither the Guomindang nor the CCP, but wanted only peace, Powell asserted. The PPC must grant it to them![28]

The People's Political Council, though no more than an advisory body, opened amidst great pressure to endorse some kind of peace plan. The Democratic League delegates, although absent from the November-December 1946 Constitutional National Assembly, took their seats in the People's Political Council. The CCP, though invited to attend, was absent. Chiang Kai-shek addressing the opening of the Council, doubtless in a gesture to public sentiment, told the delegates that "China absolutely needs peace and the government has been sincerely and tolerantly working for this goal."[29] The PPC made a radio broadcast to the CCP, urging them to resume peace talks, and formed a special commission to work out a single composite peace plan, but ultimately, was unable to agree on concrete measures.[30]

This made the June 2nd demonstrations all the more important, since this would be the last chance to pressure the Council into endorsing a peace plan before it adjourned. The government, which no more intended to pursue peace at this juncture than did the CCP, had already determined to take draconian measures to crush the planned protests.

As student activists continued publicity campaigns building support for the June 2nd demonstrations, and the PPC remained unable to agree on a peace plan, soldiers began to lay siege to university campuses. Plain-clothes police, aided by informers burst into dormitories across the nation to arrest suspected activists from prepared "black lists". All student opposition was labeled "communist planned and inspired" by the government, which intended to deport student activists to CCP base areas.[31]

In Shanghai, demonstrating students who tried to carry a petition to the Mayor were roughly handled and scores were arrested. The Wusong-Shanghai Garrison suspended three papers on May 24th because they had reported news of student strikes: *Wen Wei Bao, Xin Min Wan Bao,* and *Lian Ho Ribao.* On the morning of May 30th, police raided University Dormitories and houses all over Shanghai. Students were roused from sleep, lined up outside, and hundreds were arrested. Four news reporters were also picked up by the police for "communist activities".[32]

Other cities saw similar incidents. According to *Da Gong Bao,* one thousand persons had been arrested in Chongqing, including eight reporters from *Da Gong Bao,* four reporters from the *World Tribune,* two reporters from the *Commercial Daily,* four reporters from *China Times,* and seven reporters from *Xin Min Bao.* More than thirty reporters and staff from the *Democratic Daily,* organ of the Democratic League had also been arrested.[33]

The *Review* portrayed the early morning raids in Shanghai in nightmarish terms:

> The few Shanghailanders who happened to be awake in the early hours of May 30th heard the sirens of the police cars as they raced through the streets in the dead of night. University dormitories and private homes were broken into by tens, hundreds and even thousands of policemen, gendarmes, plain-clothes men, and secret agents. Students were pulled from their beds and stood in rows on the campus, waiting for their names to be called or their faces identified from photographs or blacklists. Women as well as men were hauled out of bed in nightclothes or pajamas with pistols pointed at their heads.[34]

Powell protested the suspension of four Shanghai papers (*Wen Wei Bao, Lian Ho Wan Bao, Xin Min Wan Bao* and *Tei Bao*) and Shanghai student arrests. He scolded the government for "launching a reign of repression," and suggested that the Central Government "might be hard pressed to put down the popular uprisings which may well break out as a result of attempts to enforce police rule in the rear areas."[35] He reminded the Government that

> News of the student arrests and suspension of papers has already been cabled around the world and certainly has not created a favorable impres-

sion, especially in Washington, towards which Nanking is today stretching a hand for financial and other assistance.[36]

At that time, U.S. Ambassador John Leighton Stuart essentially agreed with Powell's assessment. Stuart believed the demonstrations and their demands for peace were "the raw stuff out of which democracy can be given form."[37] Stuart saw student demands as an accurate reflection of public opinion and characterized the demonstrators as essentially orderly and peaceful. He believed that without doubt the deteriorating economic situation was the underlying cause of the unrest. He rejected Chiang's contention that the demonstrators were part of a Communist plot. And, like Powell, Stuart felt that things would quickly get out of hand if the situation in the cities became violent, since there would not be enough military reserves to handle it. Also like Powell, he urged Chiang to recognize the legitimate aspirations of his people to democratize the government and to open peace negotiations with the Communists.[38]

"President Chiang has a supreme opportunity to declare himself the exponent of the popular will" by seeking a cease-fire and negotiating with the CCP, Stuart wrote to Secretary of State Acheson on the eve of Chiang's repression.

> In doing so he would demonstrate his intelligent and genuine acceptance of new democratic standards and ought to rally the enlightened, forward looking elements of the people, as well as the great mass who clamor merely for peace and an opportunity to work undisturbed by conflicting factions or ideologies.[39]

*

The *Review* highlighted the widespread condemnation of GMD repression in both the liberal Chinese and foreign press. The *Shanghai Evening Post and Mercury* condemned the new repressive measures and warned of an impending popular explosion. *Da Gong Bao* labeled the government's actions "a reign of Terror," and in Beijing, Dr. Hu Shi, president of Beijing University and former Ambassador to the U.S., denied that student demonstrations had been instigated by the CCP as the government had charged.[40]

In retrospect, the *Review* came to view the brutal repression of the Taiwan revolt by Governor General Chen Yi as the first shots of an attack on the unarmed people at home, proceeding slowly in April, and then in full force by late May.[41] The Government was able to prevent the national student strike and mass demonstrations scheduled for June 2nd through the combination of preemptive arrests of potential student leaders and by sealing off campuses with armed troops. At the same time, the government drove a wedge between workers and students by inflating the Cost of Living Index by about 40 percent to give wages, which were tied to the Index, a boost, while student allowances remained at the same low levels. But the underlying problems remained unresolved, Powell warned, and with the war's continuation, would only worsen.[42]

"The Central government-to the surprise of many observers-appears to have weathered, at least temporarily, the national crisis scheduled for June 2nd", Powell wrote shortly afterwards. He attributed the economic decline that underlay the crisis to the Civil War. The government spent an increasingly large part of China's GNP on the war effort. As a result, the standard of living fell and investment capital disappeared.

> As the total production declines and as more and more is required for the war, the economy rapidly recedes, until it has shrunken to the point where, faced with actual starvation, the general populace becomes completely dissatisfied and balks.
>
> This is the period we are now facing…Historians in the future will assuredly look back upon this day in China and call it the period just before the collapse.[43]

Powell felt that "The crisis is so acute that a general breakdown of authority in the rear areas can come at almost any time."[44] Yet he recognized that like the Manchus in the late Nineteenth Century, the Nationalists might be able to hold on to power for some time after their real ability to control the country had ceased.

Student anti-war activity did not end in Shanghai after the government suppressed the June 2nd demonstrations. Repressive measures continued throughout the summer and fall of 1947. By Mid-July student leaders, in spite of increasing raids and arrests by the police and military, had consolidated local Anti-Hunger, anti-Civil War protest committees into a unified All-China Students Association.[45] All through the summer and early fall, the *Review* was filled with letters from students and feature articles reporting incidents of military or police repression at universities and middle schools in Shanghai and other cities.

In Shanghai, parents formed the "Union of Family Elders of Arrested Students of Shanghai" in July to pressure the Shanghai High Court and military garrison into releasing fifty students who had been held since May.[46] The *Review* published the group's three-page appeal recounting their futile attempts to intervene with the Mayor of Shanghai and the Central Government in Nanjing.[47] It published a "Teachers' Manifesto" signed by seventy-five college and middle school teachers, which condemned the government's high-handed repression of the students. Students engaged in peaceful, orderly activities were beaten, arrested, and even occasionally murdered by the police and military for seeking to save education in China, the Manifesto charged. It demanded the students' release, protection for basic human rights, an increase in the educational budget, and an end to the Civil War.[48]

Among the many missives in the "Letters From the People" section, the *Review* published a letter signed by internationally acclaimed Communist writers Guo Moro, Mao Dun, and other prominent intellectuals decrying the government's use of force against the students. The letter called on the government to stop the Civil War, end restrictive laws, meet the students' demands, to set free all jailed newspapermen and reopen closed newspapers.[49] Mao Dun, an early member of the CCP, was "one of the two or three foremost novelists in modern Chinese literature," while poet and playwright Guo Moro was a major figure in the Communist Party's efforts to appeal to intellectuals.[50] In spring 1950 Guo would be one of the chief editors of *People's China*, an English-language journal through which the CCP hoped to reach and influence the American public. Their choice of the *Review* as a vehicle to air their views was telling.[51]

Powell published a declaration signed by five hundred eighty-six University professors from schools across North China. "The situation is no less critical than in France on the eve of the French Revolution, or that in Russia just preceding the October Revolution", the professors warned.

> We are on the verge of political, military, economic, and cultural collapse. Disaster is at our very door. If the government continues to meet the situation with evasion and procrastination, and refuses to take decisive, effective measures, there can be only one result-total ruin for all of us.[52]

Numerous feature articles in the *Review* continued to document the extent of student unrest and of government counter-measures. An article by Henry Lee recounted the history of the May-June 1947 student protests in Nanjing, and of the government's repression. Charles J.Canning contrasted student demonstrations on the eve of the Guomindang's 1926 Northern Expeditional Campaign to unite the country, with current student unrest, and concluded that the May 1947 student movement was the largest in China's history. An article by Jefferson Cath recounted police repression at Sun Yat-sen University that extended to faculty as well as students. A grisly *Review* photo feature on three students killed in a police raid on Wuhan University drew information from *Reuter's*, *United Press*, and the GMD's own *Central News Service*. S.E. Shifrin compiled an account by Nankai University students of the May 20th demonstrations in Tianjin, and of police repression.[53]

The volume of mail reporting government repression expanded to such an extent that the *Review* had to increase the number of pages devoted to its "Letters From the People" section. Even so, the journal was only able to publish one out of every ten letters received.[54] A barrage of letters told of police raids on Henan National University, Wuhan University, Jiangsu College (the "Xuzhou Incident"), and at Fudan National University, along with individual accounts of arrest and mistreatment.[55]

The May tide of student protests and the government's response to them marked the final alienation of most Chinese intellectuals from the government.[56] Powell and the staff of the *Review* shared that sentiment by the late summer of 1947.

*

CRITICISM OF THE COURT

At the same time that Powell was reporting on the suppression of the Taiwan revolt and the swelling student movement in Shanghai, he raised the issue of the lack of judicial due process in China's courts and the tendency of the military to intervene during trials. As government repression of student protesters intensified, so did Powell's criticism of Chinese legal practice. His criticism of the courts, like his expose on the Taiwan repression, did not go unnoticed in government circles. The President of the Shanghai District High Court, Judge Zha Liangjia, attacked both Powell and the *Review*, and threatened the editor with a contempt of court citation for his criticism.[57]

Powell's complaints, to a considerable degree, echoed those which European and American entrepreneurs had been making for more than a hundred years. Since the late eighteenth century, Westerners had been highly critical of China's legal practices, which were fundamentally different from those of Western Europe and the United States. Chinese law had developed over the centuries primarily as an administrative tool of government. The legal tradition and thinking which the Nationalists had inherited strongly favored the state and the Confucian social order, and had not developed the tradition of a legal profession operating through a system of independent courts, nor a clear concept of the rights of the individual. The lack of due process to protect defendants, the practice of arbitrary detention, the assumption of guilt, the lack of legal council for the accused and of a reasonable chance to prove one's innocence in court,[58] were some of the reasons the Great Powers, in the unequal treaties of the nineteenth century, had insisted on extraterritoriality: the right to try their own citizens in their own consular courts for crimes committed in China. Although extraterritoriality had been abolished by 1943 and China had taken steps toward adopting Western-style judicial institutions, these reforms remained largely superficial.[59]

*

Powell had pointed out as early as November 1946 that China's new Constitution did not provide for an autonomous judiciary which might serve as custodian of the peoples' rights. Rather, the courts in China were subject to the orders of the military high command.[60] In April, 1947, Powell used the case of Frederick Meysberg, the Dutch manager of the American owned Abis Company, to illustrate his point.

On March third, 1947, twenty police "Waving drawn pistols in the faces of the employees" raided the Abis Company, seizing records, gold and cash from the company vault and arresting Meysberg and four other employees. They were charged with violating emergency economic measures of February 16, 1947, restricting foreign currency transactions. Meysberg was refused bail and sentenced to one year in prison. The company's funds were confiscated.[61]

What most concerned Powell was a trend he perceived toward arbitrary military and political control of the courts and the strong-arm methods of military authorities. He observed that during Meysberg's trial, Colonel Zhang Yaming, head of the Wusong-Shanghai Garrison's Economic Section, ignoring normal court procedure, had jumped to his feet several times to deliver angry speeches whenever witnesses or the defense council said anything displeasing to him. Toward the end of the trial, he castigated the defense attorney, Dr. D.S. Zhen, telling him that by defending a foreigner he had become a traitor to China. Powell felt the colonel had succeeded in intimidating the court.[62]

In early May, as student demonstrations rocked China, the *Review* stepped up its attack on the courts, causing local authorities alarm. China had no substantive judicial system, Powell charged, and its courts had made little progress since the 1920's. Neither Chinese nor foreigner could expect fair trials, he asserted. The military garrison, acting on orders from Nanjing party chiefs, typically arrested a defendant, announced his guilt to the press, followed him into the courtroom and interrupted proceedings at will, often lecturing the judge. Consequently, he concluded, the courts were afraid to render a verdict that went against any strong military or political group's wishes.[63]

Powell pointed out that although China had no lack of educated judges and lawyers, its courts were not free agents. Rather they were tools of the military. He also attacked the physical conditions and administrative corruption of China's prison system, noting that incarcerated foreigners often became sick and died.[64]

An article by K. C. Zhen amplified the attack. China's habeas corpus law, promulgated eleven years before, was supposed to have been put into effect March 15, 1946, according to the agreements of the People's Consultative Conference. Yet, during the government's attempts to suppress the student movement, China witnessed a wave of "kidnapping-like" arrests by non-uniformed agents, without warrants or any post-arrest notification to families. In effect, Zhen argued, this put China's habeas corpus law itself on trial. Was China to have government by law or by terror, he asked?[65]

The government, now trying to suppress the growing Anti-Hunger, Anti-Civil War Movement, took offense at Powell and the *Review*'s remarks. It had been only one month since Powell had embarrassed the Chinese Government before the whole world over its Taiwan policy, and official agencies were in no mood to ignore the *Review*'s attack on judicial practices.

Judge L. C. Zha, president of the Shanghai District High Court, issued a public statement labeling Powell's editorials inappropriate and defamatory.

Zha claimed the criticisms which the *China Weekly Review* aimed at the judicial structure were tantamount to contempt of court.[66] The *Central Daily News*, an official GMD organ, demanded that Powell bear the full criminal responsibility for his remarks. The journal *Fei Bao* reported that judge Guo Yongguan of the High Court, and the Chief of the Shanghai Office of Foreign Affairs, Chen Guoliang, had inspected Shanghai's jails and denied Powell's assertion of their squalor and mismanagement. Unless Powell printed a retraction, the journal reported, the Foreign Office would lodge a protest with the U.S.Consulate.[67]

Powell did not print a retraction, but rather printed a full text translation of Judge L. C. Zha's broadside: "A Review of 'China's Courts', An Editorial of the *China Weekly Review*, By the Secretariat of the Shanghai High Court."[68] Zha accused the *Review*'s editor of relying on ". . . rumors or unfounded or malicious statements" for his information, and essentially accused him of exaggerating or lying in his editorials. Powell prefaced the High Court's manifesto with a disclaimer indicating that "Publication of this article does not mean that the views expressed therein are either partially or wholly endorsed by the editor of the *Review*."[69]

Nor did Powell tone down his criticism of the lack of due process and habeas corpus. Throughout the summer and fall of 1947, as government repression of students and faculty became the order of the day, the *Review* continued to raise the issue. Powell quoted from the 1926 *Extraterritoriality Commission Report* and from Dorothy Borg's *American Policy and the Chinese Revolution*[70] to show that martial law provisions had always been a grave menace to proper administration of civil law in China.[71] ". . . China is a place where there are no civil liberties" charged former Deputy Director of the UNRRA's China Office, Douglas B.Falconer, in a speech which the *Review* published verbatim. "In March, in Peiping, 3,200 people disappeared, taken by the secret police. There is no trial, no charge, no opportunity for counsel."[72]

The *Review* published two articles by Dr. S. Francis Liu, a graduate of Oberlin College and Yale University and a judge on the Shanghai High Court. Liu recounted the most common abuses in China's legal system: incomplete transcripts of evidence, inadequate case preparation by lawyers, witnesses trying to mediate rather than testifying to the truth, and overcrowded dockets. Liu criticized Chinese judges for being overly sensitive to the opinions of others, and easily manipulated by superiors.[73]

In the fall of 1947, after three student activists from Zhejiang National University were sentenced to seven years in prison, and a fourth reportedly committed suicide while incarcerated, Powell criticized their trial and the methods used to convict them. He pointed to the complete lack of evidence and questioned the reliability of their written confessions, suggesting they may have been obtained under duress.[74] "Standing on trial together with the three students is the integrity and competency of China's judicial system," Powell editorialized.

The Hanchow high court may render its decision on the students but the students all over the country and world public opinion will hand down their verdict on China's courts.[75]

The Nationalist Government's actions silencing student and faculty protests over mismanagement of the economy, political liberalization, and the war, and its suppression of the Democratic League and the Taiwan revolt, were the context of Powell's criticism of the courts and judicial system. By the end of 1947, the Guomindang had shown itself illiberal, cynical, repressive, intent on holding on to power regardless of the consequences for the Chinese people. Whatever favorable disposition Powell may have held in 1946 toward Chiang Kai-shek's government, the events of 1947 swept it away entirely.

*

THE *REVIEW*'S CHANGING VIEWS ON DECOLONIZATION

The final aspect of change in the editorial policy of the *Review* during these years was the position it took on decolonization in South and Southeast Asia. Between 1946 and 1948, the *Review* shifted away from support for moderate negotiated solutions, and toward support for indigenous liberation struggles, and opposition to the Truman Doctrine of containment of Communist expansion. This shift of views on international issues paralleled its growing disillusionment with the GMD's handling of the student movement, the Taiwan Revolt, and the banning of the Democratic League. In the long run, this transition would help ease the ideological reorientation which the *Review* underwent after the Communist victory in 1949 (see Chapter Seven) by creating a partial convergence of its views and the anti-imperialist ideology of the new Chinese Communist government.

At the close of World War II, Powell believed American foreign policy was consistent with the national aspirations of colonial peoples of South and Southeast Asia. Here European colonialism had been interrupted by Japanese occupation (or in the case of India, pressured by the threat of Japanese invasion). After Pearl Harbor, the United States had helped to arm, train and supply indigenous anti-Japanese resistance movements. The Four Freedoms of the Atlantic Charter seemed to imply American approval for the national self determination of former colonial peoples.

President Roosevelt and Secretary of State Hull favored the break-up of colonial trading systems and hoped for a post-war world without colonies or trade barriers. Roosevelt wanted the French out of Indochina and tried to elicit a promise of Indian independence from Prime Minister Churchill.[76]

Many American Office of Strategic Services (OSS) officers in Indochina, India and elsewhere shared these views as they trained native resistance forces. Leaders of Asian national independence movements, especially those who fought as U.S. allies against Japan, such as Ho Chi-Minh in

Vietnam, hoped for American recognition and support for their fledgling republics at war's end.[77] Even the Chinese Communists looked forward in the late winter and early spring of 1944–1945, to a closer relationship with the United States.[78]

In the *China Weekly Review*, Powell initially counseled negotiated solutions and gradualism as a principle by which both former colonizers and colonials could solve the colonial imbroglio.[79] Powell's analysis of colonialism was non-Marxist: he saw no intrinsic disadvantage in labor and resources exchanged when an underdeveloped country traded raw materials or agricultural products for finished industrial goods from an industrialized nation. He therefore assumed that with independence, large scale foreign trade with the United States would be an unalloyed benefit to the former colonial nations.

Favoring a negotiated solution and a moderate path towards independence, Powell condemned the violent French recolonization of Indochina and the Dutch recolonization of Indonesia. By the same token, he applauded the American grant of independence to the Philippines and the British negotiated withdrawal in Burma and India. As the *Review* followed the developing crisis of colonialism in Vietnam, Malaya, Indonesia, Burma, India, and Korea, it increasingly sided with the national aspirations of the native peoples.

By late 1947, Powell's initial optimism faded as moderation gave way to extremism among the colonial powers and the national liberation movements. The United States became more involved in underwriting the cost of recolonization for its Cold War European allies France and the Netherlands. The *Review* warned that America was squandering its reservoir of post-war goodwill among Asian peoples, and was in danger of being branded the primary supporter of "semi-feudal", reactionary regimes the world over. Powell pointed out the danger of over-extending U.S. power, and warned that these neo-colonial regimes were often hated, corrupt, and decrepit, unable to stand on their own.

By 1948, as events in China clearly pointed to the impending demise of the Nationalist government, Powell called on the United States to remember its own anti-colonial past, to renounce the politics of reaction, and to become the champion of independence and self-determination that it ought to be. He believed that the United States, because of its unrivaled economic power in the post-war world, was in a position to force European decolonization, and that it was in America's national interest to do so.

*

The *Review* initially lauded the November 1946 Linggadjati Peace Accords, which effected a truce in the fighting between the Netherlands and the fledgling Indonesian Republic. Powell explained developments leading up to the accord:

The Military collapse of Japan in August, 1945 left a bigger political vacuum in Asia than any formed in a century. In Burma, Siam, Indochina, Indonesia, Malaya, and Borneo the controlling hand suddenly vanished and in its wake sprang up native movements aimed at destroying the old, pre-Pearl Harbor order.[80]

Indonesian leaders had quickly seized the opportunity to declare their country independent and set up the Indonesian Republic. But with the return of Dutch military forces, Powell noted, independence proponents were struggling to preserve what they had won.

The beauty of the Linggadjati Peace Accords according to the *Review*, was that they granted the Indonesian Republic "greater recognition and powers than any previous accord" while at the same time allowing the Netherlands sufficient overall political control. Powell granted that they failed to satisfy "radical nationalists" on either side, yet without the accords "the war between the Netherlands and Indonesian nationalists would still be going on, with bloody battles on a par with those continuing in Indochina."[81]

He saw the Peace Accords as the product of courageous moderates on both sides standing firm against the more volatile elements in their respective camps. "Radical nationalists on both sides attempted from the very inception of the peace talks to undermine the agreements reached," he recounted. Dutch "nationalists" felt they were giving up too much while Indonesian "extremists" complained the Peace Accords "smacked too much of the old regime."[82]

In the showdown that followed, Indonesian Premier Sultan Sjahrir and Dutch Governor Van Mook were able to prevail over the more extreme elements in their respective governments. "Without farsighted, moderate politicians like Van Mook, the Netherlands would have committed itself to a never-ending colonial conflict," Powell declared. "Without men the caliber of Sjahrir, Indonesian fanatics would jeopardize the gains already made." In Powell's view,

> The lesson for Western Powers still possessing colonies, as for the native peoples struggling to gain a greater voice in their own government, is therefore clear. For the West the message is: He who gives in time gives doubly. For the East the message is: Learn to walk before you try to run.[83]

Powell believed that it was

> recognition of the basic truth contained in these phrases which has prevented rebellion and bloodshed in India and Burma. And it is unwillingness to recognize the basic truth of these policies which has brought bloodshed to Indochina.[84]

Powell's faith in the practicability of the moderate approach would only last three months. By June, 1947, during the same period that student demonstrations and police repression were rocking Shanghai and most of

GMD controlled China, in the former Dutch East Indies, the provisions of the Linggadjati Accords providing for the emergence of the United States of Indonesia by January (1947) had not been implemented. Renewed fighting seemed certain.

In a more somber mood, Powell reassessed his earlier measure of the Accords. "The Linggadjati Agreement is an ambiguous document," he admitted. "Observers have noted that its terms cover considerably more concessions than the Dutch are actually willing to grant, and substantially less than the Indonesians have been seeking."[85] The Indonesians wanted complete, not partial independence whereas the Dutch were willing to change the form of their rule as long as it allowed continued colonial exploitation. Once fighting reached a decisive stage, Powell could see only two possible courses: Either "complete independence for the young republic, or its temporary subjugation by the Dutch."[86] History, he felt, was on the side of the Indonesians.

Shortly thereafter, Powell decried the demise of the spirit of moderation. All over Asia, he wrote, the forces of extremism were triumphing over the voices of moderation. In Indonesia, in spite of an agreement signed by both parties, Dutch military forces launched an attack on the makeshift forces of the Indonesian Republic. In Burma, extremists had assassinated moderate pro-independence Premier U.Aung Sam. In India, Powell worried that extremism between Muslims and Hindus together with possible disintegration of the Indian state only played into British plans for reconquest.[87]

In Powell's view, India's "moderates", Gandhi and Nehru, wanted a United India. Within it, they hoped to fashion a moderate kind of socialism to raise Indian peasants out of their poverty and suffering, he conjectured. But the storm had already broken in Indonesia and Burma, and in India, moderates were losing ground rapidly, he noted.

The West should have had a policy of transformation for all Asian nations and peoples from colonialism to independence, from exploitation to sufficiency, Powell declared. By failing to take this course, the West

> not only refused to spare the native populations which came under its control, but the youth of Western nations who would have to die in tropical jungles for the greater profit of reactionaries at home.[88]

Western "extremists", or colonial proponents, having originally used force to acquire their empires, now sought to retain them through force, Powell observed. The natives, in response "had to fight fire with fire, had to turn to extremist forces in order to throw off the yoke of foreign oppression." Hence, in Powell's view, Western extremism and reaction bred Eastern extremism and reaction. The Western powers should pursue a course of autonomy and moderation, he counseled. This was the only way to avoid war and bloodshed.[89]

The *Review* was initially hopeful on the prospects for United Nations arbitration of the Indonesian war, and noted that the Dutch would have preferred American good offices whereas the Indonesian Republic preferred an international body.[90] When the United Nations arranged a cease fire in Indonesia, Powell pointed out that the Indonesians had requested arbitration. Instead, the U.N. had arranged a cease fire while the Netherlands had set up a puppet federation of outlying, sparsely inhabited territories. The Dutch Federation was nothing more than a thinly veiled attempt to suppress the Indonesian Republic, he declared.[91]

*

The *Review* paid particular attention to the French attempt to reimpose colonial authority in Indochina. Numerous articles by correspondents in Hanoi, Saigon, Paris, and elsewhere provided detailed analysis of many aspects of that conflict. The *Review* strove to give a balanced presentation, although Powell's editorials left no doubt that he favored independence. An article by Caroline Cooley, an American journalist who had interviewed Ho Chi-Minh and spent several months in Vietminh-held areas, offered a good example of this balance.[92]

In Vietminh-held Tonkin, Cooley described government-run schools, hospitals, markets, and other aspects of a society under full war-time mobilization. She noted the positive aspects of social welfare measures, an increased literacy rate, flexible government price ceilings, and considerable latitude for private businesses.

On the other hand, she also observed that with the central government in hiding, its ministers had to travel, often with great difficulty, to supervise local, mainly military governments. Consequently, local governments enjoyed great latitude. With higher government officials absent most of the time, it was difficult for individuals to challenge a local official. The most important result of the war, Cooley reported, had been "the crushing of personal liberties and the elimination of any opposition within the government" for the sake of unity.[93]

In August, 1945, the Vietnamese government had been a simple coalition of various parties united by a common desire for independence, she recalled. But the struggle against the French had changed all that. In the current government, she noted, all twenty-two ministries were held by Communists. With unity being a paramount concern, Cooley noted, the secret police were the real rulers. "Either you are for the [revolutionary] government or you are against it", she stated. "But if you value your life, you are with it."[94]

Cooley recalled that during the closing months of the Second World War, American OSS officers had worked closely with Ho Chi-Minh. America was popular with Vietnamese nationalists and was commonly identified with the struggle for democracy. Great hope was placed in the Atlantic Charter. Since the end of World War II and the outbreak of the anti-French war, she reported, Ho Chi-Minh had noted the changed direction of U.S. policy and had serious doubts about expecting any help from America.[95]

The *Review* ran a constant stream of articles on the war in Indochina, which although balanced in their presentation, could hardly say anything good about the conflict. Peggy Parker reported that the United States was sending military supplies to the French. She noted that American pro-independence sympathies clashed with French efforts at recolonization.[96] Andrew Roth wrote three articles highlighting the savage nature of French repression of the independence movement. He contrasted French ideals at home with French actions in Indochina, and criticized French support for the puppet government of Bao Dai, the last Nguyen emperor, installed by the French in 1948 to help impart legitimacy to the colonial regime.[97]

Walter Briggs believed the French were concerned with redeeming "lost face". Unwilling to risk reforms which might endanger profits or eliminate their own administrative positions, French colonial officials, through their ruthless treatment of malcontents, only produced more opposition.[98] An article by J. Hendrick underscored the contradiction between the French public view of themselves and the reality of French policies in Vietnam.[99] A series of articles by William Johnson explored the history of French colonization in Vietnam during the nineteenth and twentieth centuries and traced the development of the National Liberation Movement in opposition.[100]

*

As the Cold War heated up and the Truman Doctrine and Marshall Plan were announced, Powell searched for a more positive policy toward the national aspirations of former colonial peoples. In the summer of 1947, he reminded his readers of America's revolutionary, anti-colonial genesis. In America, the individual enjoyed greater rights and freedom than any place else on earth, he declared. But America was at a serious turning point in its history. It had not yet become a symbol of reaction and the status quo, but was already advancing well along that road, he warned. The United States, by failing to take a stand against British, French, and Dutch recolonization, was in danger of becoming just one more Western Imperialist nation herself.[101]

Powell warned in another editorial that by underwriting recolonization in Asia, the United States was taking on an unlimited economic liability which would ultimately produce only bitter fruit:

> Both the French and the Dutch are second rate colonial powers who are keeping a last grip in Asia mainly through the courtesy of the British and the Americans. It is high time for the United States to realize that unless she is prepared to underwrite these two countries, both in Europe and Asia almost indefinitely, they will eventually be thrown out by their subject peoples. When that day comes, America will not be any better liked by the Indo-Chinese and Indonesians because she has helped the old masters retain their hold a little longer.[102]

There was no moral justification for colonialism, and certainly no economic advantage to be gained by backing the recolonizers, Powell admonished. However, by reversing this policy, American trading companies might open up new vistas for themselves, he pointed out.

> From the point of view of gross self-interest, the United States is making a great mistake in supporting these two colonial powers. With these characters out of the way, the U.S. businessman, who has few equals these days, could do a land office trading business in both countries.[103]

Powell criticized an article by former Ambassador to the Soviet Union William Bullitt which had appeared in *Life Magazine* in January, 1948. Bullitt had advised the French government to grant Vietnamese independence while cutting out Ho Chi-Minh and his followers from any involvement, in spite of his support among the people. This would only amount to setting up yet another puppet government, Powell asserted. He pictured Ho as a nationalist and denied that there was any evidence that he was currently a Communist.[104]

French and Dutch expatriate nationals and companies whose interests in Indonesia and Indochina were tied to the colonial regimes, resented the *Review*'s opposition to Dutch and French recolonization. They wrote angry letters to the editor, canceled advertizing contracts and subscriptions. Powell said that he was "upset to see how bitter the French and Dutch have become." He had been told that the French authorities had a black list of writers and journals and that the *Review* and Powell were on it.[105]

Powell lamented that because of his criticism of recolonization, he had been painted as a "communist" by French Colonial authorities.

> The authorities there, it is reported, 'explain' our critical attitude toward themselves by saying that we are Communists. The logic is simple. The [Vietminh] [are] against the French and there are said to be considerable Communist elements within the [Vietminh]. The *Review* occasionally criticizes the French and therefore must be presumed also to be "against" the French, then it, too, must be Communist.[106]

In reply to these critics, the *Review*'s editor clarified his position:

> The whole colonial problem in Asia seems quite simple to us. The French and Dutch ought to go home. They arrived uninvited and they are still unwelcome. They have investment which they must protect. They should try to get a settlement from the local peoples for them; failing this they should write them off as risks which didn't pan out.[107]

By the fall of 1948, Powell and the *Review* proposed a new foreign policy for the United States, that would allow America to reclaim its anti-colonial position. In a November editorial, Powell recalled America's long-standing sympathy for anti-colonial struggles. During World War II, the United States had promised to help the Indochinese and Indonesians to gain their independence. But since the start of the Cold War with the Soviets in Europe, the United States had been more concerned with bolstering the Dutch and French economies.

France and the Netherlands were the worst examples of colonizing powers in Asia, Powell asserted. Currently, America supplied arms to the French and Dutch to help them subdue their former colonials and to reassert their overlordship. This was a bad policy. America had stood up against colonialism in the past. Only the United States had the economic clout to force these two powers out of their colonies in Asia, he asserted. Since the Soviet Union lacked similar economic power, and would not be able to compete in trade and economic assistance, the U.S. could gain an advantage over the Soviets in Southeast Asia through this anti-colonial policy.[108]

After war again broke out in Indonesia, Powell restated his thesis in a more developed form. By this time, the impending collapse of the Guomindang government in China was evident and formed the backdrop. Now was a good time for the United States to reconsider its whole position in Asia, Powell declared. For three years America had been consistently backing the wrong horse in nearly every part of East and Southeast Asia. In China, America's proxy was about to lose, and the French would soon start packing up in Indochina. The days of the Dutch in Indonesia were also numbered. The era of white overlordship in Asia was ending and if the United States wished to get in on the ground floor it must act now, Powell asserted. Delay, he warned, would only cause Asia to orient itself in Moscow's direction.[109]

America should begin championing the cause of independence movements, even if only for materialistic considerations, Powell urged. The Netherlands was financing its military effort with U.S. dollars provided through its participation in the Marshall plan. The Dutch military was outfitted with American lend-lease hardware originally intended to help them fight Japan. It was now being used against Indonesians. Economic pressure from the United States, Powell asserted, could easily force the Dutch to stop their war.[110]

America also had the power to force France to halt its war in Indochina, Powell believed, since France too received large amounts of U.S. goods and dollars under the Marshall Plan. Neither France nor the Netherlands could long sustain a colonial war without American aid, since its withdrawal would soon cause hardship for Dutch and French nationals in Europe, Powell asserted.[111]

By the end of 1948, Powell had moved full circle from informing native peoples struggling for independence to "learn to walk before you try to run," as he had when he endorsed the Linggadjati Agreement and gradualism in early 1947. Gradualism had not worked, and here too, as in Shanghai, he was thrust into a world of competing extremist combatants.

CHAPTER NOTES

1. Suzanne Pepper, *Civil War in China, The Political Struggle, 1945–1949*. (Berkeley: University of California Press, 1978.) p.58.

2. Monthly Report, CWR, 31 January 1948; *Ta Kung Pao*, 26 February 1947; John K. Fairbank and Albert Feurwerker, eds. *The Cambridge History of China, Volume 13, Republican China 1912–1949, Part 2*.(New York: Cambridge University Press, 1986.) p.737–751.

3. Chou Shun-hsin, *The Chinese Inflation: 1937–1949*.(New York: Columbia University Press, 1963), p.24; Dr.D.H.Fong, "China's Postwar Economy", CWR, 31 January 1948, p.262.

4. A.Doak Barnett, *China on the Eve of Communist Takeover*.(New York: Praeger, 1963) p.20; Chiang Kia-Ngau, *The Inflationary Spiral, The Experience in China, 1939–1950*. (New York: The Technology Press of Massachusetts Institute of Technology and John Wiley and Sons, Inc., 1958.)p.71–74; *The Cambridge History of China, Volume 13*, p.741–746.

5. Chou Shun-hsin, *The Chinese Inflation*, p.350.

6. *Ibid*, p.351–2.

7. *Ibid*. p.252.

8. Pepper, *Civil War in China*, p.59.

9. C.C.Liang, "Terror on the March", CWR, 21 June 1947,p.78–9; Pepper, *Civil War in China*,p.60.

10. *Ibid*.

11. Powell,ed. "Teacher's Salaries", CWR, 12 April 1947,p.166–7; Yin-yuen Wang, "The Cost of Living Index for Military-Official-Educational Classes in Nanking Since May 1946",CWR, 12 April 1947, p.188–9.

12. C.Y.W.Meng, "China's Hyper Inflation: How to Stop It", CWR 10 May 1947, p.288–9.

13. C.C.Liu, "Education In China Great Failure; Teachers And Textbooks Inferior",CWR, 10 May 1947, p.296.

14. Chang Lien-hua, "I Accuse", CWR, 19 April 1947, p.210; Powell, ed."Dangerous Signs", CWR, 22 March 1947, p.86–7.

15. Frank L. Tsao, "Hunger on the March, A Review and Analysis into the Current Student Movement in China", CWR, 24 May 1947, p.348–9.

16. Powell, ed. "Crying For Peace", CWR, 24 May 1947, p.340; Fairbank and Feuerwerker, eds. *The Cambridge History of China, Volume 13*. p.561. The People's Political Council (Kuo-min ts'an-cheng-hui) was supposed to provide a platform for popular input, though it had no real power, and was not part of the new Constitutional machinery.; See also: Huangdah Chiu, "Constitutional Development in the Republic of China in Taiwan", in Steve Tsang, ed. *In the Shadow of China, Political Developments in Taiwan Since 1949*.(Honolulu: University of Hawaii Press, 1993.) p.17, 23. Although a new National Assembly, Legislative Yuan, and Executive Yuan were elected in 1947 and 1948, these would not actually begin sitting until 1948. Chiang Kai-shek superseded these institutions with provisions allowing direct presidential rule under martial law (Temporary Provisions Effective during the Period of Mobilization for the Suppression of the Communist Rebellion), passed by the National Assembly in December, 1946, and reaffirmed by the new National Assembly in 1948. They remained in effect until 1987.

17. Powell, ed. "Crying For Peace", CWR, 24 May 1947, p.340.

18. *Ibid.*

19. Pepper, *Civil War in China*, p.61–3; C.C.Liang, "Terror on the March" *CWR*, 21 June 1947,p.78–9; "Students Demand End of Civil War;Popular Support Seen", *CWR*, 24 May 1947,p.359; Frank L.Tsao, "Hunger on the March, A Review and Analysis Into the Current Student Movement in China", *CWR*, 24 May 1947, p.348–9.

20. Powell, ed. "The Student Crisis", *CWR*, 24 May 1947, p.341–3.

21. *Ibid.*p.341.

22. *Ibid.*p.342.

23. "Students Demand End of Civil War; Popular Support Seen", News of the Week, *CWR*, 24 May 1947, p.359.

24. Pepper, *Civil War in China*, p.62–3; Powell, ed. "Freedoms Restricted", *CWR*, 31 May 1947, p.371; Duncan C. Lee, "Rule of Force Continues in China", *CWR*, 31 May 1947, p.375; Jeffrey N. Wasserstrom, *Student Protests in Twentieth-Century China, The View from Shanghai.*(Stanford, Ca.: Stanford University Press, 1991.) p. 266–7. Neither Pepper, nor Wasserstrom mentions the PPC. Although they mention the demonstrations planned for June second, they fail to note their connection to the adjournment of the PPC.

25. As the value of the *fapi* declined, the GMD resorted to forced requisition of rice and other cereal crops to feed its troops. This contributed to the difficulty of provisioning urban centers by removing large quantities of grain from the market.

26. Bureaucratic capitalists were those who used public office for personal business and profit. Often it referred to important associates close to Chiang Kai-shek, like his brothers in law, the financiers T.V.Soong and H.H.Kung.

27. "Students Demand End to Civil War; Popular Support Seen", *CWR*, 24 May 1947, p.359; Frank L. Tsao, "Hunger on the March", *CWR*, 24 May 1947, p.348–9.

28. Powell, ed. "Crying for Peace", *CWR*, 24 May 1947, p.340.

29. "Generalissimo Stresses Peace Desire", from *Central News Service*, *CWR*, 31 May 1947, p.389; "Peace Move Spreading", *CWR*, 24 May 1947, p.359. Chiang said that peace depended entirely on the Communists and asked the PPC to think of methods to implement the new Constitution.

30. "PPC Invites Reds", *CWR*, 31 May 1947, p.391.

31. *Cambridge History of China, Volume 13*, p.746–7; Pepper, *Civil War in China*,p.62–66; Wasserstrom, *Student Protests in Twentieth-Century China*, p.267–8.

32. C.C. Liang, "Terror on the March", *CWR*, 21 June 1947, p.78–9; *China Press*, 29, 30 May 1947; Powell, ed. "Freedoms Restricted", *CWR*, 31 May 1947, p.371.

33. *Ta Kung Pao* (Chunking) 2 June 1947; "Arrest of 1,200 Suspects Breaks up Scheduled June 2 Rallies", *CWR*, 7 June 1947, p.27; C.C. Liang, "Terror on the March", *CWR*, 21 June 1947,p.78–79.

34. C.C.Liang, "Terror on the March", *CWR*, 21 June 1947, p.78–79.

35. Powell, ed. "Freedoms Restricted", *CWR*, 31 May 1947, p.371.

36. *Ibid.*

37. The Ambassador in Nanking (Stuart) to the Secretary of State, 30 May 1947, United States Department of State, *Foreign Relations of the United States,Diplomatic Papers,1947,Volume 7, the Far East: China.*(Washington D.C.:

Government Printing Office, 1972.) p.154–5.Hereafter cited as: *FRUS,1947,Volume 7.*

38. *Ibid.*

39. The Ambassador in Nanking (Stuart) to the Secretary of State, 30 May 1947, *FRUS 1947,Volume 7.* p.155.

40. "Courting Disaster", *Shanghai Evening Post and Mercury*, 31 May 1947; "Arrest of 1200 Suspects Breaks Up Scheduled June 2 Rallies", *CWR*, 7 June 1947, p.27; Henry Lee, "Behind the Demonstrations of Nanking's Students", *CWR*, 7 June 1947, p.16–17.

41. C.C. Liang, "Terror on the March", *CWR*, 21 June 1947, p.78–9.

42. Powell, ed. "Crisis in China", *CWR*, 7 June 1947, p.12.

43. *Ibid*, p.11.

44. *Ibid.*

45. Pepper, *Civil War in China*,p.66–7.

46. Pepper, *Civil War in China*,p.67; *Letter*, Union of Family Elders of Arrested Students of Shanghai to General A.C.Wedemeyer, Shanghai, 29 July 1947, "Parents Protest", *CWR*, 3 August 1947,p.246–8

47. *Ibid.*

48. *Letter*, (signed by seventy-five teachers), Shanghai, 1 June 1947, "Teachers' Manifesto", *CWR*, 7 June 1947,p.5.

49. *Letter*, Kuo Mo-jo, Mao Tun, et al.to ed., Shanghai, 1 June 1947, "Repression Scored", *CWR*, 7 June 1947, p.7–8.

50. John K.Fairbank and AlbertFeuerwerker, eds. *The Cambridge History of China, Volume 13, Republican China 1912–1949, Part 2.*(Cambridge: Cambridge University Press, 1986.) p.448,458,463.

51. No doubt Powell was happy to feature a letter signed by two such illustrious writers. At this time the *Review* did not carry the speeches or writings of prominent Communist leaders and of course had no affiliation with the CCP. A little more than a year and a half later, however, after the Communist takeover of Shanghai, all papers, including foreign journals, had to carry and comment on important speeches and party documents, as chapter seven of this dissertation explains.

52. *Letter*, Ching-yuen Yen,translator, to ed., Peiping, 31 May 1947, "586 Professors", *CWR*, 14 June 1947,p.36.

53. Henry Lee, "Behind the Demonstrations of Nanking's Students", *CWR*, 7 June 1947, p.16–18; Charles J.Canning,"Present Student Movement Held Greatest in China's History", *CWR*, 14 June 1947, p.48–9; Jefferson Cath,"Terror Reigns at Sun Yat-sen University", *CWR*, 14 June 1947, p.50; "Three Hankow Students Slain" (Photo Story), *CWR*, 14 June 1947, p.51; S.E.Shifrin,"Nankai Students' Version of May 20 Demonstrations in Tientsin", *CWR*, 7 June 1947, p.21.

54. "Increased Mail", *CWR*, 21 June 1947, p.68.

55. *Letter*, C.Y.Chang to ed., Kaifeng, 1 June 1947,"Terror in Honan" *CWR*, 14 June 1947,p.35; *Letter,*Yong Keng to ed., Shanghai, 15 June 1947, "Guns, Grenades", *CWR*, 21 June 1947,p.61; *Letter*, H.T.P. to ed., Hsuchow, 22 June 1947, "Hsuchow Incident", *CWR* 5 July 1947,p.126 ; *Letter*, Lee Shyue-Keao to ed., Hangchow, 25 May 1947, "Tears of Grief", *CWR*, 7 June 1947,p.6; *Letter*, 'A Student of Fuh Tan' to ed., Shanghai, 28 May 1947, "Special Students", *CWR*, 7 June 1947,p.7; *Letter*, Hopkin Chang to ed., Nanking, 1 June 1947, "How It All Started", *CWR*, 14 June 1947,p.38; *Letter*, K.C.Sha to ed.,Wusih, 2 June 1947, "Sad Situation", *CWR*, 14 June 1947,p.38; *Letter*, Illingsworth to ed., Chungking,

2 June 1947, "Chunking Arrests", *CWR*, 14 June 1947,p.38; *Letter*, Hsu Shih-Chen to ed., Kaifeng, 31 May 1947, "Honan Horrors", *CWR*, 21 June 1947,p.63–4; *Letter*, Hue Chen-Kuo to ed., Nanchang, 7 June 1947, "Crisis in Nanchang", *CWR*, 21 June 1947,p.66; *Letter*, Chang Huai-Yu to ed., Chungking, 29 June 1947, "Why Not Freedom?", *CWR*, 5 July 1947,p.125; *Letter*, Students' Association of National Fuh Tan University to ed., Shanghai, 29 May 1947, "Students Assaulted", *CWR*, 7 June 1947, p.8.

56. Pepper, *Civil War in China*. p.69.

57. "Court Official Flays *China Weekly Review*", *North China Daily News*, 17 May 1947,p.3; Powell, ed. "Independent Courts", *CWR*, 24 May 1947,p.339–340; *Fei Pao* 15 May 1947.

58. John King Fairbank and Merle Goldman, *China, A New History*.(Cambridge, Mass.: The Belknap Press of the Harvard University Press, 1998.) p.183–5.

59. John K.Fairbank and Albert Feuerwerker, eds. *The Cambridge History of China, Volume 13, Republican China 1912-1949*.(London: Cambridge University Press, 1986.) p.533; Fairbank and Goldman, China, A New History. p.259. "All Chinese constitutions have listed many rights but only as programmatic ideals, not necessarily as laws to be enforced. Behind this Chinese version of liberalism lay the prior assumption that the ruler's power was unlimited, still autocratic. His devices of statecraft might expand to include constitutions, parliaments, and citizens' rights (as well as duties), all to improve the state's stability and control. Typically, rights were guaranteed 'except as limited by law,' that is, by the fiat of the authorities."

60. Powell, ed. "China's New Constitution", *CWR*, 30 November 1946, p.383.

61. Powell, ed. "China's Treaties and Laws", *CWR*, 5 April 1947, p.137–8; The Secretary of State to the Ambassador in China (Stuart),Washington, 25 June 1948, United States Department of State, *Foreign Relations of the United States, Diplomatic Papers, 1948, Volume 8, The Far East: China*.(Washington D.C.: Government Printing Office, 1973.)p.576. Cited hereafter as *FRUS,1948, Volume 8*.Mentions the Meysberg case, also in n.39; The Ambassador in China (Stuart) to the Secretary of State, Nanking, 17 February 1947, *FRUS,1947,Volume 7*. p.1071–1074.Gives the economic security measures that Meysberg would violate.

62. Powell, ed. "Court Behavior", *CWR*, 12 April 1947,p.167.

63. Powell, ed. "China's Courts", *CWR*, 3 May 1947, p.257–9; Powell, ed."China's New Constitution", *CWR*, 30 November 1946, p.383.

64. Powell, ed. "China's Courts", *CWR*, 3 May 1947, p.258.

65. Walter K.C.Chen, "China's Habeas Corpus Law on Trial: Government by Law or by Terror?", *CWR*, 3 May 1947, p.268.

66. "Court Flays *China Weekly Review*", *North China Daily News*, 17 May 1947, p.3.

67. "Renovation of N.Chekiang Road Gaol", *North China Daily News*, 17 May 1947, p.3.

68. Chang T'ien-fu, translator. "The Shanghai Court's Reply", a translation of "A Review of 'China's Courts'-An Editorial of the *China Weekly Review*, By the Secretariat of the Shanghai High Court", *CWR*, 7 June 1947,p.24–26.

69. *Ibid*.

70. Dorothy Borg, *American Policy and the Chinese Revolution, 1925–1928*. (New York: Institute of Pacific Relations and MacMillan, 1947.); Commission on Extraterritorial Jurisdiction in China, *Report of the Commission on Extraterritoriality in China, Peking, September 16, 1926, Being the Report to the Governments*

of the Commission Appointed in Pursuance to Resolution V of the Conference on the Limitation of Armaments. (Washington, D.C.: Government Printing Office, 1926.)

71. Powell, ed. "Perpetual Martial Law", *CWR* 26 July 1947, p.222.

72. Douglas B.Falconer, "Non-Political Relief Urged: China Needs Help", *CWR*, 26 July 1947, p.234.

73. Dr.S.Francis Liu, "Some Observations on Judges, Lawyers, And Court Administration in China",Part I, *CWR*, 19 July 1947, p.194–6; Dr.S.Francis Liu, "Some Observations on Judges, Lawyers, And Court Administration in China", Part II, *CWR*, 26 July 1947,p.224–6; Powell, ed. "Perpetual Martial Law", *CWR*, 26 July 1947, p.222; Powell, ed., "Who's Kidding Who", *CWR*, 19 July 1947, p.198.

74. Powell, ed. "Dead Man's Tale", *CWR*, 29 November 1947, p.403–4 .

75. *Ibid*, p.404.

76. Patrick J.Maney, *The Roosevelt Presence, A Biography of Franklin Delano Roosevelt.* (New York: Twayne Publishers, 1992.), p.184–5.

77. R.Harris Smith, OSS, *The Secret History of America's First Central Intelligence Agency.* (Berkeley: University of California Press, 1972.), p.334–5; 341.

78. Joseph W.Esherick, ed. *Lost Chance in China: The World War II Despatches of John S.Service.* (New York: Random House, 1974.), p.378–386.

79. Powell, ed. "Showdown in Indonesia", *CWR*, 29 March 1947, p.113.

80. Powell, ed. "Showdown in Indonesia", *CWR*, 29 March 1947, p.113.

81. *Ibid.*

82. *Ibid.*

83. *Ibid.*

84. *Ibid.*

85. Powell, ed. "War in Indonesia", *CWR*, 21 June 1947, p.70–1.

86. *Ibid.*

87. Powell, ed. "Blood on the Flag", *CWR*, 2 August 1947, p.250–1.

88. *Ibid.*

89. *Ibid.*

90. Lin Wo-chiang, "Arbitration Said Best For Indonesia", *CWR*, 30 August 1947, p.381–2.

91. Powell, ed. " Pious Words", *CWR*, 24 January 1948, p.224–5.

92. Caroline Cooley, "Peace Far Away in Indochina", *CWR*, 21 June 1947, p.75–77.

93. *Ibid.*

94. *Ibid.*

95. *Ibid.* In her interview with Ho Chi-Minh, Ho nonetheless said that he would like to meet representatives of the American government to discuss future U.S.-Vietnamese relations. Ho was still asking for independence within the French trading system, and indicated that he expected to receive support from the Soviet Union in the near future.

96. Peggy Parker, "World Impressions of Saigon", *CWR*, 17 May 1947, p.324–5.

97. Andrew Roth, "The French Aren't French in Indochina", *CWR*, 7 February 1948, p.290–1; Andrew Roth, Indochina's Puppet Politics", *CWR*, 21 February 1948, p.349–350; Andrew Roth, "The French Are Fighting Maquis", *CWR*, 28 February 1948, p.376–6.

98. Walter Briggs, "French Bogged Down in Indochina", *CWR*, p.345–6.

99. J.Hendrick, "The Story of Vietnam Verses French Propaganda", *CWR*, 17 January 1948, p.198.

100. William Johnson, "Vietnam's Three Year War", *CWR*, 16 October 1948, p.178–9; William Johnson, "Vietnam Fights For Freedom", *CWR*, 4 December, 1948, p.15–17; William Johnson, "Vietnam's Fight For Freedom", *CWR*, 1 January 1949, p.109–111.

101. Powell, ed. "Independence Day", *CWR*, 28 June 1947, p.99.

102. Powell, ed. "Blessing of Colonialism", *CWR*, 26 June 1948, p.100–1.

103. *Ibid.*

104. Powell, "Bullitt Fires Again," *CWR*, 17 January 1948,p.194–5.

105. Powell, ed. "Blessings of Colonialism", *CWR*, 26 June 1948, p.100–1.

106. *Ibid.*

107. *Ibid.*

108. Powell, ed. "Doubtful Logic", *CWR*, 13 November 1948, p.277–8.

109. Powell, ed. "Dutch at It Again", *CWR*, 25 December 1948, p.83–4.

110. *Ibid.*

111. *Ibid.*

CHAPTER FOUR

SEASONS CHANGE: THE LATE FALL 1948 AND IMPENDING COLLAPSE

The first year of the Chinese Civil War had seen impressive gains by Chiang Kai-shek's forces. By December 1946 Nationalist armies had captured 165 towns and 174,000 square kilometers of land from the CCP. In March 1947, Chiang's forces achieved their greatest success when they captured Yanan, the Chinese Communist capital. As a result of these victories, a large portion of Nationalist forces were tied down in garrison duty in the re-conquered areas.

During the second half of 1947, the Communists began a successful counter offensive against the overextended Nationalists. By the middle of 1948, the People's Liberation Army (PLA) under Lin Biao had isolated the cream of Chiang's army in Manchuria. With the fall of the Manchurian fortified cities of Jinzhou (October 14, 1948), Changchun (October 18, 1948), and Shenyang (November, 1948), the Nationalist military had suffered an irreversible loss of half a million of its best American-trained and equipped troops.[1] At the same time, a Communist army under General Chen Yi captured the city of Jinan and the Shandong Peninsula in September 1948.

By October, 1948, the final great battle of the war, Huai-Hai, began near the intersection of the Huai River and the Lung-Hai Railroad. By November, two Nationalist divisions had defected to the Communists and Nationalist losses topped 100,000, though the battle would not be over until January. In December, 1948, Lin Biao's 800,000-man army, fresh from its Manchurian victories, joined the CCP's 550,000 man North China Army Group in a joint operation against Beijing and Tianjin. The GMD army opposing them numbered only half a million.[2]

The strategic north Chinese city of Xuzhou fell to the Communists on December 15, 1949. Within a matter of weeks the Battle of Huai-Hai would end in total Nationalist defeat opening the way for the PLA to cross the Yangzi into south China at its leisure. Beijing would fall January 15 and Tianjin January 23. Between September 1948 and January 1949, the GMD had lost 1.5 million troops, at least 800,000 of whom had defected to the Communists.[3]

In the United States, President Truman, on February 18, 1948, had recommended a $570 million dollar grant in aid to undergird the faltering Guomindang. Congress complied by passing a $400 million dollar China Aid Bill, the funds of which were distributed during the second half of 1948. However, by this time even massive American military intervention could not reverse the GMD's decline. As Nationalist military defeats multiplied during the late fall and the futility of added economic assistance became all too apparent, President Truman, in November and again in December, turned down two additional pleas by Chiang's government for aid.[4]

*

By late November or early December 1948, there was little doubt in the minds of Shanghai residents about the outcome of the Civil War and their impending occupation by the Communists, despite boisterous statements to the contrary by the Shanghai-Wusong Garrison headquarters. Journalists and business circles began speculating on what Shanghai residents might expect Communist rule to be like and how to prevent destruction of property and looting by Nationalist forces before their inevitable retreat.

Since numerous medium sized cities in the north had already been occupied for some months[5], there was much interest in their experience with early CCP urban rule. Positive accounts of the good conduct of the PLA, its careful respect for personal private property, and the rapidity with which the CCP restored electricity, public transport, and commerce were reassuring among non-Guomindang affiliated business circles. Numerous CCP radio messages reassured foreigners that their lives, property and legitimate business interests would be scrupulously protected by the People's Liberation Army. These pronouncements were strengthened by the positive accounts of foreign observers recounting the praiseworthy behavior of the PLA as it entered newly captured cities.

With the occupation of larger cities in 1948, the Chinese Communist Party had promoted a more conservative policy designed to reassure business interests that they had nothing to worry about from Communist rule. Leftist excesses were corrected through a rectification campaign and native and foreign capitalists were assured that their persons and property would be protected.[6] A moderate policy was adopted regarding labor issues.[7] In Tianjin, the Party sent New Year's greeting cards to companies to quiet their fears:

> We wish you long life and prosperous business. If we should take the city in this new year, do not be alarmed. We shall restore order quickly and welcome your business.[8]

Both foreign and Chinese businessmen and the urban middle classes in general had been alienated by the last six months of GMD rule, especially by the "Gold Yuan Reform." The surrender by the middle classes of their foreign currency, gold, and silver reserves for nearly worthless government gold yuan notes had embittered many. Jiang Jingguo's "tiger hunting" in Shanghai, i.e. the arbitrary draconian enforcement of price controls on rice and other basic commodities inside the city, had adversely effected local businessmen and merchants by isolating the Shanghai market from the rest of China, while leaving large speculators with government connections untouched.[9] Consequently, numerous Shanghai residents looked forward with hope to Communist pronouncements that business and commercial interests would be protected and fostered under Mao's "New Democracy."[10]

*

CCP POLICIES TOWARD RESIDENT FOREIGNERS, TRADE AND RECOGNITION

In view of the changing situation, the Chinese Communist Party had issued a number of policy directives throughout 1948 dealing with treatment of foreigners, foreign property holdings, and the question of recognition and trade with foreign nations. Generally these lent encouragement to resident foreign hopes for continuing trade and business under a CCP regime.

The Chinese Communist Central Committee, looking forward to the impending occupation of larger cities, instructed its cadres in February, 1948, on proper attitude toward foreigners and their concerns:

> We will soon come across more foreigners and have to deal with the churches, schools, hospitals, foundling hospitals, and nursing homes established by them, factories, mines and stores owned by foreign capital, and even foreign consulates and foreign banks. At present, our policy toward all these economic, cultural, and religious agencies owned or managed by foreigners is not to confiscate or abolish them, even if they are imperialist by nature. Rather, in a general sense, we will adopt a policy of protecting foreigners and foreign government agencies.[11]

As long as foreigners did not engage in military sabotage and obeyed the laws and regulations of the authorities, they were to be allowed to remain in the liberated areas "to continue their businesses and other legal activities" and were to be offered "due protection" by the government and PLA. Contracts were to be signed enabling foreign entrepreneurs to continue their operations. Foreign store owners were to continue their business under the protection of the new government. The property of foreign owners who had fled was to be held in trust to be returned if and when the owners returned.[12]

In early 1948, the Chinese Communist Party had not yet adopted the policy of refusing official status to foreign consular personnel until such time as their governments recognized the Communist government of

China. Rather, the Central Committee, perhaps anticipating foreign recognition, instructed cadres that:

> All consulates and their agents will be regarded as diplomatic representatives of their countries to maintain contact with their citizens whether or not their government has recognized our government.[13]

The Central Committee made it clear that consular officials, foreign service officers, and consular property were not to be molested in any way:

> All foreign consulates as well as consuls and other consular members should be protected. Their documents and properties should not be confiscated or damaged. The consulates must not be searched without a warrant.[14]

At the same time, wartime concerns remained paramount and cadres were instructed that consulates were not to install or operate radio transmitters while the Civil War was still in progress: "During the time of the Civil War, no consulate can install radio transmitters without the permission of our army headquarters, and offenders will be treated as criminals."[15]

Foreign residents, after first registering, were to be allowed freedom of movement as long as they had valid passports. The Central Committee admonished cadres that foreign property and civil rights were to be respected: "We should protect their lives and properties and provide them with freedom of movement. Without due reasons, they cannot be arrested and their rights are not to be violated."[16] The Central Committee cautioned cadres over the treatment of foreign and Chinese missionaries and their converts, reminding them that "We do not want people in foreign countries to believe mistakenly that we are carrying out an anti-religion policy."[17]

While the CCP was desirous of building a primary relationship with the Soviet Union to buttress the new regime against counterrevolutionary attack and to aid in building a socialist future, it also wished to establish ties with the Western nations. At a September 1948 Politburo meeting, Mao Zedong explained that peace, trade, and reaching an understanding with the capitalist nations were desirable. According to Mao, Chiang Kai-shek was counting on war between the Soviet Union and the United States to reestablish his position in China. Peace was therefore in China's interest. The postwar situation after World War II presented much greater opportunity to avoid another world war than the post-World War I situation had, Mao declared. He believed a compromise in international affairs between the socialist and capitalist blocs to avoid another World War was probable.

He pointed to trade development between the Soviet Union and France as an example to be emulated by China. While opposing compromise with the GMD and reactionaries at home, and insisting that each country had the right to choose its own political system without foreign intervention, Mao nevertheless indicated that compromise in foreign relations with the Western capitalist nations, including the United States, was desirable to promote both peace and trade.[18]

In November 1948, as President Truman and Secretary of State Marshall held emergency discussions on China policy in light of the Guomindang's rapid decline, the CCP Central Committee issued a public statement on foreign policy. Noting that the Nationalist government was about to fall, and that no amount of outside help could now save it, The Chinese Communist Party declared that it was :

> . . . willing to establish equal friendly relations with all foreign countries, including the United States ofAmerica, and protect the rightful interests of all nationals of foreign countries in China, including American nationals.[19]

The Communists made it clear that continued military and economic aid to the Guomindang government by the U.S. would be viewed as a hostile act, and warned America not to intervene militarily.[20] For the United States, therefore, the prerequisite for recognition of and trade with the Communist government was to cut off all military and economic aid to the Nationalist government.

*

To Powell and the *Review* staff, there seemed ample indication that businessmen, both Chinese and foreign, would be able to carry on their activities under Communist control. Mao had indicated that even after Communist victory, a long period of capitalist development would be necessary before China would be ready for socialism. CCP statements promising protection to foreign nationals and their property, and encouraging the uninterrupted continuation of commerce and production in Northern cities which fell under their control, further reinforced perceptions of the probability of continued business under a Communist regime. The practical tactic of limiting immediate Communist enemies to monopolistic GMD bureaucratic-capitalists,[21] while including almost everyone else, especially the "national bourgeoisie," or large capitalists, in the ranks of "the people," whose support the CCP was seeking, further assuaged the anxieties of shopkeepers, merchants, businessmen, intellectuals, and journalists.

Reports of the orderliness of the PLA's takeover of Northern cities , together with the fact that foreigners were by and large unmolested by the new overlords, helped convince the *China Weekly Review* staff that Shanghai businessmen might indeed be able to look forward for some time to continued business under the new regime. Consequently, the *Review* was quick to detect and encourage any indication that U.S. policy was about to shift toward recognition of the Communists and an end of support for Chiang's increasingly unpopular government.

ATTITUDE OF THE U.S CONSULAR STAFF AND STATE DEPARTMENT TOWARD
CONTINUED FOREIGN RESIDENCY AND TRADE AFTER CCP TAKEOVER

As early as August, 1948, U.S. Ambassador John Leighton Stuart had noticed a change in Communist policy toward greater toleration of middle class merchants, small scale industrialists, landlords, and businessmen so as to allay the fears and hostility of these groups. Stuart felt the CCP was bidding for cooperation with all liberal anti-Guomindang groups in their struggle to overthrow Chiang.[22] When the Communists entered Qingdao in Shandong Province in early October, 1948, the U.S. Consul General, William T. Turner, reported that Americans were well treated. CCP authorities told missionary school teachers to keep on teaching as before, and guaranteed religious freedom. Turner recounted that the PLA was well behaved and that the populace was much relieved after the dismal behavior of the GMD troops.[23]

A decision was made by the U.S. State Department to keep American consular officials in place after CCP takeover in order to establish working relations with the new Communist officials and to encourage Americans whose presence was essential to business and missionary interests to remain in China.[24] Consuls were instructed to seek relations with local Communist authorities on an informal and personal basis, since the United States did not recognize any Chinese Communist government.[25] On November 1, 1948, the People's Liberation Army captured Shenyang (Mukden), where U.S. Consul General Angus Ward and his staff had remained behind to test Communist intentions.

The day after the PLA occupied Shenyang, Zhou Enlai reminded cadres of their duty toward foreign consular staff. The British, American, and Soviet consulates were to be first protected by troops, and later guarded by police. Under no circumstances were foreign consuls to be searched as they entered or left their compounds nor were their consulates to be searched.[26]

As we have seen, the previous February, the Central Committee had instructed cadres that "All consulates and their agents will be regarded as diplomatic representatives of their countries to maintain contact with our government."[27] Although CCP policy would suddenly change in Shenyang on 10 November to non-recognition of Consular officials,[28] there seemed reason enough for many Americans to suppose the Communists would seek recognition and continued trade from the West.[29] American observers believed that only the United States possessed the capital required for massive reconstruction after the Chinese Civil War ended. The USSR, however much it might wish to aid China, did not have vast capital reserves.

The initial reports from Angus Ward, U.S. Consul in Shenyang, were optimistic, even enthusiastic on the possibility of working with the new regime. On November 9, 1948, the new Communist Mayor of Shenyang called on Ward. He lamented the absence of American businessmen, noted that the outside world had need of Manchuria's goods and that Manchuria needed products from the outside world. He hoped American businessmen would resume trade with Manchuria "on the basis of equality."

Ward noted that the manager of the British-American Tobacco Company had been assured by an official of the municipal government that other than taxes and duties, the new regime would "not interfere in domestic or foreign trade conducted by foreigners." All in all, Ward reported "The Mayor seemed sincere in his stated desire [for] early inauguration [of] foreign trade by Americans."[30] Ward also emphasized the efficient, professional way the Communists had quickly restored order, resumed public transportation, and encouraged the reopening of local businesses.[31]

The State Department noted the "correct" treatment of Americans in Shenyang following Communist takeover,[32] and accurately concluded that "incoming troops [were] obviously thoroughly briefed re: attitude and actions toward foreigners."[33] In general, the Department felt that the situation of Americans in Shanghai "was totally different from that obtaining in 1940–1941." The State Department believed the main danger Americans faced, came rather from the withdrawing Nationalist troops and bombing by the Nationalist Airforce afterward.[34]

*

The economy of Shanghai was the most developed in China. It was strongly tied to the world trading system, and held by far the largest concentration of foreign direct investments. The U.S. Consul General at Shanghai, John M.Cabot, was understandably concerned about the position of American businessmen and missionaries when the government of China changed hands. He advised Washington:

> With regard to American business men remaining behind to protect American interests, the Department will appreciate that many established concerns with important investments should not be left, under the circumstances, un-represented by resident Americans. This applies both in the commercial and missionary fields.[35]

While recommending that dependent women and children be repatriated, the Consul General informed the State Department that he had "encouraged American business men to leave their interests represented by key Americans remaining behind." The Consul added "that it would not be in the national interest to abandon positions held by Americans which have been acquired through patient upbuilding."[36]

Numerous U.S. companies: Pan American Airlines, Shanghai Power Company, Standard-Vacuum Oil Company, Caltex American, and Standard Oil, all large advertisers in the *Review*, informed the U.S. Consulate in Shanghai that they intended to continue operations if possible under Communist rule. They expressed concern that continued U.S. aid to the Nationalist regime would compromise their situation. This same anxiety was reflected in the editorial pages of the *Review*. Business leaders pressed the consulate for evacuation guarantees should this contradictory aspect of U.S. policy lead to trouble in the future.

Consul General Cabot in Shanghai, though recognizing the risk, still felt it ". . . undesirable for Americans to evacuate if their presence in China is essential to continued functioning of U.S. business, educational, missionary or other enterprises."[37] While unable to guarantee the evacuation of civilian personnel should the situation become ugly, the Consul General pointed out to American businessmen that trade between the U.S. and Communist Eastern Europe was already taking place under similar circumstances.[38]

The State Department acted to squelch anti-trade rumors sponsored by pro-Chiang proponents. China Lobbyist William C. Bullitt, former ambassador to the U.S.S.R. and consultant to the U.S. Joint Committee on Foreign Economic Cooperation, had informed Paul Hopkins, president of the Shanghai Power Company, that Communist occupation of Shanghai would result in the United States government adopting a "black out" policy on trade relations.[39] The Department denied this misinformation, noting that it had ". . . not yet determined policy [in] this regard" and stating that ". . . no foundation exists for Bullitt's alleged statement."[40] The policy of the State Department and Consular Service was essentially ambiguous. On the one hand, it was pessimistic about long range business prospects in China, yet willing to encourage businessmen to maintain their commercial activity, so long as the liability to the Consulate was minimal.

Reacting positively to Ward's assessment at Shenyang, and following Consul General Cabot's initiative, the State Department informed Ambassador Stuart in China that it recognized two categories of Americans in Shanghai: "Americans whose presence [in] China [is] essential [to] continue[d] functioning [of] U.S. business, educational, missionary or other enterprise[s]" and those who were not essential and "who had no compelling reason to remain in China." While holding that the latter group should be advised to leave China, the Department believed it was "undesirable" to encourage the former group to evacuate since it would jeopardize established American interests in Shanghai.[41]

*

We have seen that CCP regulations forbade foreign consulates from installing and operating radio transmitters as long as the Civil War was in progress. On November 2, 1948, the U.S. State Department, though aware of these regulations, chose to interpret them as not applying to the Consulate in Shenyang. In violation of the new CCP directives, U.S. Consul Angus Ward and his staff were instructed to draw no attention to their radio transmitter, to continue broadcasting and to code all messages.[42] Since the U.S. was still the mainstay of the Nationalist Government which was at war with the CCP, and in view of Communist suspicions about the United States, these directives seem to have been ill-advised.

On November 18, the Shenyang Military Control Commission shut down Ward's transmitter, ending his contact with other U.S. Consulates.[43] Under house arrest by CCP authorities who took no steps to inform the State Department of his circumstances, Ward's detention became an impediment, especially for the American side, to improving Sino-American relations.

Throughout the talks between U.S. Ambassador John Leighton Stuart and Nanjing Foreign Resident Affairs Director Huang Hua, from early April to early July, 1949, Ward's detention loomed in the background. When Communist authorities in North China made allegations on June nineteenth that an American spy ring had been operating out of the Shenyang Consulate, Ambassador Stuart categorically denied the charges.[44] Finally, on October 24, 1949, after a year of detention, Ward was charged with assaulting a Chinese employee over the issue of severance pay, found guilty, given a suspended sentence, and deported.[45]

*

John W.Powell and his *China Weekly Review* believed the United States should stay engaged in China and approved of the State Department's decision to leave U.S. Consular personnel behind as the PLA advanced in North China. "It is obvious that the embassy desires to make contact with the Chinese Reds," he declared. "This is only natural since the American government (at least the civilian part of it) hopes to maintain relations with China, no matter what kind of government."[46] "Also," Powell continued,

> In the event of a Communist victory in China and eventual American recognition- a possibility which must not be overlooked- the State Department would desire to maintain consulates in as many places as possible. It would be simpler to maintain existing consulates than to apply for permission to reestablish old ones.[47]

Powell noted that many missionary groups, including Catholic orders, intended to remain after a CCP takeover, in spite of past difficulties with the Communists. Protestant missionaries, who had generally fared better than the Catholics in Communist base areas, also intended to continue functioning under Red control.[48] A second article underscored the change of attitude among many missionaries about the prospects for continuing their work under the Communists:

> Even some Catholics today talk of remaining in areas threatened by the Reds, while a year ago, all you had to do to bring forth comments . . . was to ask a Catholic priest how he liked the Reds . . . That quite a few [Catholic and Protestant missionaries] are now discussing the question of working in Communist-controlled areas indicates a partial change of attitude in a very important group of foreigners.[49]

The continued presence of American missionaries and businessmen was an unspoken argument for maintaining a U.S. Consular presence, Powell opined, since the protection of American citizens was one of the major reasons Consular offices existed in China.[50]

Powell observed that the American business community in China also wanted to continue commerce and trade, if it proved possible under Communist control. Immediately following the fall of Jinan and Shenyang, he recalled, many businessmen were enthusiastic about this possibility due to initial reports of good treatment under CCP rule, although the recent increase in anti-imperialist rhetoric by the CCP had cast a shadow over such optimism.[51] Both groups, Missionaries and Businessmen, intended to stay on in China, and had considerable influence in Washington D.C., he reminded his readers.

The *Review*'s editor in chief believed that America should follow a policy of non-intervention militarily. "Aid to the Chinese people (but not to the GMD government) should be continued," he advised, and worthwhile projects should be continued after the change in governments. Although he recognized that official diplomatic relations were not yet an option, since the U.S. still maintained relations with the Nationalist regime, he supported the attempt to establish unofficial consular working relations. Powell believed that through extending the kinds of aid that China truly needed in a friendly and forthright manner, the United States could prevent China from becoming an outright enemy:

> It is a little late for us to try to play the role of impartial benefactor in this country, since we have already rolled up a sizable record as number-one supporter of the Kuomintang, but we think we should make the attempt. We may not be able to prevent China from going Communist, but we think we can not only prevent China from becoming an enemy, but we can keep her a good friend by aiding her in those fields where she really needs help.[52]

Noting the gradual withdrawal of U.S. servicemen from China, Powell believed he detected a cooling of Republican Congressmen's ardor for increasing military aid to the Nationalists. At the very least, he believed the U.S. would not expand its aid to Chiang to the point of active participation in the Civil War.[53] Winding down U.S. involvement in the Civil War would allow America to begin bridging the gulf that separated it from the CCP through providing reconstructive aid to the new government, he conjectured.[54]

Powell and the *Review* had consistently opposed U.S. military aid and involvement in the Chinese Civil War, and had generally come to share the views of Chinese liberals and students: that American aid had prolonged the war and the people's suffering unnecessarily. At the same time, Powell had supported the public works and relief projects undertaken by the United Nations Relief and Rehabilitation Administration (UNRRA). From 1946 on, he had opposed the partisan way in which the Nationalist government had impeded distribution of UNRRA aid, due to corruption and a desire to prevent it from going to Communist-controlled areas. On human-itarian grounds, the *Review* had repeatedly called for the equal distribution of UNRRA aid to all parts of China, without reference to politics. Powell recognized that the Nationalist government, by preventing all but a trickle of UNRRA aid from reaching CCP-held areas, had effectively politicized it.

When UNRRA aid was discontinued, the U.S. replaced it with its own aid program, the Economic Cooperation Administration (ECA), which un-like the United Nations' aid program, had never been intended as other than partisan aid to GMD-held China. With Nationalist government con-trol of China rapidly crumbling, Powell proposed that the United States, by extending ECA aid to Communist-held areas, could indicate its interest in friendly contact, trade, and assistance to the new regime.

Powell recounted a recent speech by Harland Cleveland, special Economic Cooperation Administration representative from Washington, which in-formed the Shanghai press that the replacement of the current government with a new Communist regime would not necessarily mean the end of ECA assistance for China. The bilateral agreement which underlay ECA would still be in effect, Cleveland had pointed out, as long as the new government gained U.S. recognition.[55] Although Powell felt that "the U.S. would not be in any hurry to recognize a Communist regime in China," he interpreted Harland's ambiguous statement to indicate that policy makers were holding the door open to possible continuation of ECA aid to China.

Powell pointed hopefully to ECA Chief Administrator Paul G. Hoff-man's statement in a December 1948 speech delivered in Shanghai, that the U.S. might be willing to continue its ECA programs if the coalition govern-ment which replaced the Nationalist regime did not suppress individual freedom. The speech itself was ambiguous. Hoffman had cautioned that if the coalition was obviously CCP-dominated, the chances were the U.S. would extend no more aid. But for Powell, the important point was that it indicated the U.S. government was considering a change in policy.[56]

At the same time that Powell was suggesting the continuance of ECA aid in areas that fell under Communist control, Consul General O. Edmond Clubb in Beijing proposed a similar course to the U.S. Secretary of State.[57] Suggesting that the discontinuance of the ECA food provisions after a CCP takeover would lead to a negative Chinese public reaction, Clubb believed that continuation of the food supply program might provide a point of de-parture for future U.S. policy in North China. He pointed out that mission-aries and American commercial concerns would remain even after CCP authority was established. In Clubb's view, continuation of aid after the CCP takeover entailed little risk in return for the possibility of substantial political gain in the future.[58]

The suggestion that ECA food and medical aid be continued in areas newly under Communist rule was taken up by Roger D. Lapham, Chief of the ECA China Mission, who included oil and other commodities in the proposal.[59] The project was placed before the Congressional Joint Committee on Foreign Economic Cooperation and the National Security Resources Board, both of which showed preliminary interest in the idea.[60]

Ambassador Stuart, although initially supporting a flexible approach toward ECA aid, strongly opposed the plan, which would have continued the supply of food, fertilizer, cotton, and petroleum products to Communist-controlled areas through April 3, 1949.[61] Ultimately the matter was decided by President Truman, who declared, after a Cabinet vote, that all aid would stop once an area fell under Communist control. Supplies which were already landed could be distributed, but shipments en-route were to be diverted.[62]

*

POWELL'S SUPPORT FOR CONTINUATION OF THE USIS AND RELATED SERVICES IN COMMUNIST DOMINATED AREAS

Powell, who had worked for the United States Office of War Information through December, 1945, kept contact with its successor, the United States Information Service (USIS). Mary Barrett, who joined the *China Weekly Review* staff as assistant editor on January 1, 1949, was also a news editor for the United States Information Service, where she edited the daily report for release to Chinese newspapers.[63] When the USIS was finally forced to close by the Communists in July, 1949, Barrett remained an important *Review* editor until the journal was reorganized as a monthly in September 1950.[64]

From 1946–1948 Powell defended the USIS against all critics, be they U.S Congressmen, American newspaper chains, or the Chinese Communists. He viewed the agency as a positive source of shared information with a great potential to promote understanding and mutual goodwill between the U.S. and China. Hence, Powell felt it was important that USIS and related services be continued throughout China after the Communists came to power.[65]

As early as February, 1946, the *Review* had written enthusiastically on State Department plans to develop a worldwide information disseminating and gathering service. Powell saw the United States Information Service as the logical outgrowth of the wartime OWI. The USIS program would include exchange of scholars and students, lectures, radio programs, a bulletin, etc. It would be non-military in nature, would not be a "cloak and dagger" operation, but would be open and frank in nature. The *Review* thoroughly supported the project.[66]

In his editorials, Powell made a sharp, distinction between the benign information gathering of the OWI / USIS, which he saw as the most important aspect of intelligence work, and the terroristic activities of the Chinese military's Bureau of Investigation and Statistics (BIS), which the U.S. unfortunately had a role in establishing. Powell wanted the BIS dissolved, and labeled its brand of "gestapo-like" World War II spy activities a failure.[67]

To attract better qualified personnel, Powell advocated raising U.S. Foreign Service pay. He lauded the actions of John King Fairbank, director of the new United States Information Service, for the concern he demonstrated for the widow of a USIS Chinese colleague.[68] The *Review* examined various aspects of U.S. government sponsored dissemination of propaganda and news in a series of editorials in late winter 1947.[69]

An article by Francis Fang, a cultural worker in the U.S. Information Service, outlined the positive contributions which the USIS made. China suffered from a "famine of books" on medical and technical information, which the USIS American library in China tried to remedy by filling various service requests. Fang lauded the USIS "Aid to China" campaign, which provided education on various aspects of sanitation: "a farsighted and important program which will help the progress of science and education in China."[70]

As economic conditions in North China began to deteriorate in the face of continued civil war, *Review* correspondent S.E. Shifrin decried a proposal by the cost-conscious U.S. Senate to shut down the Tianjin branch of the USIS in late summer, 1947, noting that it was the only official U.S. news agency operating in North China.[71] If its reading room and library were shut down, the quantity of books and magazines from the United States reaching North China would be greatly diminished, he pointed out.

On the home front, Powell attacked Congress's policy of curtailing the activities of the USIS by cutting into its budget, and defended the value of this "descendant of the wartime Office of War Information."[72] In January, 1948, Powell defended the USIS against attacks in Congressional hearings and by *Time* and the Scripps-Howard newspaper chain. He lauded passage of the Mundt Bill by Congress, which created the Office of International Information and Educational Exchange under the U.S. Department of State.[73] Shortly afterward, the *Review* published an article by John Melby describing the operation of the United States Educational Foundation in China and the implementation of the Fulbright Act, which provided for exchange of scholars and students.[74]

From this cursory sketch it is clear that Powell and the *Review* consistently supported and defended USIS activities in China: the gathering and dissemination of information and the exchange of students and scholars. As already noted, in mid-November, 1948, Communist radio broadcasts charged that local officials in Shenyang had uncovered a huge network of U.S. spies, employing secret radio transmissions,etc.[75] These charges were related to U.S. Council General Ward being held incommunicado by Communist authorities, immediately following their seizure of the illegally operated transmitter in the U.S. Consulate.[76]

Powell and the *Review* immediately took issue with Chinese Communist claims concerning the alleged spy network. Espionage currently consisted mostly of clerks going over foreign newspaper and radio broadcasts, he maintained. The "huge network" and "secret radio transmitters" described by CCP radio were ridiculous. Either the CCP was extremely naive or was disregarding the truth, he editorialized. Real information gathering was a completely open kind of activity, not secret. Powell was disappointed because in his view, the CCP was usually realistic- but this kind of manipulation of the truth was "impossible to justify."[77]

In spite of the Communists' spy allegations, Powell hoped the United States and China could continue their friendly relations. His assumption that Communist leaders were usually realists gave him hope that this was still possible. Many businessmen were thinking of staying after the Communists took power in Shanghai, Powell observed. The U.S. would do well to recognize the new regime and get along with it. Cooperation was possible, he believed, if the United States would only meet China halfway.[78]

To counteract the Communists' spy charges, and to demonstrate the positive role which the USIS could play in promoting Sino-American understanding, Powell asked the United States Information Service in China to prepare a summary of its activities and history. The agency complied with his request, and Powell published an account which detailed USIS operations and explained its counter-propaganda activities as well.[79]

Powell worried that the advent of Communist control would lead to the demise of the Fullbright Scholarship program in China, and called for some way to continue the program. In a December, 1948 article, he noted twenty-eight Fullbright scholars currently in China, studying and doing research. The program was supposed to last 20 years, and was an important step toward improving East Asian studies at U.S. universities. It was supported by allocating a small portion of U.S. surplus property sales payments in China, which the Nationalist government in turn distributed in the form of monthly living allowances and salaries to American scholars. Since the CCP could not reasonably be expected to foot the bill for Guomindang munitions and surplus war materials payments, of which the scholarships were a part, Powell worried that the program would end when the Communists took over.[80]

For the sake of promoting good relations between China and the U.S., Powell felt it "would be more important than ever for scholars to spend time studying (China's) new institutions and ways so that future teachers will be well informed."[81] Although he did not know just how the Fullbright scholarship program could be revived under a Communist regime, he believed that it was vital that a similar substitute program should be arranged.[82]

In regard to programs like the USIS, the CCP displayed a certain amount of ambiguity. The Chinese Communist Party Central Committee in January, 1949, gave local officials directives for dealing with foreign cultural agencies, which would seem to apply to the USIS as well. After a period of investigation, according to the specific situation, they might be supervised, transformed, or even taken over as the situation required.[83] In March, 1949, Mao, addressing the Central Committee, called for the abolition of all Imperialist propaganda agencies in China. Yet, in spite of this, the United States Information Service remained untouched by local authorities in CCP-held areas for a considerable time thereafter. The Shanghai, Tianjin and Beijing USIS and the United States Information and Education program, in fact, remained active up to their closure by Communist authorities in late July, 1949.[84]

On July 15, 1949 the Shanghai Military Control Commission ordered the acting director of the USIS in Shanghai (John W. Henderson) to suspend all activities, since the U.S. and China had no formal diplomatic relations. All USIS publicity operations, including news distribution, libraries, concerts, and movies were to be stopped.[85] On July 19, the Beijing Military Control Committee delivered a similar message closing the Beijing USIS for the same reason. USIS officials were enjoined to: "cease activities, including the printing and distribution of news copy, display and presentation of books and periodicals, affixing of charts and pictures, showing of motion pictures, giving of musical concerts, together with other external activities."[86] Three days later, the USIS in Tientsin received a similar directive from the Military Control Commission of Tianjin, closing it because of the lack of diplomatic recognition between the People's Republic and the U.S.[87]

All of this occurred after Ambassador John Leighton Stuart declined a proposed visit to Beijing for an informal meeting with Zhou Enlai and Mao Zedong (treated in chapter 6), and not long after Mao's famous "Lean to One Side" speech, outlining the intent of the CCP to steer China's foreign policy in an anti-imperialist direction. U.S. Consul General Clubb at Beijing and Minister-Counselor Clark at Guangzhou (Canton) both believed the Communist closure of the USIS and USIE programs were an attempt to "pressure the United States into early de jure recognition after [the] formation of [a] new government" and to force withdrawal of support from the Nationalist government.[88]

*

PLANS FOR KEEPING ORDER DURING THE INTERIM PERIOD IN SHANGHAI

In early December, 1948, Shanghai businessmen and merchants became alarmed over the prospect of possible looting, arson, destruction of property and rioting in the interim period between Nationalist withdrawal and the arrival of the People's Liberation Army. Radio and newspaper stories of the destruction of buildings and wide-scale looting by retreating Nationalist troops in Jinan, followed by rioting, fueled such speculation.[89] Shanghai businessmen were further worried by the rather sudden declaration by the Kuomintang government of a "scorched earth policy," and the subsequent destruction of the British-owned Kailan Mining Administration's harbor installations at Qinhuangdao by withdrawing Nationalist forces.[90]

This fear gave rise to an ongoing discussion by foreign and Chinese businessmen about what might be done to protect property and insure social order in Shanghai in the period between Nationalist withdrawal and Communist assumption of control. In the course of this debate, in which the *Review* took part, an emerging consensus was apparent, not just among foreign and Chinese businessmen but also between the U.S. State Department and the Chinese Communist Party.

Along with Chinese and foreign property owners and businessmen, the Chinese Communist Party also had a big stake in trying to prevent the destruction of businesses and facilities that employed the urban masses in the cities falling under their control. Large-scale destruction of plants, shops, and other facilities would compound urban unemployment and further disrupt the economies of cities already suffering separation from their economic hinterlands as a result of civil war. It would multiply the difficulty of managing and reconstructing the battered urban economies, making it much more difficult to strengthen and consolidate CCP urban control.[91]

Accordingly, the Communist-sponsored Sixtieth All-China Labor Congress (August 1948) issued a directive specifying that in areas soon to fall to the PLA:

> All workers should energetically protect all the public land and privately owned enterprises, factories, machinery, and materials from Kuomintang destruction and wreckage, especially on the arrival of the People's Liberation Army. They should unite people of all walks of life to keep counter-revolutionary elements under surveillance, maintain social order, and await the establishment of a new order.[92]

General Headquarters of the Northern China People's Liberation Army issued an order on November 1, 1948, proclaiming the destruction of buildings, machinery, or other property to be a serious war crime.[93] A public directive signed by PLA Commander-in-Chief Zhu De and Marshal Peng Dehuai was aired on CCP radio November 12, reiterating that those urban dwellers who destroyed property, facilities or machinery would be punished, while those who averted such damage would be rewarded.[94] Urban residents in cities soon to fall to the Communists were informed in December, 1948, by CCP radio that all residents bore responsibility to preserve and protect property and order against disruption.[95]

Reports of massive intentional destruction of buildings and property by withdrawing Nationalist troops in Baoding, on November 22, 1948, prompted the *China Weekly Review* and Shanghai's foreign community to join discussion on what might be done to avoid the same fate in Shanghai. On December 9, an alarming *New China News Agency* English broadcast from North Shaanxi described the plundering of the Hebei provincial capital, Baoding, where withdrawing Nationalist soldiers had burned schools, factories, and other public institutions. The property destroyed by the GMD 272nd Division in Baoding included Hebei University, the Army Hospital, the city electrical plant, the Chen Yi Flour Company, a match company, the railroad station, and other buildings and equipment belonging to the municipal government, communications installations, and other public and private enterprises.[96] Other reports claimed that the Guomindang was planning to destroy the Kalgan Coal Mines at Tangshan as its forces pulled out.[97]

The *Review's* lead editorial two days later decried the Nationalist's destruction of the Kailan Mining Administration's harbor installations at Qinhuangdao as a direct reversal of Nationalist policy and proof that the GMD had given up on retaking areas now falling to the CCP. Powell warned that capitalist nations like Britain and the United States would not take the wrecking of their industrial investments lightly. The Destruction of Kailan coal stores could lead to the stoppage of electric power plants, which in turn would adversely effect a large number of other industries and manufacturing plants. If the Nationalist government persisted in its policy of destroying painfully acquired industrial installations, plant and stores, the *Review* warned, the blow to the Chinese people would be crippling.[98]

A second editorial probed the question of how this destruction might be avoided in Shanghai, and attempted to promote public discussion of the issue.[99] Powell pointed out that if similar tactics were employed in Shanghai, it would mean the destruction of the American-owned Shanghai Power Company facilities, the Shanghai Water Works, the Shanghai Gas Company, and the public transit systems, all of which represented heavy foreign investments. Such action would cause chaos in heavily populated industrial Shanghai, already swollen with refugees, by suddenly throwing thousands out of work. Without jobs, light, water and gas, riots and further destruction might quickly follow. Powell called for some kind of agreement between GMD and CCP forces to avoid fighting in the city and felt that public pressure would push both sides into such an arrangement.

To prevent rioting, looting and the destruction of factories and shops by the city's unemployed in the interim period between a GMD pullout and the PLA's entry, Powell suggested that residents organize themselves. He felt that the workers in local labor unions and guilds had much to loose if their places of employment were destroyed, and that they should be organized by their employers to protect their plants and workshops.[100]

Assuming that Shanghai passed through the interim period unscathed, Powell pointed out that the city would still face depression if some way to import foreign oil for the Shanghai Power Company were not insured. He anticipated that the Guomindang would blockade the port with vessels supplied by the Americans and British, a strategy that would not make life any easier for American residents. He reminded his readers of the economic strangulation that they had briefly tasted under Jiang Jingguo's short rule in the fall of 1948, during the Gold Yuan Economic Reform, and warned that the GMD had the power to cut off Shanghai from its hinterland through naval blockade of the coast, and aerial disruption of the railroads and highways.[101]

In the same issue, the *Review* published an article by an American businessman, that proposed a more specific plan to save the city from destruction.[102] The article rejected the use of U.S. Marines (waiting on shipboard in Shanghai harbor) to preserve order, as being prejudicial to the long range interests of resident American businessmen. On the other hand ". . . if the civilian population of Shanghai organizes itself to keep the peace, the Communists cannot justly retaliate for our temporary assumption of the reins of government."[103] The article called for a meeting of the various chambers of commerce, with the city's Chinese Chamber of Commerce taking the lead, in cooperation with the French, British and American Chambers of Commerce. It looked to the business community to provide the necessary leadership in organizing temporary volunteer fire and police forces and in persuading workers to protect their plants.

Because labor in Shanghai was "restless" and "given to capriciousness and instability" in the author's view, it was:

> . . . more important than ever that some attempt be made to impress upon labor its stake in the Shanghai industrial plant. The question of ownership of property such as factories is of no importance at the moment. The important thing is to prevent its destruction. Labor has as much at stake in this as management. The story to be firmly implanted in labor's mind is: If your factory is damaged or destroyed, you will lose your job.[104]

In a following issue, an anonymous Chinese university professor joined the debate with an article on behalf of Chinese businessmen and laborers. He praised the basic ideas presented by Powell and "An American Businessman". His article declared that:

> Considerable thinking has already taken place in many Chinese circles. Shanghai industrialists have had this idea in mind for quite some time and many of them have already made arrangements with their workers for protection of factories and other installations.[105]

The author argued that foreign chambers of commerce should initiate talks on the subject rather than the Chinese Chamber of Commerce, since it would not be safe for Chinese to raise the question. "The authorities would be certain to view such actions with hostility and would undoubtedly term them Communist-inspired propaganda designed to weaken public morale."[106]

The most dangerous period would be immediately after Nationalist soldiers realized that all was lost, the author stated. He assured the *Review*'s foreign readers that Shanghai's workers could be counted on to protect their "rice bowls" and noted that workers had already defended their plants in other cities after nationalist withdrawal. The proposal to dispatch

U.S.Marines to Shanghai under Admiral Badger to protect American lives and installations, such as the Shanghai Power Company, showed an unfortunate disposition to interfere unnecessarily, the author felt. The Communists had much to gain and too much to lose by antagonizing the U.S. he believed, and would not mistreat foreigners.

The author was optimistic that disaster could be avoided in Shanghai. Local groups were already discussing ways to bridge the interim period. Workers could be counted on to defend factories from mobs, and businessmen and industrialists would cooperate with labor. He noted that the Communists had promised lenient treatment and rewards for officials and others who protected property and punishment for those who destroyed it. The author believed that Communist broadcasts warning against disorder would have a salutary impact on those inclined to commit acts of destruction. "What was needed now [was] more consultation between foreigners and Chinese to exchange ideas, information, and plans of action."[107]

Especially interesting was the author's portrayal of what might be expected after the Communists restored order in Shanghai. His predictions were directed toward ". . . our foreign friends, especially the Americans." The Chinese Communists were realistic people, who would proceed slowly and cautiously with reform and eventual socialization of society, he opined. Social change would be gradual so as not to arouse undue opposition, and would "not be of a particularly socialistic nature" for quite some time.

"During this period of reconstruction and modernization, China will need her foreign friends' aid and advice more than ever," the author declared. "For this, if no other reason, realistic Chinese Communists will welcome legitimate foreign enterprise and will do nothing to drive away those foreigners already here."[108]

In the *Review*'s lead editorial "After the Interim Period," Powell echoed many of the same themes: the despicable behavior of demoralized nationalist troops in Jinan, the necessity of businessmen, industrialists and laborers organizing to defend Shanghai's industrial plant and business enterprises against destruction, and the likelihood of slow, gradual Communist reforms thereafter. Powell, while granting that the Chinese Communists really were communists, pointed out that many of the CCP's reforms, such as rent reduction and land redistribution, were not particularly "socialistic." He noted the total lack of collective state farms in CCP areas, a development which was surely a prerequisite to socialism, and speculated that progress toward communism probably would be slow. Foreign interests would most likely be able to carry on their businesses for many decades to come.[109]

The U.S. Consulate in Shanghai monitored and was drawn into participation in plans by American and foreign business interests and their Chinese counterparts to protect property and order during the city's fall. On December 10, Consul General Cabot cabled Washington the details of a plan for the peaceful turnover of Shanghai to Communist control. Police and firemen were to be subsidized in rice by the ECA to remain on the job after Nationalist withdrawal, and to do nothing to oppose the entry of the PLA into the city. Foreign and Chinese businessmen were to fund in part the efforts of police and firemen to keep order. There was to be no sabotage or destruction of buildings or property, and no removal of property. Nationalist troops were to be persuaded to evacuate the city peacefully and the Communist forces would be be persuaded to allow safe passage to those government officials who wished to leave.

Cabot urged the State Department to make an effort to establish "some understanding with the Communists" on the matter, and suggested the British in Hong Kong might serve as go-between. He informed the Department that the American Chamber of Commerce and various Chinese businessmen were already discussing how to put the plan into effect.[110]

The following day, the U.S. State Department gave cautious approval to Cabot's requests. Acting Secretary of State Robert A. Lovett agreed to have ECA subsidize the fire and police but warned Cabot to keep a low profile. Planning and implementation were to be kept in the hands of foreign and Chinese residents. "There would be no objection [to] your suggesting [the] matter to civilian groups, such as Chambers of Commerce, Rotary Club etc.," Lovett informed Cabot. "But you should remain in the background giving personal and unofficial advise in your discretion and as deemed appropriate."[111]

In early spring, 1949, mindful of these efforts, the CCP Central Military Commission instructed PLA forces that ". . . as Shanghai's bourgeoisie does not favor fighting in Shanghai, it is quite possible that Shanghai can be taken over in a peaceful way."[112] When Shanghai finally fell, May 25–27, 1949, over 60,000 residents had participated in the volunteer "Peoples Peace Preservation Corps," guarding buildings and property, preventing sabotage and looting during the transition. Two days later, Communist authorities ordered the "People's Peace Preservation Corps" to cease its activities and to disband.[113]

In spite of the *Review*'s frequent suggestions to the contrary, the ECA stopped all shipments of rice, cotton, oil, and fuel as soon as Shanghai fell to the Communists, thus adding temporarily to inflation and triggering an immediate shortage of these commodities in the city.[114] The opportunity to use the situation to "reach some kind of understanding with the Communists," as Cabot had urged, was not exploited.[115]

To recapitulate, amidst declining Nationalist military prospects and political support in late 1948, a perceived liberalization of Communist policy towards Chinese and foreign business interests led both the U.S. State Department and the *China Weekly Review* to conclude that continued American business and trade under a Communist regime would be both possible and desirable. Nationalist reverses led President Truman to rethink continued emergency military aid in November and December, and U.S. Consular officials were instructed to stay put as northern Chinese cities changed hands.

Powell saw this as a move toward eventual U.S. recognition and one which would facilitate continued Sino-American trade. He advocated the extension of ECA economic aid to the emerging Communist regime, and the continuance of the United States Information Service and related educational programs as a way to promote understanding and the development of positive Sino-American relations.

By participating in the movement to protect Shanghai's commercial property and industrial machinery from destruction by retreating Nationalist military units, the *Review* was marching in step with the U.S. State Department and the resident American business community. Yet, it was also facilitating CCP objectives of organizing urban residents, Chinese and foreign, management and labor, to protect property. The ambiguities and temporary local congruence in U.S. and CCP policy allowed room for cooperation, giving a measure of hope to Powell and the *Review* for the future of American interests in Shanghai. What might this future entail?

CHAPTER NOTES

1. Immanuel C.Y.Hsu, *The Rise of Modern China*, (New York: Oxford University Press, 2000.)p.630–633; John F. Melby, *The Mandate of Heaven, Record of a Civil War, China 1945–49*, (Toronto: University of Toronto Press, 1968.)p.285–290; U.S. Department of State, *United States Relations with China, with Special Reference to the Period 1944–1949*.(Washington D.C.: U.S. Government Printing Office, 1949.)p.334–5.

2. Hsu, *The Rise of Modern China*, p.632.

3. Suzanne Pepper, *Civil War in China, The Political Struggle, 1945–1949*. (Berkeley: University of California Press, 1978) p.411; Mao Tse-tung, *Selected Works of Mao Tse-tung, Volume 4*.(Peking: Foreign Language Press, 1969.) p.271

4. Hsu, *The Rise of Modern China*, p.634.

5. Pepper, *Civil War in China*, p.350. Among the larger cities held by the Communists in 1948 were Harbin, Hebei, Liaoyang, Yingkou, Luoyang, Jilin, and Shenyang.

6. Pepper, *Civil War in China*, p.351.

7. *Ibid*, p.369.

8. Anna Louise Strong, *The Chinese Conquer China*. (New York: Doubleday, 1949), p.259–260.

9. Shun-Hsin Chou, *The Chinese Inflation, 1937–1949*. (New York: Columbia University Press, 1963) p.25–26; A.Doak Barnett, *China on the Eve of Communist Takeover*. (New York: Frederick A.Praeger, 1968) p.73; Freda Utley, *The China Story*. (Chicago: Regency, 1951) p.107; Jack Belden, *China Shakes the World*. (Beijing: New World Press, 1989), p.408–9; Pepper, *Civil War in China*, p.121–126; Lloyd E.Eastman, *Seeds of Destruction: Nationalist China in War and Revolution, 1937–1949*. (Stanford, Ca.: Stanford University Press, 1984), p.180–5. Jiang Jingguo (Chiang Ching-kuo), son of Chiang Kai-shek, tried to enforce price controls inside Shanghai, while the same restrictions were not applied outside the city. The result was artificially low prices within the city , a stoppage of the flow of rice and

other basic commodities into the city, and skyrocketing black market prices for the same products.

10. By "New Democracy", Mao meant that the equivalent of a bourgeois-democratic revolution, a pre-requisite for the development of socialism in a semi-colonial, semi-feudal country like China according to Marxist thought, would be carried out under the direction of the Communist Party, rather than the bourgeoisie. Toward this end, the Party acting in the name of the proletariat would unite all the revolutionary classes of China, workers, peasants, petty bourgeoisie and national bourgeoisie, under its own leadership to accomplish the task of capitalist development within a framework of Communist control.

11. Instruction, CCP Central Committee, "How to Treat Foreigners in China", 7 February 1948, Shuguang Zhang and Jian Chen, eds. *Chinese Communist Foreign Policy and the Cold War in Asia, New Documentary Evidence, 1944–1950.*(Chicago: Imprint Publications,1996.) p.85–7. Hereafter cited as CCF-PCWA.

12. *Ibid.*

13. Instructions, CCP Central Committee, "How to Treat Foreigners in China", 7 February 1948, *CCFPCWA*,p.86.

14. *Ibid.*

15. Ibid.

16. Instruction, Central Committee, "How to Treat Foreigners in China", 7 February 1948, *CCFPCWA*, p.87.

17. Ibid. p.87.

18. Speech, Mao Zedong to Meeting CCP Central Committee Politburo, 8 September 1948, *CCFPCWA*, p.89.

19. CCP Central Committee public statement of foreign policy in "Red's Warning", News of the Week, (*United Press*) CWR 27 November 1948,p.144; Charles J.Canning, "Notes on China's Domestic and Foreign Policy", *CWR* 16 July 1949,p.144.

20. *Ibid.*

21. Represented mainly by the Guomindang's "big four families": Kung, Soong, Chiang and Chen. Kung and Soong were financiers related to Chiang as brothers in law, who had held various positions within the GMD, the Chen brothers comprised a military clique which strongly supported Chiang, and of course there was Chiang's own family.

22. The Ambassador in China (Stuart) to the Secretary of State, 24 August 1948, United States Department of State, *Foreign Relations of the United States, Diplomatic Papers, 1948,Volume 7, The Far East: China.* (Washington D.C.: Government Printing Office,1973)p.431. Cited hereafter as *FRUS,1948,Volume 7.*

23. The Consul General at Tsingtao (Turner) to Secretary of State, 11 October 1948, United States Department of State, *Foreign Relations of the United States, Diplomatic Papers, 1948, Volume 8, The Far East: China.* (Washington, D.C.: Government Printing Office, 1973),p.847. Cited hereafter as *FRUS,1948, Volume 8.*

24. The Consul General at Shanghai (Cabot) to the Secretary of State, 30 November 1948, *FRUS,1948,Volume 8*, p.900–3; The Acting Secretary of State to the Consul General at Shanghai (Cabot), 2 December 1948, *Ibid*, p.907–10.

25. The Acting Secretary of State to the Consul General at Mukden (Ward), 2 November 1948, *FRUS 1948,Volume 7*, p.826.

26. Telegram, CCP Central Committee to Northeast Bureau, 1 November 1948 (Extract), *CCFPCWA*, p.91–2.

27. Instruction, Central Committee, "How to Treat Foreigners in China," 7 February 1948, *CCFPCWA*, p.86.

28. On November 1, Zhou Enlai had advised the CCP Northeast Bureau to protect the U.S., British, and Soviet consulates in Shenyang and to respect the person, property, and freedom of diplomatic personnel to come and go. Only nine days later, the CCP Central Committee ordered the Northeast Bureau to follow a policy of non-recognition of foreign consulates and diplomats, who were to be treated as ordinary foreign citizens. The reason given was that these governments had not yet recognized the Chinese Communist government. By the seventeenth, a policy of squeezing American, French and British consulates out of Shenyang had been approved by the Central Committee. The Soviet representative I.V. Kovalev had tried to convince the CCP leadership that the United States had been involved in espionage from its Mukden consulate. Chinese leaders, though skeptical, were concerned to allay Stalin's suspicions that they might follow a Titoist middle path between the capitalist West, led by the United States, and the socialist block, led by the Soviet Union. See: Telegram, CCP Central Committee to CCP Northeast Bureau, 1 November 1948 (Extract), *CCFPCWA*, p.91–2; Telegram, CCP Central Committee to CCP Northeast Bureau, 10 November 1948 (Extract), *Ibid.*, p.92; Telegram, Mao Zedong to Gao Gang, 17 November 1948, *Ibid.*,p.92; Jian Chen, "The Ward Case and the Emergence of the Sino-American Confrontation, 1948–1950," *Australian Journal of Chinese Affairs*, no. 30 (July 1993); Sergei N.Goncharov, John W.Lewis, and Xue Litai, *Uncertain Partners, Stalin, Mao, and the Korean War*. (Stanford: Stanford University Press, 1993.)p.33–34.

29. Telegram, CCP Central Committee to CCP Northeast Bureau, 10 November 1948,(Extract), *CCFPCWA*, p.92. Here Zhou Enlai writes: "As the British, French, and American governments have not recognized our government, we should not recognize the official status of Western consulates either."

30. Consul General at Mukden(Ward) to the Secretary of State, 9 Nov.1948, *FRUS,1948,Volume 7*, p.830.

31. The Consul General at Mukden (Ward) to the Secretary of State, 16 November 1948, *FRUS,1948,Volume 7*, p.571–3.

32. *Ibid.*

33. The Acting Secretary of State to the Ambassador in China (Stuart), 23 November 1948, *FRUS,1948,Volume 8*, p.893.

34. *Ibid.*

35. The Consul General at Shanghai (Cabot) to the Secretary of State, 23 November 1948, *FRUS, 1948, Volume 8*, p.894.

36. *Ibid.*

37. The Consul General at Shanghai (Cabot) to the Secretary of State, 22 November 1948, *FRUS,1948,Volume 8*, p.891; The Acting Secretary of State to the Ambassador in China (Stuart),23 November 1948, *Ibid* p.892–4; The Consul General at Shanghai (Cabot) to the Secretary of State, 23 November 1948, *Ibid*,p.894–5; The Consul General at Shanghai (Cabot) to the Secretary of State, 26 November 1948, *Ibid,* p.897; The Consul General at Tientsin (Smyth) to the Secretary of State, 27 November 1948, *Ibid,* p.898–9; The Consul General at Shanghai (Cabot) to the Secretary of State, 29 November 1948, *Ibid*, p.899–900.

38. Memorandum of Conversation, by the Assistant Chief of the Division of Chinese Affairs (Freeman), 30 November 1948, *FRUS 1948,Volume 8*, p.905.

39. The Acting Secretary of State to the Consul General at Shanghai (Cabot), 2 December 1948, *FRUS,1948,Volume 8*, p.908.

40. *Ibid.*

41. The Acting Secretary of State to the Ambassador in China (Stuart),23 November 1948, *FRUS,1948,Volume 8*, p.892–3.

42. The Acting Secretary of State to the Ambassador in China (Stuart), 2 November 1948, *FRUS,1948,Volume 7*, p.827; The Consul General at Mukden (Ward) to the Secretary of State, 15 November 1948, *Ibid* p.834–35.

43. The Council General at Shanghai (Cabot) to the Secretary of State, 18 November 1948, *FRUS, 1948,Volume 7*, p.837.

44. United States Department of State, *Bulletin* 11 July 1949, p.36; "Angus Ward Summarizes Mukden Experiences", United States Department of State, *Bulletin*, 26 December 1949, p.955–957.

45. Mary Barrett, "The Ward Case", *CWR*, 14 January 1950, p.104–6.

46. Powell, ed. "American Dilemma", *CWR*, 4 December 1948,p.7–10.

47. *Ibid.*

48. *Ibid.*

49. Powell, ed. "America's China Policy", *CWR*, 6 November 1948, p.249–51.

50. *Ibid.*

51. Powell, ed. "American Dilemma", *CWR*, 4 December 1948, p.7–10.

52. *Ibid*,p.10.

53. Powell, ed. "America's China Policy", *CWR* 6 November 1948, p.250–251.

54. *Ibid.*

55. Powell, ed. "America's China Policy", *CWR*, 6 November 1948, p.250–1.

56. Powell, ed. "Coalition Government", *CWR*, 18 December 1948, p.69.

57. The Consul General at Peiping (Clubb) to the Secretary of State, 24 November 1948, *FRUS, 1948,Volume 8*, p.652–3.

58. The Consul General at Peiping (Clubb) to the Secretary of State, 24 November 1948, *FRUS,1948,Volume 8*, p.652 ; The Consul General at Peiping (Clubb) to the Secretary of State, 26 November 1948, *Ibid*, p.653.

59. The Chief of the ECA China Mission (Lapham) to the ECA Administrator (Hoffman), 26 November 1948, *FRUS,1948,Volume 8* p.654–8.

60. The Director of the ECA China Program (Cleveland) to the Chief of the ECA China Mission (Lapham), 2 December 1948, *FRUS, 1948,Volume 8*, p.658–662.

61. The Ambassador in China (Stuart) to the Secretary of State, 9 November 1948, *FRUS, 1948,Volume 8*, p.674; The Ambassador in China (Stuart) to the Secretary of State, 4 December 1948, *Ibid*, p.662–3.

62. Memorandum by the Director of the Office of Far Eastern Affairs (Butterworth) 3 December 1948, *FRUS, 1948,Volume 8*, p.667–8; Memorandum Presented to Cabinet Meeting, 14 January 1949, annex to: Memorandum by the Director of the Office of Far Eastern Affairs (Butterworth),14 January 1949, United States Department of State, *Foreign Relations of the United States, Diplomatic Papers,1949,Volume 9,The Far East:China.* (Washington, D.C.: Government Printing Office, 1974.)9:614–615. Hereafter cited as *FRUS,1949,Volume 9*.

63. Walter Simmons, "Shanghai", *Washington Times-Herald*, as reproduced in: John W.Powell, "Reply to an Attack on the Review", CWR, 25 March 1950, p. 54; "China Weekly Review Index for January 1, 1949", CWR, 1 January 1949, p.99.

64. "The China Weekly Review Index for January,1949", *CWR*, 1 January 1949, p.99; "China Weekly Review Index August 5,1950", CWR, 5 August 1950, p.163; "China Monthly Review Index September 1950", *China Monthly Review*, September 1959, p. 1.

65. Application for exit visas by Americans after the Communists came to power could become complicated by past relations they had had with the kinds of organizations and activities Powell was defending. For example, Allyn and Adele Rickett, two Fulbright scholars who occasionally provided informal observations on political and economic events in China to their superiors, were charged with espionage after applying for exit visas. They spent four years in Communist prisons. John Dunlap, son of the former Dean of the Beijing Union Medical College, was advised not to apply for an exit visa because it would reveal that he had once been connected to the U.S. Military Attache's Office, and might be arrested as a spy. According to his father, as long as one did not apply for an exit visa, these things did not come to light. John Powell contemplated closing the *Review* in August, 1949, and again in July, 1950, after the start of the Korean War. In both cases, he changed his mind, ultimately continuing his journal until July, 1953. He may have considered that investigation following his application for an exit visa would have revealed his connection with OWI, and may have suggested a continuing link with the USIS through his assistant editor Mary Barrett. See: Allyn and Adele Rickett, *Prisoners of Liberation*. (New York: Cameron Associates, Inc.,1957.) p.16–80; A.M. Dunlap. *Behind the Bamboo Curtain, The Experiences of an American Doctor in China*. (Washington D.C.: Public Affairs Press, 1956.) p.3.

66. Powell, ed. "Information Agencies", CWR, 2 February 1946, p.163–4.

67. Powell, ed. "Death of Tai Li", CWR, 30 March 1946, p.91–2. The National Military Affairs Commission's Bureau of Investigation and Statistics (BIS) was headed by Nationalist General Tai Li. According to the article, during World War II, Rear Admiral Milton S. Miles' inland naval group, SACO, trained Tai Li's subordinates in assassination, terrorist tactics, etc. to be used against the Japanese in a counteroffensive which, because of Japan's surrender, never came.

68. Powell, ed. "Diplomatic Pay", CWR, 13 April 1946, p.138–9; Powell, ed. "The State Department's Unburied Dead", CWR, 11 May 1946, p.228.

69. Powell, ed. "US Propaganda" CWR, 8 February 1947, p.265.

70. Francis Fang, "Cultural Needs in West China", CWR, 31 May 1947, p.385.

71. S.E. Shifrin, "Conditions Worsen in Tientsin", CWR, 26 July 1947, p.231–2.

72. Powell, ed. "Short Sighted Policy" CWR, 9 August 1947, p.280–1.

73. Powell, ed. "Who's Slanting What?" CWR, 31 January 1948, p.254–5.

74. John Melby, "The United States Education Foundation in China", CWR, 21 February 1948, p.347.

75. Central Intelligence Agency, Foreign Broadcast Information Branch, *Daily Report, Foreign Radio Broadcasts, Far Eastern Section, China, Communist Controlled*, 12 November 1948, CCC3.

76. Mary Barrett, "The Ward Case", CWR, 14 January 1950, p.104. The Chinese claimed to have uncovered an espionage ring directed by the U.S. Army Liaison Group and the U.S. Consulate in Shenyang.

77. Powell, ed. "Modern Espionage", *CWR*, 20 November 1948, p.299–300.

78. *Ibid.*

79. USIS, "The United States Information Service in China", *CWR*, 13 November 1948, p.281.

80. Powell, ed. "Fullbright Scholarships", *CWR*, 18 December 1948, p.52–3; Allyn Rickett and Adele Rickett, *Prisoners of Liberation.* (New York: Cameron Associates, 1957.), p.16. The Ricketts, who were arrested and charged with espionage after the outbreak of the Korean War, had been studying at Qinghua and Yenching Universities under this program. The kind of information they gathered as a result of their studies was limited to general economic and political analysis-exactly the type of information gathering that Powell was defending.

81. *Ibid.*

82. *Ibid.*

83. Instruction, CCP Central Committee, "On Diplomatic Affairs," 19 January 1949, *CCFPCWA*, p.97.

84. Edwin W. Martin, *Divided Counsel, the Anglo-American Response to Communist Victory in China,*(Lexington:The University Press of Kentucky,1986.) p.49; The Consul General at Peiping (Clubb) to the Secretary of State, 19 July 1949, *FRUS, 1949,Volume 8*, p.1095; The Minister-Counselor of Embassy in China (Clark) to the Secretary of State, 20 July 1949, *Ibid*, 1095–6: The Ambassador in China (Stuart) to the Secretary of State,22 July 1949,*Ibid*, p.1097–8; The Consul General at Tientsin (Smyth) to the Secretary of State, 23 July 1949, *Ibid*, p.1098.

85. The Consul General at Shanghai (Cabot) to the Secretary of State, 15 July 1949, *FRUS, 1949,Volume 8*, p.1232–33.

86. The Consul General at Peiping (Clubb) to the Secretary of State, 19 July 1949, *FRUS,1949,Volume 8*, p.1095.

87. The Consul General at Tientsin (Smyth) to the Secretary of State, 23 July 1949, *FRUS, 1949,Volume 8*, p.1098.

88. The Minister-Counselor of Embassy in China (Clark) to Secretary of State, 20 July 1949, *FRUS, 1949,Volume 8*, p.1095; The Consul General at Peiping (Clubb) to Secretary of State, 21 July 1949, *Ibid*, p.1096–97.

89. Anonymous ('Chinese Professor'), "The Interim Period—-And After, Public Order Can Be Preserved And Prosperity Will Follow" *CWR*, 25 December 1948, p.85–6.

90. Powell, ed. "Scorched Earth Policy", *CWR*, 11 December 1948, p.29–30.

91. Suzanne Pepper, *Civil War in China*, p.386–394. Pepper writes that in Shanghai, from August, 1948, CCP cadres had infiltrated the work forces of a number of large, essential companies, including the American owned Shanghai Power Company, in order to promote the factory protection movement.

92. CIA, Foreign Broadcast Information Bureau, *Daily Report, Foreign Radio Broadcasts*, FESCCC. 2 December 1948, p.CCC1. Condensation of Resolution Passed by 60th All-China Labor Congress, August,1948.

93. CIA, FBIB, *Daily Report Foreign Radio Broadcasts*, FESCCC. 9 December 1948, p.CCC4.

94. CIA, FBIB, *Daily Report, Foreign Radio Broadcasts*, FESCCC. 12 November 1948, CCC3.

95. CIA, FBIB, *Daily Report Foreign Radio Broadcasts*, FESCCC. 27 December 1948, CCC4.

96. CIA, FBIB, *Daily Report, Foreign Radio Broadcasts, FESCCC,* 9 December 1948, p.CCC4.

97. CIA, FBIB, *Daily Report, Foreign Radio Broadcasts, FESCCC.* 6 December 1948, p.CCC4.(North Shensi, *New China News Agency*, 4 December 1948.)

98. Powell, ed. "Scorched Earth Policy", *CWR*, 11 December 1948, p.29–30.

99. Powell, ed. "What About Shanghai?", *CWR*, 11 December 1948, p.30–31.

100. *Ibid.*

101. Powell, ed. "What About Shanghai?", *CWR*, 11 December 1948, p.30–31.

102. American Businessman, "The Interim Period, How Can Public Order Be Preserved in Shanghai?", *CWR*, 11 December 1948, p.33.

103. *Ibid.*

104. *Ibid.*

105. Anonymous ('Chinese Professor'), "The Interim Period - And After, Public Order Can Be Preserved and Prosperity Will Follow", *CWR*, 25 December 1948, p.85.

106. *Ibid.*

107. *Ibid*,p.86.

108. *Ibid.*

109. Powell, ed. "After The Interim Period", *CWR*, 25 December 1948, p.81–2.

110. The Consul General at Shanghai (Cabot) to the Secretary of State, 10 December 1948, *FRUS, 1949,Volume 8*, p.926–927.

111. The Acting Secretary of State to the Consul General at Shanghai (Cabot), 11 December 1948, *FRUS, 1948,Volume 8*, p.931–2.

112. Instruction, CCP Central Military Commission, "On Preparations for Taking Over Shanghai," 27 April 1949, *CCFPCWA*, p.109.

113. *Liberation Daily* (Jiefang Ribao). Shanghai, 28 May 1949, as quoted in Richard Howard Gaulton, "Popular Political Mobilization in Shanghai 1949–1952." (Ph.D. dissertation, Cornell University, 1981.) p.92–93.

114. Gaulton, "Popular Political Mobilization in Shanghai", p.93.

115. The question of whether to continue ECA commodities distribution in Chinese cities where Nationalist control had disintegrated was first raised October 12, 1948, in relation to Nationalist military reverses in North China and Manchuria. An attempt to give U.S. Ambassador Stuart broad discretionary powers in this matter was rejected by the State Department on November ninth because of the need for prior Congressional consultation and the fact that aid was distributed through private channels. Moreover, pricing, fund allocation, and distribution were all supposed to be carried out in cooperation with the Nationalist government. After Consul General Clubb raised the issue again in late November, ECA officials outlined four possible courses of action which would be placed before President Truman and his Cabinet for a decision: (1) to complete the commodity program as long as Communist officials observed certain minimal conditions (2) to permit the distribution of foodstuffs and commodities already landed or being unloaded from ships only (3) to cancel or divert all shipments already en route to China (4) that U.S. authorities try to repossess goods already landed or distributed. The ECA, which had already taken steps to limit the amount of commodities that might fall into Communist hands by stipulating that no more than four weeks of supplies would be warehoused in Chinese cities under siege, submitted the above

four policy choices to a Cabinet meeting on December 30, 1948, with a recommendation that policy (2), permitting the distribution only of commodities already landed or being unloaded, was the best choice. President Truman reaffirmed the U.S. commitment to the Nationalist government, but decided to allow the distribution of ECA supplies already landed or being unloaded in areas that fell to Communist control. Supplies already en route were to be diverted and ECA aid to these areas was to be terminated. No attempt was to be made by U.S. officials to repossess ECA supplies in CCP held areas. See: The Consul General at Tientsin (Smyth) to the Secretary of State, 12 October 1948, *FRUS, 1848, Volume 8*,p.639; The Ambassador in China (Stuart) to the Secretary of State, 7 November 1948, *Ibid.*, p.645–646; The ECA Administrator (Hoffman) to the Chief of the ECA China Mission (Lapham), 9 November 1948, *Ibid.*,p.647–649; The ECA Administrator (Hoffman) to the Chief of the ECA China Mission (Lapham), 13 November 1948, *Ibid.*, p.649; The Chief of the ECA China Mission (Lapham) to the ECA Administrator (Hoffman), 26 November 1948, *Ibid.*, p.654–658; The Director of the ECA China Program (Cleveland) to the Chief of the ECA China Mission (Lapham), 2 December 1948, *Ibid.*, p.658–662; Memorandum by the Director of the Office of Far Eastern Affairs (Butterworth) to the Acting Secretary of State, 28 December 1948, *Ibid.*, p.666–667; Memorandum by the Director of the Office of Far Eastern Affairs (Butterworth), Memorandum for the Record, 30 December 1948, *Ibid.*, p.667–668.

CHAPTER FIVE

PLUMBING THE UNKNOWN: THE MONTHS PRIOR TO TAKEOVER, JANUARY-MAY, 1949

As the new year 1949 dawned, during the four months before the Communists entered Shanghai, most of the city's newspapers and journals not connected to the GMD began to slant more toward the left.[1] This phenomenon was apparent in the articles and editorials of the *China Weekly Review* also, as it began to clarify a policy which would allow it to survive within the new political climate.

Of necessity, the *Review* began to advocate that America cease all military aid to the Guomindang, now beyond salvation, and continue civilian aid and relief programs in all parts of China. The journal called on the United States to seek trade and friendly relations with the new government, to eliminate conflict whenever possible between itself and the USSR to avoid world war, and to refrain from propping up failing colonial powers in Southeast Asia. The *Review* speculated on what the policies of a Communist government might entail for foreign businessmen, based on reports from correspondents in the larger cities under Communist control. And finally, Powell tried to develop a compromise editorial policy that would allow the *Review* to adapt and survive in the new political environment without surrendering its principles. This chapter will highlight attempts by the *Review* to anticipate, and adapt to what it believed the new order would be.

*

With the backbone of the Nationalist armies broken, Chiang Kai-shek, under great pressure within his own party resigned on January 21, 1949, allowing his vice president Li Zongren to assume control of the Nationalist government. Li then initiated a bid for peace negotiations with the Communists, hoping to reach agreement with the CCP on a division of China along a Yangzi River line.[2] In spite of pressure from Soviet leader Joseph

Stalin to explore the peace plan, Mao Zedong and his party rejected it, insisting on what amounted to unconditional surrender by the Guomindang.

Reacting to initial reports in the *China Press* of GMD peace feelers, the *Review* pointed out that the CCP was much stronger than it had been in 1946. Consequently for the GMD to offer essentially the Political Consultative Conference arrangements of that year would no longer suffice.[3] Powell saw negotiations as virtually impossible with a CCP victory in sight. Rather he pictured the call for peace as an attempt by some GMD generals to disassociate themselves as much as possible from the Nanjing government.[4]

Review contributing editor Charles J. Canning, commenting on the failure of attempts to initiate GMD-CCP mediation by a third party, pointed out that the Nationalist government's policy of stamping out the slightest opposition had made it virtually impossible for any really independent third parties to exist. Canning pointed out that both the Young China Party and the Democratic Socialist Party had discredited themselves by their uncritical support for the Guomindang's Civil War policies. The top leaders of both these parties were on the CCP's war criminals list[5]

Powell speculated that the Nationalist regime was making arrangements to move its capital to Taipei, but also noted there were indications it was getting ready to relocate to Guangzhou (Canton).[6] Both observations proved to be correct. Three days after the PLA crossed the Yangzi (April 24, 1949), the Nationalist government abandoned Nanjing for Guangzhou. By December, what was left of the Nationalist regime withdrew from the mainland to Taiwan, relocating the capital in Taipei.

Tianjin fell to the PLA January 15, 1949, and Beijing by January 22. Reporting from Beijing during and soon after its fall (January 19–22), frequent *Review* contributor Andrew Roth captured the general attitude of the populace. He reported that "Students and professors have turned strongly pro-Communist in the last year, more because of complete disgust with the Guomindang Government than because of love for the Communist program."[7] Roth reported that many Beijing residents felt the Communists would make Beijing the capital once again. Most residents welcomed the Communists because it meant the Civil War was nearing its end.

Roth noted that the PLA had restored electric power by the twenty-second, and had called on people to continue their lives and jobs as usual. It proclaimed the property of foreigners and foreign university degrees would be respected, urged newspapers to continue publishing until a registration could be carried out, guaranteed religious freedom, and resumed the postal and telegraphic services. "Skeptical, worldly-wise, Peiping is not yet sure it will prefer the Communist's 'Brave New World' to the old world, but it is certain it prefers peace to war," Roth concluded.[8]

The *Review* increased its attacks on the anti-communist political culture developing in the United States, which it saw as pushing America into further involvement in European recolonization and anti-insurgency in Asia. Powell believed that the rapid demise of the Nationalist Government should have caused a day of reckoning for die-hard China Lobby proponents William Bullitt, GOP Congressman Walter Judd, and Alfred Kohlberg. He was appalled when Judd, in a *United Press* interview refused to admit he had supported a losing cause in Chiang Kai-shek, and tried to shift the blame for Nationalist demise to President Truman and Secretary of State Marshall.[9] Refuting Judd's charges one by one, Powell none the less worried that they would affect the U.S. electorate who knew little of the true circumstances in China.

Outlining essentially a modern Cold War revisionist history of American involvement in East and Southeast Asia, Powell worried that the United States was in danger of finding itself on the ultra-reactionary side of the fence all over the world, in the wake of a complete CCP victory in China. In Southeast Asia, were it not for U.S. aid, he opined, Holland and France would have been forced to recognize the inevitability of independence for their colonies, or at least some kind of compromise. Britain, while granting India and Burma independence, had opened military operations against rebels in Malaya. These European countries, Powell said, seeking increased U.S. funds and military aid to prolong their colonial rule, now proclaimed they were fighting Communism in Southeast Asia. America, they insisted, having failed to stop Communism in China, must build up anti-red fences in other parts of Asia.

The only morally justifiable position for the U.S. to follow, Powell insisted, should be that of direct opposition to French, British and Dutch colonialists and support for the subject peoples. Support for independence of European colonies in Asia would provide the U.S. with "greater opportunities for trade." It would preserve the U.S. "as a symbol of freedom" for colonial peoples, and prevent them from turning to the Communists as the only alternative.[10] Powell warned his readers:

> It is all very well to be opposed to Communism (as sincere democrats, we don't approve of Communism either), but one should move with caution in attempting to build a fence around Communist countries. If America is not careful, she may end up with her side of the fence overly well stocked with ultra-reactionaries, former fascists, and other undesirable elements.[1]

In early spring, Powell opposed the formation of the Southeast Asian Treaty Organization (SEATO), viewing it as an attempt by the European colonial powers to further involve the U.S. in helping to preserve faltering colonialism. Powell singled out the French as particularly active in generating stories of the "red menace" in Asia to elicit American intervention.[2]

Although America was not a colonial power, Powell noted in another article, it operated on much the same economic principles. Hence America reacted in a manner similar to one when it saw a market about to be eliminated or controlled by its native inhabitants. Now the colonial powers, having wasted themselves in the great wars of the twentieth century, were offering to share colonial markets with the U.S. in return for American rescue of their declining position in their colonies. Powell hoped the U.S. would not be foolish enough, with all the signs of colonial demise so apparent, to take them up on their offer.[3]

Echoing much the same theme, Andrew Roth pictured the Western powers at a dead end in Asia. Anti-colonial and Communist uprisings in the Philippines, South Korea, Vietnam, Burma, Malaya and Indonesia, were all encouraged by the victory of the CCP in China. Reviewing each case, Roth noted that the Western powers seemed incapable of formulating an adequate response.[4]

Review contributing editor C. Y. W. Meng reminded Americans that their traditional sympathies had been with colonial revolts, and that many anti-colonial uprisings drew from the U.S. example. In the case of Asian revolts, there had been only tyranny and no freedom prior to the uprisings. Colonials were underprivileged, underfed, uneducated, and concerned most with the basic necessities of life. Poverty, hunger, and neglect were more the cause of their revolt than the Communists, Meng indicated.[5]

He warned that the American policy of countering the Reds at any cost led to alliances with the former enemy (Japan, Germany), with rightists, reactionaries, and corrupt regimes. In China's case, he pointed out, there had been no democracy - only one party rule, no real freedom of speech, press, or association. Concentration camps abounded, packed with political prisoners. Cities were filled with starving and miserable people. Meng cited John King Fairbank, from his recently published book, *The United States and China*, to the effect that China was bound to experience a revolution due to its terrible social conditions, even without the Communist party.[6]

The opposition of Powell and other *Review* writers to American support of neo-imperialism and the domestic anti-communist agenda did not mean they supported or trusted the Soviet Union. Sporadic criticism of the USSR appeared throughout the *Review* from 1946 through 1949, touching on the lack of press freedom, Russian expansionism in China during the nineteenth and twentieth centuries, the Berlin Crisis of 1948–9, the Soviet refusal in 1948 to allow nation-wide elections in Korea, and other matters.

In April, 1949, Powell was particularly critical of the Soviet Union's aggressive role in accelerating the Cold War. He could see no real basis for conflict between the U.S. and the USSR.[7] He believed that neither country really wanted war, and yet their rhetoric seemed to draw them closer to conflict. While fully recognizing American antagonism toward the Soviets, Powell resented the insulting language and what he felt was the hypocrisy of Soviet anti-American rhetoric:

The most insulting statements are made about the United States, and at the same time hurt and alarm are expressed over the 'unjustified' criticism by America of Russia. Exactly the reverse takes place almost every morning in the United States.[8]

He feared there was real danger that escalating levels of suspicion, insults, threats and counter threats between the two powers might reach ". . . a state where neither behaved entirely rationally,"[9] and war could erupt.

Powell opposed the Cold War not just to avoid World War III, but because he had hoped the United States and the Soviet Union would be able to join their efforts in aiding China after the end of its Civil War. This was a proposal which had first been raised by failed presidential contender Henry A. Wallace, whom Powell and the *Review* had supported.[10] An end to the Cold War, combined U.S.- Soviet assistance for the New China, American friendship toward former colonial peoples in South and Southeast Asia, and Sino-American trade and commerce: these were the kernels of the *Review*'s editorial stance in the spring of 1949.

*

CCP TRADE POLICY IN EARLY SPRING, 1949

During the period before the takeover of Shanghai, Powell argued that foreign businessmen would be able to do business with the new Communist government. But did the CCP have any real interest in continuing foreign trade with anybody outside the Soviet bloc? The answer was yes. Previous to the Nationalist naval blockade (imposed on Shanghai from June, 1949), the CCP was interested in developing foreign trade through China's seaports to facilitate economic recovery and to help build up the economy. Although the Party believed that ideally all foreign trade should be conducted by the state, Communist cadres lacked the business connections and expertise to do so. The CCP therefore decided to revive the import-export trade as soon as possible under private management.

In February, 1949, after the takeover of Tianjin opened up to the Communists the possibility of international sea-borne commerce, the CCP Central Committee declared that "The rapid recovery and development of New China's national economy will also be based on the development of trade. Therefore, we should start New China's foreign trade immediately."[11] On the 16th of February, The party took a series of concrete steps to make this possible. In summary, those were:

    1. The CCP Central Committee would allow private management of the import-export trade.
    2. It would allow foreign firms to send representatives to China, and to set up offices, or to work through foreign concerns already in China.

3. The Foreign Trade Bureau (created specifically to coordinate foreign trade) could dispatch representatives to foreign countries and establish agencies there.

4. The Central Committee ordered the rapid development of practical procedures for loading and unloading foreign ships, for leasing warehouse and dock space to foreign vessels, for clearing foreign vessels in Chinese inland and coastal waters, for renting berths in harbors and inland rivers to foreign concerns, etc., all patterned on previously established procedures. Previously existing tariff rates would remain in effect, to be revised at a later date after careful study.

5. The Central Committee decreed the setting up of postal relations, specifically for foreign trade, with those foreign ports which traded with China in the past.

6. A national bank was set up to handle all the foreign exchange needs of foreign trade, including the buying and selling of foreign currencies, loaning foreign currency on security, etc., all based on past practices.

7. To develop a wider range of exportable materials, local governments were directed by the Central Committee to pay attention to developing exportable staple crops and products such as cotton, soy beans, salt, peanuts, tobacco, silk, fur, exportable handicrafts and manufactured goods. Loans and other incentives were to be used to encourage the increased production of exportable goods.[12]

On April 28th, in Tianjin, the CCP Ministry of Industry and Commerce commissioned the U.S. representative of the Far Eastern Trading Company to work out arrangements to export a large quantity of salt, coal, soybeans, and soy cakes in return for machine parts, radio and telecommunications equipment, paper, railroad materials like switches, locomotive parts, ties, and copper wire.[13] On the same day, Yao Yilin, CCP Minister of Industry and Commerce, sent a representative to speak with U.S. Consul General Edmund Clubb in Beijing, to initiate trade with the United States and Japan.[14] The CCP Minister of Industry and Trade wanted to restore Sino-American commerce to its pre-war level, and stated that Mao's thinking in this regard was moderate, along the lines set out in "New Democracy".[15]

On the American side, in response, the National Security Council had decided to allow trade with Communist China in all but strategically sensitive goods. The main purpose of this policy was "to prevent China from becoming an adjunct of Soviet power." Moreover, General MacArthur agreed to begin a large-scale trade between Japan and China, believing this would take some of the economic pressure off the U.S. Occupation.[16]

Most of these arrangements and hopes would later be thwarted by the Nationalist blockade. Yet, in light of these facts, the *Review*'s insistence that foreign businessmen would be able to do business with the new regime, importing at least some of its reconstruction needs was not wide of the mark, at least at the time.

The *Review* spent considerable time speculating on what Communist control might mean for foreign businessmen, Shanghai, and China. An article by Andrew Roth characterized Mao's "New Democracy" as a "transition stage of Communist-supervised economic capitalism and Communist led bourgeois democracy." Roth also correctly surmised that the CCP intended to withdraw China from the U.S. side of the Cold War.[17]

The *Review* reprinted an article from the *China Economist* which attempted to measure the degree of freedom allowed to private enterprise in Communist areas.[18] Citing the CCP's May 1948 Industrial and Commercial Conference of the North China Liberated Area, the *China Economist* noted that all industries and trades were to be open to private parties or joint private-public participation. Heavy industry would be mainly public while light industry would be mainly private, with the Government operating only that light industry which the private sector was incapable of running.[19]

Citing Mao Zedong's Report to the CCP Central Committee of December 25, 1947, the *China Economist* concluded that the transition period before all private businesses were socialized would last perhaps a generation. Meanwhile the Government's task would be to help private industry to grow. The *China Economist* noted that so far, no limit had been set to the CCP's often stated right of entrepreneurs to a "legitimate profit," It forecast that the Communist trade policy would comprise free trade internally, and controlled foreign trade, geared toward acquiring the materials necessary for reconstruction. The *China Economist* felt that the CCP would encourage the export of light industrial and agricultural products to gain the foreign exchange needed for economic reconstruction.[20]

Powell looked forward to a relative improvement of Shanghai's economy with the advent of the new regime. He did not think commercial activity would further deteriorate once the Communists took control. "Rather, we think China will experience mild prosperity." The huge expenditures of the war years would be eliminated, foraging by large masses of soldiers would cease, and waste would disappear. The new younger administration would be much more vigorous than the old GMD bureaucrats, and corruption would end, he speculated.[21]

Once unfair taxation, usury, and high rents were removed, farmers' productivity would increase considerably, Powell felt. Restored transport facilities would also improve economic conditions, would make raw materials available again, and allow finished products to move between the town and countryside. Rice would again flow into the city and manufactured goods would be shipped out in exchange.[22]

Powell believed that China's dependence on foreign cotton, coal, and other raw materials would be greatly reduced.[23] A revival of foreign trade would follow with export materials from Red areas being available to foreign buyers at the Shanghai, Tianjin, and Guanzhou docks once again. With peace, inflation would slow down at last and the new government would be able to balance its budget. With inflation more gradual and predictable, idle capital would return to productive investments rather than speculation.[24]

Yet, for all the relative prosperity, Powell reminded his readers that because China remained a poor country, the path to real development, even above 1936 levels, would be slow and difficult. At year's end, even with relative prosperity, there would not be enough surplus left over for the new government to invest in building up the kind of primary capital industries which future economic development depended on.[25] Without saying so directly, Powell was underscoring the reason why American development capital should prove attractive to Communist leaders.

In another article, Powell suggested to the CCP leadership the primary desirability of a massive hydro-electric power project in the Yangzi Valley region, near Ichang. It would provide a source of never ending cheap power, improve inland navigation, and aid in flood control. However, it would have to be financed by government capital since China had no large middle class to invest in it. Unspoken but obvious in the article was the positive role U.S. financial and technical aid could play. Powell insisted the exploitation of China's water resources should come at the top of the CCP's list of reconstruction projects once the war ended.[26]

In the past, the *Review* had covered the UNRRA's "Yellow River Project" wherein 330,000 Chinese workers directed by the American engineer, Oliver J. Todd, using largely U.S. capital, machinery, and engineering expertise, had redirected the course of the Yellow River back into its original pre-1938 channel. It had also reported flood prevention measures on the Qiantang River. Unfortunately, the Yellow River project, which required the cooperation of authorities in both GMD and CCP controlled portions of Honan and Shandong, had been plagued by the escalating conflict of the Civil War.[27]

The plan for construction of a mammoth Yangzi Valley Dam, irrigation, transportation and hydro-electric project, which Powell now cited, was first put forward in 1946 by Dr. John Savage, Chief of the United States Reclamation Service. Savage's Yangzi River Project, as reported in the *New York Times*, called for the building of a huge dam across the Yangzi River near Ichang which would be 750 feet high, and would create a 250 mile long reservoir at the cost of one billion dollars. It would generate 10,560,000 kilowatts of power, twice the electrical potential of America's Grand Coulee, Boulder, and Shasta Dams combined, and could accommodate more generating units as China's industrial capacity grew. It would provide irrigation for ten million acres of farmland, and its power lines would reach a population greater than that of the entire United States.[28] The overall desirability of this proposal was confirmed half a century later by the Three Gorges Dam hydro-electric project currently being built on the Yangzi by the People's Republic.

The *Review* cited a China National Relief and Rehabilitation Administration (CNRRA)[29] estimate that China needed the construction of over ten million houses to relieve overcrowding. Powell saw this as one of the first problems that should be tackled after the Civil War ended, and concluded that "This will be a major task for the authorities and if some assistance can be obtained from abroad, it would indeed be a good cause."[30]

A common theme in the *Review*, (which appeared in many domestic American journals as well) was the assumption that because the Soviet Union did not have sufficient economic resources to underwrite China's economic reconstruction, Mao and the CCP would have to turn, at least in part, to the United States for financial help. The corollaries to this were the relative independence of the CCP from Moscow's control, and the idea that the CCP would try to avoid excessive reliance on the Soviet Union.

Review Correspondent S.E. Shifrin recounted this view in the remarks of Clayton Lane, Executive Secretary of the Institute on Pacific Relations (IPR). "The Chinese Communists will be adverse to us and our principles, but the compulsion of their requirements will make them turn to us," Lane had stated. Mao Zedong would have to turn to the United States for the large amounts of capital China needed for long term modernization. Lane believed this would ". . . provide opportunities for material benefit and cooperation, both economically and politically."[31] Shifrin concluded his article with a positive argument for a U.S. policy of economic and political engagement with Communist China.

The *Review* reprinted an article by Owen Lattimore, at the time a professor at Johns Hopkins University. Lattimore had been the director of the Far Eastern Section of the Office of War Information during World War II. Commenting on the precariousness of the U.S. position in China, Lattimore still felt: "We have one advantage -if we are willing to use it. China, India, and colonial Asia need machinery, capital, and technology to speed up their development. Russia cannot supply these in large quantities. We can."[32]

Edgar Snow, a frequent pre-war contributor to the *Review*, reassured readers of both the *Saturday Evening Post* and the *Review*, that the Chinese Communist Party, though a loyal ally of the Soviet Union, would rule with China's own national interests in mind. The USSR would have no power to dictate policy in China as she did in Eastern Europe, Snow believed.[33] In Snow's opinion:

> If the new regime is to make a speedier success of modernizing China than its predecessors, it will have to seek aid wherever practicable, rather than abide by ideological preferences. China will need at least a businesslike understanding of America, and equable trade and credit arrangements. . . The roots of anti-Americanism are not deep in China. They will diminish in proportion as the need of American help becomes more urgent.[34]

On May 21, four days before the Communist takeover of Shanghai, the *Review* reprinted a comprehensive analysis of China's rural and urban economic situation by Dr. Gerald F. Winfield, formerly with the Office of War Information in China. China's huge population and limited land resources, its primitive productive and manufacturing methods, all kept living standards at marginal levels. Economic exhaustion due to the Civil War exasperated the already bad situation. Ultimately Winfield insisted that:

> China will have to attract large sums of outside capital if it is to build an industrial plant large enough and quickly enough to break away from the drag of its expanding population and really raise standards of living. Any government, to be long successful, will therefore have to renew normal economic and political relations with the rest of the world and will have to create conditions that will make outside capital willing to take the risks of coming to China. Finally, China must have the active technical cooperation and assistance of the more advanced nations.[35]

This assessment largely reflected Powell's own assumptions about China's reconstruction and developmental needs.

*

THE QUESTION OF A FREE PRESS

The question of the press in Communist areas was of profound importance to the *Review*. Of all areas of the CCP's initial polity, press policy was the least agreeable and certainly the most difficult to which Western journalists had to adjust. In comprehensive instructions drafted by Zhou Enlai and revised and approved by Mao Zedong, the CCP Central Committee on January 19, 1949 instructed cadres that foreign news agencies and foreign news correspondents were not to be allowed to dispatch news reports from China nor to operate radio transmitters.[36]

This did not pertain to foreign newspapers and journals published within China. These would be allowed to continue publishing after registering and providing authorities with a one-year file of past publications. Then, "After a period of investigation and with the approval of the Central Committee" foreign newspapers and journals would no longer be registered and would cease publication. Yet, even then, a select few would be allowed to continue: "For the special ones, we may not interfere with their publication for a while, or allow them to be taken over by Chinese citizens."[37] Ultimately the *Review* would fit into this latter category.

A week later, the CCP Central Committee reiterated that "For the time being we will not interfere with the activities of foreign correspondents, including American correspondents, in Beijing and Tianjin, and we will observe their activities and the reports they make."[38] Although foreign correspondents could not send telegraphic dispatches outside China, they could cable reports to Nanjing or Shanghai (not yet in Communist hands).

Copies of their cables were to be forwarded then to CCP military representatives. The Central Committee again indicated that "After a period of observation and investigation, with the approval of the Central Committee, we will then order all foreign correspondents to go through registration and examinations." The CCP would then grant the right to gather news and send dispatches to "some foreign correspondents who will fit our needs"[39]

The *Review* monitored as best it could the position of the independent press in Nanjing, Tianjin, and Beijing after these cities fell to the Communists, and tried to lay out a strategy of partial compromise while holding to its basic journalistic principles. It would tone down its criticism, take a more constructive tack, and advocate greater care by foreign journalists in checking the accuracy of their news reports. The *Review*, which intended to continue operations under the new regime, also worried about the increasingly anti-Communist tone in the English language press. Ultimately, the *Review*, because it was determined to stay, had little choice but to follow the path which many Chinese liberals and Shanghai residents had already begun to tread.

With the defeat of all of Chiang's major field armies and the fall of most of the large northern cities, it was apparent that the CCP would soon be China's new ruler. Price levels at the end of 1948 had risen to eight million times their 1936 base level. The Gold Yuan currency was almost worthless and the city's economy was at a virtual standstill. Farmers had no intention of transporting their grain to Shanghai and exchanging it for worthless currency. It took 813,880 Gold Yuan notes to buy one U.S. dollar that January in Shanghai.[40] Residents who had surrendered their gold and foreign currency reserves in August (as the law required) at the rate of four Gold Yuan notes per one U.S. dollar were understandably bitter, and favorably disposed to take a second look at the Communists. Virtually the whole population of Shanghai had given up on the Nationalist regime.[41] Chinese liberals had gradually shifted their view of the Chinese Communists from disapproval to resigned support by 1949. Mao's 1941 essay "On New Democracy", a promise to include all cooperative classes in the new government under CCP leadership, helped convince many intellectuals to extend qualified approval to the Communist's program.[42]

Early accounts of the press in newly liberated Communist areas evidenced the same hopeful optimism as that engendered by the courteous behavior of the PLA as it occupied Northern cities, or the assurances the Communists extended to urban businessmen. In mid January, the *Review* printed an account by Mark M. Lu sketching initial Communist policy toward the local press in liberated Chengzhou.[43] After the PLA entered the city, wall posters were put up declaring the Communists "would protect newspapermen and implement freedom of the press." Soon after liberation, CCP cadres visited local newspapers, asked editors to continue publishing and brought in supplies of rice, flour, paper and other necessities.

Whereas all five local papers during the last period of GMD occupation had reflected the Government's rhetorical line of 'fighting the Communists to the death', Lu reported that they now praised the Communists and life after liberation.[44]

Indeed, the Communists had taken immediate steps to provision the city, enforce order, lower commodity prices, control inflation, restore rail transportation between Chengzhou and Kaifeng, and to encourage government workers to stay at their posts. Perhaps because all of these policies were heartening, it took several months for Western journalists to realize that press freedom within the CCP areas would be contained within ideologically defined parameters. Meanwhile, the increased incidence and seriousness of press censorship by desperate GMD authorities was only too evident.

Longtime *Review* contributing editor C. Y. W. Meng noted a decline in the number of popular magazines in Shanghai during the months prior to liberation. The more liberal and progressive the journal, the better its circulation tended to be, Meng recounted. Yet it was precisely this kind of publication which the government Ministry of the Interior repeatedly closed down. Meng focused on the banning of three independent liberal Chinese journals, the *University Review*, the *Outlook Weekly*, and especially *The Observer*, edited by Professor Zhu Anping, a prominent, Chinese liberal.

The Observer had been banned December 26, and seven staff members, including an assistant editor, had been arrested. Meng reflected the concern of other Chinese journalists when he pointed out that editor Zhu Anping had left Shanghai and that his whereabouts were unknown.[45] Meng called on the government to grant true freedom of discussion and publication to the people, to lift the ban on the Democratic League, and to release political prisoners. He urged the government "to gather together the leading liberals, non partisans and social leaders to act as a bridge over which the two opposing parties can negotiate peace."[46] But it was already too late for this kind of exhortation in the eyes of most of China's liberals, who had by this time given up on the Guomindang and put aside, out of necessity, their considerable apprehensions about the CCP.[47]

In fact, Zhu Anping had crossed into Communist China, along with other liberal journalists, to attend a preparatory meeting for the CCP's projected New Political Consultative Conference (PCC), scheduled for later that year.[48] Perhaps Meng did not yet know this. A Communist radio broadcast that January had announced that Zhu Anping and Wang Yunsheng, editor of another well known independent liberal newspaper *Da Gong Bao*, had joined other liberal intellectuals in the liberated areas to attend preparatory meetings for the new PCC.[49]

In the following months, a clearer picture of the press in the Communist controlled areas began to emerge. *Review* correspondent Andrew Roth, in Beijing, noted that all the city's newspapers save one, continued publication after the Communists took over, "but most thought it advisable to use the Communists' *New China News Agency* instead of the Guomindang's *Central News Agency*."[50] Roth commented on the smoothness and rapidity of the transformation, even in the most extreme cases: "One day Peiping's best newspaper plant was turning out the Guomindang's *North China Daily*. The next day its newsboys were delivering to its subscribers the Communist *People's Daily*."[51]

The *Review* reprinted an article by former Qinghua University professor Wu Han, who had recently joined other Chinese liberals behind CCP lines. Wu gave his impressions of newspapers there, pointing out their overwhelmingly didactic and utilitarian function:

> What you will feel more strange are the papers published here. At first you may not be used to them, but gradually you will think they are really papers of the people and for the people. They are concerned with experiences acquired from land reformation, explanations of commercial and industrial policies, and criticisms of the execution of these policies. There are also questions asked by the people, the government's answers to these questions, and other items of a similar nature.[52]

By mid February, Powell began to speculate that after the conclusion of the Civil War, a change in editorial policy would be necessary. Characterizing the *Review's* editorial policy under the GMD as "a continuous diet of complaint," Powell explained that he expected to see genuine progress toward a decent material life for the Chinese people under the new regime. While making it clear that the *Review* was not relinquishing its right to criticize injustices, Powell intended his journal to follow a more positive, constructive policy.

> While we are not by any means relinquishing our right of returning to a diet of complaint- it has almost gotten to be a habit- we are looking forward to the time when we can start suggesting ideas for things which need to be done and know, we hope, that we are not merely wasting newsprint.[53]

The editorial went on to suggest a number of projects which it felt the Communist government might want to consider. All of those suggested by Powell implied the benefits which U.S. financial and technological backing might be able to contribute.

At the end of February, Powell charged that Shanghai's English-language newspapers, because of their dependence on the Nationalist news agencies, were full of distortions which unconsciously conveyed "the line of some group or individual with a large stake in the Civil War."[54] He complained that too much personal bias was being expressed in news columns, and that anti-red stories were played up while items reflecting credit on the Communists were often buried. "It is all very well for an editor to be opposed to Communism- we prefer a different system ourselves- but the editor should attempt to keep his political and economic views under restraint when it comes to the news columns."[55] Powell felt this to be particularly true of times like the present, when readers were in need of all the information they could get.

In April, *Review* correspondent Hugh Deane, traveling into Communist Shandong, recounted the use of newspapers in PLA study groups to educate the troops. With the papers used as textbooks, instructors explained various articles, and discussion followed. Deane commented that "A half dozen copies of the *China Weekly Review* which we brought with us were read avidly and numerous articles from them translated."[56] The author felt the soldiers showed a real interest in outside events. This was perhaps the first time the *Review* had been used in a Communist study group.

The *Review's* most detailed pre-liberation article on the press in Communist China was written by frequent contributor Andrew Roth in early May, a little more than two weeks before the PLA entered Shanghai. It frankly noted the tendency of all papers in Red areas to echo the Communist line, and pointed out the dangers inherent in regularly reporting distortions of the news. Roth examined the way the CCP had fundamentally reorganized the press in the Tianjin-Beijing area, using the former liberal independent *Da Gong Bao* in Tianjin as an illustration.[57]

Roth reported that the CCP organ, *People's Daily* had announced on March 10 that all Chinese newspapermen and publications had to register with the Communist authorities "in order to protect freedom of speech for the people" and "to suppress counter-revolutionary speech and publication." All foreign correspondents in Beijing had been ordered to stop news gathering and filing stories from the 27th of February.[58] The only journal the Communists did not close was the extremely anti-Guomindang *Xin Min Bao* of Beijing. Four journals were allowed to reopen after reorganization and the Communists started another four of their own newspapers out of formerly GMD-affiliated operations.[59]

The well known liberal journal *Da Gong Bao* reopened under the new name *Jinbu Ribao* (*Progressive Daily*), with the same staff. Underscoring its new operating philosophy, the *Progressive Daily* stated that newspapers did not exist in a metaphysical vacuum, but reflected economic and political trends and class orientations. "On the one hand it may be the instrument of the oppressor class to control the people, but on the other hand it may be the weapon of the people to oppose oppression."[60] The new journal pledged itself to carry out the latter policy, and to serve "China's new master, the laboring people." Roth related that under this paradigm, "news and information become not objective reproductions of life, but instruments for changing life."[61]

All of the licensed papers in the Tianjin-Beijing area participated in the current anti-American campaign, portraying the United States as internally weak and decaying, Roth noted, while holding the Soviet Union to be a bastion of peace and prosperity. Articles routinely included serious distortions. Roth complained that "these articles go far beyond any factual data or even sober Marxist analysis."[62]

Roth reported that many "liberal left" Chinese newspapermen were greatly dismayed by the degree of distortion in their journals. One liberal editor who agreed with Communist objectives, but disagreed with their methods in the press for achieving them, told Roth: "Our paper is so full of propaganda now that there is scarcely any news. . . When I argue with the Communists they say that the function of the press in the New China is to teach, not to inform."[63] Feeling that there was no reason that the press could not do both, the Chinese editor had joined with four other editors in an effort to convince the authorities in Beijing to loosen their press policy.

When Roth worried "that a steady diet of distorted information might result in mistaken decisions," an American-educated left-wing professor replied that a free press was a luxury that only wealthy countries like the U.S. and Britain could afford. The main problem in China was not freedom of the press, he told Roth, but rather "achieving freedom from want for its 400,000,000 impoverished people."[64]

The *Review* on the eve of Communist takeover was neither naive nor overly optimistic about the challenges they would face as an independent English-language journal under Communist control. Willing to modify its editorial policy, the *Review* nonetheless hoped to maintain its integrity. We have seen that not all journals actually stopped operation prior to reorganization and licensing. The order for all foreign journalists to stop gathering and filing news stories was apparently meant to apply mainly to foreign wire services. Neither the *China Weekly Review*, nor the *Shanghai Evening Post and Mercury*, nor the British owned *North China Daily News* ceased gathering and filing news stories after coming under Communist control, apparently because they were published only within China.[65] As we have seen, CCP policy was to leave foreign journals published in China relatively untouched for the time being.

By suggesting to the Communists the advantages of U.S. technical and financial help, and by trying to promote the possibility of continued trade, eventual recognition and friendship to American businessmen, Powell and the *Review* tried to steer Sino-American relations toward a normal, non-confrontational course. The Communists were interested in establishing informal trade relations, especially in their port cities, with western countries, including the United States. In this regard, there was a certain amount of synergy between the *Review*'s editorial stance and some of the CCP's policy goals, which may have contributed to the *Review*'s survival as an independent foreign journal in Communist China after others had ceased publication.

The chief editor of the *Shanghai Evening Post and Mercury*, Randall Gould, maintained that during the months following the fall of Shanghai, the Communists did not interfere in any way with the operation of the *China Weekly Review*.[66] Powell's own testimony in later years stated that editorial authority for the *Review* throughout its publication in Communist Shanghai, remained entirely in his hands.[67] We may assume therefore that the *Review* came to be regarded by the CCP as a special category that fit their needs.[68]

This may have reflected the Chinese Communist's desire, in these pre-GMD blockade days, to reestablish trade relations and eventual diplomatic relations with the West, including the United States. There is evidence to suggest Communist leaders in early spring, 1949, were thinking along these lines. Mao Zedong, on April 28, advised the Central Military Commission: "The old U.S. policy of assisting the GMD and opposing the CCP has failed. It seems that its policy is changing to one of establishing diplomatic relations with us." The Communist leader referred to secret meetings which had been held a month earlier (March 25–26) between U.S. Ambassador John Leighton Stuart and Chen Mingshu, a pro-Communist third party figure. Mao stated:

> Now the American side is asking a third party to contact us for establishing diplomatic relations. Britain is eager to do business with us. We believe that if the United States (and Britain) cut off their relations with the KMT, we can consider the question of establishing diplomatic relations with them.[69]

In the secret Chen-Stuart talks (March 25–6), Stuart had indicated that under certain conditions, the U.S. would be willing to maintain a friendly relationship with the CCP and help in China's economic recovery and reconstruction. On April 9, Mao informed Joseph Stalin that the CCP was preparing to adjust its foreign policy by initiating informal contacts with the West, including the United States.[70] Stalin replied (April 19) through his representative: "We believe that China's democratic government should not refuse to establish formal relations with capitalist countries, including the United States" provided these countries gave up their support for the Nationalist government. Stalin went on to inform Mao: "We believe that, under some conditions,[the CCP] should not refuse to accept foreign loans or do business with capitalist countries."[71]

Although the CCP intended to build a primary diplomatic relationship with the Soviet Union, Chinese Communist policy would seem to have been flexible enough to contemplate trade, loans and diplomatic relations with America and the capitalist west. By the time of the famous Stuart-Huang Hua talks in June-July, however, the Guomindang blockade, continued U.S. aid to the Nationalists, and increasing Sino-American hostility had certainly lessened, though not yet ended, this possibility.

The *Review* had moved toward adjusting its expectations and policy in anticipation of life under the new regime. It had surveyed the implications of Mao's New Democracy for private and foreign enterprises and concluded that businesses would be allowed to prosper for a fairly long time under Communist rule. Powell had adopted a hopeful stance which envisioned U.S. trade, American businessmen and capital playing a significant role in the New China's reconstruction needs. The *Review* had realistically noted the changes in function and freedom of the press in Communist controlled areas, and Powell had begun formulating a new editorial policy which would allow his journal to adapt to the political demands of Communist rule while still holding on to his basic journalistic principles. With an open mind and the best of intentions, and having contributed to local efforts to minimize destruction of property during the changeover,[72] the *Review* staff awaited the inevitable fall of Shanghai.

Chapter Notes

1. Ruth Beverly Crone, "An Inquiry into a Possible Relationship Between Propaganda and the Fall of Shanghai, 1949," (Ph.D. dissertation, New York University, 1960.) p.71–75; Richard Howard Gaulton, "Poular Political Mobilization in Shanghai 1949–1952" (Ph.D. dissertation, Cornell University,1981.) p.147–148.

2. Li Tsung-jen and Tong Ke-tung, *Memoirs of Li Tsung-jen.* (Boulder: Westview Press, 1979) p.484–495, 499, 508–513, 522, 554, 550–552. Li was highly critical of Chiang, accusing him numerous times of undermining attempts to defend south China through interference in the positioning of troops. He pointed out that Chiang had no Constitutional right to resume the presidency, and asserted that the Generalissimo, in an attempt to gain sole custody of forthcoming American aid, had promoted the fall of the last two Nationalist-controlled mainland provinces, Guangdong and Guangxi, so that Li, as president of the mainland government, could exercise no control over the funds.; Immanuel C.Y. Hsu, *The Rise of Modern China.*(New York: Oxford University Press, 1990.) p.633.

3. *China Press,*3 January 1949. The *China Press* was a Guomindang-affiliated journal which was mainly owned by H.H.Kung, a Western-trained financier favored by his brother-in-law Chiang Kai-shek.; Powell,ed. "Political Front Active", *CWR*, 8 January 1949,p.133–5.

4. Powell, ed. "The War Will Go On", *CWR*, 29 January 1949,p.208.

5. Charles J. Canning, "Can Shanghai Have a Localized Peace?", *CWR*, 5 February 1949,p.239.

6. Powell, ed. "Where Will Nanking Go?", *CWR*, 15 January 1949,p.161.

7. Andrew Roth, "The Fall of Peiping", *CWR*, 5 February 1949,p.241–2.

8. *Ibid.*

9. Powell, ed. "Day of Reckoning", *CWR*, 1 January 1949,p.105–6.

10. *Ibid.* Powell was not above appealing to the predatory sentiment of U.S. businessmen, in the name of anti-colonialism: "If the colonies are independent. . . with the huge industrial machine of the U.S. behind us, we naturally can take away any open markets we wish."

11. *Ibid.*

12. Powell, ed. "Pacific Pact", *CWR*, 2 April 1949,p.99–100.

13. Powell, ed. "Backward Areas", *CWR*, 16 April 1949,p.147.

14. Andrew Roth, "Dead End in Asia for the West", *CWR*, 16 April 1949, p.151.

15. C.Y.W. Meng, "A Chinese View of American Aid", *CWR* 19 March 1949,p.59–60.

16. *Ibid.*

17. Powell, ed. "Who's Expanding?", *CWR*, 4 October 1947,p.130. ". . .if we examine the facts dispassionately, it will become evident that there is no basis for a war between the United States and the Soviet Union. . . .The *Review* is firmly convinced that there is no real basis for another war, especially a war between the United States and the Soviet Union."; Powell, ed. "Irresponsible Behavior", *CWR*, 9 April 1949, p.125. "If war comes tomorrow it will not be because Russia or America actually wanted to begin a conflict that would be sure to cost far more than either could gain. It would be because both nations, behaving at times in the most childish manner, have insulted each other so extensively, laid down so many ultimatums and in general progressed so far toward an open rupture that they had reached a state where neither behaved entirely rationally. . . .A war between the East and the West is as unnecessary today as it ever was. There are few basic differences that could not be solved by men of common sense and good will sitting around a conference table."

18. Powell, ed. "Irresponsible Behavior", *CWR*, 9 April 1949,p.125.

19. *Ibid*.

20. Powell, ed. "Abundance For All", *CWR*, 9 April 1949,p.123.

21. Instruction, CCP Central Committee , "On Foreign Trade Policy," 16 February 1949, in Shuguang Zhang and Jian Chen, eds. *Chinese Communist Foreign Policy and the Cold War in Asia, New Documentary Evidence, 1944–1950*. (Chicago: Imprint Publications, 1996.) p.101–104.Hereafter cited as *CCFPCWA*. The provisions on trade in this document present a convincing case for Communist intentions to revive trade with China's previous trading partners as soon as possible in the newly conquered port cities, and to pattern its trade policies on previously existing practices.

22. *Ibid*. p.101–4.

23. The Consul General at Peiping (Clubb) to the Secretary of State, 30 April 1949, United States Department of State, *Foreign Relations of the United States, Diplomatic Papers, 1949, Volume 9, The Far East: China*.(Washington D.C.: Government Printing Office, 1974.) p.974–6 Hereafter cited as *FRUS, 1949, Volume 9.*; William Costello, "Japan and the Chinese Communists", *CWR*, 7 May 1949,p.218. Costello, the CBS Far East News Director, noted the importance of China as a source of soybeans, iron ore, coking coal, and salt to Japan. He asserted that Prime Minister Yoshida was eager for trade with China in spite of his dislike for the Communists.

24. The Consul General at Peiping (Clubb) to the Secretary of State, 30 April 1949, *FRUS, 1949, Volume 9*: p.976–7.

25. *Ibid*. See Chapter 3, p.136 n.10 of this dissertation for an explanation of Mao's "New Democracy".

26. Note by the Executive Secretary of the National Security Council (Souers), on the United States Policy Regarding Trade With China,28 February 1949, [Annex]Draft Report by the National Security Council on United States Policy Regarding Trade With China, *FRUS,1949,Volume 9*, p.826–34; The Department of the Army to the Supreme Commander for the Allied Powers in Japan (MacArthur), 7 May 1949, *FRUS,1949,Volume 9*, p.977–9; The Secretary of State to the Consul General at Peiping (Clubb), 8 May 1949, *FRUS,1949,Volume 9*, p.980; The Acting Secretary of State to the Consul General at Peiping (Clubb), 27 May 1949, *FRUS,1949,Volume 9*, p.985–6.

27. Andrew Roth, "The Bitter Pill of Mao Tse-tung", *CWR*,29 January 1949, p.209–10.

28. "Economic Policy in Communist Areas" summarized from the *China Economist*, in *CWR*, 5 February 1949,p.246–7.

29. *Ibid.*

30. *Ibid.*

31. Powell, ed. "Postwar Development", *CWR*, 5 February 1949,p.237–8.

32. *Ibid.*

33. *Ibid*, p.238. Of course, China had huge reserves of coal and produced its own cotton and rice, but according to the editorial, the production and flow of these commodities to the cities from the hinterlands had been cut-off by the civil war in many places, causing an undue reliance on foreign sources. With the civil war's end, the flow of commodities and finished goods between the countryside and city would resume, reducing China's over-reliance on foreign suppliers.

34. *Ibid*; Powell'ed. "Red Drive for Production", *CWR*, 16 April 1949,p.149. Powell repeats his belief that the mere ending of the Civil War would result in considerable economic improvement. He expects the per-capita national income to rise after the Civil War is over.

35. *Ibid.*

36. Powell, ed. "China's Untapped Power", *CWR*, 12 February 1949,p.263–4.

37. Duncan Lee, "Rediversion of Yellow River Poses Many Big Reconstruction Problems", *CWR*, 17 May 1947, p.319; Chen Chi, "As I Saw the Flooded Area", *CWR*, 21 June 1947,p.87; Ling Ching,"The Sorrow of China, the Story of the Yellow River and the Betrayal of a Mission", *CWR*, 12 July 1947,p.165–6; Powell, ed."UNRRA's Failure", *CWR*, 1 March 1947,p.7–8; Dick Wilson, "Taming of Chientang Under Way", *CWR*, 24 May 1947, p.346–348; "Chinese Strive to Curb Yellow River, 330,000 Workers Will Shift Yellow River to Old Course to Reclaim Vast Farm Area", *New York Times*, 20 January 1946, p.20; Tillman Durdin, "Closing of Dikes Opposed in China", *Ibid.*, 6 January 1947, p.5; Henry R.Lieberman, "Nationalists Bar China Reds' Fund, Block Accord for Delivery of Cash for Yellow River Dike Repair - UNRRA Aid Slowed", *Ibid.*, 14 February 1947, p.13. The one mile gap in the dike cut by Nationalist soldiers in 1938 to slow the Japanese advance was successful closed by the UNRRA, and the Yellow River diverted back into its old channel on March 15, 1947. However, lower dike repair in CCP-held sectors was retarded by Nationalist air raids and the withholding by the Nationalist government of UNRRA funds intended to aid dike repair and resettlement.

38. Willard R.Espy, "Dams for the Floods of War", *The New York Times Magazine*, (section VI) 27 October 1946, p.12–13.

39. The China National Relief and Rehabilitation Administration was a Nationalist-controlled body created to conjointly oversee the pricing and distribution of United Nations Relief and Rehabilitation Administration aid, projects, and materials in GMD-controlled China.

40. Powell, ed. "Ten Million Houses", *CWR*, 12 March 1949,p.30–1.

41. S.E. Shifrin, "Letter From Seattle", *CWR*, 12 March 1949,p.34.

42. Owen Lattimore, "China Crisis and the U.S.", *CWR*, 18 December 1948, p.55–8.

43. Edgar Snow, "Will China Become A Russian Satellite?" *Saturday Evening Post*, 9 April 1949; Snow's article was reprinted at same time in *CWR*, 9 April 1949, p.127–131.

44. *Ibid.*

45. Gerald F. Winfield, "China's Basic Problems", *CWR*,21 May 1949, p.256–8. reprinted from *Foreign Policy Reports.*

46. Instructions, CCP Central Committee, "On Diplomatic Affairs," 19 January 1949, *CCFPCWA*,p.97.

47. *Ibid.* The regulations would tend to freeze out all but a few selected foreign journalists.

48. "Telegram, CCP Central Committee to Tianjin and Beijing Municipal Committees", 25 January 1949, *CCFPCWA*, p.100.

49. *Ibid.* p.100.

50. Wu Cheng-hsi, "Chinese Banking and Inflation", *CWR*, 1 January 1949, p.117–118; Chang Kia-ngau, *The Inflationary Spiral,The Experience in China, 1939–1950.*(New York: The Technology Press of Massachusetts Institute of Technology and John Wiley and Sons, Inc., 1958.) P.84.

51. Suzanne Pepper, *Civil War in China, The Political Struggle, 1945–1949.* (Berkeley: University of California Press, 1978.) p.121–126; John King Fairbank and Albert Feuerwerker,eds. *The Cambridge History of China,Volume 13,Republican China,Part 2.* (Cambridge, U.K.:Cambridge University press, 1986.) p.745,782.

52. Pepper, "Socialism,Democracy, and Chinese Communism", in Chalmers Johnson,ed. *Ideology and Politics in Communist China.* (Seattle: University of Washington Press, 1973.) p.217.

53. Mark M. Lu, "Fall of Chengchow", *CWR*, 15 January 1949, p.165.

54. *Ibid.*

45. C.Y.W. Meng, "Popular Magazines Vanish", *CWR*, 29 January 1949, p.214–5.

56. *Ibid.* In respect to the GMD's last ditch call for peace negotiations, Powell had already pointed out in his editorials that the CCP had no incentive by this time to negotiate, being fairly close to final victory. Meng seems to have still seen a negotiated settlement in which Chinese liberals would put together a government as possible. Most other Chinese liberals, however, had given up on exhorting the Nationalist government to do anything, and now turned their attention to the Communists, who, like it or not, would soon be their new rulers. Since the CCP had indicated its desire to incorporate liberal parties and groups in some fashion into the new People's Government, it only made sense, assuming one intended to stay, to open contact and begin work toward a new Communist sponsored coalition government.   Liberal editors Zhu Anping and Wang Yunsheng, though wary of the Communists and strongly committed to the principle of a free press, in the end had little choice but to swallow their scruples and come to terms with the Communists. Meng and the *Review*, would eventually follow this path too.

57. Suzanne Pepper, *Civil War in China*, p.194–5;218; Suzanne Pepper,"Socialism, Democracy, and Chinese Communism", in Johnson, ed. *Ideology and Politics in Communist China*, p.217.

58. Suzanne Pepper, *Civil War in China*,p.195,218; Mao Tse-tung, "Address to the Preparatory Meeting of the New Political Consultative Conference", *Selected Works of Mao Tse-tung, Volume 4.*(Peking: Foreign Language Press, 1968.) p.405,409 "Notes".

59. Pepper, *Civil War in China*,p.195.

60. Andrew Roth, "Peiping's New Look", *CWR*, 19 February 1949, p.290.

61. *Ibid.*

62. Wu Han, (traslation by Tu Ting-mei) "Life in Red China: A Chinese Professor's Report", *CWR*, 26 February 1949,p.317. The article also appeared in: Shanghai *Shang Pao*, 13 February 1949.

63. Powell, ed. "China's Untapped Power", *CWR*, 12 February 1949, p.263–4.

64. Powell, ed. "What Is Communist Policy?", *CWR*, 26 February 1949, p.308.

65. *Ibid.*

66. Hugh Deane, "Journey to Red Shantung", *CWR*, 2 April 1949, p.103–104.

67. Andrew Roth, "The Place of the Press in Communist China", *CWR*, 7 May 1949, p.220–221.

68. *Ibid.*

69. *Ibid.* The Communist journals were *People's Daily (Renmin Ribao)*,the Party organ for all north China; The *Masses Daily (Dazhong Ribao)*,aimed at the working people locally; the *Tianjin Daily (Tianjin Ribao)*,for the Tianjin vicinity; and the *Beijing Liberation Daily (Beijing Jiefang Ribao)*, for the Peiping vicinity.

70. *Ibid.*

71. *Ibid.*

72. *Ibid.*, For example, Roth cited a Beijing *People's Daily* article that reported poverty was so bad in the U.S. that workers were reduced to selling their eyes to rich blind people to survive, while their counterparts in the Soviet Union had only to work five or six hours a day to enjoy a life of plenty.

73. *Ibid.*

74. *Ibid.*

75. The *Shanghai Evening Post and Mercury* had been published in New York during the war years, while Shanghai was under Japanese occupation. With the War's end, its publication in Shanghai resumed in 1945, and after 1946 the New York edition was ended.

76. John William Powell, Testimony, United States Senate, Subcommittee to Investigate the Administration of the Internal Security Act and Other Internal Security Laws of the Committee on the Judiciary, Interlocking Subversion in Government Departments, 83 Congress, 2 Session, Washington D.C., 27 September 1954, p.1887; *Letter*, Randall Gould to Benjamin Mandel (Director of Research), 29 August 1954, Subcommittee to Investigate the Administration of the Internal Security Act and Other Internal Security Laws of the Committee on the Judiciary, 27 September 1954, Washington D.C.,pgs.1897–1899.

77. John William Powell, Testimony, United States Senate, Subcommittee to Investigate the Administration of the Internal Security Act and Other Internal Security Laws of the Committee on the Judiciary, Interlocking Subversion in Government Departments, Washington D.C., 27 September 1954, pgs. 1863; 1864; 1882; 1895.

78. Instruction, CCP Central Committee, "On Diplomatic Affairs," 19 January 1949,in *CCFPCWA*, p.97;Telegram, CCP Central Committee to Tianjin and Beiping Municipal Committees, 25 January 1949,*Ibid*.p.100.

79. (Mao Zedong) Instruction,Central Military Commission, "Our Policy Toward British and American Citizens and Diplomats", 28 April 1949, *CCFPCWA*, p.110–111.

80. Chen Jian, "The Myth of America's 'Lost Chance' in China: A Chinese Perspective in Light of New Evidence," *Diplomatic History*, vol.21 no.1 Winter 1997, p.84.

81. Ibid.
82. See chapter 3 of this dissertation.

CHAPTER SIX

SHOCK AND ADJUSTMENT TO THE NEW ORDER:
THE COMMUNISTS ENTER SHANGHAI, MAY–SEPTEMBER, 1949

On the eve of Communist takeover, foreign and native business interests, and the CCP Central Committee looked forward hopefully to restoration of trade and commerce in the disrupted economy of Shanghai. Communist officials, after entering the city, took steps to elicit the confidence and co-operation of the urban business community in achieving these goals. Within little more than a month, however, natural calamities, coupled with Nationalist efforts to prevent the revival of international trade in Shanghai aggravated the already strained economy, triggering a wave of uncontrollable labor disputes adversely effecting Sino-American relations. This chapter examines these events and their impact on the *China Weekly Review* and the foreign press, as it struggled to define its position within the new revolutionary situation.

*

On the 24th of May, Nationalist military began withdrawing from Shanghai, the local police following along with them. The next morning, the first units of the People's Liberation Army entered the city quietly and for the most part, unopposed.[1] There was no final fight to the death, as the local garrison had promised, much to residents' relief. The foreign community in Shanghai was also inclined to breathe a sigh of relief over the peaceful change of authority in the city. Randall Gould, editor in chief of the *Shanghai Evening Post and Mercury*, a perceptive observer, explained:

> It was by no means with complete dismay that Shanghai's foreign community viewed the approach of the Chinese Communists in May 1949. Together with the Chinese population, though in a considerably less degree, we had suffered increasingly from mal-administration by most of the dominant figures of the Nationalist regime. It was true we had not been robbed of our life's savings, as had the Chinese middle class when forced to hand over its gold, silver, and foreign currency in exchange for the new "Gold Yuan" currency which replaced the worthless former "Chinese

national currency" in the summer of 1948, but which lost its initial value to drop disastrously. Neither had we been subjected to all the rigors of the Nationalist police state, including mass executions. . . But all in all, we had enough of the Nationalists.[2]

American Ambassador John Leighton Stuart, recalling the takeover, pointed out that "A large number of foreign diplomats, businessmen, and missionaries were confident that the new regime was and would be a great improvement on the old." He noted that among Chinese, ". . . a majority of the articulate intellectuals welcomed the advent of the Communist regime with enthusiasm."[3] Certainly this was the case for the foreign and Chinese staff of the *Review* as well.

When the PLA approached the city in mid-May, they found that Nationalist military and government authorities had erected a flimsy wooden fence on three sides of Shanghai, and vowed to "fight to the death". Suspected political prisoners, students who had been rounded up as a precautionary measure, and others in jail for petty crimes, were summarily yanked out of prison and executed by GMD troops on the city's sidewalks, their bodies left as a warning to the general population.[4]

Nationalist soldiers earlier in the month, had broken into the homes of two members of the U.S. consular staff, looting at gunpoint clothing, home furnishings, and other valuables.[5] Shanghai's economy had rapidly disintegrated, as the populace lost all confidence in the central government's authority.[6] Foreign residents, who "had feared days of lawless disorder,"[7] were therefore greatly relieved to wake up on the 25th and find the changeover already (for the most part) peacefully accomplished.

Shanghai urbanites, used to the bullying and arrogance of undisciplined Nationalist troops, were favorably impressed by the discipline, honesty and helpful attitude of PLA soldiers. Whereas GMD troops had once commandeered homes as sleeping quarters, and other privately owned goods, PLA troops refused to accept any gifts, slept outside on the sidewalks, and were careful to pay for anything they took.[8] Recalling their entry into the city, Randall Gould observed:

> Whereas ill-paid and undisciplined Nationalist troops had constantly created trouble through forcible occupation of public transport, places of amusement, and residences, these new soldiers were a refreshing change. They had money to pay their way, and they insisted on paying for whatever they took. Though silent, unsmiling and disinclined to fraternize, they showed no unfriendly spirit toward anybody. Their discipline was superb. At times they set their shoulders against hand-carts to help over a bridge, or otherwise showed sympathy with the lot of the Chinese worker.[9]

According to Gould, most businesses had reopened, and the city was back to normal within a few days. All Chinese-owned journals were closed "for examination" by the CCP, while the *Shanghai Evening Post and Mer-*

cury and the British owned *North-China Daily News*, together with the *China Weekly Review*, ". . . continued as usual, minus even the censorship which the Nationalists had imposed."[10] Businesses and missionary enterprises were allowed to continue without interference. Peace and order were upheld, foreigners were protected, the military maintained a low profile, and Communist officials enforced ". . . only the most elemental restrictions." Gould recalled that "Far from finding ourselves beset by a Gestapo, we could hardly locate officials of any sort."[11]

The basic framework for CCP policy toward private industry had been established prior to the takeover of Shanghai. At the Second Plenary Session of the Seventh Central Committee of the CCP in March, Mao had stressed that the Party's attention would shift to learning the complex tasks of administering the economies of the cities. The most developed sector of the urban economy, which had been held by GMD-affiliated bureaucratic-capitalists, would devolve to state :control, where it would allow the CCP to influence and control the overall economy. But China's private industry, held by the individual capitalists of the "national bourgeoisie" and its representatives, was identified by Mao as a progressive element which must be encouraged to expand and grow, within prescribed boundaries. Seen as oppressed and harried by Imperialism and bureaucratic capitalism, in Mao's view:

> The national bourgeoisie of China and its representatives have often taken part in the People's democratic revolutionary struggles or maintained a neutral stand. For this reason and because China's economy is still backward, there will be need, for a fairly long period after the victory of the revolution, to make use of the positive qualities of urban and rural private capitalism as far as possible, in the interests of developing the national economy.[12]

Although affirming that private capitalists would be regulated through tax policies, market prices and labor conditions, Mao stipulated that "We must not restrict the private capitalist economy too much or too rigidly, but must leave room for it to exist and develop within the framework of the economic policy and planing of the People's Republic."[13] Mao reiterated his government's intention to engage in trade with the Western capitalist countries: "As for doing business with foreigners, there is no question; wherever there is business to do, we shall do it and we have already started; the businessmen of several capitalist countries are competing for such business."[14] Of course China would seek trade with the socialist countries first, Mao affirmed, but "at the same time we will also trade with the capitalist countries."[15]

In Shanghai, the Communist Party acted quickly to gain the confidence and involvement of important business groups. Within days of the takeover, the CCP's Military Control Commission and the new Communist mayor, General Chen Yi, called several conferences of all Shanghai's businessmen, engineers, financial staff, and managers. Over 250 corporate and company directors and managers attended one such meeting. At these conferences, Communist authorities declared that they valued and welcomed the suggestions of the business groups, and solicited their advice on a range of specific policies.[16] The results prompted a feeling of optimism among foreign residents and businessmen.

"We had a meeting of the General Committee of the American Association today," reported American Doctor A.M.Dunlap, who had lived in China for forty years and was a member of that body, ". . . and everyone was most hopeful for the future."[17] Years later he recalled:

> There is no doubt that the Communists went out of their way to reassure the populace of Shanghai that all would be well. There was little interference with private business concerns and it was announced that exports and imports were to be continued as soon as all China was under a single administration.[18]

Paul S.Hopkins, the president of the Shanghai Power Company, the largest American-owned private investment in China, although initially suspicious of the Communists, was won over by the Party's attitude and policies during the month following takeover. The (Communist) People's Bank of China advanced Shanghai Power four loans during June to help pay its bills; the Communists then granted Shanghai Power a 700 percent rate increase on July 1, and another rate increase of 450 percent July 25, to further ease its economic situation.[19] Hopkins was thereafter understandably impressed by the Communists and confident of Shanghai Power's prospects under the new regime.[20] It seemed as though the party had made a good beginning of things.

Like Powell and the *Review*, Hopkins came to oppose the Truman administration's continued aid to the Guomindang, and the American refusal to extend ECA aid to Communist areas of China. He condemned the Nationalist bombing of Shanghai in July and called for American pressure to lift the Nationalist blockade of China's ports, initiated June 26, 1949. As the blockade brought all sea-born commerce in Shanghai to a halt, deteriorating economic conditions and lack of adequate CCP control over unions resulted in extreme labor unrest. Hopkins urged the State Department to open negotiations to ease Sino-American relations.[21]

*

In general, the party placed great importance on reviving trade and industry in Shanghai. Official policy was to benefit both management and labor equally, to maintain wage levels at or slightly below current levels, to revive production, to ensure markets for goods, to reconnect the city to its economic hinterland, to secure stocks of raw materials for industry, to advance loans to employers, to halt inflation, and to reverse unemployment.[22] Early conferences with Shanghai businessmen were intended to make them privy to and part of these efforts. Unfortunately, events would conspire to make these goals extremely difficult to achieve.

In Shanghai, the Communists marched into a city largely cut off from raw materials, food, and markets. Rising food prices pushed labor costs upward. Lack of raw materials added to production costs, with many goods being sold at a loss. Machine production was on the verge of collapse; business and industry were at a standstill; more than half of the city's businesses and shops were closed; customers were few; and only ten percent of its flour mills were operating. Shanghai itself was swollen with over a million refugees, who added to the large-scale unemployment problem[23]

Shortly after liberation, with GMD labor controls no longer in effect and the CCP's control over labor as yet non-existent, labor unrest in the form of strikes, sit-ins, work slow downs, and employer harassment, broke out all over the city as workers took the opportunity to press for improvement of their precarious situations. By the end of June, the Nationalist Blockade of Shanghai cut off all shipping to and from the city, the city's lifeblood, and Nationalist air raids added to the Shanghai's isolation. Local Communist authorities, short on trained urban cadres, had not yet gained control over the labor force. After conferring again with Shanghai business leaders in mid-August, the party passed measures designed to end labor disturbances and to loosen restrictions on management. In desperation, the party conceived plans to deport the refugee population back to their hometowns and to move selected factories out of Shanghai, closer to sources of raw materials. Slowly, the number of disturbances began to decline in September.[24]

Unfortunately, these labor incidents, the GMD blockade, and the almost daily bombing of Shanghai, formed the backdrop for a deterioration of Sino-American relations just at the moment when many resident foreign businessmen had hoped a new beginning might be possible. The *China Weekly Review*, the *North China Daily News*, and the *Shanghai Evening Post and Mercury* were part of these events and effected by them.

The labor disturbances themselves, together with losses incurred as a result of the blockade, ultimately prompted many American businessmen to opt for leaving China. Local authorities, still hoping to restore trade, tried to slow the exodus by delaying exit visas. By early fall and the inauguration of the People's Republic of China, Sino-American hostility was all but solidified.

*

Independent foreign journals remained free from government interference during the months following the Communist takeover of Shanghai. The Press Administration of the Central People's Government, which monitored all journalistic activity, including foreign publications, would not be established until February, 1950.[25] Yet, the editors of all three foreign-owned English language journals in Shanghai, the British *North China Daily News*, the American *Shanghai Evening Post and Mercury* and the

China Weekly Review, ran into difficulties which underscored the new revolutionary sensitivity of the urban Chinese population, and the intent of local Communist authorities to see that foreigners observed the rules.

On June 17th, R.T. Peyton-Griffin, editor of the *North China Daily News*, drew the anger of local authorities over his story of the GMD mining of the mouth of Wusong harbor, and was forced to print a public apology for his "rumor mongering." On June 24th, Randall Gould, editor of the *Shanghai Evening Post and Mercury*, was confined in his office by irate Chinese employees in a dispute over closing the paper and severance pay.

Review editor John W. Powell's problem occurred before the troubles of the other two editors. It took place during and immediately after the fall of Shanghai. Powell and his wife were trapped in their apartment building, which became the center of a three day shoot-out between isolated GMD troops and the PLA. While no direct account of it appeared in the *China Weekly Review*, Chinese criticism revolved around Powell and foreign press coverage of the three day siege, which marred the otherwise peaceful takeover of Shanghai.

As with Peyton-Griffith and Gould, Powell's chastisement also involved a public apology of sorts, although no newly issued rules had been broken. Because of it, Powell came face to face, at an earlier time than the other two editors, with the altered revolutionary sensitivity of Shanghai Chinese to any hint of arrogance or manipulation by foreigners. Surrounded by Chinese staff, and personally enlightened by this incident, his reporting of the later troubles faced by Peyton-Griffith and Randall Gould reflected understanding of the need to be aware of the Chinese point of view, to proceed slowly and to present a more balanced interpretation of events. (Later on, the *Review*'s balanced presentation of the *Shanghai Evening Post* crisis was resented by Gould, who saw it as traitorous to the Millard publishing interests, from which the *Review* had originally sprung.) To understand the evolution of Powell's difficulties, requires a closer look at part of the takeover process.

*

Shanghai was bisected in the north By Suzhou Creek in a meandering east-west line. The bridges crossing this creek, especially in the Hongkew district, where the American and British consulates were located, comprised the two main escape routes to Wusong, Shanghai's outlet to the ocean. It was an area where many foreign residents and wealthy Chinese lived.

On any given day, as Powell and his wife crossed the bridge in the Hongkew district, they could see the shape of their British owned apartment high-rise, the seven story Embankment Building, the tallest in Shanghai, where it stood on a solid rocky outcrop on the north bank of Suzhou Creek. Partly as a result of British evacuation plans, on May 25th, it housed over one thousand foreign and Chinese nationals, some of whom had abandoned their homes for the presumed safety of the structure. No doubt Powell's apartment, in the upper portion of the Embankment Building, had a fine view of the city.

On May 24th, Nationalist forces held a victory parade, and Fang Zhi, secretary general of the Political Council of the (GMD) Army, told a Shanghai press conference that government forces would not tolerate Communist entry into the city and promised: "We will fight to the bitter end- to the last drop of blood."[26] Even as he spoke, a fleet of GMD evacuation ships waited at the Wusong docks, and Nationalist troops, trucks, tanks, and artillery, began a mass exodus north, along the two roads leading to the port. By noon on the twenty-fifth, Communist forces, which had entered Shanghai from the southwest, had peacefully occupied most of the city up to Suzhou Creek.

To screen their retreat, Nationalist troops on Tuesday, the 25th, threw up a makeshift line on the north side of Suzhou Creek, which centered on the bridges, the Post Office, and a number of other buildings, including the Embankment Building. Two hundred soldiers barricaded themselves on the first two floors of Powell's apartment building, fortified the structure with machine guns and mortars, and placed snipers on the roof. Long after PLA troops had flanked the Suzhou Creek line and GMD supporting troops had withdrawn, and for three days after the rest of Shanghai had been occupied, the Nationalist soldiers in the Embankment building continued fighting. The Communists drew up heavier guns on the opposite bank, firing into the building and issuing an ultimatum, as snipers on the roof of the Embankment Building fired on nearby GMD troops trying to surrender.

Powell and his wife found themselves trapped, along with 1000 other civilian occupants, roughly half foreign (Mostly British but including Americans, French, Dutch and Portuguese) and half Chinese. The residents remained concentrated in the interior hallways of the fourth and fifth floors for three days, constantly scrambling from one side of the building to the other, as the incoming fire shifted. While the rest of Shanghai and the world looked on helplessly, the frightened troops in the Embankment Building, now surrounded, cut off from higher authority, and believing that they would be killed by the Communists if they surrendered, continued to resist.

By telephone Powell got in touch with Associated Press correspondent Morris Harris, to deliver a message reassuring relatives in the States that he and Sylvia were all right. On May 26th, the press publicized the fact that the *Review*'s editor and his wife were among the residents trapped in the Embankment Building:

> An estimated 500 British, American, Portuguese, Netherlanders, French and Chinese. . . are caught in Embankment Building, a seven story business and apartment building, British owned, at Honan road and North Soochow road. The building has been splattered and already is within stone's throw of the prime target, the post office, in the direct line of fire

beyond Honan Bridge. In it is John W. Powell, editor of the *China Weekly Review*, son of the famed American John Powell, who lost his feet from maltreatment at a Japanese prison camp and Mrs. Powell, former Sylvia Campbell, of Portland Oregon. Over the telephone, Powell told the Associated Press this morning, "We tried to sleep in a hall as far from the bridge as we could get."[27]

From that time on, the *North China Daily News*, the *Shanghai Evening Post and Mercury* and various American papers featured information supplied by Powell on the situation in the Embankment Building.[28] He was directly quoted in a number of Associated Press stories:

> For 48 hours my wife and I lived in a building that was the target of the Chinese civil war- the Embankment Building on Soochow Creek- where 1,000 civilians were trapped. You could follow the surge of battle by walking through the halls. When the fire came from the front, everybody crouched in the back halls but when it shifted everyone rushed to the front halls, keeping as many walls as possible between them and the guns.[29]

When apartment residents finally persuaded the Nationalist soldiers that the PLA did not kill prisoners and that they should surrender, Powell was again quoted in Associated Press accounts:

> Powell's Part In Embankment Surrender
>
> Even more bizarre was the final surrender at nearby Embankment Building where 1000 civilians were trapped with a few hundred Nationalist soldiers. Here American John Powell, editor of the *China Weekly Review* and son of the man who lost his feet from maltreatment in a Japanese prison camp, and other foreigners and Chinese civilians, managed during the night to get all the Nationalists concentrated on one floor of the building and convinced them the jig was up. ". . . It was heartbreaking," said Powell. "They all wanted to quit and were afraid to. We finally got them to disarm themselves. Then I went upstairs to see how my wife was getting along and then made another try to get the rooftop Nationalists to listen to reason."[30]

Dr. A.M. Dunlap was one of those following the Suzhou Creek standoff through the papers. "Friends and newspaper editors are in touch by telephone with foreigners living in buildings right on Soochow Creek," he wrote. "Sir R. found this morning that all resistance at the Soochow Creek bridges had ceased and tonight our evening paper tells us that the Nationalists gave up during the night. The foreigners in the area got in touch with the Communists by telephone and arranged the surrender of Nationalist officers."[31]

The undue focus on Powell by the Associated Press and resident foreign news media seemed to distort the importance of the foreign hand in resolving the Hongkew stand-off. It proved offensive to the Embankment Building's Tenants' Association, most of whom were Chinese, who did not want to be seen by their new overlords as silent partners to foreign manipulation. Because Powell had been an important source of information and had been prominently featured in AP news articles, he suddenly found himself in a compromised situation.

The Tenants' Association complained to the *North China Daily News* that "A distorted picture of the Embankment scene had been presented by a foreign news agency which had approached merely one resident for his views of what occurred."[32] Not willing to be robbed of rightful credit, the Tenant's Association detailed all its activities during the siege, and its role in the surrender. It praised the dedication, discipline, and hard work of its own members in protecting the resident foreigners.[33]

The protests of the Embankment Building Tenants' Association and the wire service's own concern that their coverage had inadvertently placed Powell in an awkward situation, led the Associated Press to issue a public apology on May 30th. Powell was allowed to clarify his own position within the A.P. statement, which was featured in Shanghai's English Dailies:

> The Associated Press has been informed that the Tenants' Association of the Embankment Building was considerably upset with this news agency's account of events taking place in that apartment building during the fighting along Soochow Creek. . . The tenants..wished to emphasize that their efforts were of a collective nature involving the hard work of a large number of individuals of several nationalities.
>
> Mr. Powell, who was the source of much of the information received by the Associated Press has stated that in general he agrees with the position taken by the Tenants' Association. He further stated that he had been considerably embarrassed by the large share of personal publicity given him in the Associated Press stories, pointing out that he was merely one of the residents of the building. . . He said that he felt it was particularly regrettable that so much emphasis had been placed upon the activities of the foreigners resident in the building since the Tenants' Association is made up of all residents, of which the vast majority are Chinese.[34]

The news agency statement ended with an apology (which appeared twice within the same article):

> The Associated Press naturally regrets that its account of the fighting along Soochow Creek has resulted in discomfiture to some of the people actually participating in the negotiations which ended hostilities[35]

The foreign press coverage of the Embankment Building stand-off, and Chinese sensitivity over it, forced Powell and the *Review* to come to terms with the essence of the changes occurring, and the shortcomings of foreign perceptions of the same. It may also have inadvertently exaggerated the perceived symbolic prominence of Powell and the *Review* in Communist eyes, since they had been featured so prominently in Associated Press news coverage.

Having every intention of continuing the *Review* in Communist controlled Shanghai, Powell exerted himself to prevent the Embankment reporting from prejudicing his journal in the eyes of the new authorities. He did so by trying to awaken in foreign residents a sensitivity toward the changed attitude of Shanghai Chinese in the wake of the victory of the Revolution. In an editorial following the siege, he chided the foreign community for failing to recognize that Shanghai had been returned to the control of the Chinese people. The prominent position that foreigners had once held, due partly to the Guomindang's reliance on foreign aid, had changed forever.

While Powell believed modernization meant foreign skills, and technical expertise would still be needed in China, he noted that it was ". . . already evident (foreigners) will no longer receive the preferential treatment which they enjoyed in the past." More ominously, he speculated that the new government might even go out of its way to impress upon foreigners "that they are no longer first class citizens, but rank with and, perhaps in some instances, after the people of China."[36]

The emphasis which the international press had placed on incidents involving foreigners during the changeover in Shanghai was "telling evidence" in Powell's opinion, that many international residents did not yet understand the nature of the revolutionary change that had occurred. Powell complained that:

> Local English dailies, as well as the foreign press associations, have written reams of copy about how this or that foreigner was beleaguered in this or that section of the city. For example, great prominence was given to the doings of the editor of this newspaper-whose activities were almost entirely misrepresented-while scarcely a few lines was devoted to the fact that more than 100 Chinese civilians lost their lives during the fighting.[37]

Powell reminded his readers that after all, the fate of five million Chinese urban residents was of far greater importance than that of five thousand foreigners. The *Review*'s accounts of Shanghai's liberation accordingly made no mention of the siege of the Embankment Building, other than this veiled reference.[38]

*

When Shanghai's Chinese journals appeared the morning of the 25th, they had judiciously switched to the Communist news services rather than the Nationalist news agencies they had formerly used.[39] Almost immediately the PLA had closed the Nationalist affiliated *China Tribune* and the *China Press*, where Powell had worked during his college days under editor Wu Giadang.[40]

On May 28th, the Military Control Commission of the People's Liberation Army in Shanghai issued a nine-point set of regulations governing Chinese-owned newspapers and journals. These forbade fabricating ru-

mors, libeling people's democratic principles, and revealing military secrets. As in other cities, the stated purpose of these directives, which were
drafted by the People's Publication Control Commission, was to "uphold
freedom of the press." All Chinese owned papers were to temporarily suspend operation, submit information about their ownership and a back file
of issues for the past year, before they could obtain an operating license to
reopen.[41] Foreign-owned journals would be governed by a different set of
regulations to be issued in the future. Yet events showed that these regulations, in spirit if not in the letter of the law, demarcated the limits of foreign press decorum as well.

Point five of the new regulations stated, among other things, there would
be "No rumor mongering." Newspapers and journals which violated this
stipulation would be subject to "a warning, suspension, or closure," and
could even face criminal proceedings.[42] Although this regulation was intended for Chinese newspapers, local authorities were quick to respond
when a story in the *North China Daily News* endangered the regime's hopes
for rapidly restoring ocean-born trade.

A *North China Daily News* headline of June 10th announced "Shipping
Suspended Here As River Entrance Feared Mined."[43] The article, which
was based on speculation over the behavior of Nationalist ships at the
Yangzi River's mouth, claimed that the Yangzi had been mined, and noted
that all shipping along the Huangpu River had been stopped. Soon the
Shanghai Evening Post and Mercury, the United Press, and the Associated
Press picked up on the story.[44] Within hours, the world believed the
Yangzi's entrance to be unsafe.

Shanghai had become the city that it was largely because of shipping
and trade. Tens of thousands of jobs, not to mention the city's overall prosperity, were shipping-related. As news of the mining rapidly spread, it
brought Ocean-born commerce to a halt. Among the ships which were diverted because of the story was an oil tanker with forty-six days of fuel oil
needed by the Shanghai Power Company to ensure the city's electricity.[45]
The possibility of the Yangzi being mined, largely inspired by the June 10th
headline, was enough to keep the harbor empty through June 18th.[46] In the
mind of at least one prominent American, U.S. Ambassador John Leighton
Stuart, the economic damage done by the mining story may have provided
the inspiration for the Nationalist naval blockade of Communist port
cities, which began later that month.[47]

When the story proved untrue, the Shanghai Military Control Commission took action against the paper by issuing a serious reprimand for inciting the false rumor. In reparation, *North China Daily News* editor R.T.
Peyton-Griffin printed a front page public apology in the June 25th issue,
along side the warning from the authorities.[48] The statement of the Military Control Commission insisted that it was dealing "leniently" in the
case.

In retrospect, considering the magnitude of the potential damage, this seems true. In fact, government action appears quite moderate when seen against the campaign in the Communist press, which depicted the mine laying rumor as part of an intentional conspiracy by the imperialist countries, and called for severe punishment of the *North China Daily News*. The CCP Central Committee, in a telegram to the Shanghai authorities drafted by Mao, expressed approval of the moderate measures which had been taken, but also evidenced a tendency to view events as part of an intentional strategy by the Imperialist West.[49]

Liberation Daily (Jiefang Ribao) on June 21st had accused the *North China Daily News* of intentionally starting the rumor that the Yangzi was mined, as part of a well planed British-American Imperialist plot to create havoc in Shanghai. The editorial claimed that the plot was intended to manipulate the People's Government into asking foreign naval intervention to clear the mines. (The June 10th *North China* article had mentioned the possibility of calling on foreign naval expertise.) It claimed the people of Shanghai were irate about the fabrication of the mining story and demanded that the government severely punish the *North China Daily News*.

On June 23rd, a New China News Agency (Xin Hua) radio broadcast reiterated much of the same in an attack on the *North China Daily News*, charging that British and American imperialists were acting together with the Guomindang to spread the rumor about the mines. The broadcast noted that the American owned *Shanghai Evening Post and Mercury*, the United Press, the Associated Press, and the *China Daily Tribune* had quickly joined in, further spreading the rumor. New China News Agency was sure this was an intentionally coordinated attempt by the imperialists to create chaos and hardship in Shanghai. It classified the incident as espionage, and called on the government to "investigate the criminal acts of the British and American papers."[50]

On the day of Peyton-Griffin's public apology, Powell and the *Review*'s response was two-fold. On the one hand, he was mildly critical, urging foreign editors to be much more careful and circumspect in their reporting, and observing that it might take some time for foreigners to adjust to the loss of their privileged positions. On the other hand, he was critical of the new regime for not being available to foreign reporters to corroborate or deny news leads. At the same time, Powell tried to present the *North China Daily News* in a positive light, quoting and referring to *North China Daily News* articles which were enthusiastic about the new government and the prospect of renewed trade.

Refusing to take sides on the harbor mining story, Powell singled out several items in the daily English press which could easily have led to misunderstandings akin to the story of the mining of the Yangzi. In each case, the events were either distorted or presented in a negative light. Powell wished to make editors more aware of the adverse reaction of the Chinese community and press, which believed the stories had been fabricated by the foreign press to serve its own interests. "While we differ with this view, and believe there is enough evidence to show that the papers were guilty only of error," the *Review*'s editor declared, "it is important to note the reaction of some of our Chinese friends."[51]

The unequal status of foreigners in the treaty ports for the past hundred years, meant they were used to receiving immediate answers to their questions and special consideration. Now, they had to adjust quickly to the new situation, and were having difficulty, Powell noted. "As foreigners, we have to make an abrupt readjustment. The realization must come that henceforth we are guests who stay at the pleasure of the Chinese."[52]

Foreign editors, in Powell's view, would have to be especially careful to corroborate news stories and to view not just foreign concerns, but the concerns of the larger society:

> In the matter of the foreign-owned, foreign language press, editors are going to have to be extremely careful. We would be the last to suggest that the *North China* or the *Evening Post*, or the *China Weekly Review*, for that matter, should embark on a program of flattering the new authorities and suppressing anything which might conceivably be construed as "offending" the new regime. Rather, we believe that we can continue as usual, except that we should proceed with a bit more care, especially in the matter of accuracy.
>
> We should, we believe, continue to adhere to our traditional concept of a free and responsible press and fight evil and injustice wherever we find it. However, we should remember that a newspaper is supposed to be operated for the benefit of society as a whole, and is not supposed to represent the special interests of any minority group.[53]

A large part of the readership of English-language journals was Chinese, Powell asserted, and while editors had a duty to inform the foreign population of happenings in China and in their home countries, they had to balance the interests of these two groups carefully.

Powell was critical of the Communist authorities for not making news available to the foreign press and to foreign correspondents in Shanghai. This, after all, might have helped avoid mistakes like the harbor-mining report. He pointed out that the new authorities had not provided any guidelines, regulations, or registration for foreign journals or newspapermen, and called on the government to clarify whether it intended to allow the continued publication of foreign-owned journals in China:

> So far all foreign papers have been operating without specific official recognition. It is true that we have not been told to close or to conform to any special procedures, but it is also true that we have not been told to continue operations as usual. If it is the intention of the authorities to permit continued publication of foreign language journals owned by foreigners, it might save future difficulties to have some official go ahead sign from the powers that be.

A large part of the problem, Powell believed, especially in regard to the story on the mining of the Yangzi, was the fault of the authorities for not being available so that foreign newspapermen might check out their stories in advance. To prevent future misunderstandings, he urged the People's Government to set up an office through which foreign newsmen could confirm or deny news leads before publication.

> Perhaps all of the instances of false or undesirable reports which we cited in the foregoing could have been prevented or at least prevented from appearing in a harmful fashion if there were some official agency which could be approached by foreign newsmen. For instance, in the case of the rumor of the mining of the Yangtze, the story could have been officially denied and never have reached the pages of the press if there had been some method of checking the report. We can hardly believe that any foreign papers here would have failed to check such a report with official quarters if there had been any method of doing so.[54]

Rather than take issue directly with *Liberation Daily's* charges, Powell chose to reinterpret the accusations in a less threatening light. In his version, the sinister intent largely disappeared in an effort to smooth over differences. Whereas *Liberation Daily* said:

> The British and the United States imperialist elements take to base espionage activities to concoct all kinds of rumors to frighten the Chinese people into their trap. This is why they made the suggestion of British and United States help for sweeping the mines soon after the rumor.[55]

Powell's interpretation of the same events and charges rendered them benign and almost well intended as he tried to find a common, less judgmental basis for mutual understanding:

> The arguments of *Jiefang Ribao*, it would appear, may be summarized as follows: ... In an effort to establish contact with the new authorities under favorable conditions, they (the British and Americans) started the false rumor that the mouth of the Yangtze was mined. At the same time they pointed out the difficulties and dangers of inexperienced people attempting to sweep mines. They then came forward with an offer to lend technical and material assistance to sweep the mines away, hoping thereby to establish official contact with the new people's regime, which would then be indebted to the foreigners.[56]

Elsewhere in the *Review's* editorial pages, Powell uncharacteristically paraphrased the *North China Daily News'* coverage of a speech by the British Consul-General in an effort to portray the newspaper in a favorable light before the new regime:

> As the *North China Daily News* said in its introductory paragraph, Mr. Urquhart emphasized the positive aspects of the present situation. This is something we need more of, rather than a constant carping about such

matters as the recent gas shortage, the lack of industrial raw materials, etc.[57]

A different strand in the same editorial again asserted a positive view of the *North China Daily News* : " A few days prior to the British Consul General's speech our eye was caught by a story in the *North China* head-lined, 'Recognition Of New Government Will Aid Foreign Trade.'" The ar-ticle contained the opinions of several British and American businessmen who all favored their countries dropping any connection with the former Nationalist government and recognizing the new People's Government.

*

The Closing of the *Shanghai Evening Post and Mercury*

A few days after the story of the Yangtze delta mining drew fire from Shanghai officials, a labor dispute broke out at the American-owned *Shanghai Evening Post and Mercury* over adjusting wages to the new Communist currency. When *Post* editor Randall Gould threatened to close the paper rather than settle the matter, his Chinese employees resorted to a series of short "lock-ins", preventing Gould and the *Post* business manager from leaving their offices. The issue changed to one of severance pay with the paper's closing, and the controversy dragged on from mid-June until mid-September. Closely monitored by the United States Consulate staff in Shanghai, and widely reported in the U.S. domestic press, the incident served to dampen the hopes of those Americans who wished to continue doing business under Communist rule, and to re-confirm the hostility of those who wanted nothing to do with the People's Government.

Gould's experiences, personalized for American readers through news-paper accounts, occurred at the same time that U.S. Ambassador John Leighton Stuart was being indirectly contacted by Mao Zedong and Zhou Enlai for informal talks in Beijing, capital of the new People's Republic. Sensitivity to political pressure at home, from the "China Lobby" and pro-Chiang Senators, and GOP attacks on the State Department for the "loss" of China, ultimately led President Truman to order Stuart not to visit Bei-jing. Ironically, while the *Post* dispute was in progress, Shanghai Commu-nist leaders went out of their way to impress upon Stuart, who was visiting that city, their desire for trade and their concern to put an end to labor unrest.[58]

Many Americans suspected that the CCP had fomented this and other labor disputes, to curry favor with urban laborers. The tardiness of Com-munist officials in intervening helped to reinforce this impression among Americans, although there were good reasons for moving slowly and care-fully.[59] Gould himself reflected this belief.[60] This perception did harm to prospects for normalized Sino-American relations and trade. Here, we will first look at the *Shanghai Evening Post* management-labor dispute, and its relation to the *Review*. We will then seek to place it in proper context as one among hundreds of similar disturbances, and to examine Communist labor policy as it pertained to these cases.

*

Standard Vacuum Oil Company and the *Shanghai Evening Post and Mercury* were the first two American firms to suffer lock-ins. While the former was handled in a low key fashion, not so the latter. Lack of flexibility by the editor and president of the *Shanghai Evening News and Mercury*, Randall Gould, readily engendered a political situation ripe with symbolism for both sides. For Gould, the issue was editorial freedom to publish without meddling by the employees, the union, or the government. For his employees, the issue was Gould's shirking of his responsibility as an employer by closing the paper.

These issues were transformed into potent political symbols which had a negative impact upon relations between China and the United States. Gould's experiences and treatment, featured in the pages of the *New York Times*, became the archetype of what all Americans who wished to do business with China might expect. His behavior in closing the plant, as portrayed in the Chinese press, became an archetype for the Chinese of a greedy foreign imperialist, totally lacking in benevolence and caring nothing for the Chinese people.

Powell and the *China Weekly Review* tried to steer a course between these two distortions by reducing the issue to its bare facts, and by refusing to condemn either Gould or the union. The outcome of the controversy directly effected the future of the *Review*, since it was printed on the *Shanghai Evening Post*'s presses. After Gould closed the daily, it was essential for Powell to maintain a working relationship with the union, which remained in control of the plant's printing operations. At the same time, he did not wish to offend the *Post*'s editor, who had been a long-time friend of his late father, J.B. Powell.

During the *Shanghai Evening Post* labor troubles, Shanghai's Chinese journals were full of vituperative attacks on Gould. Peyton-Griffith and the *North China Daily News* obtained a full expose of events from Gould by phone, but was pressured by its printers' union not to publish the account.[61] Among both Chinese and foreign journals in Shanghai, only the *Review* had the courage to publish Gould's own narrative of events, balancing it with two other accounts: one by the workers, and another by the *Post*'s business manager, Fred T.Douglas.

THE *SHANGHAI EVENING POST* Crisis and the *Review*

Labor troubles began at the *Shanghai Evening Post and Mercury* on June 14th over the workers' mid-month payment in the new Communist currency, the "renminbiao". In the absence of the former GMD cost of living index, management, represented by business manager Fred T. Douglas, and workers were unable to agree on a basis for wages in the new currency. The frustrated employees responded by holding Douglas captive in his office.

Douglas phoned *Post* editor Randall Gould, who immediately joined his business manager. After half an hour of fruitless negotiations, Gould, who was also barred from leaving the newspaper office by the employees, declared the plant officially shut down. Intervention by the city's General Labor Union late that night persuaded the workers to release editor Gould, business manager Fred T.Douglas, and Charles S.Minor (the representative of the *Post*'s owner, C.V.Starr) in return for Gould's promise not to close the paper.[62]

But the following day, the union's objection to an editorial written by Gould, which was critical of both the union and of the government for not establishing a uniform cost of living index for wages, halted the paper's publication.[63] On June 15th Gould ordered employees not to report to work. Rather than resolve the wage issue, he resigned as chief editor on June 22nd, and announced the *Shanghai Evening Post and Mercury*'s official closure on June 23rd at a press conference.

Ignoring the wage issue which had precipitated the crisis and whose resolution would delay his departure from China until September, Gould invoked principles of free speech and infringement upon editorial prerogative as his reason for closing the *Post*. By his own account, there had been no interference or regulation by the new government, the PLA or the Communist party. Rather it came from the *Post*'s union; Gould's quarrel from start to finish remained with the union.[64]

The role of municipal, and local party leaders, although not prompt, was to attempt arbitration and to try to facilitate a solution. U.S. Ambassador John Leighton Stuart was in Shanghai during this time and spoke with American businessmen, missionaries, Chinese businessmen, and Shanghai Communist authorities. He reported that "Foreign and Chinese employers alike worry over labor troubles. New authorities thus far seem more conservative than employees in individual factories." Stuart felt there was danger the CCP could wind up alienating both labor and management[65] He noted that the *Post*'s employees had objected when Gould suggested the matter be referred to the municipal authorities.[66]

During the crisis at the *Shanghai Evening Post*, the problem of renegotiating the employees' wages and pay scales in terms of the new currency was also at issue at the *North China Daily News*. As previously noted, the blockade, typhoon and flooded countryside all contributed to rising prices, forcing thousands of employers in Shanghai, both foreign and

Chinese, to deal with similar issues.[67] In the case of the *North China Daily News*, management and labor were able to work out an agreement.[68]

The *Post*'s business manager, Fred T. Douglas, believed the decision to close the *Post* was precipitous and unnecessary. He disputed Gould's contention that the real issue was freedom of speech. Along with Gould, Douglas had participated in discussions with the union, had been detained, and represented management. Douglas faulted Gould's account of the controversy:

> I can state categorically that the closing of the newspaper was entirely unnecessary, that the decision to close the newspaper was premature and ill-advised since all possible means of settlement had not been thoroughly explored.

According to Douglas, "The problem originally was, and still is, one of negotiating a new basis for wages and salaries but it has been represented by the editor as an issue of freedom of the press."[69] Douglas maintained that there had been neither government interference nor censorship of the *Post*, a view in basic agreement with Gould's own statements.[70]

The *China Weekly Review* had always been printed on the presses of the *Shanghai Evening Post and Mercury*. When Gould, as president of the publishing company, gave the order to close down the printing plant (July 1), it adversely effected the *Review*. Up until this time, there had been a very general agreement in the views of the two American journals, the *Post* having shared many of those expressed by Powell over the years. The bewilderment of readers of both journals over Gould's sudden closing of the *Post* was reflected in letters to the *Review*'s editor.[71]

After Powell published three different accounts (July 16) by Gould, Douglas and the *Post* employees describing the wage dispute issue, Gould reacted by trying to halt publication of the *China Weekly Review*. He recalled, years later, that:

> Our printers were going through the motions of filling job-printing undertakings, notably publication of the Communist-sympathetic *China Weekly Review*, owned and edited by John W. (Bill) Powell, an American and son of the late J.B. Powell, a strong pro-Nationalist. Despite written notice to Powell, he persisted in using our print-shop to issue his magazine through July and August, paying the union.[72]

When agreement was finally reached (30 July 1949) between the *Shanghai Evening Post* employees and management over terms closing the Mercury Press printing plant,[73] two issues of the *Review* lay partially completed (those of July 30th and August 6th). The printing plant had been submerged by flooding from the typhoon. To finish publication of these last two issues, Mercury Press employees worked two days beyond the date covered by their wage settlements, having to first repair the water damage before printing and binding the *Review*. The two issues were then mailed out together to subscribers.[74] Powell henceforth turned to the British-owned presses of the *North China Daily News* to print and bind the *Review*, breaking the connection which had existed since 1917 with Millard Publishing.[75]

*

COMMUNIST POLICY TOWARD URBAN LABOR

What was the CCP's policy toward labor during the *Post* crisis? When workers staged widespread strikes in Shanghai during the spring of 1947, Communist pronouncements had expressed sympathy and support. However, once the Communists were able to hold large cities on a permanent basis, their policy shifted to discouraging labor unrest in cities under their domination. In the spring of 1948, after the capture of the city of Luoyang, Mao had cautioned cadres against fomenting labor unrest lest it adversely effect production:

> On entering a city do not lightly advance slogans of raising wages and reducing working hours. In wartime it is good enough if production can continue and existing working hours and original wage levels can be maintained. Whether or not suitable reduction in working hours and increases in wages are to be made later will depend on economic conditions, that is, on whether the enterprises thrive.[76]

This directive was applicable to all newly liberated cities, and was sent concurrently to all "leading comrades" throughout China.[77]

In April, 1949, Liu Shaoqi, First Vice Chairman of the CCP Central Committee, took measures in Tianjin to stop cadres who had ignored the Party's warning against fomenting class strife between urban workers and employers. Liu's actions prohibiting labor agitation were subsequently adopted as a model for all other cities under CCP control.[78] The labor disputes following liberation in Shanghai were primarily related to economic conditions, not CCP agitators.

A smooth restoration of production and commerce to revive Shanghai's economy were important goals of the Shanghai Military Control Commission and the Shanghai People's Government. General Chen Yi, Mayor of Shanghai and head of the Shanghai Military Control Commision (SMCC), stated that in trying to restore factory production and foreign trade, and to arbitrate labor disputes, he and the SMCC had ". . . closely followed the policy of Chairman Mao Zedong, namely, 'to develop production, to prosper the economy, to benefit both labor and capital and to give equal consideration to public and private interests.'"[79] Disruption of production and trade represented a threat to the goal of reviving the economy.

During the years previous to Communist takeover, there had been thousands of labor disputes in Shanghai as a result of runaway inflation and the disintegrating economy. Although inflation now slowed under Communist control, it remained problematic. Price increases were fueled by the Nationalist blockade and by the flooding of Shanghai's economic hinterlands due to a typhoon. The consequent shortage of raw materials impeded production even as it drove the cost of raw materials up. Unemployment remained high throughout the summer of 1949, with much of the work force putting in only three days labor per week.

In the two months following the takeover, with Nationalist restrictions of labor no longer in place, new labor disputes mushroomed, as impoverished employees seized opportunities to demand pay raises, better working conditions, and guaranteed employment. Mayor Chen Yi, reported that in the month of July alone there had been over two-thousand labor disputes in the city, including strikes, sit-ins, and lock-ins.[80] These ran counter to the Communists' preoccupation with reviving production and had to be addressed by the summer's end.

The Nationalist blockade, effective from the end of June, aggravated the effects of typhoon and flood, further disrupting production and trade, and putting an end to any early hope for a rapid economic recovery. In an emergency bid to stem growing unemployment and further dwindling of production, the Communist government of Shanghai, throughout June and July, forbade employers from shutting their operations down.[81] Although government officials did not raise the issue, the *Shanghai Evening Post*'s editor was violating this directive when he closed his newspaper and printing plant.

In August, Communist authorities, reacting to the complaints of employers, lifted the ban. The consequent actions of businessmen to reduce wages, fire workers, or stop production, set off a second series of labor disputes. The government, short on urban cadres and still forming the General Labor Union of Shanghai, was as yet unable to channel and control laborers' demands.[82]

Lock-ins of employers by employees, a wide-spread labor tactic throughout the summer, were prohibited by the government in the early fall.[83] The Shanghai Military Control Commission, through the Labor Bureau of the Shanghai People's Government, introduced two methods of avoiding labor disputes: collective industry-wide agreements between industrialists and laborers culminating in yearly contracts, and Labor-Capital Consultative Conferences.[84] This was essential to avoid further disruption of production.

The general essence of the Government's labor policy was: Workers must not ask for wage increases that management could not afford and management must not pay less than it formerly paid. Management must do whatever it could to improve working conditions, and the People's Government would do everything in its power to help management secure operating capital (loans), raw materials, and favorable conditions and markets. Management was given the right to appeal unreasonable wage demands before the Labor Bureau.[85]

*

AMERICAN BUSINESSES AND THE LABOR TROUBLES

A number of American-owned firms and concerns were engulfed in the widespread labor disputes of the summer, especially after authorities lifted the ban on companies closing down. The Texas Oil Company, the American Consulate, the United States Information Service, Standard-Vacuum Oil Company, American Asiatic Underwriters, and the *Shanghai Evening Post and Mercury* all suffered lock-ins as a result of wage and severance pay disputes. U.S. Ambassador John Leighton Stuart observed that lock-ins were common experiences for Chinese and American employers at this time.[86] The lock-in involved employees refusing to allow employers to leave their offices in an effort to apply pressure to redress grievances. Uppermost in these cases, was the workers' desire to prevent the closure of their places of employment.

American businessmen in Shanghai, through the American Chamber of Commerce and otherwise, urged the State Department to sever its support for the GMD and to pressure the Nationalists into lifting the blockade.[87] When it became obvious that the U.S. Government had no intention of doing so, many American businessmen, convinced that the situation could only get worse, elected to close operations and to apply for exit visas. The Chinese employees of these companies (virtually all major American concerns by October)[88] sought to prevent the departure of key American personnel, citing issues of severance pay, in an attempt to insure continued employment.[89]

U.S. Consular officials believed Communist authorities desired American businessmen to stay, that they were "jarred" by the large number requesting exit visas, and that they feared the end of oil deliveries if all American executives repatriated. The Consular staff noted that Shanghai authorities had rejected a proposal to turn management over to Chinese Management Committees, which coupled with pressure from labor, would have allowed the authorities to take over businesses as soon as American managers departed.[90] Rather, Communist officials in Shanghai seemed to be deliberately limiting the exodus of American businessmen by delaying exit visas.

*

The *Shanghai Evening Post* crisis forced the *China Weekly Review* to reevaluate its function and mission, and to face the possibility that it too might have to close in the near future. Powell noted the flagging revenues from advertising and subscriptions. Advertising had shrunken from a pre-takeover high of fifteen pages of advertisements per issue, to a mere three pages. Similarly, subscriptions had also fallen considerably from the previous high of ten-thousand.[91] This made it increasingly difficult to continue publication and raised the possibility ". . . that the *Review* may in the not-too-distant future be forced to close, or at least to suspend publication temporarily".[92]

In the past, Powell observed, the *Review*'s function had been to provide a relatively untouchable forum for disseminating news and opinions which otherwise would have been suppressed by Nationalist authorities. "In those days of brutal suppression by the KMT, the *Review* frequently was almost the only medium through which uncensored news could be disseminated throughout the country." Now, with most of China no longer under GMD control, "the need for the *Review* is obviously much less great," Powell opined.[93]

Eleven days earlier, Powell had made it clear the *Review* was not a vehicle to represent the special minority interests of resident foreigners. With the Chinese English-reading community comprising more than half of the *Review*'s readership, Powell felt a responsibility to this group, as well as a duty to inform foreigners who did not read Chinese of events in China and news of home.[94]

During this period of uncertainty, Powell sought the advice of Chinese friends on the matter.[95] One of these may have been Liu Zunji, an associate of Powell during the former's war-time days with the OWI, and a prominent Communist journalist who would soon emerge as one of the editors of *People's China*.[96]

Ultimately, Powell concluded that ". . . the *Review* could continue to perform a useful function in interpreting the West to its Chinese readers and in interpreting China to its Western readers." Proclaiming this goal as the *China Weekly Review*'s new mission, Powell solicited the opinions and advice of his subscribers on the matter, as well as their active support in terms of finding new readers or patrons.[97]

Many of the obstructions to economic recovery and improved Sino-American relations could be dealt with more effectively if normal diplomatic relations were established between the two countries. Powell shared this opinion with numerous resident American businessmen and local Consular officials. Accordingly, the *Review* redoubled its efforts to encourage American recognition of the new central people's government as soon as it was formally established. In the meantime, Guomindang pilots continued dropping American bombs from American supplied bombers over Shanghai, while the Guomindang navy, using American-supplied warships, continued the blockade.

CHAPTER NOTES

1. Mary Barrett, "The Liberation of Shanghai", *CWR*, 4 June 1949, p13.
2. Randall Gould, "Shanghai During the Takeover, 1949",("Report on China"),*The Annals of the American Academy of Political and Social Science*, 277: 182.(September, 1951).

3. John Leighton Stuart, *Fifty Years in China, The Memoirs of John Leighton Stuart, Missionary and Ambassador.* (New York: Random House, 1954.)p.282–3.

4. Gould, "Shanghai During the Takeover",p.183; Mary Barrett, "The Liberation of Shanghai", *CWR*, 4 June 1949, p.13; Powell, ed. "Final Proof", *CWR*, 4 June 1949, p.7.

5. The Consul General at Shanghai (Cabot) to the Secretary of State, 8 May 1949, United States Department of State, *Foreign Relations United States, Diplomatic Papers, 1949, Volume 9, The Far East: China.* (Washington D.C.: Government Printing Office, 1974.) p.1256. Hereafter cited as *FRUS, 1949, Volume 9.*

6. Gould, "Shanghai During Takeover",p.183.

7. *Ibid.*

8. Suzanne Pepper, *Civil War in China, The Political Struggle, 1945–1949.*(Berkley: University of California Press, 1979.) p.388–390.

9. Gould, "Shanghai During the Takeover, 1949",p.184.

10. *Ibid.*

11. *Ibid.*

12. Mao Tse-tung, *Selected Works of Mao Tse-tung, Volume 4.*(Peking: Foreign Language Press, 1969), p.367.

13. *Ibid*,p.368.

14. *Ibid*,p.371.

15. *Ibid.*

16. Millard Publishing, *Daily Translation Service*, (Shanghai), 6 June 1949, p.5; Gaulton,"Popular Political Mobilization in Shanghai", p.90.

17. *Letter*, A.M. Dunlap to Donald and Helen Dunlap, Shanghai, 6 June 1949, in A.M. Dumlap, *Behind the Bamboo Curtain, the Experiences of an American Doctor in China.* (Washington, D.C.: Public Affairs Press, 1956.) p.22.

18. A.M. Dunlap, *Behind the Bamboo Curtain*, p.23.

19. Warren W.Tozer, "Last Bridge to China: The Shanghai Power Company, the Truman Administration and the Chinese Communists", *Diplomatic History*, Volume 1, Number 1 (winter 1977), p.70.

20. *Ibid.*p70; p.76. In fact, the American owned and directed company was singled out by Zhou Enlai as late as May, 1950, as an example of a well run private firm. It was not until a month after the intervention of Chinese volunteers in the Korean War (November, 1950), that the Communist government took control of Shanghai Power (28 December 1950).

21. *Ibid.*p.71.

22. Suzanne Pepper, *The Civil War in China*, p. 394–398.

23. Pepper, *Civil War in China*, p.401.

24. *Ibid.*,p.398–405.

25. Frederick T.C. Yu, Chief Contributor, Intelligence Research Branch, Chinese Documents Project, *The Propaganda Machine in Communist China-with Special Reference to Ideology, Policy, and Regulations, as of 1952,*(Lackland Airforce Base, Texas: Airforce Personnel and Training Research Center, 1955.) p.32.

26. Walter Sullivan, "Communist Army Enters Shanghai", *New York Times*, May 25, 1949,p.1,3.

27. Fred Hampton (AP), "Foreigners Trapped in Hongkew Buildings", *North China Daily News*, 27 May 1949, p.1.

28. "Nationalist Stand on Soochow Creek Disturbs Change-Over", *North China Daily News*, 27 May 1949,p.1; "Trapped Foreigners In Hongkew Regain

Liberty",*North China Daily News*, 28 May 1949,p.1; "Powell Tells of Life Under Siege", *North China Daily News*, 29 May 1949p.3.

29. "Powell Tells of Life Under Siege",(AP), *North China Daily News*, 29 May 1949,p.3.

30. "Trapped Foreigners In Hongkew Regain Liberty",(A.P.), *North China Daily News*, 28 May 1949,p.1; Besides direct quotes and narratives by Powell, information was published in which Powell was the implied source. For example: "Nationalist Stand on Soochow Creek Disturbs Change-Over", *North China Daily News*, 27 May 1949, p.1. "It is reported that a foreign resident in the Embankment Building asked one of the soldiers there why he continued fighting, offering him and his comrades clothes if they wanted to flee. The soldier's reply was 'If we retreat we shall be shot. If we surrender we shall be shot. We might just as well die bravely fighting to the last.'"

31. *Letter*, A.M. Dunlap to Donald and Helen Dunlap, Shanghai, 27 May 1949, in A.M. Dunlap, *Behind the Bamboo Curtain*. p.16–17.

32. "Embankment Building's Ordeal Described", *North China Daily News*, 29 May 1949, p.3.

33. *Ibid.*

34. "A.P. Statement On Emb't Bldg Battle", *North China Daily News*, 30 May 1949, p.2.

35. *Ibid.*

36. Powell, "Misplaced Emphasis", *CWR*, 4 June 1949, p.9–10.

37. *Ibid.*

38. Mary Barrett, "The Liberation of Shanghai", *CWR*, 4 June 1949, p.12–13; "People's Liberation Army Takes Shanghai, Nanchang And Sian", *CWR*, 28 May 1949, p.277.

39. Walter Sullivan, "Communist Army Enters Shanghai", *New York Times*, 25 May 1949 p.3; "Shanghai's Millions Quickly Swing Into Line Behind the Communists", *New York Times*, 27 May 1949, p.4.

40. Sullivan, "Communist Army Enters Shanghai", *New York Times*, 25 May 1949, p.3; United States Civil Service Commission, Washington D.C. *"Temporary Appointment, Transfer, Reinstatement, Or Promotion, Etc."*, Exhibit No. 462-A, p.1853, in United States Senate Subcommittee To Investigate the Administration of the Internal Security Act and Other Internal Security Laws of the Committee of the Judiciary, 27 September 1954. Powell worked as a reporter, rewriter and proof-reader for Woo Kya-tang of the *China Press*, from October 1940 to July 1941; The Consul General at Shanghai(Cabot) to the Secretary of State, 3 December 1948, *FRUS, Vol.8*, p.911–912. Cabot asked the U.S. State Department to evacuate Woo Kya-tang, then an editor with the *Shanghai Evening Post and Mercury*, for humanitarian reasons.

41. Walter Sullivan, "Communists Set Up Shanghai Rule; Report 40,000 Nationalists Taken", *New York Times*,29 May 1949, pgs.1, 17; "Rules Issued Governing Chinese-Owned Press", *North China Daily News*, 29 May 1949, p.3.

42. "Rules Issued Governing Chinese-Owned Press", *North China Daily News*, 29 May 1949, p.3; Sullivan, "Communist Rule of Shanghai Set Up", *New York Times*, 29 May 1949, p.17.

43. "Shipping Suspended Here As River Entrance Feared Mined", *North China Daily News*, 10 June 1949, p.1.

44. Powell, ed. "Shanghai's Foreign Press", *CWR*, 25 June 1949, p.70; *Shanghai Evening Post and Mercury*, 11 June 1949; *United Press*, 13 June 1949; News of the Week, *CWR*, 25 June 1949, p.84–5.

45. "Shipping Suspended Here As River Entrance Feared Mined", *North China Daily News*, 10 June 1949, p.1.

46. "Shallow Draft Craft Sent to Sweep Estuary", *North China Daily News*, 17 June 1949, p.1; "Yangtze Estuary Reported Clear", *Ibid*. p.1.

47. John Leighton Stuart, *Fifty Years in China, Memoirs of John Leighton Stuart, Missionary and Ambassador*. (New York: Random House, 1954.) p.253."The harm done to Shanghai by the mere rumor that its estuary had been mined may have led the defeated Nationalist leaders to announce the closure of all Communist-held ports."

48. E.T.Peyton-Griffin, "An Apology"(23 June), *North China Daily News*, 25 June 1949, p.1; Chen Yi, Chairman, Shanghai Military Control Commission, "Order for British-Owned *North China Daily News*"(24 June), *Ibid*.

49. (Mao Zedong) Telegram, CCP Central Committee to CCP Shanghai Municipal Committee, 23 June 1949, Shuguang Zhang and Jian Chen, eds. *Chinese Communist Foreign Policy and the Cold War in Asia, New Documentary Evidence, 1944–1950*.(Chicago: Imprint Publications, 1996.) p.117. Hereafter cited as *CCFPCWA*.

50. CIA, Foreign Broadcast Information Branch, *DRFRB*, China, 24 June 1949, BBB 1–2.

51. Powell, ed. "Shanghai's Foreign Press", *CWR*, 25 June 1949, p.71.

52. *Ibid*.

53. *Ibid*.

54. *Ibid*. p.72.

55. *Ibid*.; CIA, Foreign Radio Broadcast Information Branch, *DRFRB*, China, 24 June 1949, BBB 1–2.

56. Powell, ed. "Shanghai's Foreign Press", *CWR*, 25 June 1949, p.71.

57. Powell, ed. "Realistic Approach", *CWR*, 25 June 1949, p.72–3.

58. The Ambassador in China (Stuart) to the Secretary of State, 19 June 1949, United States Department of State, *Foreign Relations of the United States, Diplomatic Papers, 1949, Volume 8, The Far East: China*. (Washington D.C.: Government Printing Office, 1978.) p.763. Hereafter cited as *FRUS, 1949, Volume 8*.

59. Pepper, *The Civil War in China*, p.399–400; Ch'en Yi, "Mayor Ch'en Yi's Report to the Shanghai People's Conference (16 October 1950)", *China Monthly Review*, December 1950, (Supplement to CMR, December 1950) p.1–2.; Gaulton, "Popular Political Mobilization in Shanghai, 1949–1952", p.128–137.The sheer magnitude of the labor unrest dictated a cautious approach by the new government.

60. Randall Gould, "Shanghai During the Takeover, 1949", *The Annals*, p.188; Randall Gould, Randall Gould, "Statement by Randall Gould, Former Editor, *Shanghai Evening Post and Mercury*", *CWR*, 23 July 1949 p. 164–5.

61. Randall Gould, "Shanghai During the Takeover, 1949", *Annals* p.187.

62. Gould, "Shanghai During the Takeover", p. 184–187; *New York Times*, 24 June 1949.

63. Randall Gould, "Statement by Randall Gould, Former Editor, the *Shanghai Evening Post and Mercury*", *CWR*, 23 July 1949, p.164–5; Gould, "Shanghai During the Takeover", p.186; Fred T.Douglas, "Statement by Fred T.Douglas", *CWR*, 23 July 1949,p.165.

64. *Ibid.*: See also: Suzanne Pepper. *Civil War in China.* (Berkeley:University of California Press,1978.) p.399–400.

65. The Ambassador in China (Stuart) to Secretary of State, 19 June 1949, *FRUS, 1949, Volume 8*, p.763.

66. Stuart, *Fifty Years in China, the Memoirs of John Leighton Stuart, Missionary and Ambassador.*(New York: Random House, 1954) p.253.

67. Gaulton, "Popular Political Mobilization in Shanghai, 1949–1952," p.97–100; Ronald Hsia, *Price Controls in Communist China.*(New York: Institute of Pacific Relations, 1953),p.81.

68. Fred T. Douglas, "Statement by Fred T. Douglas", *CWR*, 23 July 1949, p.165.

69. Fred T. Douglas, "Statement By Fred T. Douglas", *CWR*, 23 July 1949, p. 165.

70. Randall Gould, "Statement By Randall Gould", *CWR*, 23 July 1949, p. 164; Gould, "Shanghai During the Takeover,1949",p.184–5.

71. "Shocked", *CWR*, 6 August 1949, p.180. "As a faithful reader of the *Shanghai Evening Post*, I much appreciated the original intention of Mr. Gould 'to stick it out' and to try his best in working for peace and a better understanding between America and the new Chinese democracy. Therefor when I read in your July 23rd issue the statements about the wage dispute between the editor and the workers of the *SEP* it was a shock to me to see how little self-restraint and practical wisdom Mr. Gould showed in handling this case." ; Chang Pei-lin to editor, "*Evening Post Dispute*", *Ibid*, p. 178–180. This letter lauded Douglas's middling position, and defended the fact that authorities had not announced a new wage formula (Gould's initial criticism) since conditions varied so much from plant to plant.

72. Gould, "Shanghai During the Takeover, 1949", p.188. ". . . The Communist-sympathetic *China Weekly Review*". This account was written in 1951, two years after Gould's return, during the Korean War and Senator Joseph McCarthy's rise to prominence. Though Gould could accurately call the *China Monthly Review* pro-Communist in 1951, it is doubtful that he would have seen *CWR* as such in June-July, 1949.

73. The *China Weekly Review* had been printed by the Mercury Press, 19 Chung Cheng Road (Eastern), Shanghai.

74. Powell, ed. "To Our Readers", *CWR*, 6 August 1949, p.182; "Our Thanks", *Ibid*. p.183.

75. From August 13, the *China Weekly Review* was printed by Millington Limited, 117 Hongkong Road, Shanghai.

76. Mao Tse-tung, "Telegram to the Headquarters of the Loyang Front After the Recapture of the City", 8 April 1948, *Selected Works of Mao Tse-tung, Volume 4*, p.248.

77. *Selected Works, Volume 4*, p.248, footnote.

78. Frederick C. Teiwes, "The Establishment and Consolidation of the New Regime, 1949–1957" in Roderick MacFarquhar,ed. *The Politics of China 1949–1989* (New York: Cambridge University Press, 1993.) p.25.

79. Ch'en Yi, "Text of a Report on the Work of the Shanghai Military Control Commission and the Shanghai People's Government for June and July submitted by General Ch'en Yi, Mayor of Shanghai, to the Shanghai People's Conference, August 3, 1949," *CWR*, 20 August 1949, p.219–221.

80. Ch'en Yi, "Inaugural Address at the Opening Session of the Second Shanghai Conference of People's Representatives," 5 December 1949, in all Chinese Papers, U.S. Consulate General, Press Translation Service, Shanghai, China, *Chinese Press Review*, 15 December 1949 ; Pepper, *Civil War in China* p.339

81. Chieh-fang jih-pao she, *Shang-hai chieh-fang i-nien*, pt. 1, p.61 in Richard Howard Gaulton, "Popular Political Mobilization In Shanghai, 1949–1952", p.123–4.

82. Gaulton, "Popular Political Mobilization in Shanghai", p.95–6. It should be noted as well that throughout the first three months of Communist rule, the Military Control Commission and Shanghai People's Government (as per instructions by the Central Committee) had been preoccupied with establishing firm control over (formerly GMD) large-scale public enterprises and bureaucratic-capitalist holdings. Perhaps this imperative delayed the authorities from paying adequate attention to controlling the labor situation in Shanghai; Pepper, *Civil War in China*, p.403–4.

83. Gould, "Shanghai During the Takeover, 1949", p.191; Powell, "New Labor Rules", *CWR*, 3 September 1949, p.3; Sheila Watson, "Labor, Management In Shanghai", *CWR*, 8 October 1949, p.78–80.

84. *Ibid*.

85. Julian Schuman, *Assignment China*,(New York: Whittier Books, 1956.) p.53; Sheila Watson, "Labor, Management In Shanghai", *CWR* 8 October 1949, p.79–80.

86. John Leighton Stuart, *Fifty Years in China, The Memoirs of John Leighton Stuart, Missionary and Ambassador*. p.253.

87. The Consul at Shanghai (McConaughy) to the Secretary of State, 11 August 1949, *FRUS,1949,Volume 9*, p.1290: The Consul at Shanghai (McConaughy) to the Secretary of State, 3 August 1949, *FRUS,1949,Volume 9*, p.1283; The Consul at Shanghai (McConaughy) to the Secretary of State, 15 August 1949, *FRUS, 1949, Volume 9*, p.1293.

88. The Consul at Shanghai(McConaughy)to the Secretary of State, 5 October 1949, *FRUS,1949,Volume 9*, p.1350–52. These included American executives from Schelke,Anderson,Meyer and Company, Chase Bank, National City Bank, Northwest Airlines, BOTRA, Shanghai Warf Warehouse, Shanghai Power Company, Shanghai Telephone Company, Caltex, Standard Vacuum Company, and the American Express Company.

89. The Consul at Shanghai (McConaughty) to the Secretary of State, 7 October 1949, *FRUS, Volume 9, 1949*, p.1352–3.

90. The Consul at Shanghai(McConaughy) to the Secretary of State, 7 October 1949, *FRUS,1949,Volume 9*, p.1352–1353; The Consul at Shanghai(McConaughy) to the Secretary of State, 5 October 1949, *FRUS,1949,Volume 9*, p.1349–52.

91. Powell, ed. "To Our Readers", *CWR*, 6 August 1949, p.182. Exactly what the figures were, Powell did not say; only that subscriptions had ". . . declined steadily," and that the Review was ". . . far from its previous peak of some 10,000 subscribers."

92. *Ibid*.

93. *Ibid*.

94. Powell, ed. "Shanghai's Foreign Press", *CWR*, 25 June 1949, p.70–2.

95. *Ibid*.

96. Harold R. Isaacs, *Re-Encounters in China, Notes of a Journey in a Time Capsule* (New York: M.E. Sharpe, Inc., 1985) p.95–6. In 1944, Liu was chief of the Chinese staff of the United States Office of War Information in Chongqing. He was a member of the Journalists' delegation to the People's Political Consultative Conference in 1949. According to Isaacs, Liu became head of the China Information Bureau and of the Foreign Language Press which published *People's China* and *Peking Review*. He helped set up the English section of *Xin Hua*. During the Anti-Rightist Campaign of 1957 and again during the Cultural Revolution of 1966, Liu was banished to a labor camp, and later imprisoned.; Stephen R. MacKinnon and Oris Friesen, *China Reporting, An Oral History of American Journalism in the 1930s and 1940s*. (Berkeley: University of California Press, 1987) p.196–8. Here John William Powell says much the same thing about Liu Zunji. In 1985 Powell visited Liu in Peking. where after political rehabilitation, he had helped found *China Daily*, another English language publication.

97. *Ibid.*

CHAPTER SEVEN

THE *REVIEW*'S CAMPAIGN FOR RECOGNITION, JUNE, 1949 – JULY, 1950

Before the fall of Shanghai, Powell supported the actions of United States Consular officials, who remained in cities taken by the PLA, as a logical first step toward establishing diplomatic relations with the new regime. He urged the U.S. government to sever its relations with the dying Nationalist cause, a condition which Communist authorities insisted upon for the establishment of normal relations. He was aware that John Leighton Stuart was in contact with the new Chinese authorities. Diplomatic relations, Powell believed, would facilitate commerce and trade, and help American businessmen to protect their interests from possible British encroachment.[1] He felt America had much to offer China as it began to reconstruct, and believed the new government would want to encourage the revival of trade in Shanghai.

As the first months of Communist control passed, labor problems, a stagnant economy and a number of xenophobic incidents underscored the importance, for resident businessmen, of early recognition of the new regime and the establishment of normal diplomatic relations between China and the United States. After Stuart's return to the United States and the publication of the State Department's China White Paper severely critical of both the GMD and the CCP, Powell worried about gathering indications that America intended to write off China as it had the Eastern European countries.

He began a campaign to convince returning businessmen and resident Americans to speak out to Congressmen and the folks back home about the changes actually taking place in hope that it might allay their misgivings. As American China policy became less ambiguous and more hostile to the new government, Powell fought all the harder to try to prevent policy makers from irrevocably identifying China as a new Cold War enemy. Here we will consider this effort from the creation of the People's Republic of China in October, 1949, through Britain's recognition of the PRC in

January, 1950, the seizure of U.S. Consulate buildings in Peking by the People's government in February, up to the outbreak of the Korean War in June, 1950. Before looking at Powell's efforts on behalf of recognition, we must first consider the attempts of both governments to gauge the intentions of each other.

THE STUART-HUANG HUA TALKS: HOSTILITY CONFIRMED

Throughout the summer of 1949, U.S. Ambassador John Leighton Stuart delayed his departure from China, awaiting the result of talks that representative Chen Mingshu of the Revolutionary Committee of the Guomindang, a non-Communist political party of leftist GMD members, had with Mao Zedong and Zhou Enlai. In March, Stuart had outlined the U.S. position and related concerns in secret talks with Chen, so that he might carry these views to the Communist leadership.[2] The CCP leadership was a party to these talks, and believed they signified U.S. interest in establishing diplomatic relations and trade.

Moreover, Chen was scheduled to take part in the Pre-Political Consultative Conference in Beijing, and Ambassador Stuart wished to ascertain just how "democratic" the emerging coalition would be.[3] Stuart therefore regarded it as a good sign when Chen, after discussions with Mao and Zhou Enlai and with their knowledge, advanced his return date and requested Stuart to delay his departure so that they might talk.[4]

Later discussions between Stuart and Nanjing Foreign Resident Affairs Director Huang Hua resulted in an invitation to Stuart to visit Beijing for an informal meeting with Mao and Zhou. The Stuart-Huang meetings coincided with the Guomindang blockade, which the U.S. seemed to tolerate, economic crisis in Shanghai, the well- publicized labor disputes, especially the *Shanghai Evening Post* affair, and rising anti-Communist sentiment within the United States.

Although Consul General John M.Cabot in Shanghai pointed out that a meeting between Mao and the American ambassador would have been welcomed by resident American businessmen and employers, fear of anti-Communist backlash at home prevented it from taking place. According to Ambassador Stuart, the U.S. rejection of the invitation caused a loss of face among chagrined Communist leaders, and was taken by them as a confirmation of American hostility.[5] At the very least, the U.S lost an opportunity to begin an earnest Sino-American dialogue.

Ambassador Stuart had remained behind when the Nationalists had evacuated Nanjing in April. Stuart did so to observe Communist intentions and to give the Communists the chance to discuss Sino-American diplomatic relations.[6] In spite of the CCP's refusal to recognize foreign diplomatic officials until their governments recognized the new People's Government (which was not formally established until October), CCP leaders paid careful attention to Stuart's presence. When PLA soldiers broke into the ambassador's residence during the liberation of Nanjing, Mao Zedong himself drafted an angry telegram scolding the officer in charge:

> The day after the 35th Army arrived in Nanking, its units, without asking for instructions, sent troops to enter [John Leighton] Stuart's residence. This incident not only proves that your troops have committed a mistake by acting without asking for instructions in such an important matter; this also indicates that you have failed to educate your subordinates on diplomatic affairs in advance. This matter must be brought to your immediate attention. Otherwise, your troops could commit bigger mistakes in the future.[7]

Mao instructed Military Control Commissions to educate troops on protecting foreign residents and diplomats ". . . especially those from the United States and Britain." Mao explained that "The old U.S. policy of assisting the GMD and opposing the CCP has failed" and that the United States was changing its policy ". . . to one of establishing diplomatic relations with us." Because of this, he did not think the U.S. would make a major issue out of the intrusion into Stuart's residence ". . . so long as we do not allow similar incidents to happen in the future".[8] Later on, PLA General Liu Bozheng, the Communist mayor of Nanjing, called on Stuart to apologize for the PLA soldiers who had broken into his residence during the first days of liberation.[9]

When the Central Committee appointed Huang Hua director of the Foreign Resident Affairs Office of Nanjing on April 25th, they did so because he was a graduate of Yenching University and a former student of John Leighton Stuart. They consequently reasoned he would be in a particularly good position to contact the ambassador and former president of Yenching University[10].

The Central Committee commissioned Huang to hold talks with Stuart, which lasted throughout May and June. Mao himself drafted the written instructions to Huang, and commented on Huang's transcripts of their dialogues. The purpose of the meetings was to "detect the intentions of the U.S. government." Future diplomatic relations necessitated cessation of interference in China's internal affairs, and had to be based on "equality, mutual benefit, mutual respect for sovereignty and territorial integrity."[11] Mao instructed Huang to "listen more and talk less," to adopt an attitude "of being both serious and cordial," and to make it clear to Stuart that the talks were informal since neither side as yet had formal diplomatic relations.[12]

Mao's commentary strove to insure that Huang communicated the CCP's views accurately and to avoid possible misrepresentation in his dialogues with Stuart. The key issue was for the U.S. to sever its ties with the Guomindang:

You stated in your telegram that "It is no use for the Americans to make empty statements; rather, as the first step, it is necessary for the United States to do more things that are beneficial to the Chinese people.". . . If the U.S. government is willing to consider establishing diplomatic relations with us, it should cease all support to the GMD and cut off its connections with the reactionary GMD remnants. Your statement may give the Americans the wrong impression that the CCP hopes to get American aid. The key issue now is that the U.S. government should stop supporting the GMD.[13]

Stuart was aware that Huang was in constant contact with the top Communist leadership, believed they had consented to his talks, and correctly assumed that Huang reported his conversations to them.[14] Through Huang, Stuart had informed Mao that he wished to remain the accredited U.S. ambassador to China, and to begin renegotiating a new Sino-American commercial treaty. Mao agreed, instructing Huang Hua:

In response to Stuart's desire, as expressed to you by [his secretary] Philip Fugh, to remain the ambassador to deal with us and to revise the commercial treaty [between China and the United States], you should not reject it.[15]

At the June 15th opening session of the Preparatory Meeting for the new People's Political Consultative Conference, Mao Zedong again reiterated his government's willingness to establish diplomatic relations with all countries on the basis of equality, mutual benefit and respect for territorial sovereignty. But those governments must be willing to sever relations with the Nationalists, and to cease helping or working in collusion with them. The *Review* published the full text of Mao's speech in translation.[16] Concerning the restoration of international trade, the Chinese Communist leader stated that the Chinese People were

. . . willing to carry out friendly cooperation with the people of all countries in the world in restoring and developing international trade relations so as to favor the development of production and the bringing about of a flourishing economy.[17]

At about the same time, Huang Hua arranged a visit to Shanghai for Stuart, where the ambassador spoke to U.S. businessmen, and to Communist Mayor General Chen Yi and members of the Shanghai Military Control Commission. In spite of the labor troubles then plaguing foreign businessmen, Stuart informed Secretary of State Dean Acheson that Shanghai's Communist leaders were eager to resume Sino-American trade and hoped for a resumption of friendly diplomatic relations:

This trip to Shanghai gave me ample evidence local CCP authorities [are] anxious [to] develop international trade and make utmost use [of] Shanghai for promoting industry. . . To this end they especially want friendly relations with [the] USA.[18]

The Stuart-Huang talks had materialized because both sides wanted to sound out the other's intentions in regard to possible diplomatic relations. Hence one of Stuart's goals was to establish direct high-level contact with the CCP leadership. That this objective soon came within reach was an indication that some kind of Sino-American accommodation seemed possible. Such contact would doubtless have been positive for the Shanghai foreign business community, and might have accelerated the Communist authorities' efforts to control the city's restive labor force. A major irritant to Sino-American relations, the lock-ins of American employers and the negative publicity they produced in the U.S. domestic press, might have been eased somewhat.

The invitation to meet with Mao and Zhou occurred in early April, after Stuart's secretary, Philip Fugh informed Huang Hua that the ambassador would like to visit his old university in Beijing. Huang said nothing at that time, but on June 18th asked Fugh if Stuart might delay his return to the U.S. long enough to visit Beijing? Less than a week later,(June 24) Chen Mingshu, back from Beijing, briefed Ambassador Stuart on his talks with Mao and Zhou and urged Stuart to delay his departure.[19] Stuart anticipated that this might culminate in some kind of contact from the Communist leadership.

On June 28th, Huang called on Stuart with an invitation to visit Beijing. The ambassador informed the secretary of state that Huang "had received [a] message from Mao Zedong and Zhou Enlai assuring me that they would welcome me to Beijing if I wished to visit Yenching University." Stuart told his superiors "I can only regard Huang's message as [a] veiled invitation from Mao and Zhou to talk with them while ostensibly visiting Yenching."[20]

Stuart observed that the meeting would allow him to outline American anxieties over Communist rule and to gain an authoritative view of CCP intentions. He thought that it would offer a "step toward better mutual understanding," a chance to express American open-mindedness toward changes occurring in China, and might help counter Soviet influence within the CCP. Stuart believed this was a "unique opportunity for [an] American official to talk to top Chinese Communists in [an] informal manner which may not again present itself," and assumed it would have a "beneficial effect" on future Sino-American relations.[21]

On the negative side, the ambassador worried that the talks would result in the U.S. being the first to break the American-sponsored diplomatic "united front" strategy toward the new regime[22]. Stuart believed his talks with the CCP leadership, for better or worse, would be "the second step" toward recognizing the new government.[23] Although he had given Huang no answer to the invitation, Stuart told his superiors he had "received the clear impression that Mao, Zhou, and Huang are very much hoping that I make this trip".[24]

The general opinion among Consular officers was that Stuart should go to Beijing and that the advantages to be gained from so doing far outweighed its disadvantages. Consul General O. Edmund Clubb in Beijing recommended that Stuart meet with Mao and Zhou; Minister-Counselor Clark in Canton felt the benefits to be gained by Stuart meeting with top CCP leaders "were obvious."[25] Consul General Cabot in Shanghai perhaps stated the strongest case:

> We strongly suspect Western interests in Shanghai would welcome Ambassador's proposed trip with open arms as first means of putting Western viewpoint before top Communist leaders and therefore of protecting those interests.[26]

Cabot noted the labor troubles foreign firms were experiencing and the Communists' increasing concern over Shanghai's economic difficulties and suggested that Mao and Zhou might want to address these matters.

The chief difficulty of Stuart's proposed visit to Beijing lay in the realm of U.S. domestic politics. Bad press back home over labor lock-ins was not the only factor influencing American public opinion and domestic politics.[27] As the Nationalists' grasp of China rapidly crumbled in early 1949, their lobbyists in Washington D.C. stepped up efforts to promote the notion that the United States was mainly responsible.[28] In April, pro-Chiang Senators Styles Bridges, Pat McCarran, and William F. Knowland, had attacked the State Department in Congress and called for a joint Senate-House investigation of its handling of China policy.[29] On June 24th, four days before Huang presented Mao's invitation to visit Beijing to Stuart, sixteen Republican Congressmen and five Democratic Congressmen published a joint open letter to President Truman asking that he not recognize Communist China.[30]

State Department Policy Planner John P. Davies acknowledged the difficulty of Stuart's accepting the Beijing invitation in a message to his superior, George Kennan. Davies cited the opinion of the Director of the Office of Far Eastern Affairs, W. Walton Butterworth, that "The ultimate decision turns on an estimate of American domestic reaction."[31]

Butterworth, fearing a violent reaction to Stuart's visit, had linked the trip to so many prior conditions as to surely make it unacceptable to the Communists. Flying in his own plane, Stuart must first pick up Consul Angus Ward and his staff who had been detained in the Mukden Consulate since November, 1948. Only then and in their company might he stop in Beijing on his way home to meet Mao and Zhou.[32] Thereafter, Stuart was to stop by Taiwan to speak to the Communist's arch-rival, Chiang Kai-shek.[33]

At the time of the Stuart-Huang talks and the Beijing invitation, Butterworth was under attack by pro-Chiang U.S. Senators Knowland, Arthur H.Vandenberg, Owen Brewster, and Bridges, who were trying to block his confirmation as assistant secretary of state for Far Eastern affairs.[34]

Davies' own solution for quieting domestic opposition was that the Department of State should issue a statement that "Stuart had not gone to Beijing to play footy-footy with the Communists but had gone there, as would be the fact, to read them the riot act."[35]

Davies need not have worried. On July 1st, Secretary of State Acheson, after consulting the president, instructed Stuart that "under no circumstances" was he to visit Beijing.[36] Ten days later, President Truman ordered the ambassador to visit the Nationalist government in Canton before returning home, so as to avoid confusing or arousing the indignation of the American people.[37] Stuart successfully resisted the latter order, seeing it as pointlessly damaging any possible future relations with China, and liable to place Americans still in China in an even more uncomfortable position.[38]

Stuart was aware of the potential damage that the last minute scuttling of the informal Stuart-Mao-Zhou talks might cause. For months negotiations and feelers had been in progress. These had convinced the Communists that the U.S. was interested in opening relations. Eventually the CCP leadership had been drawn into issuing an informal invitation only to have the United States abruptly decline.

As we have seen, Mao originally made it clear to Huang Hua that the purpose of his talks was to determine American intentions. The Communists had believed that reopening trade relations with the capitalist countries was both possible and desirable. Mao believed the British and Americans were interested in this, and certainly it was true that both British and American businessmen were initially attentive. The attitude of the United States would have great influence on whether or not this could be carried out.

While the Huang-Stuart exchanges were taking place, the Nationalists had declared CCP-held port cities to be under blockade. Although the State Department had protested the blockade as illegal, the CCP suspected that it was being carried out with tacit U.S. approval if not outright support. Under the circumstances, Stuart surmised that his refusal to visit Beijing for informal talks with Mao and Zhou would be seen as confirmation that the U.S. intended to pursue a hostile policy toward the new government:

> All reports that I have from Peiping and indications from local Commie authorities confirm that Mao and Chou have lost face, are chagrined at my rejection of their "invitation" to visit Peiping and consider it a clear indication of American policy.[39]

From Shanghai, where the GMD blockade had dried up trade, and labor disputes and lock-ins plagued foreign employers, threatening to further poison Sino-American relations, Council General Cabot expressed disappointment to the secretary of state over the lost opportunity to open talks with high CCP officials:

I must candidly state that, viewed from Shanghai, I consider [the] decision conveyed by Deptel 775, July 1, 6 p.m. to Nanking to be disastrous. We have certainly rejected [an] opportunity to place [the] foreign viewpoint and problems before top Communists and to establish some local working contacts which are so needed and so lacking in [the] present ominous situation.[40]

He pointed out the contradictory and irresponsible aspect of a foreign policy which first encouraged American businessmen to continue their activities in China, and then assumed a hostile political stance toward the new government:

If we are to pursue a positively antagonistic policy towards [the] Chinese Communists, we have no right to leave Americans and their property in Communist-held China subject to Communist retaliation.[41]

*

Two weeks after the establishment of Communist rule in Shanghai, an article by Charles J. Canning reiterated the *Review*'s basic position on diplomatic relations. Recognition was a "must" if the United States wished to protect its interests and did not intend to pull out of China totally. There was no doubt in the author's mind that diplomatic relations would be established: "All indications are the United States government will eventually recognize the new government and establish diplomatic relations with it."[42] The only question was how soon.

Canning noted that Ambassador Stuart had already started working with Huang Hua, the Foreign Affairs Bureau representative of the Communist government. He recalled that the British Foreign Office had stated on April 20th that it planned to establish friendly relations with the new Government of China. The U.S. State Department too had indicated that it wished to develop "working contacts" with the new regime.[43]

Recalling the conditions laid down by PLA General Li Tao for establishing diplomatic relations, the same official conditions Mao had commended to Huang Hua, Canning surmised that Britain would recognize the new government before the Americans, since the British put forward the principle of the regime holding "paramount power" as a precondition. In contrast, Secretary of State Acheson had informed the U.S. Senate that America would not recognize the new government while Chiang still maintained a foothold on the Mainland.

Canning worried that British businessmen would increase their market share at the expense of American counterparts. The British were eager to do business with the new regime and already involved in trade with North China through Hong Kong, he noted. British banks had remained in Tianjin after the Communists arrived, while American banks withdrew. British businessmen seemed better able to pressure their Foreign Office into "playing ball" with the Communists, he observed.

The CCP's plans for reconstruction and expansion of the economy meant large amounts of foreign materials and technical know-how would be needed. Although China could get along without assistance from the West, Canning opined, they would not want to, as this would retard the progress of reconstruction.[44]

Powell's outlook was gloomier. He worried that the Truman Doctrine would eventually be applied to China; that the Truman Administration would try to surround China with potential enemies. He complained: "It is probably too much to expect that the men who have designed policy in the past . . . suddenly will. . . attempt to make a friendly and cooperative approach to the new regime."[45] He lauded the British policy of making technical skills and materials available and agreed wholeheartedly with those British and American businessmen in Shanghai who felt that recognition of the new government would aid foreign trade.

Powell assumed China's new rulers would eventually seek foreign help, that the U.S. should cut its dealings with the GMD, accept things as they were, recognize the new regime, and get ready to do business.[46] As the fourth of July approached, Powell hoped that a year from that date, American and Chinese diplomats would be well settled in, and diplomatic relations an established fact.[47]

After the Truman Administration vetoed Stuart's meeting with Mao Zedong and Zhou Enlai, Mao announced China's alignment with the Soviet Union (July 1) in his address, "The People's Democratic Dictatorship," commemorating the 25th anniversary of the CCP's founding.[48] A *Review* article by Canning refuted the assumption that Mao's "Lean to one side" policy, set forth in the address, meant the CCP intended to shut out the West.

Canning noted Mao's reassertion in the speech that China intended to establish diplomatic relations with all countries, to open trade and cooperation with all peoples in order to help expand production and to pursue a flourishing economy.[49] He pointed out that the U.S. was still actively aiding the Nationalist government. The key, Canning asserted, was to sever relations with the Guomindang.[50]

By August, several incidents that occurred in July persuaded the State Department to begin closing down U.S. Consulates in Dihua, Guangzhou, and four other cities before they came under Communist control.[51] This partially reversed the stay-put policy the United States had followed since the fall of Mukden in October, 1948. The controversy over employee severance pay and other matters which had delayed Ambassador Stuart's return, the Closing of the United States Information Service offices by Communist officials, and the lock-in of Acting Consul-General Walter McConaughy in his Shanghai office by disgruntled former U.S. Naval Yard employees[52] all reinforced the decision to close the U.S. Consulates in six Chinese cities.[53]

The State Department began to encourage resident American business-men to return to the United States. American Consular officials negotiated with the Communists and the Nationalists to allow a "rescue" ship, the *General Gordon*, to pass the Nationalist blockade and evacuate those wishing to return home. Though both American and British governments had protested the blockade to the Nationalist government, the Commu-nists believed the United States actually supported it, since the ships and planes used to enforce it had been supplied by America. Ultimately the Communists approached the British for cooperation in breaking the block-ade, initially indicating they would allow British naval vessels to escort merchant ships as far as Woosung.[54]

Upset by State Department evacuation plans, Powell accused Secretary of State Acheson of exerting considerable pressure on all Americans to leave. He noted that the actual number in South China informing the em-bassy they would depart was only two hundred, of whom seventy were em-bassy personnel. In Shanghai and Nanking, Powell pointed out, more than seventy-five percent of the American residents were "staying put". Busi-nesses were paring down their staffs, but not closing their doors.[55] "I would feel like a fool if I went home now and two months later business picked up", Powell quoted one resident American businessman as saying.[56]

Powell contrasted the widening differences in American and British pol-icy, apparent by September. While the U.S. grew daily more hostile toward the new regime and sought to hinder it through restricting trade, Britain tried to carry on commercial and business relations in a normal manner in spite of the difficulties. While Washington closed consulates and evacuated diplomats in Dihua and Guangzhou, discouraged businesses wishing to trade with China, and sent a well-publicized evacuation ship to Shanghai, the British made no move to evacuate their nationals, and made no attempt to interfere with private firms doing business with China.

He noted approvingly that the British Navy had been convoying mer-chant shipping as far as possible through the blockade. Most British busi-nessmen intended to stick it out, and in spite of their losses, looked forward to friendly and profitable relations in the future. Many expected to enlarge their market share if U.S. competitors left, he warned. With the United States seeming to adopt an antagonistic policy toward the new gov-ernment, Powell feared that America would find itself left out in terms of markets and general influence in China and throughout Asia.[57]

Powell chipped away at America's lingering support for the remnant Nationalist regime, since this seemed the main impediment to recognition. An editorial entitled "World's Richest Refugees" cited recovered National-ist documents to underscore the depths of GMD corruption. The *Review*'s editor pointed to the profligate speculation and milking of the public by the GMD's "Big Four Families" through their ownership of local banks and various companies. But Powell's main fire was reserved for Chiang Kai-shek's Gold Yuan Reform of 1948, "The biggest steal of all time," which netted an estimated three hundred million dollars in gold, silver and foreign exchange from China's impoverished middle classes.[58]

Towards the end of September, Powell addressed an impassioned plea to the passengers who were to embark on the evacuation ship, *General Gordon*. He told them that their words on arrival in the U.S. and other countries would carry great weight, since they were the first large passenger ship to sail from Shanghai since the Nationalist blockade began.

> As foreigners with a special interest in China, it is particularly important that you give people abroad a well-balanced, objective picture of developments here. If you are a businessman, you will be interested in seeing your government do what it can toward restoration of normal shipping and other commercial relations with the new China.[59]

As long as foreign governments gave recognition to the GMD and its blockade, it would be difficult to resume peacetime trade relations, he pointed out.

> If you are a missionary or educational worker the continuance of your chosen line of work in this country depends upon ultimate recognition of the People's Government by your government and the establishment of normal treaty relations between the two countries.[60]

Their balanced picture of developments in China, Powell urged, would help counteract misinformation and inform public opinion abroad. Their account of changes since the establishment of Communist rule would help people in America to keep their traditional feelings of friendship for the people of China, he affirmed. "We do not ask you to do anything but tell exactly what you have seen." Powell pleaded. "You have an unequalled opportunity to tell the people the facts since you are well qualified and since everyone is anxious to listen to you."[61]

When the *General Gordon* finally arrived at Shanghai the end of September, the Shanghai General Labor Union and the Seamen's Union aranged a banquet and celebration in honor of the crew.[62] Meanwhile, Guomindang naval vessels enforcing the blockade sunk one British freighter and siezed another. Discontent over the ongoing isolation of Shanghai due to the Nationalist blockade continued to build in the British and American resident communities.[63]

Not content with journalistic efforts alone, Powell, on behalf of the *China Weekly Review*, joined with Paul Moritz of the "International Committee of the Y.M.C.A." to sponsor a petition calling the United States to break the GMD blockade. By September 21, they had collected one-hundred four signatures of American businessmen, missionaries, and educators residing in Shanghai - a "fair cross section" of the foreign community in the opinion of the *North China Daily News* - and had sent the petition to U.S. Secretary of State Dean Acheson.[64]

According to the *New York Times*, the signatories urged the U.S. government "to take measures to facilitate the restoration of shipping and trade." and to establish a "sound basis for friendly relations" with China's new government.[65] The petition asked the U.S. government to facilitate the medical, educational, cultural, and religious work of Americans in Shanghai by fostering the climate of traditional friendship between the American and Chinese peoples.[66]

Twenty days before the People's Republic of China would be inaugurated, the Communist leadership again sent word to the U.S. State Department that the new government could have diplomatic relations with the United States if the U.S. "Gave up" Chiang Kai-shek and the Nationalists. This message was delivered directly by Mao Zedong to Lo Longji, leader of the Democratic League, on September twentieth, and communicated to Washington on the twenty-ninth.[67] There was no American reply.

*

Part of the *China Weekly Review*'s campaign for U.S. diplomatic recognition of the PRC involved efforts to explain the formation of the new government to the American people. The *Review* followed events closely as the People's Political Consultative Conference (PPCC) completed its final work in creating the Central People's Government of the People's Republic of China, institutionalizing the Common Program of the PPCC and Mao Zedong's ideas on Democratic Dictatorship.[68] Articles sought to illustrate how people's democracy operated at the local and national levels, and how American and British educated Chinese intellectuals were accommodating themselves to the new order.[69]

Powell published a translation of an article by the well- known British and American-educated Chinese sociologist, Fei Xiaodong which had originally appeared in *Sin Wen Ribao*.[70] Fei had helped to launch the "December First Movement" at Lianda University in Kunming, late in 1945, to promote formation of a coalition government and to protest resumption of China's Civil War. The *Review* had followed the movement from its inception.[71]

Previously, Fei had been much impressed by American and British democracy, and believed that democracy required balloting, vigorous election campaigns, and a loyal opposition. Since none of these existed in China, Fei did not believe that the Communist party would put democracy into practice.[72] When he discerned elements of dictatorship in the new government after liberation, he doubted that it could be at the same time democratic, since he held democracy and dictatorship to be incompatible.

But his participation as a delegate in the People's Political Consultative Conference (PPCC) on September 12, 1949, changed his opinion. Although not elected, Fei found the delegates of the PPCC to be representative of the entire population. True, they did not satisfy the formal criterion of democracy that he had embraced in the past, yet he believed the delegates to be more truly representative than any elective body he had observed in either the United States or Britain.[73] "The Conference in Peiping is only the starting point of democracy in China," Fei declared, but from this beginning he looked forward to its fuller development in the future.[74]

The *Review* published an article by Lee Zongying, which documented the extent of democratic practices at the village and city level.[75] Lee described the Provisional People's Assembly which had met in the city of Jinan in Shandong province. The Assembly had lasted a week and was comprised of delegates either elected by their trade unions or nominated by the city government. After discussing government reports presented to it, the Assembly passed various recommendations, which Lee pointed out were not binding on the government:

> Of course, this was only the beginning. As mentioned above, the delegates were not yet all elected by popular votes. The Assembly still was of a consultative nature in that the resolutions it passed were not binding on the government.[76]

Yet in Lee's opinion, this was an important first step toward democracy and helped to build a bridge between the government and the masses. He pointed toward future plans for "an entirely popularly elected assembly of a legislative nature"(the All China People's Congress outlined in the Common Program of the PPCC), and felt that once this came into existence, China would be propelled into ". . . a form of democracy built on a much broader base than practiced, or rather abused, by the capitalistic countries."[77]

With an emphasis on its democratic elements, the *Review* explicated the blueprint for the new central government which the PPCC had drafted. Eventually, elections were to be held throughout China to choose an "All China People's Congress", which was to be the nation's top political organ. It would appoint a "Central People's Government Council" to supervise all administrative, judicial, and military functions.[78] But until elections could be organized for the All China People's Congress, which did not actually occur until 1954, the People's Political Consultative Conference, comprised of 662 delegates, was to act as the All China People's Congress, electing the Central People's Government Council in its stead.[79]

*

In Beijing, at the Great Hall of the People, before a tumultuous crowd, Mao Zedong proclaimed the establishment of the new Republic on October 1, 1949. On the same day Zhou Enlai, Minister of Foreign Affairs and Premier of the Political Council of the new government sent out letters to foreign governments, including the United States, announcing the inauguration of the People's Republic. He invited each to recognize China's new government and to establish "normal diplomatic relations".[80]

The U.S. State Department, responding to press queries about Zhou's letter inviting diplomatic relations, emphasized that it still recognized the

Nationalist government and had no immediate plans to answer Zhou's letter.[81] Powell felt the State Department's response ". . . stacked up to a fairly gloomy picture as regards early recognition," and one that would ". . . not be pleasing to many Americans, especially those engaged in commercial, educational, religious, and other work in this country."[82]

Even so, he underscored the ambiguities in the American position. The previous week, the Nationalists had been pressured by the State Department into releasing two American ships, the *Flying Clipper* and the *Flying Independent*, which had tried to run the blockade. The incident had occasioned angry criticism of the GMD in the U.S. Senate, and the State Department had warned the Nationalists that the U.S. would view gravely any new attack on an American ship. The United States again asserted that it considered the blockade illegal.

Powell saw this as an indication of conflict between U.S. political policy of hostility toward the new regime and the economic policy not to hinder U.S. businessmen carrying out trade in "non-critical" materials.[83] This ambiguity suggested to Powell that the question of recognition was still open. He urged a ". . . new policy, based on a clear understanding of events in this country, and taking into consideration the best interests of the American people," comprising early recognition.[84] He again urged his American readers

> . . . who are living in China and who obviously are in the best possible position to know the facts, to let their government know what they think. A cable, or personal letter, to an individual Congressman, the Secretary of State, or even the President can be effective. It is up to us to take advantage of our good fortune of being on the spot and to do what we can to urge early recognition.[85]

*

Zhou Enlai's letter served to rekindle public debate over the recognition issue within the U.S., and led the State Department to seek the council of academics, journalists, diplomats and businessmen who were familiar with China. The State Department did so through the formation of an advisory committee under the chairmanship of Dr. Philip C. Jessup, head of the U.S. delegation to the United Nations,[86] and by convening a "Round-table Discussion" of China experts in Washington D.C.[87] Although the advisory committee was divided in its overall views, academics and those participants with an in-depth knowledge of China, agreed on the desirability of recognition and diplomatic relations.[88]

Sixty-eight Protestant missionaries wrote to President Truman to warn that American mission interests in China would be compromised if the U.S. withheld recognition.[89] The *New Republic* published articles by Edgar Snow and Jack Belden, which favored recognition.[90] After Britain and

India recognized the PRC, *New Republic* urged the U.S. government to do the same to avoid isolating itself diplomatically over the China issue.[91]

Opposition to recognition was strident among Republican Senators and Congressmen, led by Representative Walter H.Judd, Senator William Knowland, Senator Arthur Vandenberg, Senator Henry Cabot Lodge, and Representative Louis B. Heller.[92] GOP Senators and Congressmen petitioned the president urging that Communist China not be recognized under any circumstances.[93] Henry Luce's publications, *Time*, *Life*, and *Fortune*, longtime supporters of Chiang Kai-shek, opposed recognition and began a search, along with GOP members of Congress, for scapegoats within the U.S. State Department to explain "the loss of China".

Secretary of State Acheson, a few days after receiving Zhou's letter, listed three test requirements which the United States would apply to the question of recognition. (1) The new government should actually control the country it claimed to rule. (2) It should accept its international obligations. (3) It should rule with the acquiescence of its people.[94] The Secretary of State did not say whether he considered the People's Republic to have met these standards. All of the Far East specialists on the Jessup Committee (formed to advise the State Department on the issue of recognizing the PRC) favored recognition, since the PRC already controlled most of China, although the Committee itself was unable to reach a unanimous recommendation.[95]

Commenting on Acheson's three prerequisites for recognition, Powell noted that the People's Republic already satisfied the first. By "international obligations" (the second criterion), did the United States mean the new government must pay Guomindang debts incurred during the Civil War, he asked? Surely no realistic American would expect the Communists to pay for the bullets and bombs used against them. It was true the Nationalists recognized their own debts, plus some of the debts of previous governments, but they did nothing to pay for any of them, Powell argued. Likewise the GMD's recognition of treaties had not insured their implementation.[96]

As for the third criterion, the acquiescence of the people, Powell believed the GMD did not even have the passive consent of those it ruled, while rule in CCP areas could more accurately be described as supported by the vast majority of the population. Powell pointed out the marked difference in people's attitudes toward the old and new regimes. He noted the all-day city wide celebration of the declaration of the PRC by more than one million participants. It would be impossible to compel so much enthusiasm from an apathetic population, he felt.[97]

The time had come for the Truman administration to face reality, Powell declared.

> China has a new government which has come into power with the support
> of the people and there is every indication that it is here to stay. Recognition
> must come. This is obvious. The only question is when. Truman and Ache-
> son can save the American government considerable future embarrassment,

and will do a real service to American business, by swallowing the bitter pill as quickly as possible and extending immediate recognition.[98]

On October 14th Guangzhou (Canton) fell to the PLA. Nationalist President Li Zongren moved his capital to Chongqing.[99] Powell noted that the fall of Guangzhou made the blockade less effective. He wondered how long the foreign powers, especially Britain and the United States, would continue their de-facto "recognition" of the blockade as the Nationalist government crumbled.[100] The *Review* pointed to the Pacific Northwest, whose lumber and other exports had been adversely effected by the blockade, and noted the large number of labor unions in the region calling for resumption of trade with China.[101]

*

One very serious impediment to better Sino-American relations was the sudden arrest on October 24, 1949 of U.S.Consul General in Mukden Angus Ward and four of his staff, who had been held under house arrest by the Communists for almost a year. Ward was charged with having assaulted an employee over a wage and severance pay dispute. At his trial, Ward was found guilty of unreasonably discharging Chinese workers, withholding their wages and severance pay, and assaulting and causing injury to the two laborers in question. He received a suspended sentence, had to pay fines, wages, severance pay, and medical expenses totaling the equivalent of $178 U.S. dollars, and was to be deported. Ward and the four others were released November 21, 1949.[102] The incident elicited widespread outrage in the United States and made the possibility of American recognition of the PRC more problematic.

The *Review*'s approach to the incident was to withhold judgment, to try and reduce the controversy to actual events, and to present the narratives of both sides through their trial testimony.[103] Its account implied that one of the workers who had slept overnight on the consulate staircase in protest of his wage settlement, fell while being pulled back down the stairs by Ward. His injuries were accidental, the result of his breaking free of Ward's grasp and falling backwards down the staircase.[104] This was a very different account from that presented by New China News Agency (*Xinhua*), which reported that Ward and four other Consulate staff members had kicked, beaten, and insulted him.[105]

The *Review* noted that President Truman had called Ward's arrest an outrage, and that Secretary of State Acheson had said the United States could not recognize China's new government as long as consular staff were subjected to this kind of treatment. In the author's view, the Ward case was "scarcely of sufficient importance to constitute a key issue in America's relations with China,"[106] and had been blown out of proportion by the press in America. The *Review* article charged that "Voice of America" radio broadcasts and the president and secretary of state's statements, by ignoring important facts, "tended to give the American public a false impression of the whole affair."[107]

In November the United States announced that it would place a ban on all "strategic" materials bound for China. For two years the U.S. had applied similar restrictions to trade with the Soviet Union and Soviet satellite countries of Eastern Europe. Powell labeled the trade restrictions "power politics," designed to slow down the economic recovery and industrialization of these countries. He pointed out the broad interpretation of materials having a "war potential": industrial lubricating oils, electric generators, transmission and distribution apparatus, large electric motors, mining and quarrying machinery, oil drilling and refining equipment, automotive replacement parts, etc.

The real meaning of the ban, he felt, was that the U.S. government had decided officially to extend the cold war to China. Powell pointed to the contradiction of the Truman Administration on the one hand negotiating with countries throughout the world to lower tariffs, while at the same time erecting trade barriers with China. From now on the kinds of industrial equipment China could purchase from America would be severely limited. The main result, Powell feared, would be to retard reconstruction and widen the breach between the American and Chinese people.[108]

With the trade restrictions and fallout from the Ward case, Powell believed he saw a shift in U.S. China policy. The attitude implied by the China White Paper, although hostile, was yet ambiguous enough to allow for change. But now He feared that Washington was embarking on a policy of active hostility.[109] Though distressed by the drift of events, he did not slacken his campaign for recognition.

*

On November 28th, the Nationalists abandoned their new capital at Chongqing and moved it to Chengdu. By December 6th, they moved their capital offshore to Taipei. Li Zongren flew to America for medical treatment, and in early March 1950, Chiang Kai-shek, who had resigned ten months earlier, resumed the post of president in Taiwan.[110] The State Department had maintained that it would continue recognition of the Nationalist government as long as it retained a hold on the mainland. Now the Nationalists no longer met that criterion. Powell responded by condeming the contradictions in State Department policy and issuing a strong editorial appeal for recognition based on self interest, directed at all Americans who had dealings with China.

Powell noted that Secretary of State Acheson in the White Paper made it clear the Nationalist government fell because it was corrupt, doomed to extinction by its own rottenness, and implied that the United States wanted nothing more to do with it. Yet the secretary of state refused to break off relations with the Nationalists. Acheson called the Nationalist blockade illegal and protested to the Nationalist government. Yet he did nothing to raise the blockade in spite of the fact that American ships had been fired on.

It was the proper task of the secretary of state to support the best interests of American businessmen abroad and help them however he could, Powell asserted. The Secretary was negotiating reciprocal tariff agreements worldwide to increase American foreign market access. Yet he urged caution and patience to U.S. businessmen who worried about the British getting in on the ground floor in the new China.[111]

Powell rejected the idea that the United States must first approve of the government of a country before it could grant recognition, and noted that the United States already recognized many regimes it did not necessarily approve of. He quoted President James Buchanan on U.S. recognition of the Second Empire of Louis Napoleon:

> In its intercourse with foreign nations, the government of the United States has, from its origin, always recognized de-facto governments. We recognize the right of all nations to create and reform their political institutions according to their own will and pleasure. We do not go behind the existing government to involve ourselves in the question of legitimacy.[112]

"The fact remains", Powell concluded, "that the people of China have changed their government and have established a new regime which in every way appears a stable one and one destined for a long life." He closed with a plea addressed to all sectors of the American population having potential interests in China:

> It is in the best interests of all the American People - traders with merchandise to sell, shippers with bottoms to fill, farmers with food to sell, bankers with money to loan, industrialists with goods to sell, workers with jobs to hold - that the U.S. recognize the new People's Government of China. So long as Mr. Acheson fails to withdraw recognition from the Kuomintang remnants and accord it to the new government, he is failing to look after the best interests of the American people.[113]

*

In mid December, the U.S. government opted to retain diplomatic contact with the Nationalists on Taiwan while ending military aid. President Truman and Secretary of State Acheson concluded that Chiang could not hold Taiwan against the PLA, and aimed to limit the damage to U.S. prestige by utilizing only diplomatic and political means to delay the Communist conquest of the island.[114] On January fifth, 1950, President Truman announced that the United States would not intervene militarily to prevent the fall of Taiwan, nor would it provide military aid or advisors.[115]

Secretary of State Acheson in a speech before the National Press Club, told reporters that both Taiwan and Korea were outside the American defense perimeter.[116] On January sixth, 1950, Great Britain announced its unconditional recognition of the government of the People's Republic of

China. Pakistan and Ceylon recognized the PRC soon thereafter. Burma and India had done so in December.[117]

Powell responded with another editorial asking how much longer the United States could delay recognition? The GMD became, with each passing week, increasingly a fiction as China's real government, he said. Its hold on Taiwan was tenuous and probably destined to be short-lived. Since the main criterion for recognition was usually that the government actually control the country it claimed to rule, there could be no doubt about which was the real government of China.[118]

With the Civil War almost over and the new government turning to reconstruction, there was nothing to be gained and a great deal to be lost by the Truman administration's stalling policy, Powell remonstrated. "The longer recognition is delayed, the longer it will be before normal commercial and other relations can be resumed." Now that Britian had recognized the new government, Powell asserted that the U.S. position had become all but indefensible. With signs the United States was slipping into economic recession, America could not afford to penalize every country that embraced Communism by slapping export restrictions on them.[119] He chided U.S. authorities:

> Withholding recognition until doomsday will not bring Chiang Kai-shek back to Nanjing, nor will it force the new government to pay all of Chiang's bad debts. . . It will, however, seriously injure the traditional friendship between the Chinese and American Peoples.[120]

On January fourteenth, the People's Government began requisitioning the part of the U.S. Consulate holdings in Beijing that had formerly contained military barracks. The United States, the Netherlands, Great Britian, and France had all recieved advance notification of repossesion of similar portions of their Consular property by the PRC on January sixth. These properties had been ceded to the Great Powers under duress following the Boxer Intervention and had symbolic significance as tokens of China's shame and humiliation at the hands of foreign imperialists. They comprised only a portion of U.S. Consular holdings in Beijing and no longer housed troops.[121]

The United States reacted to notification of the PRC's intent to reclaim the former barracks by threatening to withdraw all diplomatic personnel from China.[122] Consequently, after the property was requisitioned, President Truman ordered the removal of all U.S. Consular officials from China.[123] The seizure of part of the Embassy caused widespread indignation in the American press, which generally approved of the President's action. It also put an end to the growing debate over recognition of the People's Republic of China in the U.S. media.[124]

Powell's response to the Consulate seizure was to research the treaties. Consulting the 1943 "Treaty Between the United States of America and the Republic Of China for the Relinquishment of Extraterritorial Rights in

China and Regulation of Related Matters," Powell pointed out that the Nationalist Government had accorded the U.S. only the continued right to use the land in question, not ownership of the property. He noted that both the U.S. and the PRC agreed that the buildings on the land belong to the United States. The crux of the issue was simply that while the GMD was willing to allow the continued use of the land, the PRC was not.[125]

Once again Powell felt that the American response to the issue was out of proportion to the reality of the event:

> In any event it seems to us that Mr.Acheson's actions in ordering the recall of all American diplomatic and Consular representatives in China is an extremely severe step and one hardly justified by an argument over a piece of property scarcely totaling half a dozen acres. Recalling of diplomats is a measure usually associated in international circles with border incidents, mobilization and the like. Certainly relations between the United States and China, strained though they may be, are not in such a sorry state as this drastic action would seem to indicate.[126]

The recall of consular officials would add to the "already numerous disadvantages" facing U.S. businessmen and other residents in China, Powell felt, and further reduce American influence in Asia.[127]

Powell's arguments in favor of U.S. recognition of the PRC presupposed that such action would coincide with the establishment of normal diplomatic relations. Certainly it had worked that way when the Soviet Union had recognized the People's Republic. Normal diplomatic relations would, everyone assumed, allow resident businessmen and others to address the People's Government through their own recognized consular officials, and perhaps to get action on the many difficulties they faced. The *Review*'s initial coverage of the exchange of diplomatic notes occasioned by British recognition shows that it believed this would be the case.[128] But within a month, the *Review* quietly noted without comment that full diplomatic relations had not followed British recognition, and had yet to be negotiated.[129]

An article by professor Xiao Chien in *Da Gong Bao*, which the *Review* synopsized, explained that, while the Soviet Union had welcomed the establishment of the PRC with friendship and enthusiasm, the British did so merely to preserve their economic interests in China. Because Britain still followed the lead of the hostile United States, it likely sought diplomatic relations "as a means of undermining socialism," and had to be treated differently.[130]

British recognition did not result in any of the anticipated advantages. Businessmen were as beleaguered as before, and British consular officials were still ignored by Chinese authorities.[131] The withdrawal of American consular staff had put an end to the growing debate over recognition in the United States, and the disappointing results of British recognition rendered questionable several of the underlying premises of Powell's campaign for U.S. recognition of the PRC.

American recognition seemed ever more remote in Powell's view. He noted an increasing tendency in the American press and military circles to stress ". . . the importance of Taiwan as a base in the event of war with the Soviet Union." He saw this as the beginning of a campaign ". . . to whip up U.S. public sentiment in support of open American intervention to 'save' the island."[132] Yet, in spite of the mounting pressure for intervention, Powell believed that it was

> . . . extremely unlikely that the United States plans to risk getting its fingers burned twice. No matter how much the American government dislikes the prospect of a 'communist' Taiwan, it is obvious that nothing short of actual American participation -which would be an open invitation to war- can save the KMT's hide.[133]

Powell's last editorial on the recognition issue was written just prior to the outbreak of the Korean War, June 25, 1950, and appeared on the fifth day of hostilities. Once again he reviewed Secretary of State Acheson's three-part test for the recognition of governments, and pleaded that by any realistic interpretation of these, America should have recognized the People's Republic. Again he underscored the folly of continued recognition of the GMD as China's legal government. On the sticking point of foreign debts, he once more pointed out the injustice of expecting the PRC to assume payment of debts incurred by the Nationalist government:

> Has the American government withdrawn recognition from Britain, France or Germany because these countries defaulted on their World War I debts? Did the U.S. government accept the debts and obligations of the Confederacy following the American Civil War?[134]

By that time, of course, the outbreak of the Korean War and the U.S. deployment of the Seventh Fleet in the Straits between Taiwan and the Chinese mainland had rendered the *Review*'s recognition campaign a moot point.

*

In late March, 1950, with war clouds gathering between the two great powers, and the possibility of American intervention in Indochina, Taiwan or Korea all too apparent to the CCP leadership, Zhou Enlai addressed a challenge to PRC Foreign Ministry personnel. The U.S. imperialists hoped to mobilize Americans for a new war, he claimed. Although the American people were currently leading peaceful lives, unfortunately they were under the control of American monopoly capitalism.

> The information of our side cannot reach them. The monopoly capitalists are using vulgar culture to poison their people. It is the duty of the people of the world to awaken the American people. We Chinese people should

share this duty. . . We should influence the American people, and we should not shirk this duty.[135]

Zhou called for discrediting American efforts to organize NATO, to rearm Japan and Germany, and to mobilize the American people for war. He looked forward to restoring China's legal position in the United Nations as one step toward these ends. No doubt the appearance in 1950 of *People's China*, a government-sponsored English language journal, and the *Shanghai News*, a government- sponsored English language daily, were both related to efforts to influence the American people and international opinion in general.

The *China Weekly Review*, although moderate by Communist standards and not yet conforming to party line, had already proven itself to be a valuable ally in these efforts. Powell and the *Review* staff had devoted their efforts to documenting positive changes in the new China, explaining Chinese people's democracy in practice. They had thrown themselves into an extensive campaign for U.S. recognition of the new regime. The fact that the *Review* was American-owned and well known in the U.S. doubtless added to its utility in Communist eyes, and probably helped prolong its life.

The *Review* gradually adjusted itself. Although no oppositional press would be tolerated by China's new leaders, Powell approved of the basic reforms of the revolution, and had been able to voice restrained criticism where he felt it was justified. In his opinion, the *Review* was performing an important function by providing Americans an un-jaundiced view of the changes undertaken by the Chinese Revolution, a necessary corrective to the distortions of the pro-Chiang domestic American press.

The *Review* remained free but constricted by ideological parameters. By the eve of the Korean War, to what extent had the government and party been able to harness the press, consolidating its control and preparing the people for its domestic and foreign policy transformations? And how did this influence the editorial freedom and content of the *Review*?

CHAPTER NOTES

1. Powell believed that if American businessmen pulled out of China, their British counterparts would use the opportunity seize American market share and takeover U.S. investments.

2. The Ambassador in China (Stuart) to the Secretary of State, 13 June 1949, United States Department of State, *Foreign Relations of the United States, Diplomatic Papers 1949, Volume 8, The Far East: China.*(Washington D.C.: Government Printing Office, 1978.)p.756–7. Hereafter cited as *FRUS, 1949, Volume 8*.

3. The Ambassador in China (Stuart) to the Secretary of State, 13 June 1949, *FRUS, 1949, Volume 8*, p.756–7.

4. The Ambassador in China (Stuart) to the Secretary of State, 24 June 1949, *FRUS, 1949, Volume 8*, p.764.

5. The Ambassador in China (Stuart) to the Secretary of State, 18 July 1949, *FRUS, 1949, Volume 8*, p.791.

6. John Leighton Stuart, *Fifty Years in China the Memoirs of John Leighton Stuart, Missionary and Ambassador.*(New York: Random House, 1954.) p.241.

7. (Mao Zedong), Telegram, Central Military Commission to Su Yu, 27 April 1949 (Extract), Shuguang Zhang and Jian Chen, eds. *Chinese Communist Foreign Policy and the Cold War in Asia, New Documentary Evidence, 1944-1950,*(Chicago: Imprint Publications, 1996.) p.109. Hereafter cited as *CCF-PCWA.*

8. (Mao Zedong) Instruction, Central Military Commission, "Our Policy toward British and American Citizens and Diplomats," 28 April 1949, *CCFPCWA*, p.109-111.

9. The Ambassador in China (Stuart) to the Secretary of State, 23 July 1949, *FRUS, 1949, Volume 8*, p.799.

10. Huang Hua, "My Contact With Stuart After Nanking Liberation",trans. Li Xiaobing, *Chinese Historians 5* (Spring 1992): p. 47–56.

11. Telegram, CCP Central Committee to CCP Nanking Municipal Committee, 10 May 1949, *CCFPCWA*, p.112, n.44.

12. (Mao Zedong) Telegram, CCP Central Committee to Nanking Municipal Committee, 10 May 1949, *CCFPCWA*, p.111-112.

13. *Ibid*, p.112.

14. Stuart, *Fifty Years in China*, p.248.

15. (Mao Zedong), "Telegram, CCP Central Committee to CCP Nanking Municipal Committee, 10 May 1949", *CCFPCWA*. p.112.

16. Mao Tse-tung, "Mao Tse-tung on China's Future Government", *CWR*, 25 June 1949, p.82. Text of address to the Preparatory Meeting of the New Political Consultative Conference, 15 June 1949.

17. *Ibid.*

18. The Ambassador in China (Stuart) to the Secretary of State, 19 June 1949, *FRUS, 1949, Volume 8*, p.756.

19. The Ambassador in China (Stuart) to the Secretary of State, 24 June 1949, *FRUS, 1949, Volume 8*, p.764–5.

20. The Ambassador in China (Stuart) to the Secretary of State, 30 June 1949, *FRUS, 1949, Volume 8*, p.766-7.

21. *Ibid.*

22. The United States at first tried unsuccessfully to organize a uniform approach to recognition of the PRC among the Western powers, a "united front", so as to gain more leverage with Communist leaders in negotiating various unresolved matters, with the implied threat of isolation, should China become too close to the Soviet Union.

23. *Ibid.*

24. *Ibid*, p.767.

25. The Consul General at Peiping (Clubb) to the Secretary of State, 11 July 1949, *FRUS, 1949, Volume 8*, p.779; The Minister-Counceler of Embassy in China (Clark) to the Secretary of State, 2 July 1949, *FRUS, 1949, Volume 8*, p.770.

26. The Consul General at Shanghai (Cabot) to the Secretary of State, 1 July 1949, *FRUS, 1949, Volume 8*, p.769.

27. Walter Sullivan, "Employees in Shanghai Hold U.S. Editor In Move to Force Him to Reopen Paper", *New York Times*, 2 July 1949, p.4; Walter Sullivan,

"Shanghai Staff Accepts Apology for Scuffle Of U.S. Editor; Pattern for Foreigners Seen", *New York Times*, 6 July 1949, L,p.16; Walter Sullivan,"U.S. Editor Is Held Again In Shanghai", *New York Times*, 27 July 1949, L,p.16; Walter Sullivan, "Shanghai Staff Frees U.S. Editor", *New York Times*, 29 July 1949,L,p.5.

28. Ross Y. Koen, *The China Lobby in American Politics*, (New York: Octagon Books, 1974.) p.95.

29. *Congressional Record*, 81st Congress, 1st Session, Volume 95 (15 April 1949; 21 April 1949) p.3864.

30. *New York Times*, 25 June 1949, p.1.

31. Memorandum by Mr. John P. Davies of the Policy Planning Staff to the Director of the Staff (Kennan), 30 June 1949, *FRUS, 1949, Volume 8*, p.768-9.

32. *Ibid.*

33. The Minister-Counselor of Embassy in China (Clark) to the Secretary of State, 2 July 1949, *FRUS, 1949, Volume 8*, p. 770.

34. *Congressional Record*, 81st Congress, 1st Session, Volume 95 (24 June 1949), 8292-8293; Ross Y.Koen, *The China Lobby*,p.96; E.J. Kahn,Jr. *The China Hands, America's Foreign Service Officers and What Befell Them*. (New York: Penguin Books, 1975) p.193.

35. Memorandum by Mr, John P.Davies of the Policy Planning Staff to the Director of the Staff (Kennan), 30 June 1949, *FRUS, 1949, Volume 8*, p.768.

36. The Secretary of State to the Ambassador in China (Stuart), 1 July 1949, *FRUS, 1949, Volume 8*, p.769.

37. Memorandum by the Secretary of State of a Conversation With the President, 11 July 1949, *FRUS, 1949, Volume 8*, p.780-1.

38. The Ambassador in China (Stuart) to the Secretary of State, 18 July 1949, *FRUS, 1949, Volume 8*, p.791.

39. *Ibid.*

40. The Consul General at Shanghai (Cabot) to the Secretary of State, 7 July 1949, *FRUS, 1949, Volume 8*, p.1263.

41. *Ibid.*

42. Charles J. Canning, "The Question of Recognition", *CWR*, 11 June 1949, p. 34-5.

43. *Ibid.*

44. *Ibid.*

45. Powell, ed. "Same Old Pattern", *CWR*, 18 June 1949, p.50.

46. Powell, ed. "Realistic Approach", *CWR*, 25 June 1949, p.72-3.

47. Powell, ed. "Fourth of July", *CWR*, 2 July 1949, p.93-4.

48. Mao Tse-tung, "The People's Democratic Dictatorship", *CWR*, 9 July 1949, p.131-4.

49. Charles J. Canning, "Notes on China's Domestic and Foreign Policy", *CWR*, 16 July 1949, p.143-5.

50. *Ibid.*

51. Memorandum by the Chief of the Division of Chinese Affairs (Sprouse) to Mr. Livingston T. Merchant of the Office of Far Eastern Affairs, 15 August 1949, *FRUS, 1949, Volume 8*,p.1316-17; "The Charge' in China (Clark) to the Secretary of State", 14 August 1949, *FRUS, 1949, Volume 8*, p. 1315-6.

52. The Consul at Shanghai (McConaughy) to the Secretary of State, 19 August 1949, *FRUS, 1949, Volume 8*, p.1276-79.

53. These cities were: Chongqing, Kunming, Dihua, Qingdao, Hankou and Guangzhou. The Consulates in Shanghai, Beijing, Nanjing and Tianjin remained open. (Mukden [Shenyang] had been closed in May due to the house arrest of Ward).

54. Edwin W.Martin, *Divided Counsel, the Anglo-American Response to Communist Victory in China.*(Lexington: The University Press of Kentucky, 1986.) p.57,58.

55. Powell, ed. "The Evacuation Ship", *CWR*, 27 August 1949, p.228.

56. *Ibid.*

57. Powell, ed. "Two Policies", *CWR*, 3 September 1949, p.2; "Escort for British Ships to Shanghai", *North China Daily News*, 9 October 1949,p.1.

58. Powell, ed. "World's Richest Refugees", *CWR*, 24 September 1949, p.44.

59. Powell, "An Open Letter To Passengers On the 'General Gordon'", *CWR*, 24 September 1949, p.46.

60. *Ibid.*

61. Powell, "An Open Letter to Passengers On the "General Gordon'", *CWR*, 24 September 1949, p.46.

62. "Seamen's Union Fetes General Gordon Crew", *North China Daily News*, 25 September 1949, p.3.

63. "Nationalists Reported Tightening Blockade", *North China Daily News*, 17 September 1949, p.2; "No Solution", *North China Daily News*, 23 September 1949,p.3; "British Navy Criticized Over Blockade", *North China Daily News*, 24 September 1949,p.2.

64. "104 Americans Here Ask US to Break Blockade", *North China Daily News*, 22 September 1949, p.1; *New York Times*, 22 September 1949, 3: p.5. The *North China Daily News* reported that "Mr.John W.Powell of the *China Weekly Review*" was one of three sponsors of the petition.

65. *New York Times*, 22 September 1949, 3: p.5.

66. "104 Americans Here Ask US to Break Blockade", *North China Daily News*, 22 September 1949, p.1.

67. The Consul General at Tientsin (Smyth) to the Secretary of State, 29 September 1949, *FRUS, 1949, Volume 8*, p.542.

68. "PPCC Proclaims Republic", *CWR*, 1 October 1949, p.64. The Common Program of the PPCC, adopted in 1949, functioned as a provisional constitution, until a state constitution was promulgated in 1954. Mao's New Democracy consisted of a four-class dictatorship of the workers, peasants, petty bourgeoisie, and national bourgeoisie, in which CCP direction would duplicate the economic development that theoretically would have followed a bourgeois revolution, while at the same time repressing the reactionaries: i.e. landlords, bureaucratic capitalists, and those who favored the imperialists.

69. Lee Tsung-ying, "The New Village Democracy", *CWR*, 1 October 1949, p.61–3; Fei Hsiao-tung, "My Search For Democracy", *CWR*, 1 October 1949, p.65–6.

70. Fei Hsiao-tung, "My Search For Democracy", *CWR*, 1 October 1949, p.65–6.

71. See Chapter Two of this dissertation.

72. Fei Hsiao-tung, "My Search For Democracy", *CWR*, 1 October 1949, p. 65–6.

73. *Ibid.*

74. *Ibid.*

75. Lee Tsung-Ying, "The New Village Democracy", *CWR*, 1 October 1949, p.61–3.

76. *Ibid.*

77. *Ibid.*

78. "People's Political Consultative Council Proclaims Republic", *CWR*, 1 October 1949, p.64.

79. *Ibid.* The *Review* also printed *New China News Agency*'s English translation of the "Common Program of the Chinese People's Political Consultative Conference" on 8 October 1949, p.104.

80. The Consul General at Peiping (Clubb) to the Secretary of State, 1 October 1949, *FRUS, 1949, Volume 8,* p.544–45; The Consul General at Peiping (Clubb) to the Secretary of State, 2 October 1949, United States Department of State, *Foreign Relations of the United States, Diplomatic Papers, 1949, Volume 9, the Far East: China.* (Washington D.C.: Government Printing Office, 1974.) p.93. Hereafter cited as *FRUS, 1949, Volume 9.* In his letter to the United States government, Chou said in part: "I consider that it is necessary that there be established normal diplomatic relations between the People's Republic of China and all countries of the world."

81. Foster Rhea Dulles, *American Policy Toward Communist China, 1949–1969.*(New York: Thomas Y. Cromwell Company,1972)p.50; Powell, ed. "What will America Do?", *CWR*, 15 October 1949,p.92.

82. Powell, ed. "What Will America Do?", *CWR*, 15 October 1949, p.92.

83. *Ibid.*

84. *Ibid.*

85. *Ibid.*p.93.

86. Department of State, *Bulletin*, 15 October 1951, p.603.

87. Department of State, *Transcript of Round-table Discussions on American Policy Toward China*, (Washington D.C.: U.S. Government Printing Office, 1949).

88. *Ibid.* These included Edwin O. Reischauer, John King Fairbank, Owen Lattimore, Lawrence K. Rosinger, and many others.

89. *New York Times*, 29 April 1950, p.16; *Ibid*, 5 January 1950, p.8.

90. *The New Republic*, 7 November 1949, p.24.

91. *The New Republic*, 12 December 1949, p.52.

92. *New York Times*, 11 October 1949, p.24 (Knowland); *Ibid.*,22 December 1949, p.1 (Vandenberg); *Ibid.*, 2 December 1949, p.15 (Lodge).

93. *New York Times*, 21 October 1949, p.6; *Ibid.*, 29 November 1949, p.14; *Ibid.*, 17 January 1950, p.3.

94. Foster Rhea Dulles, *American Policy Toward Communist China*, p.50.

95. Ross Y.Koen, *The China Lobby*, p.202–3; Foster Rhea Dulles, *American Policy Toward Communist China*, p.50–1.

96. Powell, ed. "Definition of Government", *CWR*, 29 October 1949, p.128–9.

97. *Ibid.*

98. Powell, ed. "Definition of Government", *CWR*, 29 October 1949, p.128–9.

99. "Liberation of Canton", *CWR*, 22 October 1949, p.117.

100. Powell, ed. "Another Hole in Blockade", *CWR*, 22 October 1949, p.110.

101. "Blockade Hurts U.S. Trade", *CWR*, 19 November 1949, p.187–8.

102. Mary Barrett, "The Ward Case", *CWR*, 14 January 1949, p.104–6; Martin, *Divided Counsel*, p.80.

103. Mary Barrett, "The Ward Case", *CWR*, 14 January 1950, p.104–6.

104. *Ibid.*

105. The Consul-General at Peiping (Clubb) to the Secretary of State, 26 October 1949, *FRUS, 1949, Volume 8*, p.984–85. Clubb quotes a 25 October 1949, *Hsinhua* news broadcast from Peking; The Consul General at Peiping (Clubb) to the Secretary of State, 27 October 1949, *Ibid.*,p.986–7. Quotes *Hsinhua* broadcast, 26 October, Mukden.

106. Mary Barrett,"The Ward Case", *CWR*, 14 January 1950,p.106.

107. *Ibid.*

108. Powell, ed. "U.S. Trade Ban Hits China", *CWR*, 19 November 1949, p.180–1.

109. Powell, ed. "U.S. Trade Ban Will Not Cripple China", *CWR*, 10 December 1949, p.23–4.

110. Martin, *Divided Counsel*, p.95.

111. Powell, ed. "America's Best Interests", *CWR*, 31 December 1949, p.66–7.

112. *Ibid.*

113. *Ibid.*

114. The Consul at Taipei (Edgar) to the Secretary of State, 23 December 1949, *FRUS, 1949, Volume 9*, p.451–5 Edgar reported that the Nationalists had no support among the people of Taiwan and that they could not maintain their hold on the island without outside help; Memorandum by the Assistant Secretary of State for Far Eastern Affairs (Butterworth) to the Secretary of State, 28 December 1949, *FRUS, 1949, Volume 9*, p.460; *New York Times*,4 January 1950; Hungdah Chiu,ed. *China and the Question of Taiwan, Official Documents, 1662-1950.* (New York: Praeger, 1973.) U.S.Department of State, Policy Information Paper-Formosa. Special Guidance No.28, 23 December 1949. p.217–220.

115. Department of State, *Bulletin*, 16 January 1950, p.79.

116. *Ibid.*, 23 January 1950, p.111–18.

117. Martin, *Divided Counsel*, p.102–3.

118. Powell, ed. "How Much Longer?", *CWR*, 14 January 1950, p.102–3.

119. *Ibid.*

120. Powell, ed. "How Much Longer?", *CWR*, 14 January 1950, p.102–3.

121. Department of State, *Bulletin*, 23 January 1950, p.119–20; The Secretary of State to the Consul General at Peiping, 8 December 1949, *FRUS, 1949, Volume 8*, p.1121 (U.S. rationale for not paying taxes on the property); "A Peking Report of the Consular Property Dispute", *CWR*, 11 February 1950, p.168–9.

122. Memorandum by the Acting Secretary of State to the President, 10 January 1950, United States Department of State, *Foreign Relations of the United States, 1950, Volume 6: East Asia and the Pacific.*(Washington D.C.: Government Printing Office, 1976.) p.270–2.Hereafter cited as *FRUS, 1950, Volume 6.*

123. The Secretary of State to the Consul at Peiping, 10 January 1950, *FRUS, 1950, Volume 6*, p.275; The Consul General at Peiping (Clubb) to the Secretary of State, 12 January 1950, *FRUS 1950, Volume 6.*p.276–7; Department of State, *Bulletin*, 20 February 1950, p.302.

124. Martin, *Divided Counsel*, p.108–9.

125. Powell, ed. "U.S. Conulate Dispute", *CWR*, 28 January 1950, p.134–5.

126. *Ibid.*

127. *Ibid.*

128. "British Recognition", *CWR*, 14 January 1950, p.110.

129. "Diplomatic Relations", *CWR*, 11 February 1950,p.175; Martin, *Divided Counsel*, p.101–3. The British expected that their de jura recognition of the People's Republic on January 6 would also mark the beginning of diplomatic relations. But when Charge d'Affaires ad interim John C. Hutchinson arrived in Beijing, he was informed by the Chinese government that diplomatic relations would have to be negotiated.

130. *Ta Kung Pao,* 17 January 1950; *"Ta Kung Pao*: Sino-British Diplomatic Relations", *CWR*, 28 January 1950,p.145.

131. Martin, *Divided Counsel*, p.103.

132. Powell, ed. "Last Act on Taiwan", *CWR*, 17 June 1950, p.38–9; *Time*, 22 May 1950.

133. Powell, ed. "Last Act on Taiwan", *CWR*, 17 June 1950, p.39.

134. Powell, ed. "Practical Politics", *CWR*, 1 July 1950, p.74–5.

135. Zhou Enlai, "On the International Situation and Our Diplomatic Affairs after the Signing of the Sino-Soviet Alliance Treaty," 20 March 1950, CCFPCWA, p. 145.

CHAPTER EIGHT

ACCOMMODATION AND REASSESSMENT:
THE WINDS OF IDEOLOGICAL CHANGE

Between December 9, 1949, and October 28, 1950, the People's Republic promulgated the "Provisional Press Laws and Regulations of the Central Government of the People's Republic of China" regarding newspapers, and periodicals. These laws attempted to prescribe the exact role and function of the press in Communist China, to organize and coordinate all press organs under the direction of a government-controlled administration, and to harmonize the press with the policies and goals of the Communist leadership. A perusal of these regulations reveals there were no exceptions for any publications, public or private, Chinese or foreign.[1] This chapter will examine the means by which the editorial policy of the *China Weekly Review*, and its understanding of the central government's position on various issues, were brought into closer alignment.

We have seen that Zhou Enlai felt it was the Party's duty to place its case before the American people and the world. Towards this end, in early 1950 the CCP founded *People's China*, an English language monthly, and the *Shanghai News*, an English language daily. The *Review*, because it was already well known in the United States, was a potentially important vehicle in this effort.

A close reading of the *Review* during this period reveals an increasing coordination with topics and campaigns generally undertaken by the Chinese press which were guided by the central government. Some of this coordination was due to the replacement of Nationalist and Western wire services with Communist ones. But there was more. Although the power of the central government was as yet weak and a high degree of local autonomy prevailed during the first year of the PRC, by early 1950 the Central People's Government had already taken steps to harness the nation's press for didactic purposes and to mobilize support for its policies. Since these efforts effected the *Review* as well, they must be taken into account.

✻

CHANGES IN THE PRESS, MAY 1949-JUNE 1950

Shortly after the fall of Shanghai, Communist authorities took initial steps toward reorganizing the press. They set up a "Cultural and Educational Committee" of five members to investigate GMD holdings among Shanghai's publications, and to administer those confiscated. The assets of all Guomindang-owned or connected papers, or publications owned by the Guomindang's "big four" families (Jiang, Kung, Soong, and Chen) were to be seized by the government.[2]

A set of rules governing the operation of all Chinese-owned newspapers and journals was promulgated by the Military Control Commission of the People's Liberation Army in Shanghai on May 28, 1949. This nine-point set of regulations which was drafted by the People's Publication Control Commission, forbade fabricating rumors, libeling the people's democratic principles, and revealing military secrets. They required all Chinese-owned papers to suspend operation temporarily and to submit a year's file of back issues for inspection along with information on the journal's ownership before they could be re-licensed to open again.[3]

The Shanghai dailies *Shi Shi Xinbao* and the *Da Wan Bao* , both owned by the prominent GMD family of H.H. Kung, devolved into government hands. The GMD-supervised *Shun Bao* (affiliated with the Guomindang's CC Clique)[4] was taken over by the CCP which began publishing the Party's Shanghai organ, *Jiefang Ribao*, in its plant. *Sin Wen Bao*, another GMD-supervised journal, was reorganized as the *Sin Wen Ribao*, under joint government-private ownership. Most former GMD-affiliated journals which were reorganized under a new name retained their former staff, the former editors having fled or resigned. *Da Gong Bao*, perhaps the best known independently owned liberal journal, continued publishing after Wu Dingzhang, one of its stock holders who was affiliated with the Political Science Group of the GMD[5], resigned from the journal's board of directors.[6]

By July, 1949, the Central Government took a step toward bringing all journalists and newspaper employees under closer supervision when it consolidated various editors, journalists' associations, and newspaper workers' unions into a single mass National Newspaper Worker's Association. The Association's Preparatory Committee, convened in Beijing, included Powell's old friend from OWI days, Liu Zunqi, who at that time was editor of the *United Pictorial Magazine* in Shanghai.[7]

Aside from the *China Weekly Review*, there were four English- language dailies in pre-Communist Shanghai:the *Shanghai Evening Post and Mercury*, owned by the American C.V. Starr, the British *North China Daily News*, owned by the Morris family, the *China Daily Press* owned mainly by H.H.Kung, and the Nationalist Government's own *China Daily Tribune*. The two latter journals, being GMD affiliated, were confiscated, while the *Shanghai Evening Post*, as noted previously, was closed by its editor over a disagreement with its employees.[8]

While no regulations had as yet been promulgated for *foreign* journals as of summer 1949, the *North China Daily News* discovered that the authorities expected it to behave as if the decrees pertaining to Chinese journals applied to it as well. The *Review* had defended the *North China Daily News* and the *Shanghai Evening Post*, which had repeated the North China *Daily News'* harbor mining allegations. At that time Powell had pleaded for a ruling by the government that would clarify how the regime expected foreign publications to proceed.[9] But in general, as Randall Gould observed, foreign journalists during the first few months of liberation ". . . could hardly locate officials of any sort."[10]

At this early juncture it was not clear to foreign journalists what CCP policy toward the resident foreign press was, beyond protecting foreign property. In early 1949, the Chinese Communist Party Central Committee sent tentative instructions to cadres in urban centers concerning foreign-owned journals and newspapers which were similar to some of the regulations issued by Shanghai authorities during July, 1949 for Chinese owned publications. Cadres were to take no immediate action concerning foreign-owned journals but were to order them to present the year's file of issues as a condition for registration. After a period of investigation, some would be ordered to cease publication while others would not be interfered with nor would the Party allow them to be taken over by Chinese citizens.[11]

The CCP Central Committee instructed the Tianjin and Beijing Municipal Committees to refuse to grant interviews or to answer the questions of foreign correspondents. Local authorities were to be evasive: "If by chance [our people] are encountered and enquired (sic) about our attitude toward foreign correspondents, they may reply that they have not considered the question."[12] Again, after a period of observation, correspondents were tentatively ordered to go through registration and examinations, with those who "fit our needs" being allowed to remain in China, functioning as journalists.[13]

PRESS COORDINATION, THOUGHT REFORM, AND THE *REVIEW*

This uncertainty had given way by 1950 to a well developed and guided national press policy. This was due to two factors: the creation of the Press Administration of the Central People's Government, established in February, 1950; and the advent of the ideological study movement (Xuexi) in October, 1949 and the criticism / self criticism movement (Zhengfeng), in which the *China Weekly Review*, as well as the rest of the country, became deeply involved. Both of these elements were intertwined and mutually reinforcing.

The Press Administration was responsible for the political training of journalists, the supervision of newspapers, supplying guidance for the editorial policies of the nation's journals to keep them in harmony with party policies and projects, managing the CCP's official news agency *Xinhua*, and its branches, and supplying the nation's press with photos, graphics,etc. Journals were supposed to send a monthly report to the Press Administration relating any difficulties carrying out its directives.[14]

The Press Administration was also in charge of regulating propaganda to foreign countries. Jiao Guanhua directed the China Information Service which produced propaganda for consumption outside China and edited *People's China*, an English-language magazine which authoritatively covered governmental and party policies. Jiao's immediate subordinate was Powell's old friend, Liu Zunqi, who had been chief of the translation department of the United States Office of War Information in Chongqing while Powell was stationed there during World War II. According to Powell, Liu had studied in the U.S, just after the war on a scholarship.[15]

While having a friend in a position of power certainly did not garner the *Review* any special privileges nor even insure its survival, it probably did not hurt matters either.[16] Concerning the question of which foreign journals and journalists would be allowed to continue functioning in China, it no doubt helped that the Vice-Director of the China Information Bureau of the Central People's Government[17] was thoroughly familiar with the *China Weekly Review* and its editor.

A month after its founding, the Press Administration of the Central People's Government convened the National Press Work Conference, a nationwide conference of all journalists from March 29 to April 16, 1950.[18] Having created machinery capable of coordinating the nation's journals and broadcast media, both public and private with government policies, it was now time to put it into practice. At the conference, the Press Administration communicated four major directives from the Central Government of the PRC to the nation's journalists.

First, newspapers and journals were to devote more space and attention to people's labor in farm and factory, to discuss problems and successes in production. Stories about new records set by factory workers, the rebuilding of bridges, or the elimination of pests by peasants, according to Liu Zunqi, would establish a stronger link between the masses and the publication, while providing valuable instruction to the people on different methods that might be incorporated into their own work.[19]

For the next three years the *Review*'s content reflected this directive with a steady stream of articles describing the building of dams, hydro-electric projects, new apartment blocks, improvements in agricultural production, etc. Powell tacitly acknowledged this when he wrote that several American readers

> ... have said they get the impression (from the *Review*) that the Chinese people are so busy building dams, leveling mountains, and in general remaking their country that they have no time for relaxation or entertainment.[20]

Since the *Review* wished to make the positive accomplishments of the revolution known to the Western public, this directive did not clash with Powell's basic editorial policy.

Second, newspapers and journals were instructed to centralize direction and management in the hands of the editor (who might then be held more directly accountable for failing to coordinate his journal's policy with the efforts of other journals). This seemed to counter to some degree the trend toward more inclusion of pressmen, reporters, and staff in editorial decision-making that was apparent soon after the Communists came to power in Shanghai.[21] It also tends to confirm Powell's testimony before the Senate Judiciary Subcommittee in 1954, that he alone was responsible for the content of his journal.[22]

Yet, editors were by no means absolute and a large element of collective responsibility seems to have remained. According to Liu Zunqi, "Among the press workers themselves, the old division of labor had been changed. The old method of distinguishing news editing from news gathering, and writing from editing no longer holds."[23] The *Review*'s assistant editor Alun Falconer explained that

> On the typical newspaper now, the editor is the highest authority. The editor decides policy, although there are regular conferences of department chiefs. Reporters are expected to play a new role and their responsibilities have increased.It is said that the emphasis of responsibility, in comparison with American dailies, is shifting from the editorial to the reporting staff.[24]

After reporters wrote their copy, it was put before a meeting of the reporting and editorial staffs together, who decided what to use, how much to use, and what to emphasize.[25]

Falconer said that the press was supposed to treat news as an opportunity to educate the public. Referring to a recently reported case of a corrupt official, he observed "the press was expected to explain the social sources and causes of corruption in this case, as in others like it, and show how corruption can be overcome."[26] According to Liu Zunqi, both editors and reporters were to seek closer ties to the people.[27]

Third, newspapers and journals were to establish "correspondents networks" and to encourage the formation of "newspaper reading groups" whenever possible. Both of these tasks were seen as important means of securing closer ties between the journal and the masses. Correspondents might be workers writing about changes instituted in their factories or peasants reporting on the progress of land reform in their villages or individuals recounting their experiences in the political study movement.[28]

In many papers, the educational standards of worker or peasant correspondents were quite low. Although this was not so for the *China Weekly Review*, since it remained closely tied to the intelligentsia, Falconer observed that the inexperience of amateur correspondents, who were paid for their contributions, created more work for editors and reporters who had to rewrite their articles. He also noted that it had been easier to recruit correspondents in areas where literacy was high than it had been in factory and field.[29]

Falconer said the authorities attached "great political importance" to expanding the network of correspondents. They were to serve as the eyes and ears of the press in every aspect of the nation's life. Correspondents were also integrated into the institution of self-criticism, thought reform, and the study movement.[30] This became quite evident in the *Review* as well.

Newspaper reading groups, which all journals were to encourage, were an important means of ideological education in a society where illiteracy was as yet the plight of most workers and peasants. Articles were read aloud in these small groups, and then discussed. During the Korean War, the *Review* would be used in a similar fashion among American prisoners of war[31]

The fourth and final directive which the Conference placed before the nation's press was the responsibility of criticizing the failings of government agencies, administrators, economic organizations, and cadres. The practice of criticism\self-criticism was to be extended to the government itself by the people through the intermediary of the nation's journals and newspapers. In effect, the press was being asked to involve itself in party/government rectification.

On April 19, 1950 the CCP Central Committee promulgated its "Decisions Regarding the Development of Criticism and Self-Criticism Through the Press" which called on all party members to welcome and support ". . . criticism which reflects the opinions of the masses." Ignoring such criticism was "strongly condemned," as were any ". . . bureaucratic attitudes which restrict the publication of such criticism or receive it in a hostile way by counter-attack, revenge or ridicule."[32]

Xia Yan, director of the Shanghai Bureau of Cultural Affairs, said that since April, 1950, the organizations under his direction (the Bureau of Education, the Bureau of Cultural Affairs, and the Press and Publications Office of the Shanghai Municipal People's Government) had

> . . . promoted extensively the movement of self-criticism and mutual criticism in accordance with the 'Directives Concerning the Promotion of Self-Criticism and Mutual Criticism in the Newspapers and Magazines' issued by the local people's government and mobilized the people of the whole city to examine, supervise, criticize and correct the work done by the government in Shanghai as well as the working style of the cadres.[33]

The Shanghai People's Government decided that, in carrying out criticism of the government, its agencies, and personnel, editors were to work closely with government officials under the control of the Press Administration which would help them to distinguish constructive from malicious self-criticism.[34]

For a small private journal like the *Review*, the safest part of the Press Administration's fourth directive was that which enjoined editors to pay particular attention to letters to the editor. The *Review* had always done this, and soon its pages echoed with accounts of the ideological reformation of its urban intellectual readership.

*

IDEOLOGICAL RETRAINING OF JOURNALISTS

Mao Zedong, in a speech delivered to the editorial staff of the *Shansi-Suiyuan Daily* in April, 1948, indicated that CCP policy was to utilize journals as didactic instruments to help educate the people politically and to explain government directives. Because the press of China would supply most of the textual materials used in "political studies" (thought reform) by all walks of people, Mao insisted it was first necessary that journalists and editors, Communists and non-Communists alike, should reform their own thinking so as to bring it into line with the political orthodoxy of the new regime.

The Press Administration consequently established the Beijing Journalism School to systematize the training or re-training of editors and reporters. The Press Administration directed other professional journalism schools throughout the country, operated by municipal or provincial authorities, and it also cooperated with the CCP's Department of Propaganda in training editors either on the job or by establishing special short courses.[35]

Special "revolutionary" universities were established in each military control district for the ideological re-education of intellectuals, whose services the CCP needed to run the schools, universities, government bureaucracy, postal system, etc.[36] In Shanghai, the revolutionary university was called the East China University of Political Science and Military Studies.[37] Within it, by early 1950, the Press and Publications Department of the Shanghai People's Government in cooperation with the Press Administration ran a school of journalism for the political re-education of the city's editors and newspapermen.[38]

The *Review* acknowledged the establishment of the revolutionary university, and pointed out the need for such an ideological institution in Shanghai:

> There has been a shortage of journalists who could cope with the political demands of the new situation. However, there is a school of journalism in the East China University, the new politically oriented university that has been established by the government.[39]

Journalism schools in the city's established universities still retained the pre-1949 faculty, the article noted, who were undergoing the slow process of ideological remolding, and consequently could not fill the current need.[40]

The Press and Publications Department of the Shanghai People's Government also helped organize local associations of journalistic workers into groups to carry out ideological study and thought reform.[41] It held press conferences and explicated the government's policies and decrees to newsmen, who then publicized and explained them to the public. In his "Report", Xia Yan held that Shanghai, China's "foremost center of private newspapers, publications, and broadcast stations," had ". . . always been an important battle front in the ideological struggle."[42] He pledged that the Press and Publication Office would ". . . continue to organize and guide Shanghai's press, publication and broadcasting to wage an arduous ideological struggle."[43]

In Shanghai the Press and Publication Office also had the responsibility ". . . to help promising private-operated press or publication enterprises to overcome their difficulties."[44] Between December 1949 and September 1950, the Office had recommended 73 publishers to local banks for loans totaling 3,823,500,000 RMB (renminbiao) to help them weather the difficult economic times.[45] This was welcome news to many privately owned journals which, like the *Review*, had seen their advertizing revenues evaporate.

*

THE GREAT STUDY MOVEMENT OF OCTOBER 1949-JUNE 1950

According to Guo Moro, a well known Communist writer who chaired the Central Government's Committee on Cultural and Educational Affairs, "A large scale study movement was set going through the entire country after the Central People's Government was established." Invoking Mao, Guo explained that it was necessary for the people to ". . . unlearn the bad habits and thoughts acquired from the old society."[46]

Since 1942, the Party had developed and perfected the techniques for ideological reform in rectification campaigns designed to insure that diverse elements absorbed into the rapidly growing CCP conformed to Party orthodoxy and discipline. The CCP membership had grown 2000% between 1937 and 1949. Through a program of intense ideological study, small group criticism / self-criticism sessions, and work among the peasants, new cadres struggled to eradicate their non-proletarian ideas, to cement their primary loyalty to the Party, and to internalize common goals and a common ideological weltanschauung.[47]

In 1949, these same methods were applied to non-Party personnel as well: government workers, former GMD officers, factory workers, peasants, and most importantly from the *Review*'s perspective, China's urban intellectuals, including students.[48] The CCP did not have enough trained personnel to run the schools, government offices, banks, etc. with its own cadres, and would have to rely on these groups, whose loyalty was questionable, well into the foreseeable future. Many upper level intellectuals, the traditional leaders of Chinese society, had been educated either in American Universities in China or in the United States and looked to the capitalist West, not the USSR for inspiration. Since Mao had indicated that China was going to "lean to the side of the USSR" in the Cold War, it was imperative that her intellectuals reverse this bias. A Nation-wide mass study movement (Xuexi) comprising the whole population was put into effect.

Government workers came to work early to participate in daily group study sessions. University professors joined with student associations and support staff to pursue ideological remolding and self-criticism in small group discussions. Elementary and secondary school teachers attended short-term institutes and training classes for political indoctrination, and thousands of intellectuals representing many professions attended the six month training courses at the new revolutionary universities.[49] Virtually the entire population was drawn into the study movement as it gained momentum from late fall, 1949, through the spring of 1950.

Mao recommended criticism/self-criticism as the main tool to cement the revolutionary coalition of classes which the CCP claimed as its base. He also imputed to it a quasi-constitutional standing:

> To attain the objective of cementing the revolutionary united front, we must adopt the method of criticism and self-criticism according to the Common Program. The main criterion when adopting this method is our present great basic law-the Common Program. We have adopted the method of criticism and self-criticism at this meeting. This is an excellent method, which prompts everyone of us to uphold truth and correct errors. This is the only correct method for all the revolutionary people in a people's state to carry out self-education and self-reformation.[50]

Mao explained that the CCP would not use coercion among the ranks of the people. Instead it would employ the "democratic" methods of "education and persuasion." He further indicated that:

> The nature of this kind of educational work is that of self-education within the ranks of the people and criticism and self-criticism is the fundamental method of self-education."[51]

Guo Moro, in his June, 1950 Report to the National Committee of the People's Political Consultative Conference, outlined the progress of the "Great Study Movement."[52]

> Political institutes and training classes have been set up throughout the country. In universities and middle schools, political classes on the history

of social development, political economy and new democracy have been instituted and political studies have also been organized among teachers.[53]

"Self-criticism is practiced by many old-style intellectuals and government personnel," Guo reported, in order to eradicate their predilection for a "middle road" between socialism and capitalism and to encourage "the idea of serving the people" among them. He called for greater efforts "to win over all patriotic intellectuals," whose help the party would need to "reform the old educational system."[54]

To help promote the "Great Study Movement," the government had organized ". . . literary and artistic propaganda work, newspapers, broadcasts, exhibitions and published books and journals in large numbers." Guo called attention to the National Journalists' Conference called by the Press Administration in April (1950) and opined that ". . . it had established closer ties with the masses," had developed "criticism and self-criticism" and had improved all journals' foci and coverage of economic reconstruction.[55]

✻

THOUGHT REFORM AND THE *CHINA WEEKLY REVIEW*

As enquiring journalists, the *Review* staff from the very beginning sought to understand the new regime, its motivation and probable direction. Only a month after the PLA took over Shanghai, contributing editor Charles J.Canning concluded that:

> A correct and clear understanding of the Communist concept of democracy is essential if one is to follow intelligently what is happening and what is going to happen in this country. Without a background knowledge of Mao's doctrine of new democracy, it is utterly impossible to understand or judge the policies of the Chinese Communists.[56]

Accordingly, Canning quoted extensively from Mao's "On New Democracy" and "On Coalition Government".

Shortly afterward, the *Review* printed Mao's speech on the Twentieth Anniversary of the CCP, "The People's Democratic Dictatorship," an important item for small-group study. Henceforth, the *Review* published English translations of all important speeches, which were indexed and sold in reprint form. As the post office increasingly took over the sales and distribution of journals, these reprints were readily available for group study by intellectuals who wished to practice English while digesting the new ideology, and for foreigners who wished to understand the new regime.

The first description of thought reform in the *Review* appeared in mid-July, 1949. Duncan Lee, a frequent contributor, described the advent of criticism/self-criticism and small group study at the post office where he worked:

'Learn, learn again' [paraphrasing Mao] has become the slogan. In an effort to keep abreast of what has been done and is now going on in the liberated areas, and to learn about the New Democracy, some 1500 employees have banded together to learn under Communist guidance.[57]

After each task, a discussion was held and Lee ". . . began to realize that such self-criticism plays an important part in their [the Communists] success in many fields."[58]

Another article, "Why the Communists Win," outlined the practice of the "Small Group System" among new Party members:

1. Each member of the group learns from the group through self-criticism and the criticism of others. . . .
2. There is mutual supervision. The members of a group supervise one another and also encourage one another to be firm in their faith and loyalty to the party. Under this type of mutual supervision there is scarcely room for half-heartedness and corruption.[59]

That same month former *Review* correspondent H.C. Huang, who had recently joined the PLA, recounted the practice of criticism/self-criticism and ideological study among soldiers.[60]

An August 1949 feature article in the *Review* described the new revolutionary universities designed to reeducate ". . . former students, workers, government functionaries, office workers, small businessmen, and soldiers, persons of various political leanings."[61] All participants took six month courses covering Marxism-Leninism, government policies, and the history of the CCP. Each class of about two hundred-fifty persons was divided into groups of twenty-five, and further divided into guided discussion groups of eight.

In small groups what is called 'criticism and self-criticism' is practiced.One may point out his or another's defects in the meeting and suggest points for improvement, or confess what he has done during the Nationalist regime and repent.This has brought out one amusing point: The Communists are atheists, yet the very weapon of religion-confession and repentance-is used to convert their former political enemies.[62]

The author noted that "Both in teaching and study, the practice of criticism and self-criticism is used."[63]

A former Honan University student in July, 1949, related the efforts of 2,500 fellow students to reform their thinking through special political training courses. He and his fellow students ". . . joined these political training courses just last week because we realize that our education for many years has been a reactionary one." Having given up individual study for collective study, they now spent ". . . two-thirds of their time in small groups discussing whatever they have learned."[64]

Assistant Editor Mary Barret wrote an article recounting the changes in private religious colleges and universities throughout China and particularly in Shanghai. Christian Universities altered their curriculum to teach New Democracy, dialectical studies, historical materialism, and the history of social development to incoming freshmen. Second-year students studied New Democracy and the history of the Chinese Revolution. Personnel to teach these new subjects were recommended by the Shanghai Bureau of Higher Education.[65]

Another article sketched changes in the curriculum and political training of teachers in the East China region. Here 2000 university and college faculty and 4000 primary school teachers attended special courses lasting one or two months studying the principles of the New Democracy. Shanghai authorities called numerous meetings of educators as well, to keep them informed of the new government's policies.[66]

A Fudan University student told how his fellow students and their teachers organized themselves into a single body to ". . . take the fullest advantage of self-criticism and mutual criticism, the two weapons of Marxism-Leninism."[67] A future doctor at the People's Medical College reported:

> We have been studying here for half a year, in which time we have studied politics and developed a severe system of self-criticism. Now we know what we did wrong in the old days and how we can improve ourselves in order to serve the people in the future.[68]

Francis H. Chow, a frequent contributor on thought reform and teacher at Fudan University, explained the need for criticism and self-criticism:

> We must wash our faces in the morning. If we fail to do so, they will become dirty.It is obviously true that we are sometimes blind to the mistakes of ourselves. Therefore, mutual criticism is required, otherwise, we cannot be free from repeating mistakes. But sometimes our mistakes appear in such an ambiguous form that they can hardly be detected by others. It is then that self-criticism is indispensable and self criticism is also a sign of being ready to receive mutual criticism.[69]

Grace D. Liu, an American woman married to a Chinese national, explained in an article that she and her husband sent their children to ordinary Chinese schools. Now with the study movement underway, her twelve-year-old daughter was the group leader of a small gathering of three boys and three girls who discussed their own and others' shortcomings and how to change them. Her eight-year-old son also attended criticism/self-criticism meetings, and was the deputy-leader of his small group. Her sixteen-year-old daughter, away at a private boarding school for girls, was learning along with her school mates what it meant to work, since they had to clean and maintain the facilities themselves.[70]

A letter from Gao Dienge of Beijing Normal University gave a good indication of how political studies were organized at his university, and of the Party and government's control in the process. When classes began in October (1949), Communists and Youth League members promoted discussions and organized a "Students' League," which was based on the democratic centralized system. The League's main function was to lead the students in their political training and to improve their study methods.

According to Gao, all the universities and middle schools in Peking devoted at least three hours each week to political education and had divided students into small groups of six to twelve members. Professors, instructors, teachers and students were mixed together under conditions of equality in these groups. Here Students'League members guided small group discussion. Recalcitrant individuals could be sent before the university's Political Studies Committee.[71] Each holiday, the students went into the countryside to help explain the government's policies to the peasants.

Francis H.Chow outlined the mode of organization at Shanghai's Fudan University. Here the Professors' Association, the Lecturers' and Assistants' Association, the Staff Association, and the Employees' Association had all combined into a single mass union. Led by an Administration Committee and adopting the principle of democratic centralism, the union worked to promote unity, collectivity, and diligent political study of the new democratic principles.[72]

Four months later, Chow opined that political studies had reached its high-water mark at Fudan, and that other disciplines now rested on a bedrock of political understanding:

> It has been a full year since the liberation of Shanghai. In this past year we spent much time in political discussions, mutual criticism and self-criticism; thus our political consciousness has been heightened. The political work and social activities in which we engaged have created suitable and advantageous conditions for our present study.
>
> Now we have fewer meetings because the situation throughout the country has changed. We realize that no definite line can be drawn between our political work and our studies and have found it to be true indeed that political work paves the way for technical study.[73]

In July, the Education Bureau of East China convened representatives from various universities to explain the Central Government's intention to send politically advanced graduates wherever they were most needed. Chow declared that by this time, Fedayeen graduates were ready to go anyplace their country needed them. He concluded that "It is obviously true that there is no outlet for the intellectuals unless they unite themselves with the working class, the peasantry and the soldiers."[74]

Another frequent contributor, S.Y. Livingston Hu of Chongqing, formerly of the GMD Army, enrolled May, 1950, for six months in the "Advanced Research Class of the Southwest Military and Political University" (a new revolutionary university) for political re-education. Hu explained:

> By the end of six months we must show by concrete example that we have reformed our old ways of thinking; that is we must learn to view things from the standpoint of China's farmers and working class. Our studying,

therefore, is based on mutual criticism and self-criticism, dialectical materialism and linking up our studies with our daily lives.

We have to unlearn our old ways of thought before we can learn the new. We must live as the common people do and get rid of the "face" ideas, fatalism, and the gentlemen's ways that were based on contempt for the workers. Only then can we serve the government smoothly and effectively.[75]

On May 26, the Shanghai People's Government mandated that all government workers and employees of state-run enterprises in Shanghai had to engage in political study. An office worker named Wong Zeliang described a class which had been organized by the authorities and her labor union to reeducate fellow bureaucrats. They listened to lectures broadcast every Tuesday and Friday by the Shanghai People's Broadcasting Station, took notes, studied selected documents, practiced criticism and self-criticism in small groups, and were required to take three different kinds of examinations.[76]

The *Review* translated and summarized an article by Northeastern University professor Zhao Lisen, entitled "How to Comprehend and Utilize Criticism and Self Criticism." Zhao claimed that correct use of criticism and self-criticism by ordinary people to point out flaws or abuses in government or by CCP cadres ". . . consolidates the sense of being masters in the minds of the masses" and would help to prevent the growth of bureaucracy. Criticism was not intended to "bring down" government leaders, he pointed out, but to help them avoid sliding into bureaucratic practices.[77]

The *Review* summarized a speech by Dr. Fei Xiaodong, who was emerging as a leading figure in the thought reform movement, at the Higher Education Conference in Beijing. Fei, then teaching at Qinghua University, called for careful and long-term reform of higher education to transform it from a semi-colonial institution that prepared students for bureaucracy and study abroad, to one that served the people. Reform of the curricula had to be ideological, Fei declared, and before that could be undertaken, the teachers themselves had to be politically reformed. To accomplish this, teachers would study at Revolutionary Universities and work in factories during vacations.[78]

Powell had published an earlier article by Fei (discussed in the previous chapter) wherein he recounted his changed conception of democracy and criticized his previous views. Since Fei was an internationally respected sociologist and anthropologist (the author of two well known volumes published in the United States: *Earthbound China*, and *Peasant Life in China*), his self-critical confession, because of his previous identification with American and British-style liberal democratic ideals, was particularly important.[79]

Baring Nee, a middle school teacher at Changsha, explained how he and his fellow teachers were reeducating themselves in the new ideology:

At the end of last term, most of the teachers joined the Winter Learning Conference for Middle School Teachers specially to receive a course on revolutionary theory. Thus they have in this semester brought back fresh inspiration and new methods for conducting the school both in administration and in teaching.[80]

Two feature articles by Canadian professor Earl Wilmott described mass meetings by the faculty, students, and workers at West China Union University in Chengdu. Self-Criticism and patient consultations had created a vastly improved climate at the University, he reported, sweeping away differences and leading to a sense of openness and unity among university workers, faculty, administrators, and students.[81]

An article by Professor Xia Li, of the National College of Fine Arts in Hangzhou, told of ideologically reeducated art students and art faculty being transported into the countryside to stay on farms and learn from the peasants. Small group discussions and public lectures helped improve the students' and teachers' political understanding. They were currently painting scenes of farm life, tractors, etc.[82]

A feature story by H.Y. Shi, a Qinghua University student, explained how he learned the true nature of class conflict through participation in a village land reform movement. His work team of ten students was directed by a district cadre. After thoroughly acquainting themselves with the social and economic conditions of the village, they organized an agrarian society of poor peasants. In their efforts to awaken class consciousness among the reticent peasants, the students had to come to grips with their own class biases.[83]

Finally, an enthusiastic letter written by Hu Yonghua summed up the Great Study Movement, its methodology and benefits:

> China now has entered into a new era. In this era it is required that things old should be replaced by things new and that our thoughts have to be reformed too in order to enable us to gain progress and to become new men in New China. The method specifically recommended for such a purpose is "Criticism and Self-Criticism," the weapon generally recognized as powerful enough to uncover our wrong-doing and improper thinking, the existence of which would make us unable to keep pace with the conditions under Communist guidance.[84]

Not all letters to the *Review* reflected an appreciation of the new ideology. Thought reform occurred rather unevenly, being either more or less advanced from one location to the next. This reflected the relative lack as yet of strong centralized control and the large degree of regional autonomy characteristic of this early period of CCP rule.[85]

A letter by Professor G.B. Shie of Eastern Civilization College in Chengdu underscored this reality in its content. While opposing nuclear weapons as threatening to lead to World War III, and believing that there was no reason why capitalists and communists should not get along,

Professor Shie projected an older ideology and understanding. He upheld the wisdom and morality "of our ancient philosophers," who held that ". . . those who love power and money are wicked and those who loved morality and wisdom are good." In Shie's view,

> There are only two kinds of men who are leaders: the political administrators and the greatest scholars. As our classics teach us, "He who exercises government by means of his virtue may be compared to the north polar star which keeps its place and all the other stars turn towards it."[86]

*

As a result of political study, *Review* articles by regular Chinese and foreign contributors became more ideologically attuned. Stories by contributing editors C.Y.W.Meng, Duncan C.Lee, Tao Wei-lin, Mark M.Lu, Mary Barrett, Earl Willmott, Rewi Alley, and Jullian Schuman, all testified to a new political awareness and ideological sensitivity among the *Review* staff.[87] An article by Julian Schuman will serve as an example of the staff's new ideological perspective.

In May, Schuman reviewed a play, "The Voice of America," written by the Soviet playwright Boris Lavrenev, which described an American war hero's realization that his country was going down the path of fascism in its domestic and foreign policy. When he joined the opposition, the hero was branded a communist and traitor. Schuman described the play as a "medium of education."

> For Shanghai audiences, brought up to a great extent on Hollywood's bill of fare, a look at America and Americans from a political viewpoint is something new and an education in itself. The audience is given a good opportunity to view some of the more prevalent trends in America today, seen in the hounding of the hero by the House Un-American Activities Committee. the Voice of America is an attempt to overcome various notions in the minds of its audience, long subjected to American exports both physical and spiritual.[88]

*

Criticism of the *Review*'s drift to the left from the United States and from some Americans still in Shanghai was not long coming. An American reader informed the editor that he had . . .

> . . . heard a great deal of criticism of the *Review* from many of your readers since the liberation. Some of us feel that under the KMT days, you were very courageous in presenting an objective and critical view of the events taking place at that time. However, since the liberation we have seen only bouquets for the new government and we feel your magazine can no longer be considered objective and unbiased.

We also feel that you have dealt too severely with American Policy and, as far as I can remember, I have seen no criticism by you of what Russia has been doing.[89]

Powell, replying to this letter in an editorial, said that he believed the *Review* was ". . . giving a picture of events in China which is every bit as objective as in the past." In his opinion, the present government was

. . . the best regime ever to come to power in this country. It is efficient and its personnel are honest. Granted, it has its faults and defects, but to date they have been of a relatively minor nature and there has already been evidence that it is flexible enough to change policies or procedures that prove erroneous or unsuitable. What more could one expect of a government?

Considering the overall picture, we have found very little to criticize.[90]

There is no doubt that Powell had made significant enemies, first within the Nationalist government which he had embarrassed over its repression of the Taiwan revolt and the suppression of student demonstrators, secondly with the GMD's supporters in the U.S., and thirdly, among former resident Americans who resented his defense of the new Chinese government. These included former editor of the *Shanghai Evening Post and Mercury* Randall Gould. In 1950, with the advent of Senator Joseph McCarthy's anti-communist rhetoric and the Korean War, the shrillest phase of domestic anti-communist hysteria seemed to spread through American society. In the U.S., newspapers and journals that had drifted considerably to the right, became aware of Powell and the *China Weekly Review*'s drift to the left.

In December 1949, Powell published a political analysis of the deterioration of civil liberties and the decline of the position of labor at the hands of anti-communist zealots in the United States. In it he expressed apprehension that the repressive atmosphere in America might give rise to the development of a brand of native fascism, and exhorted overseas Americans to do whatever they could to oppose this trend.[91]

Ever since the American Revolution, citizens of the United States have valued their individual freedom and their personal liberties. There was a time when the United States was undoubtedly the 'freest' place on earth a man could live. However, for the past several years these freedoms have been under attack, with the result that today it is not nearly so free as in the past.

There are individuals and groups in America who are opposed to the continuance of the traditional freedoms. They wish to qualify the word freedom, reserving complete freedom of action for themselves but denying even the vestiges of such freedom to the broad mass of the population.[92]

The article, which Powell signed, reflected the editor's own ideological soul searching and frustration with what he viewed as the continuing reactionary trend of American domestic and foreign politics.

Although raising valid concerns about the health of American civil liberties, and the rising influence of the military in the U.S. government, Powell's article also clearly reflected an increasing acceptance of the Chinese Communist viewpoint—evidence that he, no less than other editors and intellectuals, was successfully internalizing the new orthodoxy. It could not have been otherwise if he intended to continue publication.

Not surprisingly, his article elicited harsh condemnation from columnist Walter Simmons of the *Washington Times-Herald*. Simmons, whose article, "Shanghai," also appeared in the *Chicago Tribune* and the *New York Daily News*, charged that the *Review* "never deviates from the communist line and apologizes continuously for the American way of life." He strongly implied that Powell, his wife Sylvia, associate editor Mary Barrett, and contributing editors Julian Schuman and William Berges were communist subversives, out to libel American and all that it stood for.[93]

Powell refuted Simmons' accusations point by point in a feature article defending past editorial statements and denying that his wife and *Review* staff members were part of a secret communist cell of some sort.[94] Meanwhile the *Review* continued to sound the alarm over the erosion of civil liberties at home.

Eleven leaders of the U.S. Communist Party were put on trial and sentenced to prison in October, 1949, for their views, now deemed illegal.[95] Powell saw this and similar attacks on Communist parties in other Western nations as the ". . . beginning of a legal assault against the free institutions of these countries."[96] The real target was not the Western Communist parties, which were marginal and held little power, but rather the people's right to question the government and consider changes in the economic system. "The fact to be remembered," he warned,

> is that once a breach is made in the fundamental laws which protect the rights and freedoms of the people, these rights and freedoms have been all but lost . . . the removal of constitutional guarantees from communists is merely the first step toward the destruction of all liberty for all the people.[97]

The *Review* noted a growing number of cases where lawyers were cited for contempt or otherwise penalized for defending leftwing clients in the United States.[98] It pointed to ten Hollywood script writers (the Hollywood Ten) who were indicted for refusing to admit or deny membership in the Communist Party. The *Review* highlighted restrictions on the right of free speech of university faculty, and decried the purging of labor organizers with leftwing beliefs from the CIO and other unions.[99]

The charges that Senator Joseph McCarthy made in the Spring of 1950 against Johns Hopkins University China specialist Owen Lattimore, Columbia University International Law professor and Ambassador-at-Large Philip C. Jessup, and Secretary of State Dean Acheson (that they had conspired to turn over China to the Communists) reflected Chinese Nationalist lobby activity, the *Review* believed. Powell charged that information and funding for McCarthy's smear campaign against ". . . public figures who are not willing to continue all-out aid to Chiang Kai-shek" came from both the GMD and pro-Chiang New York importer Alfred Kohlberg.[100] He was right: Kohlberg, head of the American China Policy Association, a network of Chinese and American supporters of Chiang Kai-shek, had provided McCarthy with many of his "documents", and Nationalist agents had indeed been the source of much of the information.[101] The goal of Kohlberg and his associates was to discredit U.S. foreign service and State Department officials who had submitted negative assessments of the Guomindang's decline and had suggested withdrawing support from the failing Nationalist cause.

*

On June 25, 1950, in response to a limited incursion of South Korean troops on the Ongjin Peninsula the night before, which served as a pretext, North Korean forces launched a well-planned and prepared invasion of the South all along the thirty-eighth parallel.[102] As South Korean forces rapidly disintegrated, the United States rushed reinforcements from its occupation forces in Japan to slow the North Korean advance. On June 27, President Truman interposed the U.S. Seventh Fleet between mainland China and Taiwan, blocking the PRC's planned invasion of Taiwan, the final battle of the Chinese Civil War. The People's Republic, while sympathizing with the (North) Korean people's desire for national unification and condemning America's intervention, was more upset that the long-planned campaign to reunite Taiwan with the mainland was check-mated by the U.S. Navy.[103]

On June twenty-sixth, the *North China Daily News* was suspended for three days by Shanghai authorities for running the headline "North Korea Declares War on South Korea," because it seemed to impute responsibility for the war to the North.[104] The *China Weekly Review* also reflected initial ambiguity over who started the war. Although the *Review* announced that

> South Korean Forces had launched a surprise attack along the entire length of the thirty-eighth parallel dividing line at dawn on Sunday . . . ,[105]

it also noted that "Dispatches from Seoul and Tokyo claimed that the attack had come from the other direction and that the North had declared war on the South."[106]

While recounting a speech by Zhou Enlai charging that Truman had encouraged South Korean President Syngnman Rhee to start the war to provide a pretext for the U.S. to block China's takeover of Taiwan (a baseless accusation), the *Review* again registered ambiguity over who started the war:

> Although the Pyongyang radio reports that hostilities in Korea had been started by Southern forces on June 25, Truman blamed the north and said..: "I know that all members of the U.N. will carefully consider the consequences of the latest aggressive act in Korea in contravention of the

U.N.Charter. In international affairs, the restoration of power rule will
have widespread repercussion. The U.S. will continue to support rule by
law." [107]

However, Powell and the *Review* had long been following the history of
the repressive regime of Syngman Rhee in the South, and generally held
Rhee and the nation which sponsored him, the United States, responsible
for the outbreak of war. He viewed the struggle in Korea as an internal civil
war which the Koreans should be allowed to settle among themselves, and
did not want the United States to become further involved.

When it did, Powell lamented that "The United States which once was
the hope of the oppressed colonial peoples of Asia has now become the
biggest obstacle to their fight for freedom and independence." [108] He
charged that President Truman had subordinated all other considerations
to the ". . . short-sighted policy of waging a world-wide 'cold war' with the
Soviet Union." Powell noted with disgust that the president had ". . . put
the United States on record as approving and supporting nearly every rotten, corrupt, feudal-fascist regime in Asia." [109]

On July 1, 1950, Mao Zedong called on all Chinese to unite against
American aggression in Taiwan and Korea. A "National Campaign Week
against U.S. Aggression in Taiwan and Korea" was initiated on July seventeenth with accusation meetings being held all over China. [110] It was against
this background of rapidly deteriorating relations that Powell announced
the *China Weekly Review* would close down with its August fifth issue, citing continuing economic problems, including currency restrictions along
with the "overall situation" in the decision to cease publication. [111]

"These are indeed sad days for the United States," he intoned:

> Long the champion of the oppressed and long the world's leading expo-
> nent of national self-determination, America has shifted course until
> today she has become the most powerful force for reaction throughout the
> world. In the grip of a carefully plotted anti-red hysteria, the American
> people are being stampeded into accepting a short-sighted policy of clasp-
> ing the hands of any and all -including some of the world's worst
> scoundrels- who profess to be against communism. [112]

Powell felt it was "tragic" that American bombs were killing thousands
of Korean civilians and that Koreans and Americans were killing one another. "All of this is being done in the name of defending democracy. All
we can say is that Truman is wrong." [113] He calculated that the Korean situation would result in the U.S. Congress accepting the huge new military
budget needed to fund Truman's Containment Policy, first put forward in
National Security Council Resolution no. 68.

"Only a drastic change in America's internal and external policies"
could alter the situation, Powell felt. Therefore, he called on all progressive
Americans at home and abroad, to put pressure upon U.S. policy makers to
stop repression at home and "adventurism" abroad. [114] He called on the

people of the United States to join the people of China and of all countries in opposing Truman's policy of "aggressive interventionism" by signing the Stockholm Peace Appeal, drawn up by the Permanent Committee of the World Peace Congress, wherein Chinese and Russian Communist interests were strongly represented.[115]

The *Review*'s interest in the peace movement was not new. In March, 1950, an article by Dr. Hewlett Johnson, Dean of Canterbury, spoke approvingly of the Soviet Union's support of the international peace movement and questioned the Western governments' hostility toward it.[116] In May, 1950, the *Review* reported enthusiastically on efforts in Shanghai to secure one million signatures in support of the Stockholm Peace Appeal.[117] Communist China became a vigorous proponent of the movement.[118]

From July fifteenth when Powell announced the journal's closure through August fifth (the last issue), he was overwhelmed by letters from readers urging the *Review* not to close, and that some way be found to keep the journal open.[119] One letter in particular suggested that the *Review* reorganize itself as a monthly, carry out retrenchment policies, and raise its price.[120] Once Powell had been convinced of the continuing need for the *Review*, that was the course he followed.

In explaining his decision to continue publication as a monthly, Powell cited three primary factors: first, the overwhelming desire of the journal's readers, as expressed in letters to the editor, that it find a way to continue publication; second, the ". . . sharpening of the conflict between the forces of peace and the forces of war"; and third, the fact that people in Western countries had ". . . few opportunities to obtain unbiased accounts of developments in this part of the world."[121]

*

A few weeks into the Korean War, *Time* magazine, which had praised Powell's work only a few short years before, bitterly attacked the editor and his journal. *Time* charged that Powell had become an ". . . outright apologist for Communism," and his father, former editor J.B. Powell, ". . . who called no man master, would have been surprised and shocked at [the *Review*'s] subservient tone." Apparently believing the *Review* should have been fighting a private war against the new regime, *Time* complained that

> After Red troops finally took Shanghai in 1949, the *Review* hailed the city's "liberation," lavishly praised "the new democracy", and began demanding Formosa's "liberation" from Chiang Kai-shek's "henchmen." The *Review*'s version of life in the U.S. became a red-and-pink patchwork quilt, sewn together from such dependably left-wing sources as the speeches of Howard Fast and George Selds' newsletter *In Fact*. Wrote the *Review*: "The United States in the eyes of the Chinese people, has become the symbol of world reaction."[122]

In essence, Powell, the *Review* and its editorial staff had been held up before the nation as potential targets for anti-communist denunciation.

With the prospect of possible war between the United States and China in Korea, the anti-colonial orientation of the *Review* now cast it in an adversarial role, in the eyes of American domestic critics.

The *New York Times*, noted almost without comment that the "leftist *China Weekly Review*" was going to cease publication August fifth due to currency restrictions.[123] After Powell announced plans to resume publication as a monthly, the *Times* ran a longer article which left little doubt about the *Review*'s ideological orientation. Amidst pages filled with photographs of embattled American G.I.'s, wounded soldiers, and the names of the dead, the paper quoted Powell as saying:

> America's adventuristic policy in Korea has misfired badly but, nevertheless, the Truman administration is doing its best to scare the American people into a state of war hysteria so they will accept a war economy as a necessary step and fail to realize that it is an illogical and, in the long run, an absolutely useless palliative for the country's basic ills.[124]

The juxtaposition against images of Americans suffering in the war made Powell's words seem insensitive and disloyal. With the *Review* locked into telling the other side of the story to an increasingly hostile Western audience, it was only a matter of time before anti-communist partisans back home had enough material to drag the editor and his associates before the inquisitor's tribunal.

The Korean war looked different from Powell's position in China. What seemed a minor war (or "police action") to contain Communist expansion from a North American perspective, was in reality a vicious, all-out civil war within Korea itself, with a civilian death toll of two million persons by the time the war ended.[125] Powell reacted with indignation to the escalating horror of the mass bombing of urban centers and the napalming of villages by American aircraft.

It was within this context that he would cover the allegations of germ warfare which figured significantly in his indictment for sedition upon his return home. The story he was running in spring 1950, of blacklisted writers, purged labor leaders, fired professors, and maligned diplomats was destined to become his own story after the war's conclusion.

CHAPTER NOTES

1. "Xin wen, xu ban: Zheng wu yuan guan yu tong yi fa bu zhong yang ren min zheng fu, ji qi suo shu ge ji guan zhong yao xin wen de zan xing ban fa," [Newspapers and Publications: Provisional Regulations of the Government Administrative Council Regarding Unifying and Promoting Important News of the Central People's Government and its Agencies]; "Di yi jie guan guo chu ban hui yi wu xiang jue yi," [First Session of the All-China National Publications Meeting, Five Decisions.] both in: *Zhong Yang Ren Min Zheng Fu Fa Ling Hui Bian, 1949–1950 Volume 1* (Beijing: Ren Min Chu Ban She, 1952). [*Central People's Government Collected Laws and Regulations, 1949–1950 Volume 1.* Beijing: People's Publishing Com-

pany, 1952.] p.617–626; 627–630. These are a series of provisional laws and directives for the organization of the press, dating from December 9, 1949, to October 28, 1950. Dr.Bau Hwa Sheieh of Western Oregon University kindly translated and commented on these pages. There were no exceptions for a foreign-owned journal like Powell's. These laws applied no less to the *China Weekly Review* than to other privately-owned publications. An English language explication is found in: Liu Tsun-chi, "The Press in New China", *People's China*, 16 December 1950. p.8–10.

2. Alun Falconer, "Changes in Shanghai's Press", *CWR*, 11 March 1950,p.26–8. The "Big Four Families": Chiang, Soong, Kung, and Ch'en. The first was Chiang's (Jiang Jieshi's) family itself, then Chiang Kai-shek's brothers-in-law, T.V.Soong and H.H.Kung, both Western trained economists influential enough to chart GMD economic policy. Each held various diplomatic and governmental positions at one time or another. Finally, the fascist-leaning Ch'en brothers, Ch'en Li-fu and Ch'en Kuo-fu, headed up the "CC Clique" within the GMD military, and were core supporters implicitly trusted by Chiang.

3. "Rules Issued Governing Chinese-Owned Press", *North China Daily News*, 29 May 1949, p.3; Walter Sullivan, "Communist Rule of Shanghai Set Up", *New York Times*, 29 May 1949, p.17.

4. See footnote 2.

5. John K.Fairbank and Albert Feuerwerker, eds. *The Cambridge History of China, Volume 13, Republican China 1912–1949.* (Cambridge: Cambridge University Press, 1986.) p.144. The Political Science Group or Political Study Clique (Cheng-hsueh-hsi) was a loose group of economists, industrialists, bankers, publishers, and intellectuals all holding similar viewpoints, who were close to Chiang Kai-shek but without strong ties to the GMD. They served as technical advisors and professional administrators.

6. Alun Falconer, "Changes in Shanghai's Press", *CWR*, 11 March 1950, p.26–8. Some other papers affiliated with the KMT included *Ho Ping Jih Pao*, a KMT Army organ; *Tung Nan Jih Pao*, KMT organ for Southeast China; *Hwa Mei Wan Pao*, affiliated with the KMT Publicity Board;*Chien Sien Jih Pao*, connected to KMT General Ku Chu-tung;*Shang Pao*, originally the commercial organ of the (KMT's) CC Clique, it remained in business after the liberation of Shanghai as a privately owned journal associated with the Federation of Industry and Commerce; *Sin Yeh Pao*, also affiliated with the KMT's CC Clique, and *Ching Yung Chi Pao*, which was connected with the "Political Science" faction of the KMT.

7. "First National Meeting of Newsmen in Peiping", *North China Daily News*, 10 July 1949, p.3.

8. Alun Falconer, "Changes in Shanghai's Press", *CWR*, 11 March 1950, p.26,28.

9. Powell, ed. "Shanghai's Foreign Press", *CWR*, 25 June 1949, p.71–2; E.T. Peyton-Griffin, "An Apology"(23 June), *North China Daily News*, 25 June 1949, p.1; Chen Yi, Chairman, Shanghai Military Control Commission, "Order for British-Owned *North China Daily News*"(24 June), *Ibid.*

10. Randall Gould, "Shanghai During the Takeover, 1949", (Report on China), *The Annals of the American Academy of Political and Social Science*, 277: 184. (September, 1951).

11. "Instruction, CCP Central Committee, "On Diplomatic Affairs," 19 January 1949,in Shuguang Zhang and Jian Chen, *Chinese Communist Foreign Policy*

and the Cold War in Asia, New Documentary Evidence, 1944–1950.(Chicago: Imprint Publications, 1996). hereafter cited as *CCFPCWA*.p.97.

12. Telegram, CCP Central Committee to CCP Tianjin and Beiping Municipal Committees, 25 January 1949, *CCFPCWA*, p.100.

13. *Ibid.*

14. Frederick T.C. Yu, Intelligence Research Branch, Human Resources Research Institute, *Research Memorandum No. 37. The Propaganda Machine in Communist China with Special Reference to Ideology, Policy, and Regulations, as of 1952.* (Lackland Airforce Base: Air Force Training and Research Center, 1955). p.32.

15. Ibid. p.33–4; Statement by John W. Powell in Stephen R. MacKinnon and Oris Friesen, *China Reporting, An Oral History of American Journalism in the 1930's and 1940's.* (Los Angeles: University of California Press, 1987).p.196–9; Harold R. Isaacs, *Re-encounters in China: Notes of a Journey in a Time Capsule.* Armonk, (N.Y.:M.E.Sharpe, Inc., 1985). has a chapter on Liu Tsun-chi.

16. *Letter*, Randall Gould to Senator Benjamin Mandel, Director of Research, United States Senate Subcommittee to Investigate the Administration of Internal Security Laws of the Committee on the Judiciary. 29 August 1954. On this question Gould said: "My impression is that the Communists actually did little if anything for him except leave him alone."

17. Liu Tsun-chi, "The Press in New China", *People's China*, 16 December 1950, p.8,(footnote).

18. Liu Tsun-chi, "The Press in New China", *People's China*, 16 December 1950, p.8–9; Yu, *The Propaganda Machine in Communist China*, p.32.

19. *Ibid.*

20. Powell, ed. "Report to Readers", *CMR*, July 1953, p.128–9.

21. Randall Gould, "Shanghai During the Takeover, 1949", ("Report on China"), *The Annals of the American Academy of Political and Social Science*, 227: p.186; Randall Gould, "Statement by Randall Gould, Former Editor, the *Shanghai Evening Post and Mercury*", *CWR*,23 July 1949, p.164–5.

22. John W. Powell, Testimony, United States Senate, Subcommittee to Investigate the Administration of the Internal Security Act and Other Internal Security Laws of the Committee on the Judiciary, *Hearings: Interlocking Subversion in Government Departments*, 83 Congress, 2 Session, Washington, D.C., 27 September 1954, p.1882, 1894.

23. Liu Tsun-chi, "The Press in New China", p.9.

24. Alun Falconer, "Changes in Shanghai's Press",p.27.

25. *Ibid.*

26. Alun Falconer, "Changes in Shanghai's Press", *CWR*, 11 March 1950, p.27; Yu, *The Propaganda Machine in Communist China*, p. 34.

27. Liu Tsun-chi, p.9.

28. Liu, "The Press in New China",p.9–10; Yu, *The Propaganda Machine in Communist China*,p.33, 35–6.

29. Falconer, "Changes in Shanghai's Press",p.27; Yu, *The Propaganda Machine in Communist China*, p.33–4.

30. *Ibid.*

31. *Ibid.*

32. Liu Tsun-chi, "The Press in New China", p.10. Liu paraphrases this directive from the Central Committee.

33. Hsia Yen, Director of the Bureau of Cultural Affairs of Shanghai, "Report on Cultural and Educational Work in Shanghai", Delivered on Behalf of the Bureau of Education, Bureau of Cultural Affairs and the Press and Publications Office of the Shanghai Municipal People's Government at the First Session of the Second Conference of People's Representatives of All Circles in Shanghai, (*Shanghai News Translation*), *CMR*, December, 1950,p.6–9.

34. "Directive from the Shanghai People's Municipal Government on Development of Self-Criticism in Newspapers", *Ta Kung Pao* (Shanghai), 16 May 1950; Yu,*The Propaganda Machine in Communist China*, p.36.

35. Frederick T.C.Yu, *The Propaganda Machine in Communist China*.p.34.

36. Theodore H.E.Chen, *Thought Reform of the Chinese Intellectuals*.(Hong Kong: Hong Kong University Press,1960).p.17.

37. *Ibid.*

38. Hsia Yen, Director of the Bureau of Cultural Affairs of Shanghai, "Report on Cultural and Educational Work in Shanghai, First Session of the Second Conference of People's Representatives of All Circles, Shanghai", *CMR*, December 1950,p.6–9.

39. Alun Falconer, "Changes in Shanghai's Press", *CWR*, 11 March 1950,p.27.

40.*Ibid.*

41. Yen, "Report on Cultural and Educational Work in Shanghai", *CMR*, December 1950, p.8.

42. *Ibid.*

43. *Ibid.*

44. *Ibid.*

45. *Ibid.*

46. Kuo Mo-jo, "Cultural and Educational Work in China", Report Delivered to the Second Meeting of the National Committee of the Chinese People's Political Consultative Conference, Peking, 14–23 June 1950, (translation by *Hsinhua*) *CWR*, 8 July 1950, p.106–7.

47. Frederick C. Teiwes, *Politics and Purges in China, Rectification and the Decline of Party Norms, 1950–1965*. Armonk, N.Y.: M.E.Sharpe, 1993. p.51–4.

48. Chen, *Thought Reform of the Chinese Intellectuals*. p.12.

49. *Ibid.*

50. Mao Tse-tung, Closing Address to the Second Meeting of the National Committee of the Chinese People's Political Consultative Conference, Peking, 14 June 1950,(translated by *Hsin-hua*), *CWR*, 8 July 1950, p. 105–6.

51. *Ibid.*

52. Kuo Mo-jo, "Cultural and Educational Work in China", p.106–8.

53. *Ibid.*

54. *Ibid.*

55. *Ibid.*p.107.

56. Charles J. Canning, "New Democracy-Theory and Practice", *CWR*, 25 June 1949,p.76.

57. Duncan C. Lee, "Changeover In the Post Office", *CWR*, 16 July 1949,p.146.

58. *Ibid.*

59. Chang T'ien-fu, "Why the Communists Win", *CWR*, 16 July 1949, p.147–8.

60. H.C. Huang, "Life in a Communist Training Camp", *CWR*, 23 July 1949, p.168.

61. Y.H. Hpain, "China's New Universities", *CWR*, 13 August 1949, p.206.(Author's name reproduced as it appears in both article and Index.)

62. *Ibid.*

63. *Ibid.*

64. *Letter*, Hsu Shih Chen to Editor, "Active Life", Kaifeng, 25 July 1949, *CWR*, 8 September 1949, p.14.

65. Mary Barrett and Kiang Chun-chang, "What's Happening at Christian Colleges", *CWR*, 29 October 1949, p. 131–3.

66. "Education in East China", *CWR*, 29 October 1949, p.133.

67. *Letter*, Francis Hanling Chow to Editor, Fuhtan University, Shanghai, 26 October 1949, *CWR*, 5 November 1949, p.143, 160.

68. *Letter*, Tuan Min-chuang to editor, "New Education", People's Medical College, Kiangwan, Shanghai, 4 November 1949, *CWR*, 19 November 1949, p.179.

69. *Letter*, Francis H. Chow to editor, Fuhtan University, Shanghai, 22 December 1949, *CWR*, 31 December 1949, p.65. Chow frequently contributes letters. See for example: Francis H. Chow, "Students' Proposals", *CWR*, 3 December 1949, p.1 (summarizing proposals made by Fuhtan University students at the Shanghai Students' Conference), or Francis H. Chow, "Fuhtan Union", *CWR* 11 February 1950, p.178 (recounting the centralization of the university community for political study).

70. Grace D. Liu, "Education in New China", *CWR*, 10 December 1949, p.25–6.

71. *Letter*, Kao Tien-ke to editor, Peking, 5 February 1950, *CWR*, 11 February 1950, p.165, 178.

72. *Letter*, Francis H. Chow to editor, Shanghai, 2 February 1950, *CWR*, 11 February 1950, p. 178.

73. *Letter*, Francis H. Chow to editor, Shanghai, 12 May 1950, *CWR*, 10 June 1950, p.19, 36.

74. *Letter*, Francis H. Chow to editor, "Jobs for Graduates", Shanghai, 20 July 1950, *CWR*, 5 August 1950, p.163.

75. *Letter*, S.Y. Livingston Hu to editor, Chungking, 9 May 1950, *CWR*, 3 June 1950, p.18; *Letter*, S.Y. Livingston Hu to editor, Chunking, 2 July 1950, *CWR*, 5 August 1950, p.163.

76. *Letter*, Wong Sze-liang to editor, Shanghai, 2 December 1949, *CWR*, 17 December 1949, p.33; *Letter*, Wong Sze-liang to editor, Shanghai, 5 June 1950, *CWR*, 17 June 1950, p.54.

77. Chao Li-sen, "How to Comprehend and Utilize Criticism and Self-Criticism", *Kwan Cha* (the *Observer*) Volume 6, no.14, summarized in "Criticism and Self-Criticism", *CWR*, 17 June 1950, p.50.

78. Fei Hsiao-tung, "Report on the National Higher Education Conference", *Hsin Kwan Cha* (the *New Observer*), 1 July 1950, summarized in "Educating the Educators", *CWR*, 29 July 1950, p.157.

79. Fei Hsiao-tung, "My Search for Democracy",(translated from *Sin Wen Jih Pao*), *CWR*, 1 October 1949, p.65–6; Powell, ed. "About the Author", *CWR*, 1 October 1949,p.65; Fei Hsiao-tung, *Earthbound China*. (Chicago: University of Chicago Press, 1945).

80. *Letter*, Baring Nee, "Min-Teh School", Changsha, 25 June 1950, *CWR*, 15 July 1950, p.126.

81. Earl Willmott, "New Deal at a Christian University", *CWR*, 8 April 1950,p.91–2; Earl Willmott, "New Democracy on the Campus", *CWR*, 1 July 1950, p. 77.

82. Hsia Li, "Art Education in New China", *CWR*, 3 June 1950, p.7–8.

83. H.Y. Shih, "Learning from the Peasants", *CWR*, 27 May 1950, p.220–221.

84. *Letter*, Hu Yung-hwa, "Powerful Weapons", Shanghai, 28 June 1950, *CWR*, 15 July 1950, p.109,126.

85. Teiwes. *Politics and Purges in China*, p.84.

86. *Letter*, Professor G.B. Shie,"Chengtu Reader", Chengtu, 6 February 1950, *CWR* 18 March 1950, p.33.

87. H.C. Huang, "Peasants Accuse Local Despots", *CWR*, 18 March 1950, p.37–8; H.C. Huang, "Letter From the Front", *CWR*, 18 March 1950,p.78; C.Y.W. Meng, "Sino-Soviet Relations", *CWR*, 11 March 1950, p.22–24; C.Y.W. Meng, "New Direction for Shanghai Business", *CWR*, 27 May 1950, p.223–6; Duncan C. Lee, "China's Changing Countryside", *CWR*, 13 May 1950, p.186; Duncan C.Lee, "Peking Panorama", *CWR*, 10 June 1950, p.29; Mark M.Lu,"The 'New Look' in Liberated Honan", *CWR*, 20 May 1950, p.206–7; Tao Wei-lien, "Land Reform Begins in the Newly Liberated Areas", *CWR*, 22 October 1950,p.111–3; Tao Wei-lien, "U.S.Trade Ban Will Not Cripple China", *CWR*, 10 December 1950,p.23–5; Tao Wei-lien, "Foreign Relief and China's Famine", *CWR*, 22 April 1950,p.126–8; Tao Wei-lien, "Western Press Distorts China News", *CWR*, 17 June 1950,p.44–6; Marry Barrett, "People's Conferences in China", *CWR*, 1 April 1950,p.73–6; Earl Willmott, "A Chengtu Diary", *CWR*, 4 March 1950,p.8–12; Julian Schuman, "The Last Act on Taiwan", *CWR*, 25 February 1950,p.222.

88. Julian Schuman, "The Voice of America", *CWR*, 27 May 1950, p.222.

89. *Letter*, American Reader to editor, "Are You Objective?", Shanghai, 18 October 1949, *CWR*, 22 October 1949, p.124.

90. Powell, ed. "Are We Objective?", *CWR*, 29 October 1949, p.129–30.

91. John W. Powell, "The American Scene", *CWR*, 3 December 1949, p.11–14.

92. *Ibid.*

93. John W. Powell, "Reply to an Attack on the *China Weekly Review*", *CWR*, 25 March 1950, p.54–56.

94. *Ibid.*

95. "U.S. Communists Sentenced", *CWR*, 29 October, 1949, p.139. They were charged with violating the (1940) Smith Act, which made it illegal to advocate overthrowing the government by force or to belong to a group which advocated the same.

96. Powell, ed. "Anti-Communist Laws", *CWR*, 24 June 1950, p.56–7.

97. *Ibid.*

98. "The Civil Rights Scene in America", *CWR*, 11 March 1950, p.24–5. The "Dennis Trial" (of eleven U.S. Communist Party leaders), the trial of labor leader Harry Bridges, and the trial of the "Trenton Six" (six African Americans on trial for murder) were the cases cited.

99. *Ibid.*

100. "KMT Lobby Busy in Washington", *CWR*, 24 June 1950, p.63–4.

101. Ross Y.Koen, *The China Lobby in American Politics*. (New York: Octagon Books, 1974.) p.122–124, 164–168; Stanley I. Kutler, *The American Inquisition, Justice and Injustice in the Cold War*. (New York: Hill and Wang, 1982.) p.187–188, 193.

102. Bruce Cumings, *The Origins of the Korean War, Volume II, The Roaring of the Cataract 1947–1950*. (Princeton, N.J.: Princeton University Press, 1990), p.615–19.

103. Sergei N.Goncharov, John W.Lewis, and Xue Litai, *Uncertain Partners, Stalin, Mao, and the Korean War*. (Stanford: Stanford University Press, 1993.) p.157–158.

104. "Paper in Shanghai Halted for Blaming North Korea", *New York Times*, 11 July 1950, p.4; *North China Daily News*, 26 June 1950, p.1.

105. Civil War in Korea", *CWR*, 1 July 1950, p.87.

106. *Ibid*.

107. "Chou En-lai Answers Truman", *CWR*, 1 July 1950, p. 84.

108. Powell, ed. "People Must Fight for Peace", *CWR*, 8 July 1950, p.92–3.

109. *Ibid*.

110. Chen, *Thought Reform of the Chinese Intellectuals*, p.24–5.

111. Powell, ed. "Review to Close", *CWR*, 15 July 1950, p.110.

112. Powell, ed. "The Lesson of Korea", *CWR*, 15 July 1950, p.110–111.

113. *Ibid*.

114. *Ibid*.

115. Roderick MacFarquhah and John King Fairbank, eds. *The Cambridge History of China, Volume 14, Part I: The Emergence of Revolutionary China, 1949–1965*. (Cambridge: Cambridge University Press, 1987.)p.260. The "Appeal" was written at the April, 1950 meeting of the Permanent Committee of the World Peace Congress in Stockholm, Sweden. Representatives from thirty countries, including all of the countries of Communist Eastern Europe, the USSR, and Communist China, took part, and the PRC became a strong proponent of the movement. Powell, ed. "The People Must Fight for Peace", *CWR*, 8 July 1950, p.92–3; Huang Tsai-liang, "Significance of the Peace Signature Movement", *Shih Chieh Chih Shih (World Culture)*, Volume 21, No.23 summarized in *CWR*, 15 July 1950, p.120; Powell, ed. "Peace Can Still Be Won", *CWR*, 29 July 1950, p.146–7. Powell saw the fact that Secretary of State Acheson had denounced the World Peace Appeal as Soviet propaganda and that Voice of America had tried to discredit the Appeal as proof that Washington leaders were concerned over the petition.

116. Hewlett Johnson, "Russia Builds for Peace", *CWR*, 4 March 1950, p.4.

117. "World Peace and the Atomic Bomb", *CWR*, 20 May 1950, p.216.

118. Speech, Zhou Enlai, "On the International Situation and Our Diplomatic Affairs after the Signing of the Sino-Soviet Alliance Treaty," 20 March 1950, CCF-PCWA, p.144. Zhou underscored the importance of working for peace and styled socialist countries the "peace camp". The Imperialists disliked revolutions and could only resort to war to put them down. Since they preferred to fight through proxy countries, mobilizing international support for world peace would help the cause of national liberation worldwide, Zhou reasoned.

119. *Letter*, "Positive Help", Chengtu, 17 July 1950, *CWR*, 29 July 1950, p.145; *Letter*, Mark M. Lu to editor, "Friend Since 1929", Kaifeng, 23 July 1950, *Ibid*; *Letter*, Y.Y.L. to editor, "Must Not Close", Shanghai, 24 July 1950, *Ibid*; *Letter*, T.H. Kwok to editor, "Willing to Help", Shanghai, 19 July 1950, *Ibid*; *Letter*, Yen

Ching-hua to editor, "I Have Learned Much", Nanking, 22 July 1950, *Ibid*; *Letter*, P.Y. Wang to editor, "Deep Regrets", Peking, 22 July 1950, *Ibid*, p.162; *Letter*, T.Y. Yang to editor, "Our Magazine", Shanghai, 26 July 1950, *Ibid*; *Letter*, Duncan C. Lee to editor, "Intimate Friend", Peking, 17 July 1950, *Ibid*; *Letter*, "Good Wishes", Peking, 20 July 1950, *Ibid*; *Letter*, "Reconsider", Peking, 20 July 1950, *Ibid*; *Letter*, Wong Sze-liang to editor, "Heavy Loss", Shanghai, 24 July 1950, *Ibid*; *Letter*, Chang Shu-chi to editor, "A Good Friend", Kaifeng, 19 July 1950, *CWR*, 5 August 1950, p. 163; *Letter*, M. Yao to editor, "Concerned Reader", Shanghai, 24 July 1950, *Ibid*,p.179; *Letter*, Jamen Moh to editor, "Disheartening", Tietsin, 17 July 1950, *Ibid*; *Letter*, Wong Ping-sen, "Fighter For Justice", Shanghai, 25 July 1950, *Ibid*; *Letter*, "Heartfelt Sympathy", Shanghai, 28 July 1950, *Ibid*; *Letter*, Cheng Yung-chung to editor, "Mission Not Over", Shanghai, 24 July 1950, *Ibid*; *Letter*, C.Y. Yen to editor, "Try to Continue", Hankow, 20 July 1950, *Ibid*; *Letter*, Baring Nee, "Closure Regretted", Changsha, 20 July 1950, *Ibid*; *Letter*, H.C. Lin to editor, "Monthly Review", Shanghai, 31 July 1950, *Ibid*.

120. Letter, H.C. Lin to editor, Shanghai, 31 July 1950, *CWR*, 5 August 1950, p.180. Lin wrote: "My humble suggestion is that, beginning from September 1950, you publish a *China Monthly Review*, carry out a retrenchment policy, and fix the price of the monthly at JMP 10,000 per copy." Except for the price, which was only raised to 6,500 JMP, this was the basis of the *Review*'s reorganization.

121. Powell, ed. "Review to Continue", *CWR*, 5 August 1950, p. 164.

122. "Dream Street, Shanghai", *Time*, 17 July 1950.

123. "*China Weekly Review* to End", *New York Times*, 26 July 1950, p.10.

124. "*China Weekly Review* to Go on Publishing", *New York Times*, 15 August 1950, p.2.

125. Bruce Cumings, *Korea's Place in the Sun, A Modern History*. (New York: W.W. Norton and Company, 1997) p.290.

CHAPTER NINE

THE BACTERIOLOGICAL WARFARE ISSUE AND THE *REVIEW*, PART I:
ANTECEDENTS AND CONTROVERSY

This chapter and the next will deal with the *China Monthly Review*'s involvement in the campaign by the People's Republic of China to publicize charges that the United States had engaged in biological warfare in North Korea and Northeast China. This chapter in particular will focus on the publicity campaign itself, and its antecedents, rather than the veracity or falsity of the accusations. The bacteriological warfare (BW) charges, made in the spring of 1951 and 1952 by North Korea and China were, and still remain, a matter of controversy.

The most recent book on the subject, *The United States and Biological Warfare, Secrets from the Cold War and Korea*, written by Edward Hagerman and Stephen Endicott (son of Dr. James G. Endicott: in 1952 a pro-Communist Canadian clergyman and a frequent contributor to the *Review*[1]) demonstrated the plausibility of the charges, and that the U.S. had the motive and means, but was unable to prove from American sources that the charges were indeed true.[2] Their study has been criticized for an uncritical reliance on North Korean and Chinese documentary sources.[3] While it is true that the book utilized the original Communist documentary evidence as a starting point[4], and that the authors spent considerable time and effort gathering materials on location in Korea and China, it is also true that they exhaustively sifted American sources in an attempt to verify the charges.

Conversely, recent attempts to demonstrate that the charges were fraudulent (Milton Leitenberg, *The Korean War: Biological Warfare Resolved* and Kathryn Weathersby, "Deceiving the Deceivers: Moscow, Beijing, Pyongyang, and the Allegations of Bacteriological Weapons Use in Korea"), have succeeded in showing that the Soviet hierarchy did not believe the charges, but nonetheless helped the North Koreans gather and fabricate evidence.[5] Soviet technicians went so far as to infect selected areas with BW pathogens so that the evidence collected would appear more authentic. The documents cited did not show that Chinese authorities shared Soviet misgivings. Although they discredit Soviet and North Korean activities, these documents are not by themselves sufficient to dismiss the allegations totally.

Whether true or not, there is little doubt that medical and military personnel, along with the peasantry in allegedly affected areas, and a large mass of the Chinese people accepted the charges as true. Organized hysteria over halting the threat of bacteriological attack, combined with trust in the honesty of government-sponsored displays of evidence,[6] and the very real health measures undertaken, including a massive inoculation drive, convinced the public of the veracity of the charges.

The role which the *China Monthly Review* played in the controversy, which quickly grew to international proportions, assured the prosecution of the American editorial staff on their return home after the war. Relying on Chinese and American news sources, the *Review*, carefully reiterated the genesis of the charges, tracing speculation in the U.S. media over American capabilities and the possible use of bacteriological weapons in Korea. It presented bacteriological warfare charges as a logical outgrowth of the savage air war then underway, and against a backdrop of atrocities committed by South Korea, with the full knowledge of the American military,[7] against pro-Communist elements of the civilian population.

An additional feature of the *Review* related to the BW issue involved its coverage of the Peace Movement among U.S. prisoners of war, another important part of the Communist propaganda effort. It published letters home and lists of POWs held in North Korean and Chinese POW camps. Besides reassuring folks back home of their good treatment, POW letters, broadcasts, and testimony denounced the war and testified increasingly to the horrors of the air war in Korea. The depositions of captured U.S. flyers, presented by Communist authorities to bolster BW charges, appeared in the *Review* as an extension of the inhumanity of the air war.[8]

Congressional testimony after the war by former POWs made it clear that the *China Weekly Review*, along with *People's China*, the *Shanghai News*, and other publications, were used in POW study and discussion groups, as part of the thought reform process. This policy was beyond the *Review*'s control. Yet the journal's staff, in the person of Dr. H.C. Huang, after joining the PLA and being assigned to an American POW camp hospital, regularly reported ongoing efforts to organize the prisoners.

Ultimately, the *China Monthly Review* was forced to close in August, 1953, due to financial insolvency. Powell and the staff had devoted most of their efforts to informing the American people of the positive accomplishments of the Chinese revolution. In spite of the war, and the *Review*'s integration with the rest of the Chinese press into government-directed propaganda campaigns, most of the space in the *Review* had been devoted to that purpose. Toward this end the staff had traveled throughout China, documenting the ongoing transformation, and the people's involvement in the process. But in spite of this effort, the *Review*'s American editors would be remembered largely for their expose on germ warfare in Korea, and would face prosecution at least in part because of it. ·

*

By October, 1950, American and Chinese soldiers faced each other on the battlefield. Control over Western enterprises and the financial situations of the remaining foreigners in China tightened after China entered the Korean War.[9] For the *China Monthly Review*, the hardening of the Press Administration's control and guidance into law, the continuation of thought reform, and tighter financial controls increasingly integrated its editorial policy with that of the People's Government.

From December 30, 1950 to January 4, 1951, one hundred and fifteen American-owned companies were placed under the control of the Shanghai Military Control Commission.[10] American nationals could not withdraw more than 1000 parity deposit units (PDU) per month from Chinese banks, and cash withdrawals by American business firms and personnel were also regulated.[11] All foreign- owned or subsidized educational, cultural, religious or relief organizations in Shanghai had to register with local authorities.

The Shanghai Military Control Commission created a Registration Department subdivided into various divisions, including a "Publications Division," and stipulated seven classes of foreign-capitalized enterprises which had to register with them. The fifth of these included ". . . newspapers, printing factories, publishing houses, bookstores, and broadcasting stations."[12] The *China Monthly Review*, as a foreign-owned enterprise receiving remittances from sales and subscriptions in the United States, needed to register. The *Review* and other foreign publications had to report their financial dealings twice yearly to the division.[13]

Thought reform intensified during the Korean War in the form of the *San Fan* or "Three Antis" movement: anti-corruption, anti-waste, and anti-bureaucracy, and the *Wu Fan* or "Five Antis" movement: anti-tax evasion, anti-bribery, anti-theft of government property, anti-use of government economic information for speculative gain, and anti-cheating on government contracts through provision of sub-standard goods.[14] The *Review* continued to interpret and justify thought reform to the West.[15]

> The greatest national mass movement is that of thought reform. In some ways it is different from previous mass movements in that it deals primarily with habits and patterns of thinking, with philosophical concepts. . .
> For readers abroad, one of the first distinctions which should be made is between "Thought Reform" and "Thought Control"- a distinction which the Western press has almost universally been at great pains not to make! China's Thought Reform Movement, very simply, is the result of the recognition that every type of society is both the producer and is itself based upon definite types of thought or philosophy . . . Old ideas, old concepts, old philosophies, ranging from those hangovers of feudalism on down to Chiang Kai-shek's imported fascist theories- are being carefully

examined. Such an examination is necessary for a nation setting out on the road to socialism, a new social system.[16]

The "Decisions Regarding the Promotion of Presswork," which were promulgated by the Press Administration of the Central People's Government, and the "Decisions Regarding the Development of Criticism and Self-Criticism Through the Press," which the Central Committee of the CCP promulgated, were all enacted into the Provisional Laws of the Central People's Government. They comprised a set of six statutes which were incorporated into law between December 9, 1949, and October 28, 1950. These statutes effectively placed the press under the direction of the Press Administration, and gave the force of law to the directives already considered in Chapter Seven. There were no exclusions made for the foreign press.[17]

This meant that henceforth the *Review* would serve a function specialized to its particular audience, would participate in nationally directed campaigns, that Powell would as editor bear primary responsibility for this, but would also be free to decide how this should be done. Throughout the Korean War, the overwhelming majority of articles in the *Review* focused on documenting the positive changes which the Revolution was instituting in the lives of rural folk, urban factory workers, educators, and churchmen. The pervasiveness of the new democratic spirit in all strata of society, the construction of new apartment blocks, factories, floodwater control projects, and the improvement of conditions in factory and field filled most of its pages.

This represented the journal's primary specialization and accorded well with Powell's stated desire to give an accurate picture of the transformations underway to offset distortions in the Western press. The various national propaganda campaigns which the *Review* reflected: the campaign to document the "democratic" reorganization of churches and affiliated bodies and of private sectarian universities, the campaign to encourage the peace movement, to document bacteriological warfare, to convince the world of the humane treatment of prisoners of war (POW's), were all secondary to this primary concern.

The second most important focus of the *Review* during the Korean conflict was on American prisoners of war. Next to stories of New China's achievements, articles concerning the POW's: their disgust with the war, their confirmation of alleged atrocities committed by U.N. forces, their participation in camp anti-war activities, and their good treatment, were the second most common focus in the *China Monthly Review*.[18] Other English language publications, *People's China*, the *Shanghai News*, and the *North China Daily News*, contained similar articles on POW's and many of the same photographs, but the proportional amount of journal space devoted by the *Review* to this issue surpassed that of either of the other two, even after the bacteriological warfare issue became prominent in the spring of 1952.

With the emergence of the bacteriological warfare matter to center stage, no English-language journal came close to the CCP's own *People's China* in terms of the quantity of material published in support of the germ war charges. It published virtually all confessions by captive American airmen, various Chinese and Soviet-sponsored investigative commission reports, government statements, and virtually all the major documentary evidence, comprising several hundred pages. However, the sheer volume of material in *People's China* did not mean that it rendered a more effective presentation than did Powell's journal.

During spring, 1952, bacteriological warfare became the third most important focus of the *China Monthly Review*. The monotony of page after page of fine print supplements was not, however, an option for the *Review*, with its limited format and page size. Powell judiciously highlighted only the most important parts of Commission reports, was more selective in the choice of captured airmen's confessions, and skillfully mixed photos so that they augmented the text, giving a more human face to the individuals concerned. Better known in the United States than Communist Party publications or the ex-patriot British press, the *Review*'s coverage of the BW issue could be taken in at a glance, used photos to stimulate curiosity, and was available to a U.S. public beyond its individual subscribers through university, college, and public libraries.

*

Although bacteriological warfare allegations surfaced during the Korean War and became a major international controversy during 1952–53, the roots of the allegations, whether true or not, pre-dated the war. They grew out of the Soviet investigation of the bacteriological warfare activities of Unit 731 of the Japanese Imperial Army, the American refusal to prosecute the leaders of this unit as war criminals, and the mutual suspicion and mistrust of the growing cold war. The allegations were the culmination of a considerable paper trail which must be taken into account.

Five years after the Japanese Guandong Army seized Manchuria and five years before the bombing of Pearl Harbor, Japan began a program to develop and manufacture biological weapons. Under the supervision of General Ishii Shiro of the Army Medical College and a group of Kyoto University graduates, military personnel in Manchuria built factories to breed germ cultures, medical and surgical facilities to conduct experiments and dissections on living human victims, and crematoria to dispose of the bodies.

From 1936 to 1945 thousands of civilian Chinese, Koreans, and even American prisoners of war were routinely infected with enhanced disease germs, observed as the disease ran its course, and sometimes vivisected to gain a better understanding of the internal pathology of the ailment. Field trials of various types of germ bombs were undertaken, again with living victims, and villages and even cities were used to test deadly contaminants and the ability to create epidemics.[19]

In October, 1981, almost three decades after the Korean War, *The Bulletin of the Atomic Scientists* published an article by John William Powell exposing Japan's development of biological weapons using live human victims, including American prisoners of war, during World War II. It recounted not only the horrendous experiments of Lt.General Ishii Shiro and his medical staff, but also documented the American decision to shield Ishii and his subordinates from prosecution as war criminals in return for access to the results of their experiments, which because they could not be duplicated in America for obvious moral reasons, were militarily quite valuable.[20] By that time, the doings of Ishii's Unit 731 outside Harbin, Manchuria, from 1936–1945, had already been aired on Japanese television by producer Yoshinaga Haruko over the Tokyo Broadcasting System.[21]

All the essential elements of Powell's 1981 article had appeared much earlier in his *China Monthly Review* by April, 1952, including the fact that some of the victims of Unit 731 had been Americans and that many of those responsible were working in the United States on the American BW program.[22] Most of the information about Ishii and his activities derived from the December 20–25, 1949 Soviet trial in Khabarovsk, Siberia, of twelve captured members of Ishii's Unit 731.[23] In 1949 The *China Weekly Review* had noted those proceedings and the fact that the Soviet Union had turned over materials from them to U.S. occupation authorities in Japan (Supreme Commander of Allied Powers - SCAP).[24]

By the outbreak of the Korean War, a summary transcript of the trial had been published in the Soviet Union and was widely circulated outside the U.S.S.R. The basic details of Japan's biological warfare research, development, and deployment during World War II were consequently well known in all the Communist countries by the time the Korean War erupted. Equally understood in the USSR, China, and North Korea was the fact that the United States had chosen not to prosecute those who had been in charge of germ warfare experiments, in spite of evidence which the Soviets had passed to SCAP.

Frustrated by the American refusal to prosecute high- ranking members of Unit 731 residing in Japan, Communist authorities in the months preceding the Korean War had turned the issue into a minor campaign. In early 1950, the Soviet Union and China, at Soviet instigation, both called for the appointment of a "Special International Military Court" to put the Japanese Emperor (Hirohito), Lieutenant Generals Ishii Shiro and Kitano Masajo of the Medical Service, Major General Wakamatsu Yujiro of the Veterinary Service, and General Kasahara Yukio, Chief of Staff of the Guandong Army, on trial for the crime of bacteriological warfare.[25] The details were widely disseminated through the Chinese national press, and appeared in the *China Monthly Review* in the form of a special supplement.[26]

*

The Communists were also well apprised of U.S. efforts to develop germ weapons. American reports on germ weapons production were reflected in the Chinese Communist news media often enough to prove they were paying attention. Information on the American Bacteriological Warfare program from the end of World War II to the outbreak of the Korean War had been widely reported in the U.S. press, including the U.S. employment of Japanese germ warfare technicians.

In 1946, *Life* magazine had outlined the research and production of bacteriological weapons at Ft. Detrick, Maryland; Virgo, Indiana; Pascagoula, Mississippi; and Dugway, Utah.[27] That same year, the *New York Times*, reporting on the U.S. program, asserted that bacteriological weapons could "wipe out a city at a single blow,"[28] while *Time* magazine thought American bacteriological weapons research held even greater promise than the atomic bomb, since such weapons did no damage to buildings and other property.[29] The *New York Herald Tribune*, the *New York World-Telegram*, *Science Illustrated*, *Newsweek*, *Collier's*, *New Masses*, and the *Bulletin of the Atomic Scientists* all published articles exploring the subject of U.S. biological weapons development in 1946.[30]

The United States government itself started the speculative ball rolling on January 3, 1946, when it released a report to the Secretary of War, prepared by George W. Merck, on the American biological warfare program.[31] Merck's "Report" was published in the *Bulletin of the Atomic Scientists*, in the journal *Military Surgeon*, and in the *New York Times* in a condensed version.[32] Nor did interest die down in the following years in spite of the government's decision to black-out future news of the program's development.[33]

The most important book-length treatment of bacteriological warfare during the inter-war period in the United States was Theodor Rosebury's *Peace or Pestilence, Biological Warfare and How to Avoid It*, which appeared in 1949. Rosebury, a bacteriologist involved with the American BW program from its inception, was one of the authors of the Rosebury-Kabat-Bolt Report, an extensive exposition on the principles of Bacteriological warfare which was not made public until 1947.[34]

By 1949, Rosebury had accepted a teaching and research post at Columbia University, and was internationally recognized as the leading American expert on bacterial warfare. Communist authorities in 1952 referred to Rosebury's work several times within the evidence considered by the "International Scientific Commission for the Investigation of the Facts Concerning Bacterial Warfare in Korea and China,"[35] in an effort to calibrate their findings in Korea and China with knowledge of the American and Japanese BW programs.

Rosebury's book came out the same year the USSR put members of Japanese Unit 731 on trial for World War II BW experiments. This coincided with a period of heightened anxiety within the United States over an assumed Russian BW capacity, spurred by escalating Cold War tensions. In 1949 *Newsweek* magazine prefaced an article on Rosebury with an imaginary scenario describing a Soviet bacteriological attack on the United States. This set a tone for other articles on germ warfare up through 1951, well into the Korean War. The emphasis was always on a possible Soviet or North Korean germ attack on the United States, or on U.S. forces in Korea: how to detect such an attack and take defensive measures against it:

> You are sitting at home listening to your radio or looking at television. It's a baseball game, which suddenly gives way to a solemn announcement: "We interrupt this program with an important news bulletin. The president has just signed an executive order giving Surgeon General Blank of the United States Public Health Service special powers to mobilize all necessary resources to combat the epidemic that started last Wednesday in St. Louis. There have been more than 4,000 deaths in the city in five days, with a peak of 2,439 yesterday. Cases of what is thought to be the same disease have been reported from Chicago, Milwaukee, Memphis, Kansas City, and Indianapolis.
> The source of the disease has not yet been discovered. The allegation made yesterday on the floor of the House by Representative Dash that this is a germ warfare attack of Russian origin has not been substantiated. If it proves true, we are assured by the Army High Command that extreme retaliatory measures will be taken."[36]

Although the United States had not been a signatory to the 1925 Geneva Protocol condemning the use of bacteriological weapons, since 1943 it had a public policy of no first use of such weapons.[37] The problem posed by the *Newsweek* article, namely of detection and defense against BW attack, rather than speculation on BW as an offensive weapon, became the subject of numerous articles in popular American scientific journals, right up to the time of the first North Korean charges of BW use by the U.S. in Korea.

Rosebury, in the 1949 *Newsweek* article, and in his book *Peace or Pestilence*, debunked earlier *New York Times* reports that the United States had developed a biological toxin so powerful that a single ounce could wipe out all of the United States and Canada. The 1946 *New York Times* news stories which had featured this sensational claim had resulted in misleading speculation that biological weapons were even more powerful than the atom bomb.[38] Rosebury sought to puncture this inflated view of the potential power of BW in the press, by assuring the public: "There is no single biological agent . . . that I can imagine capable of wiping out all forms of life in any area, large or small."[39]

Sensational speculative reports in the U.S. press over the "super toxin" and the power of biological weapons were clearly reflected in the Chinese Communist press. The *North China Daily News*, citing *Xinhua*, declared that mankind was in danger from bacteriological weapons developed in the United States. Only seven ounces of a destructive biological agent which the Americans had developed was capable of killing everyone on the planet, and rendered the atomic bomb obsolete, according to the report.[40] The following day, a second *Xinhua* story in the *North China Daily News* quoted a speech by a Soviet bacteriologist who condemned the super poison, and stated that science should not be employed to create BW weapons at all.[41]

The original 1946 *New York Times* articles were clearly reflected in the *Xinhua* reports. The authorities in the Soviet Union and China were obviously paying attention to BW items in the American media. At the time of the *Xinhua* articles, preparations for the Soviet trials of twelve captured Japanese members of Unit 731 (which would be held in December, 1949) were underway. Soviet prosecutors were by then in possession of considerable information about the Japanese development and testing of bacteriological weapons in Manchuria. Meanwhile, deteriorating Sino-American relations in 1949 gave way to war in Korea by June, 1950, and an ever-widening air war against North Korean targets by 1951.[42] In light of the escalating conflict, what would Chinese and North Korean authorities have seen in the U.S. press, between late 1949 and the first germ warfare charges, that would have heightened their suspicions?

*

A series of articles in the prestigious American journal *Science News Letter* and other popular scientific magazines from 1949 to 1951 kept bacteriological warfare in the public spotlight. An article in June 1949, asserted that in the event of another war, bacteriological weapons would be used. In the article, Dr. Theodor Roseburg warned that U.S. defenses against a biological warfare attack were woefully inadequate, and noted that the ultimate practicability of germ weapons could only be proven by their use in war.[43]

On the first of October, 1949, another article noted the difficulty of keeping actual trials of BW secret even though it would be easy to mask germ production facilities as plants "producing vaccines for peacetime protection of the population against smallpox, diphtheria, and so on."[44] The article was concerned about the production and testing of biological weapons by the Soviet Union and whether field tests could be detected.

Later that same month, Dr. Victor H. Haas, director of the Microbiological Institute of the National Institutes of Health, revealed that federal agencies were currently training scientists in germ warfare detection techniques as part of the U.S. Civil Defense program. Haas admitted the inadequacy of current methods for detecting BW attacks, and indicated that the first signs would probably come "some days after the attack has taken place and will depend on the appearance of illnesses resulting from exposure to the germs or toxins."[45]

Soon after the start of the Korean War, *Science Newsletter* suggested that: "Germ warfare may get a trial very soon if the fighting in Korea continues." Superficially the article worried the Soviet Union might take advantage of the fighting to stage a trial of BW in Korea, but in effect, it seemed to invite the same action by the United States. The source of this speculation was a paper delivered by Dr.Joseph F. Smadel of the U.S.Army Medical School to an American Medical Association meeting in San Francisco.[46] Dr. Smadel asserted the practicability of bacterial warfare and assured his audience that "The risks associated with the limited geographic use of such methods are no more hazardous to persons directly exposed than are the effects of high explosives or nuclear weapons."[47] Smadel also dismissed the risk that a man-made epidemic might rebound against its initiator.

In December 1950, the U.S. journal *Science Digest* reprinted an article from the British magazine, *Discovery*, which recounted the drawbacks of bacteriological warfare and its limitations. It called attention to the Soviet account of Japanese biological warfare experiments near Harbin during World War II as well as to American BW research at Camp Detrick, Maryland. According to the story, the United States had come very close to initiating BW against Japan at the close of the Second World War, sending a "shipment of synthetic hormones . . . to the Pacific for use against the rice crop in the Japanese homeland."[48]

In January 1951, Dr. Norman H. Topping of the U.S. National Institutes of Health, Bethesda, Md., outlined research on new defensive concepts to counter a Soviet BW attack on a large-scale basis which relied on:

> Finding specific treatments for diseases caused by the smaller viruses, learning how to sterilize large masses of air and methods of mass immunization less cumbersome than injection of each individual . . .[49]

The United States Federal Civil Defense Administration published and distributed a booklet in February, 1951 to alert the public to the possibility of a BW attack and to acquaint citizens with defensive measures they might take against it.[50] It attempted to answer basic questions about biological warfare and gave precautionary measures pertaining to cleanliness, food supplies, and drinking water. *Science Newsletter* reviewed the main features of the BW Civil Defense pamphlet and elaborated on various diseases which might be employed in a germ war attack.[51]

In May, 1951, the press reported a national effort to systematize civil defenses against biological warfare. Public health officials from thirty states met with representatives of the U.S. Public Health Service, the National Institutes of Health, and the Civil Defense Administration at the United States government's Communicable Disease Center in Atlanta, Georgia. The delegates created a system for monitoring the daily absentee rates in offices, factories, and schools as a method of determining whether the country was under biological attack.[52]

In the context of the Korean War, American preparations for defense against BW at home was seen by Communist authorities and the *Review* as indicative of plans to add germ weapons to the rain of destruction already falling on North Korean targets. The intense focus in the American press over preparations for biological warfare, together with the Soviet account of Japanese BW development (technology now inherited by the United States), predisposed Communist authorities in China and North Korea to view a bacteriological attack by the United States as a real possibility.

Had not American specialists affirmed the desirability of field-testing bacteriological weapons, and stated that they would no doubt be used if the fighting in Korea continued?[53] Had they not indicated the difficulty of detecting these weapons?[54] And was not the United States already conducting an inhumane air war against the Korean people and the Chinese People's Volunteers? And might not the intensified activity to create a BW defense within the United States, and the fear of Soviet retaliation, be, in fact, a reflection of imminent plans to use germ warfare in Korea? In March, 1951, the Chinese press recalled that:

> During World War II, the Japanese army used bombs with bacteria of bubonic plague and typhus after their invasion of northern and central China. . . After the defeat of Japan the war criminals enjoyed MacArthur's protection and were not punished.

And it warned that:

> U.S. authorities assigned Ishii Shiro, leading Japanese bacteriological warfare expert, to develop bacteriological weapons to be used against us, instead of punishing him as a war criminal.[55]

*

As United Nations' forces retreated through devastated portions of North Korea during the harsh winter of 1950–51, major epidemics of smallpox broke out among the local population.[56] On May 8, 1951, North Korea lodged an official protest to the United Nations. According to North Korean Foreign Minister Bak Hun Yung, the contagion had been intentionally planted among the Korean civilian population, the Korean People's Army, and Chinese military forces by American troops throughout their line of retreat in December, 1950.

Seven to eight days after the Americans passed through, Bak reported, smallpox broke out and increased to 3,500 cases by April, 1951. He said there were no cases in districts which had not been occupied by U.S. troops. He accused the U.S. of "openly collaborating with Japanese Bacteriological war criminals" (Ishii Shiro, Wakamatsu Jiro, and Kitano Masajo), who had been protected by the U.S. from prosecution for war crimes committed in China during World War II.[57] He pointed to American news reports of a U.S. Navy epidemic control ship lying off the North Korean Coast as proof the Americans were following in Japan's footsteps by performing BW experiments on North Korean and Chinese captives.[58]

Throughout March, April, and May, 1951, the bacteriological warfare charges reverberated briefly in the Chinese and Russian print and broadcast media, and then faded.[59] Then, after a hiatus of almost a year, a more concerted campaign of BW charges began which would quickly reach world-wide proportions and echo through the world press, the British Parliament, the U.S. Congress, and U.N. Security Council Debates.

The *China Monthly Review* became an important part of the bacteriological warfare propaganda blitz emanating from the Communist countries from the spring of 1952, largely because it was the only independent, Western-owned and controlled journal left operating in China. While the next chapter will focus on the *Review*'s involvement in the BW propaganda campaign, before concluding, I will summarize the extent and importance of the international controversy which the BW charges engendered throughout 1952–53, the context of the *Review*'s activities.

*

At the end of February, 1952, the North Korean Foreign Minister made detailed charges to the United Nations Secretariat alleging bacteriological attacks by the U.S. Airforce on eleven different sites in North Korea.[60] His accusations were fully supported before the United Nations by Chinese Foreign Minister Zhou Enlai, who shortly thereafter charged that American aircraft had conducted numerous bacteriological attacks on locations within China itself.[61] Soviet Press and radio broadcasts editorialized the charges, condemning the United States for its barbarous acts against humanity in Korea and China.[62]

Similar condemnations soon appeared in Communist journals in France, India, Brazil, and Canada. Reports of the allegations reverberated in major newspapers and journals all over the world. The BW charges were discussed in Parliament by the British House of Lords.[63] The United Nations representative of the Soviet Union, Yakov Malik, who served as president of the U.N. Security Council in June, introduced the BW allegations into Security Council debate, and into the U.N. Disarmament Commission, of which he was also a member.[64] The Red Cross Societies of China, Rumania, Hungary, Bulgaria, and Poland all protested alleged U.S. bacteriological weapons use to the International Committee of the Red Cross (ICRC) in Geneva.

After Zhou Enlai endorsed the North Korean BW charges, diplomats from India, Pakistan, Indonesia, and Burma all expressed anxiety to the British Charge at Beijing, Lionel Lamb. The British, concerned over the effects of the accusations on other Asian countries, urged the U.S. Secretary of State to call for an impartial investigation by some "neutral" agency, such as the International Committee of the Red Cross.[65] The following day, March 4, 1952, Secretary of State Dean Acheson stated that the biological warfare charges were "categorically and unequivocally" false.[66] The Secretary General of the United Nations, the United Nations Commander in Chief, and the United States Secretary of Defense also made statements denying the charges.

Following the suggestion of the British Ambassador, Acheson sent a request (March 11) to the ICRC in Geneva asking them to investigate, and informed President Truman that:

> The Communist campaign against us, charging that we have engaged in biological warfare, has been making headway in the Asian countries. We thought it necessary to take some further step to counter-act it. After conferring with General Ridgeway, I sent off last night a letter to the President of the International Red Cross, the text of which follows this message to you. We plan to plug this heavily on the Voice of America and other media.[67]

Acheson requested that the ICRC determine the extent of the epidemics which he assumed were in progress in North Korea. He believed the results would provide ". . . additional evidence of the falsity of the biological warfare charge." Scientific experts from neutral Asian countries were to be included in the ICRC's scientific investigating committee.[68]

At almost the same time (March 4), the Soviet leadership sponsored the investigation of the Commision of the International Association of Democratic Lawyers (treated in chapter 9), which was similarly commissioned by the Soviet government to ". . . investigate and establish the crimes committed by the interventionalists in Korea."[69] On March 14, the USSR introduced the bacteriological warfare allegations into the United Nations' Disarmament Commission, and repeatedly injected the BW issue into the United Nations Security Council proceedings.[70]

Chinese Foreign Minister Zhou Enlai on March 8, 1952, only four days after the initial U.S. denial of BW use in Korea, accused the United States of flying a total of 448 missions during a six day period over Northeast China and dropping diseased insects over several Chinese cities, including Qingdao. At a Joint meeting of the U.S. State Department and the Joint Chiefs of Staff (March 19), the Deputy Assistant Secretary of State for Far Eastern Affairs (Nelson T. Johnson) and the Assistant Secretary of State (H. Freeman Matthews), sought assurances from the military that no U.S. planes had been in the vicinity of Qingdao at the time BW attacks were alleged to have taken place. The Joint Chiefs' response at best projected uncertainty born of wartime confusion, and at worse could be interpreted in a more cynical vein.

> *Mr. Matthews:* . . . The Chinese Communists have specifically charged that on 6 March three U.S. planes dropped canisters containing germ-laden flies on Tsingtao. The Chinese Communist Foreign Office states that these canisters and their contents are now being scientifically studied at Peking medical center. The Chinese Communists state that this is the first time U.S. planes have attacked China proper. They further state that similar canisters have been picked up near Panmunjom and elsewhere in North Korea.

Mr. Johnson: The Chinese Communist radio has elaborated this theme. It has reported that a U.S. plane flew over Tsingtao and that all kinds of bugs were released-ants, beetles, flies, fleas, etc.

Mr. Matthews: Of course we know that no bugs were dropped but we want to be sure before replying to New Delhi that no U.S. planes were over Tsingtao on reconnaissance missions.

General Vandenberg: Certainly no such flights have been authorized. If you wish, I can query to determine whether any flights were undertaken on local authority.

Mr. Matthews: Do they have local authority to make such flights?

General Vandenberg: They are doing some reconnaissance over Manchuria.

General Lee: They have no authority locally to fly over the area you mentioned.

Mr. Johnson: It would be helpful if we could state categorically that no planes were over the area.

Admiral Fechteler: If any were flying over they were only taking photographs. I doubt that there were any there.

Mr. Matthews: Is it your answer that there were no planes there?

General Vandenberg: I recommend that you state categorically that none were there whether or not any were there. I do not think any were there.[71]

In the United Nations Security Council and in the U.N. Disarmament Commission, Yakov Malik, the Soviet Union's representative in both bodies, repeatedly accused the United States of using bacteriological weapons and demanded that the Security Council and Disarmament Commission call the Americans to account for such actions. He pointed out that the United States had not signed the 1925 Geneva Protocol banning bacteriological weapons, a point meant to lend credence to BW charges, and which forced onto the United States the defensive task of trying to explain how the isolationism of the 1920's, coupled with concerns over the treaty's lack of enforceability, had prevented its ratification.[72]

On March 12, the International Committee of the Red Cross agreed to investigate the bacteriological warfare charges and the United States quickly accepted the offer. Nations aligned with the United States tried to pressure the USSR's representative (Malik) into using the good offices of the Soviet Union to encourage China and North Korea to accept the ICRC's investigation. France and Britain accused the Soviets of making the serious charges of bacteriological weapons use without any evidence whatever to back it up. The issue of proof, or the lack thereof, was now pushed forward for both sides.[73]

As Albert E. Cowdrey has shown, evidence gathered by U.S. intelligence sources indicated that the epidemic environment of 1951 had cleared up in North Korea by 1952.[74] Perhaps unaware of this information, Secretary of State Acheson (March 1952) accused the Communists of trying to cover-up their own inability to deal with naturally occurring disease outbreaks by blaming it on the United States. He noted that both the Red Cross and the United Nations' World Health Organization had offered to lend assistance to the Communists in fighting epidemics in North Korea and China.[75]

Following the U.S. lead, Great Britain, France, Brazil, Chile and Taiwan (the Republic of China) all accused the Communists of using the "big lie" technique to distract attention from epidemics they were unable to control in China and Korea. The British representative, Sir Gladwyn Jebb, recalled that in 1948 the Soviets had blamed a potato crop failure in Czechoslovakia on the United States as well, claiming American planes had dropped potato bugs.[76]

In response, the North Korean and Chinese governments, while playing up the barbarity of bacteriological attacks, refused to make any casualty figures available and insisted that anti-epidemic mobilization efforts had thwarted the worst effects of the attacks. Offers by the World Health Organization and the ICRC to help fight epidemics in North Korea and China were depicted as crude attempts by the United States to gauge the effects of BW attacks.[77]

On March 26, at a Disarmament Commission Meeting, Malik rejected the International Committee of the Red Cross's offer to investigate the BW charges. The ICRC was not an international organization, he asserted, but was Swiss, and as such could not be expected to be impartial or objective.[78] According to Secretary of State Acheson, the Soviet refusal to allow an investigation by the ICRC demonstrated that there was no truth to their bacteriological warfare charges.[79]

The BW issue further polarized the international community into two camps, with capitalist nations accepting U.S. assurances that the BW accusations were false, and those of the Soviet bloc just as adamantly insisting they were true. Although both sides had made arrangements to have "impartial" scientific investigations carried out by qualified personnel, only the investigation sanctioned and organized by the Communist side would be allowed to compile evidence in China and North Korea. Both China and the Soviet Union were influential in the organization that chose the personnel of the "International Scientific Commission for Investigation of the Facts Concerning Bacteriological Warfare in Korea and China," which authenticated the main body of evidence assembled by Communist authorities to support the BW allegations.[80]

To bolster the evidence which the "International Scientific Commission" would put forward in the early fall, 1952, confessions by American prisoners of war were widely publicized in the Communist media. The *China Monthly Review* was fully integrated into this propaganda effort. The *Review* highlighted articles from U.S. journals which seemed to corroborate Communist charges. Because it was American-owned and operated, and because it was well known in the States[81], it played a particularly conspicuous role in this orchestration.

Yet, the bacteriological warfare allegations as they appeared in the *Review* were a natural out-growth of the steady escalation of the air war in Korea with all its attendant horrors. Photographs and reports of numerous atrocities, evidence of the results of bombing and of the use of napalm were everywhere around Powell and his staff: in newspaper accounts, in journals, in newsreel films, and in the Communist broadcast media. Even had the *Review* not been coordinated with the rest of the Chinese media, could its editors have ignored that which was most prominent and pervasive in the journalistic world around them? The following chapter will examine the role of Powell's journal in the unfolding BW controversy.

CHAPTER NOTES

1. James Endicott, "Building a New China", *CMR*, July 1952, p.31 ; James Endicott, "The Christian Church in China Today", *CMR*, May 1952, p.430; James Endicott, "How American Imperialism Used Religion in China", *CMR*, June 1952, p.543. Like Powell, Endicott too, on his return home to Canada found himself under attack for alleged disloyalty.

2. "Clear and identifiable evidence that the United States experimented with biological weapons in the Korean War is not available in the U.S. archives *as they presently exist* for public scrutiny." Stephen Endicott and Edward Hagerman, *The United States and Biological Warfare, Secrets from the Early Cold War and Korea*. (Bloomington: Indiana University Press, 1998),p.188.

3. John Ellis van Courtland Moon, "Dubious Allegations, The United States and Biological Warfare: Secrets from the Early Cold War and Korea," *The Bulletin of the Atomic Scientists*, May-June 1999, p.70–72; Ed Regis, "Wartime Lies?", *New York Times Book Review*, 27 June 1999,p.22.

4. The supporting evidence for bacteriological warfare allegations gathered by North Korea and China during the Korean War is treated in chapter 9.

5. Milton Leitenberg, *The Korean War: Biological Warfare Resolved*. (Stockholm: Stockholm International Peace Research Institute, 1998),p.1; Kathryn Weathersby, "Deceiving the Deceivers: Moscow, Beijing, Pyongyang, and the Allegations of Bacteriological Weapons Use in Korea", *Cold War International History Project, Bulletin No. 11*, Winter 1998; Milton Leitenberg, "New Russian Evidence on the Korean War Biological Warfare Allegations: Background and Analysis," *Cold War International History Project, Bulletin 11*, Winter 1998; Yasuro Naito, "The Use of Bacteriological Weapons by U.S. Forces During the Korean War Was Fabricated by China and Korea: Uncovered by Classified Documents of the Former Soviet Union", *Sankei Shimbun*, 8 January 1998.

6. These included bent leaflet-bomb containers, photographs of insects in the snow, microscopic photographs of pathogens allegedly disseminated, and testimony of peasants and farmers implicating U.S. aircraft.

7. "Who Commits the Atrocities?", *CMR*, January 1951, p.18; "Never Call Retreat", *CMR*, February 1951, p.70–71; "Wanton Bombing of Korean Civilians", *CWR*, 5 August 1950, p.158; Bruce Cummings, *The Origins of the Korean War, Volume II, The Roaring of the Cataract, 1947–1950*.(Princeton: Princeton University Press, 1990) p.747–756.

8. Treated in chapter 9 of this dissertation.

9. "Working Rules For Foreign Organizations", (*Hsinhua*, 15 January 1951), *North China Daily News*, 16 January 1951,p.1; "SMCC Starts Registering Foreign Cultural Bodies", *North China Daily News*, 20 January 1951,p.1.

10. "115 American Companies Placed Under Control",(*Hsinhua*, 2 January 1951), *North China Daily News*, 4 January 1951,p.1; "Shanghai Welcomes Government Control of U.S.Assets", (*Hsinhua*, 31 December 1950), *North China Daily News*, 3 January 1951,p.1.

11. "Americans May Withdraw Only PDU 1,000 Monthly", *North China Daily News*, 5 January 1951, p.1; "U.S.Residents' Firms' Bank Withdrawals", (*Hsinhua*, 15 January 1951), *North China Daily News*, 17 January 1951,p.2 ; Shun-Hsin Chou, *The Chinese Inflation 1937–1949*.(New York: Columbia University Press, 1963) p.151–5; Roderick MacFarquhar and John King Fairbank, eds, *The Cambridge History of China, Volume 14, The People's Republic, Part I: The Emergence of Revolutionary China 1949–1965*. (London: Cambridge University Press, 1987) p.150–152. Parity Deposit Units, or "PDU" were a form of foreign exchange controls to prevent the flight of foreign currency, which was badly needed to pay for imports, interest on foreign loans, etc. As an anti-inflationary device, the value of all bank deposits and bonds were in general tied to four basic commodities: rice, wheat flour, cotton cloth and coal. Previously, the Nationalist government had also tried to prevent the flight of foreign currency with its Foreign Exchange Clearance Certificate System and the Foreign Exchange Surrender Certificate System. The Clearance Certificate System was abandoned in May, 1949. The Communist government of Shanghai replaced it with the Foreign Exchange Deposit Certificate System in June, 1949. And in 1950, the Central People's Government centralized most aspects of the financial and tax system, taking it out of the control of local governments.

12. "SMCC Starts Registering Cultural Bodies", *North China Daily News*", 20 January 1951,p.1.

13. *Ibid*; "Working Rules For Foreign Organizations",(*Hsinhua*, 15 January 1951), *North China Daily News*, 16 January 1951,p.1.

14. John W. Powell, "China Cleans House", *CMR*, May 1952,p.456–464.

15. *Ibid*; Powell, ed. "Extortion Racket Exposed, Thought Reform", *CMR*, February 1952, p.117–122; Chen Ren-bing, "New China's Thought Reform Movement", *CMR* 1952,p.123–135.

16. Powell, ed. "The Month in Review, Thought Reform", *CMR*, February 1952, p.120–2; Also, Dr.Chen Ren-bing, Dean of the College of Arts at St.John's University in Shanghai, gives a much more detailed analysis of the Thought Reform Movement in: Chen Ren-bing, "New China's Thought Reform Movement", *CMR*, February 1952, p.123–130.

17. "Xin wen, xu ban: Zheng wu yuan guan yu tong yi fa bu zhong yang ren min zheng fu, ji qi suo shu ge ji guan zhong yao xin wen de zan xing ban fa," [Newspapers and Publications: Provisional Regulations of the Government Administrative Council Regarding Unifying and Promoting Important News of the Central People's Government and its Agencies]; "Di yi jie guan guo chu ban hui yi wu xiang jue yi," [First Session of the All-China National Publications Meeting, Five Decisions.] both in: *Zhong Yang Ren Min Zheng Fu Fa Ling Hui Bian, 1949–1950 Volume 1*. (Beijing: Ren Min Chu Ban She, 1952). [*Central People's Government Collected Laws and Regulations, 1949–1950 Volume 1*. Beijing: People's Publishing Company, 1952.] p.617–626; 627–630.

18. Letters expressing these themes were a sign of progress in thought reform, which all U.S. prisoners of war had to undergo. The *Review* sometimes printed these letters as part of larger feature stories. See chapter 9.

19. Peter Williams and David Wallace, *Unit 731, The Japanese Army's Secret of Secrets*. (London: Hodder and Stoughton, 1989); Hal Gold, *Unit 731 Testimony*. (Tokyo: Yenbooks, 1996); Sheldon H.Harris, *Factories of Death, Japanese Biological Warfare 1932–45 and the American Cover-up*. (London: Routledge, 1994).

20. John W.Powell, "A Hidden Chapter in History", *The Bulletin of the Atomic Scientists*, Volume 37, no.8 (October 1981)p.44–52. Although all the major belligerents during World War II were conducting research into BW weapons, Japan's program was the most advanced.

21. Yoshinaga Haruko, "A Bruise - Terror of the 731 Corps", documentary, Tokyo Broadcasting System, 2 November 1976.

22. Powell, ed. "Germ Warfare: A Sign of Desperation in Korea", *CMR*, April 1952, p.342–331.

23. *Materials on the Trial of Former Servicemen of the Japanese Army Charged with Manufacturing and Employing Bacteriological Weapons* (Moscow: Foreign Languages Publishing House, 1950).

24. "Bacteriological Warfare Charge", *CWR*, 31 December 1949, p.83; Powell, ed."Germ Warfare: A Sign of Desperation in Korea", *CMR*, April 1952, p.324.

25. Vice Foreign Minister of the People's Republic of China Li Ke-nung to Mr.P.A.Shibaev, Charge d'Affaires of the Soviet Union, Peking, 8 February 1950, "China's Foreign Relations During the Past Year,(translated by Hsinhua News Agency),Part VI.-Miscellaneous, Trial of Japanese War Criminals", in Supplement, *CMR*, October 1950, p.11–12.

26. *Ibid.*

27. Gerard Piel, "BW", *Life*, 18 November 1946.

28. "Congressmen Reveal Germ Weapon Can Wipe Out City at Single Blow", *New York Times*, 1 December 1946; "Ounce of New Superpoison Held Able to Wipe Out U.S., Canada", *New York Times*, 19 September 1946; "Waitt Confirms New Superpoison", *New York Times*, 20 September 1946; Hanson W. Baldwin, "Germ War Is Studied", *New York Times*, 27 September 1946.

29. "Better Than the Bomb", *Time*, 30 June 1946.

30. Sidney Shallet, "The Deadliest War", *Collier's*, 15 June 1946; Dyson Carter, "New Ways of Killing", *New Masses*, 3 September 1946; "Germ Weapon Called Just a Mighty Rumor", *New York World-Telegram*, 25 May 1946; Gerald Wendt, "Silent Death", *Science Illustrated*, October 1946; Special Projects Division, Chemical Warfare Service, Camp Detrick, Maryland, "Plant Growth Regulators", *Science*, 103:468, 19 April 1946; "United States Navy Coveralls for Use in Germ and Poison Warfare" *Newsweek*, 14 January 1946 (photographs p.76); George W.Merck, "Report to the Secretary of War on Biological Warfare" (summary), *Bulletin of the Atomic Scientists*, 2:16, 1 October 1946.

31. "Activities of the United States in the Field of Biological Warfare," a Report to the Secretary of War by George W.Merck, Special Consultant on Biological Warfare, Entry 488, Box 182, Records Group 165, National Archives.

32. George W.Merck, "Official Report on Biological Warfare", *Bulletin of the Atomic Scientists*, March 1946, p.16–18; George W.Merck, "Report to the Secretary of War on Biological Warfare", *Military Surgeon*, 98:237, March 1946; *New York Times*, 4 January 1946.

33. "U.S. Studying Atom and Germ Warfare Defenses", *New York Herald Tribune*, 1 December 1947; "Army Is Silent on Germ Warfare", *New York Sun*, 23 January 1947; "Army Bans News on Germ Weapons", *New York Herald Tribune*, 15 September 1947; "Hush on Germ Warfare", *San Francisco Chronicle*, 27 January 1947; "Army Secrets Get Airing in Congressional Talks", *New York Herald Tribune*, 24 May 1948; Leonard Engel, "The Scope of Biological Warfare", *The Nation*, 26 July 1947; Jerome Feiner, "If Biological Warfare Comes", *Harpers*, May 1948.

34. Theodor Rosebury, Elvin A.Kabat, and Martin H.Bolt, "Bacterial Warfare" [1942 Report to the U.S.Government], *Journal of Immunology*, 56:7, May 1947; Theodor Rosebury, *Peace or Pestilence, Biological Warfare and How to Avoid It*. (New York: Whittlesey House, McGraw-Hill Book Company, 1949).

35. "Report of the International Scientific Commission for the Investigation of the Facts Concerning Bacteriological Warfare in Korea and China", Supplement, *People's China*, 17 September 1952. See for example, p.27: "Ten years ago Rosebury expressed the view that it might be possible to spread this effectively for warlike purposes, but only in rear areas remote from the front lines owing to the great danger of the infection of friendly territory. In Korea the Commission's work has revealed repeated attempts to diffuse plague at places not far removed from the front lines, contrary to the opinion of so experienced a bacteriologist as the former Director of Camp Detrick."

36. "War by Disease", *Newsweek*, 30 May 1949, p.52–3.

37. Franklin D.Roosevelt, President of the United States, 8 June 1943, *Documents of American Foreign Relations, Volume 5*. (Boston: World Peace Foundation, 1944).

38. "Congressmen Reveal Germ Weapon Can Wipe Out City at Single Blow", *New York Times*, 1 December 1946; Ounce of New Superpoison Held Able to Wipe Out U.S., Canada", *New York Times*, 19 September 1946; "Waitt Confirms New Superpoison", *New York Times*, 20 September 1946; "Better Than the Bomb", *Time*, 30 June 1946.

39. "War by Disease", *Newsweek*, 30 May 1949.

40. "Destructive Biological Weapon", *North China Daily News*, 11 September 1949, p.2.

41. "Professor Bernal on Biological War Weapon", *North China Daily News*, 12 September 1949,p.1; "An Appeal of the World Peace Council Against Bacteriological Warfare", (Oslo, 1 April 1952), in Supplement, *People's China*, 16 April 1952, p.1. Dr.Bernal was a "Vice President" of the World Peace Council, the organization based in Prague which later organized the International Scientific Commission For the Investigation of the Facts Concerning Bacteriological Warfare in Korea and China. See "Report of the International Scientific Commission for the Investigation of the Facts Concerning Bacteriological Warfare in Korea and China", Supplement, *People's China*, 17 September 1952, p.4.

42. Besides destroying all cities in North Korea, the United States in 1951 increased the pressure on the People's Republic by bombing Dandong in Manchuria, the largest Chinese city on the north side of the Yalu river. See: Jon Halliday and Bruce Cummings, *Korea, The Unknown War*.(New York: Pantheon Books, 1988.)p.162–163.

43. "Germ Warfare Likely", *Science Newsletter*, 4 June 1949, p.359.

44. "Trials of Germ Warfare", *Science Newsletter*, 1 October 1949, p.210.

45. "Germ Warfare Detection", *Science Newsletter*, 28 October 1949,p.275.

46. "Germ Warfare in Korea?", *Science Newsletter*, 8 July 1950, p.22.

47. *Ibid.*

48. Chapman Pincher, B.Sc. "Epidemics Made to Order", *Science Digest*, April 1951, p. 52–7, reprinted from *Discovery* (London), December, 1950.

49. "Forecasts Better Weapons Against Germ Warfare", *Science Newsletter*, 31 January 1951, p.27.

50. Federal Civil Defense Administration, *What You Should Know About Biological Warfare.*(Washington, D.C.: United States Government Printing Office, 1951).

51. "Disease Danger in War", *Science Newsletter*, 24 March 1951, p.188.

52. "Warn of Germ Warfare", *Science Newsletter*, 19 May 1951, p.317.

53. "Germ Warfare Likely", *Science Newsletter*, 4 June 1949, p.356; "Germ Warfare In Korea?", *Science Newsletter*, 8 July 1950, p.22.

54. "Germ Warfare Detection", *Science Newsletter*, 28 October 1949, p.275.

55. Beijing *Jenmin Jihbao*, 7 March 1951; *Hsinhua* as quoted by Prague *Svobodne Slavo*, 24 March 1951, Central Intelligence Agency, Foreign Documents Division, "A Report on Foreign Press Coverage of Anti-U.S. CW (and BW) Propaganda", 2 July 1951, p.6,18, as cited in Albert E.Cowdrey, *United States Army in the Korean War, The Medics' War.* (Washington, D.C.: Center of Military History, United States Army, 1987)p.219.

56. Cowdrey, *United States Army in the Korean War, The Medics' War*, p.220.

57. Powell, ed. "The Month in Review, Crime Against Humanity", *CMR*, March 1852, p.226–7.

58. *Ibid.*

59. Earnest A.Gross, Deputy U.S. Representative to the United Nations, Security Council Statement, 1 July 1952, "The Soviet Germ Warfare Campaign: The Story of the Big Lie", United States *Department of State Bulletin*, 28 July 1952, p.154.

60. United Nations Document. S/2684; Powell, ed. "The Month in Review, Crime Against Humanity", *CMR*, March 1952, p.225–30; Gross, (Security Council Statement of July 1) "The Soviet Germ Warfare Campaign: The Strategy of the Big Lie", 28 July 1952, *Bulletin*, p.154.

61. United Nations Document. S/2684/Addendum 1; Powell, ed. "The Month in Review, U.S. Extends Germ Warfare", *CMR*, April 1952, p.317. Zhou alleged that U.S. planes had carried out 448 flights over Northeast China, and had carried out BW attacks on Fushun, Xinmin, Andong, Guandian, Linjiang, and Qingdao. Secretary of State Acheson vigorously denied this on March 4.

62. *Pravda*, 14 March 1952; *Izvestia* 14 March 1952, both cited in Gross, "The Soviet Germ War Campaign: The Strategy of the Big Lie", 28 July 1952, *Bulletin*, p.155.

63. *London Times*, 16 July 1952, p.16; Cowdrey, *United States Army in Korea, The Medics' War*, p.220–3; Gross, Statement, "The Soviet Germ Warfare Campaign: The Strategy of the Big Lie", *Bulletin*, 28 July 1952,p.155.

64. Ernest A.Gross, Deputy U.S. Representative to the United Nations, Statements, "U.S. Proposes Investigation of Bacteriological Warfare Charges", U.S. Department of State, *Bulletin*, 7 July 1952, p.32, n.

65. "Memorandum of Conversation, by the Deputy Assistant Secretary of State for Far Eastern Affairs (Johnson)", 3 March 1952, United States Department of

State, *Foreign Relations of the United States, Diplomatic Papers 1952–1954, Volume 15, Korea, Part 1.*(Washington, D.C.: Government Printing Office, 1984), p.73–4. Cited hereafter as *FRUS, 1953–1954, Vol.15*

66. Dean Acheson, Statement, 4 March 1952, *Department of State Bulletin*, 17 March 1952, p.427.

67. The Secretary of State (Dean Acheson) to the President, 11 March 1952, *FRUS 1952–1954,Vol.15,*p.79.

68. Ernest A. Gross, Deputy U.S. Representative to the United Nations, Security Council Statement of July 1, "The Soviet Germ Warfare Campaign: The Strategy of the Big Lie", *State Department Bulletin*, 28 July 1952,p.154.

69. *Ibid*; United Nations Document S/2684/ addendum 1, 30 June 1952; Commission of the International Association of Democratic Lawyers, "Report on U.S. Crimes in Korea", Supplement, *People's China*, 1 June 1952,p.3–19. The "Report" enumerates particular instances of alleged bacteriological and chemical attacks, as well as massacres, strafings, and other atrocities.

70. *Ibid*.p.156–7.

71. "Memorandum of the Substance of Discussion at a Department of State-Joint Chiefs of Staff Meeting," Top Secret, 19 March 1952, *FRUS, 1952–1954, Vol.15,*p.101–2. General Robert M. Lee was Director of Plans, Office of the Deputy Chief of Staff Operations for the U.S. Air Force. General Hoyt S. Vandenberg was Chief of Staff for the Air Force, and Admiral William N. Fechteler was Chief of Naval Operations for the U.S. Navy.

72. Ambassador Benjamin V. Cohen, Deputy U.S. Representative to the United Nations, Statement, "Advancement of World Peace Through Disarmament", 14 March 1952, *Department of State Bulletin*, 31 March 1952, p.506; "The United States in the United Nations", 15–27 March 1952, *Department of State Bulletin*, 31 March 1952, p.515–16.

73. *Ibid*.

74. Cowdrey, *The United States Army in the Korean War, The Medics' War.* p222–224; 225.

75. Dean Acheson, United States Secretary of State, Statement, 26 March 1952, *Department of State Bulletin*, 7 April 1952, p.529; Cowdrey, *United States Army in the Korean War, The Medics' War.* p.225–6.

76. "The United States in the United Nations", Security Council, Disarmament Commission, 20,26 March 1952, *Department of State Bulletin*, 31 March 1952, p.515.

77. Guo Moro, "Guo Moro Answers Questions on U.S. Bacteriological Warfare Put to Him By *L'Humanite*, Paris," *People's China*, 1 May 1952, p.11. "This can only be the desire of the organizers of bacteriological warfare to find out the effects of their experiment."

78. "The United States in the United Nations", *Department of State Bulletin*, 31 March 1952,p.516.

79. Dean Acheson, U.S. Secretary of State, "Further Denial of Soviet 'Germ Warfare' Allegations", 26 March 1952, *Department of State Bulletin*, 7 April 1952, p.529.

80. World Peace Council, "An Appeal of the World Peace Council Against Bacteriological Warfare",(Oslo, 29 March-1 April 1952) Supplement, *People's China*, 16 April 1952, p.1. CCP intellectuals Guo Moro and Mao Dun were leading members of the World Peace Council, based in Prague, which organized the Commission.

81. The *China Weekly Review* had an illustrious history under J.B. Powell, and his son, John W. Powell, had gained notoriety before the fall of Shanghai, through his coverage of the Taiwan revolt.

CHAPTER TEN

THE BACTERIOLOGICAL WARFARE ISSUE AND THE *REVIEW*, PART II

The first reports of bacteriological warfare in the *China Monthly Review* appeared within the context of a larger campaign calling attention to the savage nature of the air war in Korea and in the midst of charges and counter charges of atrocities. It was at first an incidental addition to a litany of horror stories, most of which involved aerial bombardment and strafing of civilian centers and the widespread use of napalm by American attack aircraft. Although most news stories were drawn from the available Communist news sources, whenever applicable, Powell utilized American press or wire service reports, along with corroborating testimony extracted from U.S. servicemen (under duress) in Chinese POW camps.

We have seen that the Chinese and North Korean charges that American forces were employing germ warfare were preceded by a lengthy paper trail from both American and Soviet sources which no doubt led Communist authorities to anticipate possible use of BW by American forces after the fashion of Japanese germ warfare in World War II. Certainly the United States was worried over the possibility of Soviet BW attacks, not just within Korea, but on American cities as well. With both sides already sensitive over the issue, and with American domination of the sky in Korea leading to an escalating air war, the stage was set for the confrontation.

As noted, previous to the BW charges, the Chinese and Soviet governments had been calling for the punishment of former Japanese military personnel who had been granted immunity from prosecution by American authorities in return for their cooperation with the American BW program. At the same time, the bacteriological warfare controversy took place during an unprecedented attempt by the Chinese Communist Party to mobilize medical resources at home to wipe out epidemic diseases in China. This medical campaign had been ongoing since 1949, and was amply covered by the *Review*. Once the Chinese and North Koreans became convinced that the United States was utilizing bacterial weapons, they adapted these mass-mobilization techniques to combat the potential BW threat in Korea.

*

In the *Review*, the peace movement, American POW testimony, and the theme of atrocities and later of bacteriological warfare emerged in conjunction with one another and were mutually reinforcing. During the first month of the Korean War, C. Y. W. Meng explaining why he signed the "World Peace Appeal" sponsored by the Stockholm Peace Congress and the Chinese government, echoed a theme Powell had already repeated: America as recent champion of democracy now fallen from grace.

> Many far sighted and progressive American statesmen and private observers have long championed the cause of the oppressed peoples of the world. For a while under the enlightened administration of Roosevelt, it appeared that the United States might become a force for progress and peace in the world.
>
> However, following the conclusion of World War II, it became clear beyond all doubt that reaction was triumphing in America and that, instead of becoming a leading force for democracy and progress, the United States was to become the fortress of reaction.[1]

Meng feared that the Korean War could be the starting spark for a third world war. He criticized the American policy of bombing Korean cities, drawing parallels with the Japanese bombing of Chinese cities during World War II. Without war, science might have turned its attention to alleviating disease and want in the world. "The great tragedy," Meng believed,

> is that the world's scientists, the pioneers of the modern world, are in greater or lesser degree forced to concentrate their efforts upon production of weapons of destruction. In America, science has been almost completely subjugated to the military.[2]

Powell editorialized on the ". . . lack of enthusiasm with which the American people have accepted this 'colonial war'," and noted that the World Peace Appeal campaign in America reported ". . . a great increase in the number of signatures in favor of peace and in favor of outlawing the atomic bomb." The use of testimony by American prisoners of war to demonstrate the immorality of the war, to contribute to anti-war sentiment, and to confirm atrocity reports began the very first month of the conflict. Powell believed that the low morale of U.S. troops in Korea and the fact that a number of American prisoners of war had collaborated with their North Korean captors demonstrated the unpopularity of the war among most Americans.

> A number of the American prisoners captured by the North Korean forces have signed a statement calling for the withdrawal of Americans from Korea and a speedy end to the war. Several of the prisoners have made broadcasts to the United States and to their fellow soldiers calling for a

halt to American participation in the conflict. This action by the American POW's is especially significant in view of the fact that it has never happened before. In no previous war have American troops, following their captors, been so ready to condemn the actions of their own government.[3]

Having to view the actions of the outside world through the prism of Communist revolution, Powell concluded that the Truman administration was going against the wishes of the American people, and most of the people of the world. He saw the actions of the POW's and the Peace Appeal as positive indications that peace could still be won. No matter how determined the Truman government was to carry out its interventionist policy in Korea, Powell warned, it would find it impossible once the American people were sufficiently aroused in opposition.[4] To inform the American people of the true nature and horror of the war in Korea became the *Review*'s purpose.

As U.S. and South Korean troops fought to maintain an ever shrinking perimeter in the face of the North Korean advance, American air and naval superiority resulted in the mass destruction of North Korean cities and towns, and heavy loss of life. These tactics developed out of World War II, were accepted without question by the American military, and increased in ferocity as the Korean War dragged on.[5] The bulk of the two million Korean civilian deaths during the war were directly or indirectly attributable to aerial bombing by U.S. forces.[6]

By August, 1950, the human cost of American bombing raids became a recurrent feature in the *Review* as it did also in the *North China Daily News*, *People's China* and the *Shanghai News*. It is well to remember, in addition to the propaganda value of the reports, the reality of human suffering behind them. Under the direction of Communist prison camp personnel, American POW's through small group discussion sessions, criticism, and self criticism, were made acutely aware of this destruction, and of the struggle of the Korean people against colonialism and for unification. Ill-prepared psychologically, and having been recently thrust into combat from the relatively comfortable task of occupation in Japan, with little understanding of Korean history, some American G.I.'s proved susceptible to Communist methods of thought reform. Statements by repentant prisoners, and even letters of encouragement from resident Americans in China to POW's who had begun taking part in the peace movement, were increasingly featured in the *Review*.

Within the first month of the war, the *Review* printed excerpts from a Pyongyang radio broadcast of July, 1950, by Sergeant Merlin J. Hamilton of the thirty-fourth U.S. Infantry Regiment of the twenty-fourth Division. "The peaceful Korean people are now being slaughtered by air raids and bombardment by American warships," Hamilton said in his broadcast. "Their homes and schools, built by their own sweat, are being cruelly destroyed." He called on U.S. forces to stop fighting and either return home or join the Korean People's Army.[7] One hundred and fifteen American POW's issued a joint statement calling for the removal of all foreign troops from Korea. Their appeal was also broadcast.[8]

"American planes are bombing the homes of the North Korean people with a horrible savagery" began a *Review* article reprinted from *Xinhua*. It described the results of bombings north of Pyongyang from July sixth through the thirteenth.

> In one congested workers' quarter an acre of ramshackle houses had been laid level by a giant bomb in the raid on the thirteenth. Men and women wandered listlessly over it, poking amid the rubble of their homes for bits of property. Over it still hung that smell of bombardment and death which is the same in any country. . . .
>
> The rescue workers had just discovered another man or women. . . , already covered with a black gauntlet of flies.[9]

News briefs on July fifteenth and twenty-second reported that the U.S. House Armed Services Committee and the State Department were considering the use of atomic bombs in Korea. The *Review* cited the *Washington Post* as its source:

> The *Washington Post*, regarded as having close connections to the State Department, said that North Korea should be warned of the likelihood of an atomic attack if communist forces did not withdraw from invaded South Korea. [10]

The *Review*'s fears were well-founded: by spring, 1951, American military leaders were in the process of moving as many as thirty-eight atomic bombs from the United States to Japan, for use in Korea.[11]

A special feature article in September told of the heavy bombing of North Korean cities and recounted the testimonies of U.S. prisoners about strafing refugees and destroying Korean villages with aerial bombing.[12] In October a pictorial spread mixed disaffected POW's with the bombing and atrocity theme:

> Captured U.S. troops . . . admit that they weren't told where they were going or what they were fighting for. Many have stated that they don't like what they are doing; they have no quarrel with the people of Korea, they say, and the people of Korea should be allowed to settle their own affairs.
>
> Meanwhile, the U.S. air force bombs peasant villages and strafes livestock, and the ground troops frequently open fire on the peasants in masses, fearful that some of them may be guerilla fighters. Young and old are rounded up and shot by America's South Korean "allies," sometimes with targets over the heart for surer aim.[13]

Another pictorial in the same issue called attention to American strafing raids on the Chinese side of the Yalu River.[14]

On August fifth, North Korean Foreign Minister Bak Hun Yung lodged a solemn protest over the American air war in Korea before the United Nations Security Council. With the full support of China, Bak demanded an immediate end to ". . . the atrocities committed by United States forces."[15] To demonstrate the deliberate distortions which were being used in the American press to justify the bombing of schools and hospitals and other civilian targets, the *Review* quoted an article in *Collier's* by Captain Walter Craig, U.S.Naval Reserve, that reflected a callous attitude toward strafing and napalming civilians and refugees.[16]

Drawing parallels to Nazi Germany, Powell argued that the article portrayed Asians as ". . . a sub-human species against whom it is both necessary and proper to practice all the barbarities which modern science has made available." However, these atrocities could be stopped, Powell asserted, ". . . if the American people sufficiently will for it to stop." He called on the U.S. press to inform the American public truthfully of the horrors of the air war being carried out in their names.

> The press, as the most important public opinion media has a duty to give the people honest information rather than the criminally misleading propaganda contained in this article. While admittedly under heavy pressure, the American press is not yet controlled in an official sense of the word. It is still possible for American editors and publishers to make a strenuous effort to tell the American people the truth.[17]

With China's entry into the war, U.S. bombing of Chinese targets increased. The *Review* documented one hundred staffing and bombing missions across the Yalu, and personalized the strafing of Kooloutzu village with an account of some of the victims and supporting photographs.[18] Another pictorial accused South Korean and American troops of carrying out large scale reprisals (mass executions) after capturing cities in North Korea and on recapturing Seoul after U.N. forces swept across the thirty-eighth parallel in September, 1950.[19]

In February, the *Review* quoted *United Press* and *Reuter's* accounts of mass killing of civilians by ROK troops in Seoul, and commented on U.S. military complicity.

> *Reuter* described one shooting of thirty-four Koreans near the camp of the Northumberland Fusiliers. They were killed without having any "special charges against them made known." Among them were two women and "two young kiddies aged about eight and thirteen." A motor truck took them, tied together in pairs, to trenches dug the day before. The Sygman Rhee guards shoved them into the trenches, made them lie down, and shot them from behind.
>
> One eye-witness, M. Brown, said, "It was disgustingly brutal. The youngest, a boy of about eight, while kneeling in a trench crying and waiting to be shot, turned his face around to the guard. The guard cuffed him across the face and then shot him."

... According to a *UP* dispatch, at least eight-hundred persons, including many women and children, were executed within five days with rifles and machine guns. It was believed women and children were being executed as members of the families of the condemned men. The same report goes on to state that "The executions have been going on almost daily since the liberation [by U.S. forces] of Seoul in September."[20]

The *Review* noted that American military authorities refused to intervene to halt the killings, claiming they lacked jurisdiction to do so, even though the U.S. military had "... undisputed reign over the entire conduct of the U.N. effort in Korea."[21]

Another article charged that "The Americans and their allies have carried on a war of 'total annihilation' in the guise of 'police action' against the Korean people and their property."[22] It documented mass executions and the intentional demolition of public buildings and more than 100,000 homes after American and ROK forces took Pyongyang.[23] The article painted a picture of the utter destruction of many Korean cities and towns by American air power:

By late October most of the cities and villages of all Korea had been razed. Yet, since then the systematic destruction of all remaining places was intensified by the Americans and their air arm. A random selection of small cities in Korea finds that in the towns of Kangke, less than 500 buildings out of 8,000 remained in December; in Sinyichu, about 1,000 out of 12,000; and in Manpochin, about 200 out of 1500. In North Korea alone, by the end of 1950, American planes had destroyed and burned down approximately 7,000 villages ... Never before has the physical make-up of one nation been so systematically and thoroughly destroyed. Hand in hand with this has been a policy of "exterminating all opposition." In many cases the opposition has been anyone who served on the public utilities under the North Korean government or the relatives, including children, of suspected communists.[24]

American POW's stated on March fifteenth that in spite of clear markings on the roof, U.S. planes strafed their camp, killing four and wounding fifteen POW's. One man complained, "They strafe indiscriminately. If something moves they shoot up the place, without bothering to see who or what it is ... We live in fear that they will use napalm bombs on us."[25] Another wrote, "Everyday they are bombing and strafing all these Korean houses and killing poor innocent victims like children and old people and when they are through all that is left is a pile of ashes."[26]

A May photo spread claimed 10,000 Korean civilians had been murdered at Hawon during its American occupation, and displayed bodies lying unburied in trenches in this and other villages as proof.[27] The *Review* noted that the *New York Times* in April had uncovered the massacre of most of the inhabitants of the village of Shim-Um Mium by South Korean troops[28]. It reported the bombing of Red Cross hospitals in Pyongyang, Thonchon, and Wonsan.[29]

*

During the American retreat of the winter of 1950–51, amidst the large scale bombing and destruction caused by embattled armies crossing and re-crossing battered North Korea, typhus and smallpox epidemics broke out in numerous locations.[30] Epidemics were reported in northern and Southern P'yongan Province, Kangwon Province, Southern Hamyong Province, and Hwanghae Province.[31] The government of North Korea would later blame these outbreaks on bacteriological attacks by American troops as they retreated through these areas. This was before the development of an "actual" operational BW capacity in Korea, according to Endicott and Hagerman.[32]

Presumably concerned over the potential spread of epidemic diseases to United Nations forces, Brigadier General Crawford Sams, chief of SCAP's Health and Welfare Section, embarked on a mission in March, 1951 to test for the presence of bubonic plague in North Korea. Sams led a laboratory-equipped landing craft into North Korean waters to kidnap and test sick Chinese or North Korean soldiers from a hospital near Wonson.[33] The results would determine whether U.S. soldiers in Korea needed to be immunized.[34] Ultimately, Sams found no evidence of plague.

On April ninth, 1951, *Newsweek* magazine, alerted to the situation, reported the "secret mission" of a "Navy epidemic control laboratory ship" which was lying off the east coast of North Korea, near Wonsan harbor. According to the article, American landing parties had been ". . . grabbing up numbers of Chinese Reds from the tiny islands of the harbor and taking them back to the ship where they are tested for symptoms of the dread bubonic plague."[35] The story explained that the purpose was to determine whether reports of plague in North Korea were true or not, so that preventive measures might be taken, if needed.[36]

The Communist press, with the activities of Unit 731 of the Japanese Imperial Army still fresh in mind, interpreted the story to mean that the Americans, like the Japanese before them, were utilizing the abductees to test biological weapons. For months the press in China had anticipated the use of BW. As early as January, 1951, the front page of the *North China Daily News,* citing *Xinhua,* noted that germ weapons production in Japan had been stepped up by SCAP, which had built a BW facility in the mountains north of Tokyo that was in constant touch with Camp Detrick, Maryland. Reportedly, the Americans had placed the Japanese facility under the direction of Ishii Shiro, who had led Unit 731 in China during World War II, and production had been "intensified to an unprecedented degree."[37] The article reminded readers of the 1949 Soviet trial of Japanese BW war criminals at Khabarovsk, and pointed out that the United States had protected Ishii from prosecution for war crimes.

On May 8, 1951, North Korean Foreign Minister Bak Hun Yung injected bacteriological warfare into his earlier atrocity charges in a cablegram to the President of the United Nations Security Council. The Foreign Minister charged the United States with using biological weapons in Korea during December 1950 and January 1951 to cause smallpox epidemics in a number of provinces during the retreat of American troops.[38] The *Review* withheld comment on the BW charges for a month, although it did mention the use of "gas bombs" which burst in mid-air, releasing a "bluish-grey heavy vapor which spread over the ground."[39]

The first accusations of bacteriological warfare in the *Review* (June, 1951) shared the page with a photograph of a girl weeping over her dead mother, killed in the U.S. bombing raid on the city of Andong, April 17, 1951.[40] Echoing *Xinhua*, the *Review* presented the Communist interpretation of the *Newsweek* article of April eighth:

> An American naval vessel masquerading as an epidemic control [ship] but actually carrying out a highly secret mission and loaded with bacteriological installations, has recently arrived at the Korean east coast harbor, Wonsan. Chinese volunteers taken prisoner have been used as victims to test bacteriological weapons.[41]

The *Review* viewed the alleged American testing of bacteriological weapons on helpless captives as one more atrocity, in line with past inhumane behavior by America and its ally, the Republic of Korea. It reported that *Xinhua* and *People's Daily* had accused the United States of using Chinese POW's for "the most inhumane type of experiments," and charged the United States with manufacturing bacteriological weapons on a large scale at Camp Detrick, Maryland, and in Minami Kondo-gun, Jodofu, Japan. These experiments were linked in the same article with the non-related alleged mass murder of 31 captured Chinese soldiers and 35 Korean civilians by American soldiers on December 1, 1950, in Kaech'on, South P'yongan province.[42]

The *Review* noted that a formal protest had been lodged by the Chinese Red Cross to the International Committee of the Red Cross and the League of Red Cross Societies. The Chinese Red Cross charged the United States with using Chinese prisoners for bacterial warfare experiments and demanded punishment for the guilty.[43] But the world paid little attention; propaganda about atrocities by both sides had become a common feature of the conflict in Korea by this time.

*

For a year nothing more appeared in the *Review* or the Communist press on the BW issue. Then from February 1952 to the end of the war in 1953, more serious and sustained charges of bacteriological warfare, backed by considerable evidence, became an ongoing feature in the *Review*, and indeed, in the press of all the Communist countries. The issue quickly became an international bone of contention with the Western bloc led by the United States on one side of the divide, and the Soviet bloc nations on the other.

The BW controversy spilled over into the United Nations Security Council, where the Soviet Union temporarily held the presidency, and made its way into U.N. disarmament talks. On one side, President Truman, Secretary of State Acheson, and the United States' representative in the U.N. emphatically denied the allegations and tried to dismiss the evidence. On the other side, Chinese and North Korean military authorities organized peasants to collect mounds of insects to be tested and sorted as part of the evidence, documented hundreds of eyewitness accounts, and organized massive immunization and sanitation drives to head off the threat of epidemics.[44]

On February 22, 1952, North Korean Foreign Minister Bak Hun Yung once again lodged official charges with the United Nations Secretariat that the United States Air Force had dropped large quantities of insects infected with deadly disease bacteria in eleven different locales in North Korea. Along with the location and date of the attacks, Bak described the use of black flies, fleas, bugs, spiders, mosquitoes, ants and other insect vectors to spread plague, cholera and other infectious diseases.[45]

Two days later, Chinese Foreign Minister Zhou Enlai issued a statement to the U.N. Secretariat supporting North Korea's charges, and demanded an immediate end to BW assaults. On 8 March 1952, he accused the United States of flying 448 sorties into Northeast China to spread germ-laden insects at Fushun, Xinmin, Andong, Guandian, Linjiang and other places.[46]

The United States was quick to respond. Secretary of State Acheson issued a statement on March fourth "categorically and unequivocally" denying that U.N. forces had used bacteriological weapons in Korea or China. Acheson said the United States would welcome an impartial investigation by an agency like the International Committee of the Red Cross, but said the Communists had refused.[47] This was because North Korea and China knew their charges to be false, Acheson claimed. He charged that the outbreak of a serious plague epidemic was the result of the inability of the North Korean regime to meet the health needs of its own people adequately.[48]

On March tenth the United States formally requested that the International Committee of the Red Cross (ICRC) investigate the charges. The ICRC contacted North Korea, the U.S., and China with the proposal. In reply, Yakov Malik, the United Nations Security Council Representative for the Soviet Union, rejected the ICRC's proposal, claiming that the ICRC was too connected to the capitalist West to be impartial.[49] China and North Korea soon did the same. In place of the International Committee of the Red Cross, Communist leaders composed two outside investigating committees of "democratic lawyers" and internationally known scientists who were sympathetic toward the Chinese Revolution.[50]

On February 22, 1952, Zhou Enlai directed the Chinese People's Committee for Defending World Peace to suggest to the communist-sympathetic World Peace Council, headquartered in Prague, that it should initiate a campaign against American use of germ warfare in Korea.[51] Chinese Communist intellectuals Guo Moro and Mao Dun both held leadership positions (respectively, Vice President and Member of the Bureau of the World Peace Council) within the Council.[52] In response to Zhou's call, the Council issued an "Appeal" condemning the United States.

Earlier, in 1951, responding to North Korea's initial charge of atrocities, another pro-Communist group, the Council of the International Association of Democratic Lawyers, had sent a Commission to collect atrocity evidence in Korea and China. As a result, the Commission delegates were in China when the main flurry of BW accusations began in March, 1952, and it enlarged the scope of its investigation to include germ warfare. Most of the scientific data utilized in this and later investigations were gathered at this time.[53]

After the Commission of the Association of Democratic Lawyers released two reports in April, 1952, one on atrocities and one on germ warfare, *People's China* reported that:

> The World Peace Council, on the proposal of the China Peace Committee, has decided to form another impartial international commission . . . to investigate all the evidence of U.S. bacteriological warfare in China and Korea.[54]

Within a month, the Executive Bureau of the World Peace Council had organized the International Scientific Commission for the Investigation of the Facts Concerning Bacterial Warfare in Korea and China. It was to be composed of "highly distinguished representatives" of the international scientific community[55] and would ultimately present the main body of scientific evidence supporting the Communist BW charges.

Most of the scientific data and specimens utilized in its investigation during the summer of 1952 had been collected and prepared earlier for the pro-communist Commission of the Democratic Lawyers. Consequently, the investigations of both bodies were thoroughly reliant on Chinese technicians for the preparation of all specimens. The International Scientific Commission did not gather or test any of the specimen evidence themselves, a weakness it acknowledged, while expressing confidence in the professional competence of the Chinese scientists who had done so.[56]

Yet, in spite of the impeccable credentials of the academic figures recruited by Communist authorities for the investigation, the validity of the ISC's report depends first of all, on the honesty and competence of the Chinese military personnel and the peasants who initially gathered the evidence, and secondly, on the objectivity and inviolability of the laboratory tests which were made: two factors which must be accepted on faith since they were beyond verification by the time of the ISC investigation.

＊

In the March 1952 issue of the *Review*, Powell reiterated the history of the charges, and repeated parts of the year-old April 1951 *Newsweek* article on the epidemic control ship:

> Last March, a U.S. naval ship, under Crawford F. Sams, chief of the Public Health and Welfare Section of the U.N. Forces General Headquarters, sailed into Wonson on the east coast of Korea. Although masquerading as an epidemic control ship, it was actually loaded with bacteriological installations and was used for testing germ weapons on North Korean and Chinese prisoners.
>
> Commenting on the activities of this ship, the April 9, 1951 issue of *Newsweek*, under the head "Bubonic Plague Ship" stated: "Look for news of the secret mission of a Navy epidemic control laboratory ship to Wonson harbor on the east coast of North Korea, where the navy has maintained a lengthy siege."[57]

Powell noted that the laboratory ship's mission involved ". . . grabbing up numbers of Chinese Reds . . . and taking them back to the ship where they were tested for symptoms of the dread bubonic plague."[58]

Powell underscored a firm connection between the activities of Japan's Unit 731 during World War II and the current activities of U.S. forces in Korea:

> The Americans have been openly collaborating with Japanese bacteriological war criminals who, through U.S. pressure, had been freed in 1950 of charges of conducting such warfare in China during World War II. Among such criminals sent to Korea by the Americans are Shiro Ishii, Jire [sic] Wakamatsu, and Masajo Kitano.[59]

In April, the *Review* bolstered Chinese BW charges, which now included photographs of insect vectors, delivery devices, microbes, and Chinese anti-epidemic prevention teams in Korea, with statements taken from the U.S. press. It quoted the *New York Times* to show that General MacArthur had, in 1946, sent ". . . eighteen Japanese specialists in germ warfare to the United States to carry out experiments in numerous laboratories and institutes of America."[60]

Utilizing testimony from the 1949 Khabarovsk trial, Powell sketched the entire history of Units 731 and 100,[61] from their inception in 1936, up to their connection with the alleged U.S. germ campaign against North Korea and China. According to the *Review*, Emperor Hirohito had ordered the creation of bacteriological weapons research in Manchuria.[62] Soon Units 731 and 100 were devising effective methods of producing and delivering enhanced diseases. Tests were done on over 3000 live human victims, mostly Chinese and Soviets, but also including Americans:

> A typical experiment was to drop thin-walled porcelain receptacles filled with plague-infected fleas on a 'proving ground' in which 'logs' (as human

experimentees were called) were chained naked to stakes. These 'experiments' were also made in Mukden on American prisoners of war to determine their immunity to infectious diseases.[63]

Capable of producing tons of deadly plague, cholera and anthrax germs by the War's end, both personnel and equipment of Units 731 and 100 were reportedly evacuated to South Korea, and then to Japan. The article noted that:

> Documents showing the BW crimes committed by the Japanese Zaibatsu-militarists were given to the chief American prosecutor at the International Military Tribunal in Tokyo after VJ Day. However they were never turned over to the tribunal. The only explanation for this is that the U.S. militarists were anxious to make use of the experience and services of their one-time enemy.[64]

According to the *Review*, "the commander of both detachments, General Ishii . . . was reported engaged in 'research' in the United States as late as the autumn of last year (1951)."[65]

Powell cited Rosebury's *Peace or Pestilence* to back-up Soviet charges that the U.S. was trying to obstruct efforts to ban bacteriological weapons, and General Henry H. Arnold's *One World or None* to show that germ weapons were on a par with atomic weapons.[66] He used George Merck's 1946 "Report to the Secretary of War on Biological Warfare" to imply that the American BW program was more advanced than had been that of Nazi Germany or Japan.[67]

For evidence of the scope and capacity of U.S. pathogen production, the *Review* cited *Life* Magazine.[68] It invoked a 1946 State Department Report to the United Nations on bacteriological warfare to prove that the United States sought to increase the virulence of disease germs.[69] Finally, Powell pointed to an article in the *New York Journal American* to show that by 1951, the American military establishment had grown increasingly restive with Roosevelt's 1943 "no first use" policy regarding biological weapons.[70]

Since January 28, 1952, the *Review* stated, the United States had been employing biological warfare on a much larger scale than previously. For three months various types of flies, fleas, ticks, spiders, mosquitoes, and ants, which laboratory tests showed to be infected with plague, cholera, and other diseases were being dropped from planes in a variety of containers.[71] A six page pictorial, which also appeared in *People's China*, displayed insects, drawings of germs, and delivery systems, reinforcing the allegations.[72]

"Pious denials by US officialdom to the contrary, the American military have been planning germ warfare for many years," the *Review* charged. Using magazine and newspaper articles, scientific, and U.S. government reports, the journal reviewed the history of American BW development by looking at ". . . their own actions and statements down through the last ten years."[73]

In May, Powell highlighted the investigation of biological warfare charges conducted by the Commission of the International Association of Democratic Lawyers submitted in Beijing, April 2, 1952, which considered the evidence, and concluded that the charges were justified. The Commission inspected the remains of germ bombs, spoke with eye-witnesses and scientific personnel, and recorded the symptoms of those infected.[74] In spite of the massive number of reported instances of alleged dissemination of bacteria, the Commission confined its investigation to only ten cases.[75]

Powell took issue with Secretary of State Acheson's charges in 1952 that epidemics in North Korea were the result of unsanitary conditions and the inability of the government to see to the people's health needs.[76] The quick mobilization of the people in Korea and Northeast China to take preventive measures had put an end to the threat of U.S. germ raids, the *Review* asserted. There were no epidemics in either region.[77]

The *Review* and the English language press in China had given close and recurring coverage to the efforts of the People's Government since 1949 to wipe out all epidemic diseases in China through massive urban inoculation campaigns.[78] Now, a general mobilization of health workers in North Korea and teams sent from the PRC orchestrated mass clean-up and inoculation campaigns so thorough that they even extended to American POWs.[79]

According to Major General W.F. Dean, the highest ranking American POW in captivity, the entire North Korean population recieved massive innoculations, and nobody could appear on the streets without an inoculation card.

> Everybody,-soldiers, civilians, adults, and children- received four separate inoculations and revaccination. They were monster shots and all of North Korea had fever and sore arms.[80]

"The success of the health campaign over the past three years has been one of the reasons why Washington's plan to win in Korea through germ warfare has failed so miserably," Powell wrote in September, 1952.

> The people's public health organizations in Korea and China have been able to deal effectively with the outbreaks of disease induced by the dropping of germs in Korea and Northeast China, resulting in a minimum of sickness and death and successfully preventing the outbreak of any widespread epidemics.[81]

U.S. intelligence sources confirmed Powell's assertions about the containment of epidemics, regardless of whether the contagions resulted naturally from the devastation of war, or from BW attacks.[82]

*

The atrocity theme continued in the *Review* in conjunction with BW charges as they proliferated during 1952–53. For example, a photo layout of napalm victims in September 1952 was cited as proof that the United States was morally capable of bacteriological warfare.[83] Eventually the themes of mass bombing of civilian targets, the alleged murder of Chinese and Korean POWs at Koje Island, and bacteriological warfare all merged in the confessions of American prisoners of war in 1952–1953.[84]

From the first month of the war, the *Review* had paid special attention to American prisoners of war. It featured stories on favorable conditions in the camps, it published letters home by POWs which urged family and friends to fight for peace, and it printed long lists of the names of POWs so that their families would know they were alive.

Review Contributing Editor Dr. H.C. Huang had joined the PLA in late 1949, and continued writing articles for the journal. By 1952, Huang had been assigned to an American POW camp hospital,[85] where he regularly sent reports to the *Review* on the men, their thoughts and activities, accompanied by photographs. Since the *Review* was sent to POW camps, which all had "libraries" of materials used in study and self-criticism, the POWs could read about their own basketball, soccer and football games, along with Thanksgiving and Christmas preparations.[86]

Huang was able to establish a seemingly close rapport with some of the men, and his articles focused on the human dimension, with political sentiments being almost incidental.[87] By June, after several months of work, Huang had organized a POW peace committee within the camp, and peace demonstrations by most of the camp's 2000 inmates.[88]

The *Review* carried a story by Frank Noel, a Pulitzer prize winning Associated Press photographer who was captured November, 1950, along with marines from the First Marine Division. Noel described the structure and self-government of POW camps, along with diet, medical care, entertainment, clothing issues, and sanitary conditions.[89] Another article compared the brutality faced by North Korean and Chinese POW's in South Korea with the athletic program organized for American prisoners in Chinese and North Korean POW camps.[90]

As former POW testimony before Congress later attested, conditions in Chinese prisoner of war camps improved by 1952, and sporting equipment had indeed been provided for athletic activities at least in some camps.[91] The propaganda opportunity this represented was not neglected by the English language press in China.[92] A pictorial in the *Review* showing POW's in clean, white jerseys playing baseball, basketball, and soccer asserted that:

> North Korean and Chinese authorities have gone to considerable pains to provide educational and recreational facilities for the POW camps in North Korea. Books, sporting equipment, musical instraments not to mention such essentials as food, clothing and medical supplies are shipped in from hundreds, sometimes thousands of miles, to the camps.[93]

Intramural sports matches between the camps had grown so popular with the POW's, said the *Review*, that "periodic all-camp Olympics" were now held.[94]

*

In May, 1952, *People's China* printed depositions by two captured U.S. Air Force officers, First Lieutenant Kenneth Lloyd Enoch, a navigator, and First Lieutenant John Quinn, a pilot, both shot down 13 January 1952. These proved to be the first of a series of confessions by U.S. airmen admitting to the charges of dropping germ bombs on North Korea and Northeast China.[95] By summer, 1953, the Chinese people's government had collected similar statements from nineteen more American airmen, totaling over 66 pages of written testimony, all recounting in detail the history of their involvement in germ warfare.[96]

The first indication of POW corroboration of germ warfare charges in the *Review* appeared in June, 1952 in a report that secret inoculations and protective masks had been issued to American G.I.'s.[97] But the *Review* avoided direct coverage of POW germ warfare confessions that summer in order to focus its attention on preparations for the approaching Asia and Pacific Regions Peace Conference to be held in Beijing during the last week of September.[98] Powell and his wife Sylvia began making arrangements to attend the Conference as delegates.

Their attendance was noted in the United States. The *New York Times*, informed by a Beijing Radio broadcast of September twenty-seventh, reported that

> John W. Powell, editor of the *China Monthly Review* in Shanghai and his wife, Sylvia Campbell Powell, had arrived in Beijing to join seven other American delegates participating in the "Asian and Pacific Peace Conference" there.[99]

In the same column, the *Times* noted that Secretary of State Acheson had labeled the Asia and Pacific Regions Peace Conference ". . . an obvious propaganda operation," and warned that Americans who attended it would be liable to prosecution under U.S. passport laws.[100] The State Department had already identified fifteen American participants.

Powell published a special "Peace Conference Issue" (November-December 1952) wherein the *Review* summarized the work of the International Scientific Commission (ISC) for Investigating the Facts Concerning Bacteriological Warfare in Korea and China. The Commission's 300,000-word report provided the primary documentary support to the BW charges. Without mentioning the role of the PRC and the USSR in organizing the Commission (a significant oversight), the *Review* stressed its international complexion, with photographs and biographies of six of the members. These included Dr.Andrea Andreen of Sweden, Dr.Joseph Needham of the U.K., Dr. Oliviero Olivo of Italy, Professor Jean Malterre of France, Dr.

Samuel B. Pessoa of Brazil, and Dr. N.N. Zhukov-Verezhnikov of the USSR, who had been the chief medical expert at the Khabarovsk biological warfare trial of the twelve members of Japanese Unit 731.[101]

The *Review*'s summary of the itinerary and work of the Commission was adapted from the ISC's official report, which had appeared as a supplement in *People's China*.[102] The Commission had examined the sites of the alleged use of germ warfare in Korea and China, had spoken with Chinese scientists who had prepared specimens, had interviewed hundreds of witnesses, and had spoken with captured U.S. airmen who had confessed to dropping germ bombs.[103] Because the International Scientific Commission had stated that its report was based on a mass of evidence which was entirely circumstantial, and often incomplete,[104] corroborating testimony by American POW's became an important buttress to the BW allegations.

Letters published in the *Review* from Quinn, Second Lieutenant Paul R. Kniss, and Second Lieutenant Floyd B. O'Neal to the U.S. delegation of the Asian and Pacific Regions Peace Conference mixed the themes of atrocity and biological warfare in their denunciation of the war. John Quinn related stories of strafing children and dropping bombs on peaceful villages before calling on the delegates to convince the people back home of the reality of germ war attacks. "You've seen the proof of it. But the people back home don't know about it. We're counting on you to prove it to them." [105]

Floyd O'Neal condemned ". . . the mass bombings of civilian towns, the murdering of Chinese and Korean POW's on Koje Island" and urged the delegates to make the crime of biological warfare known to the American people.

> Have you seen the exhibits on germ warfare and heard our testimonies? Good, for then you know the truth. I had an opportunity to tell the International Scientific Commission Investigating Germ Warfare about my part in it. Get a copy of the Commission's Report and take it back with you..there are still 149,000,000 U.S. citizens who don't know the truth about the crimes that are committed in their names.[106]

The *Review* complemented the letters with an interview with Wifred Burchett, Paris *Ce Soir* correspondent who had been present when the International Scientific Commission had questioned four American POW's on their depositions. Burchett spent several days living and speaking with lieutenants Kenneth L. Enoch, John S. Quinn, Floyd B. O'Neal, and Paul R. Kniss to determine why they made depositions admitting participation in germ warfare. He concluded that disillusionment over the war and with their superiors, revulsion at the slaughter of civilians, and surprise over their humane treatment by their captors had led the men to confess.[107]

The Interview did not refer directly to the process of thought reform which led to these confessions. Although Burchett throughout the interview was describing the state of mind of each of the captive airmen at various stages of the thought reform process, the process itself was the element left unspoken. Yet, the long arduous road toward the final statement: of study, questioning, writing, criticism, self-criticism, rewriting, over and over, until the captors felt the prisoner's statement left nothing untold and the captive himself had gone through an epiphany of sorts, was reflected in Burchett's account of the airmen's replies. Describing the stages Lt.Quinn went through before his final confession, Burchett related:

> . . . he was given books to read-a great variety of books. Books by Americans and about America that had never been in his hands before-Dreiser and Fast and others. He read about the Chinese Revolution from American writers and about the War of Resistance. The disillusioning process continued. The whole pattern of the lying propaganda in the press, in the films, on the radio, became clear to him. And everything he read and experienced supplemented his own doubts and questionings of American policy from the time he arrived in Korea.[108]

Yet Quinn continued to resist for a variety of reasons which Burchett denoted, until finally:

> His awakened moral feelings overcame his personal fears and he decided to take a stand. So Quinn spoke out. He, like all of these airmen, told me of a great sense of calm- the absolute certainty of having done the right thing-which swept over him as soon as he had taken the decision to give his testimony.[109]

Most previous POW testimony, however, lacked convincing technical detail. Burchett recognized this problem in his interview:

> I think they were told only part of the truth about germ warfare by their superiors-Lt. Kniss, for instance, told me several times that he was convinced that the lecturers and briefing officers only told them the minimum necessary information to satisfy their curiosity. . . . But I did have the feeling that these men did tell everything that they knew.[110]

All that changed in mid-summer, however. By far the most persuasive evidence of bacteriological warfare usage came from the depositions of two senior U.S. Marine Corps officers captured in July, 1952. Colonel Frank H. Schwable, Chief of Staff of the First Marine Aircraft Wing, and Major Roy H. Bley, Ordnance Officer of the First Marine Aircraft Wing, gave such detailed technical, logistical, and operational information about how germ attacks were carried out, and by which units, and for what purposes, that it was difficult to dismiss their accounts.

The BW program that Schwable and Bley described was incidental to conventional bombing, was small in scale, and experimental in nature. Though it gave the Communists the technically informed accounts they had lacked, it was a far cry from the vast conspiracy against humanity which the press of the Soviet-bloc countries had been claiming. Still, Schwable and Bley named high ranking military personnel who had been involved in the operations and indicated the Joint Chiefs of Staff had on one occasion, issued a directive stating that if the experimental use of BW warranted it, the program could be expanded at a later date.[111] The *Review* printed both accounts in full.

Schwable avoided the language of thought reform which had marked other confessions. Rather, he defended the honor of the Marine Corps and the loyalty of the officers he served with. "I believe without exception, we came to Korea as officers loyal to our people and government." To a man, officers had expressed surprise and dismay upon learning they would be dropping various types of experimental bacterial bombs along with their regular loads. Schwable placed the onus upon germ weapons themselves, and opined that they had not been worth the effort or the risk to the honor of the United States.

> When I took over from Colonel Binney, I asked him for results or reactions up to date and he specifically said, "Not worth a damn." No one that I know of has indicated that the results are anywhere near commensurate with the effort, danger and dishonesty involved, although the Korean and Chinese authorities have made quite a public report of early bacteriological bomb efforts.[112]

As the war was approaching its conclusion, Powell quoted the *Associated Press, United Press* and *Time* magazine in the July 1953 issue of the *Review* to show that the American government was worried over what returned U.S. prisoners of war might say upon arriving home. United States military authorities, according to U.S. sources, had set up ". . . a program to 'reorient' to the American way of life any released prisoners of war who may have succumbed to Communist propaganda."[113] And indeed, upon their release after the war, airmen who had confessed to dropping germ bombs were secluded from reporters, and kept under close surveillance as hospital patients. Under threats ranging from indictment for treason to dishonorable discharge, pressure was put on them to write recantations.[114]

Because the accounts of Schwable and Bley were particularly convincing, both men came under extreme pressure on their return home. Voices from the Justice Department, the Senate Armed Services Committee, and the Department of Defense demanded that Schwable and other POW's who had confessed to BW, be put on trial for treason.[115] General Lemuel G. Shepherd, the Marine Corps commandant, denounced Schwable as ". . . an instrument, however unwilling, of causing damage to his country," and the Marine Corps convened a Court of Inquiry to look into his case.[116]

Both Schwable and Bley recanted their earlier testimony, as did most of the former POW's who had made BW depositions. The United States then submitted to the United Nations the recantations, wherein the flyers denied they had been involved in bacteriological warfare, and charged that their former false confessions had been extracted through coercion.[117]

A year later, after the Court of Inquiry decided against disciplinary action, the commanding general of the Atlantic Fleet Marine Force, Major

General Clayton Jerome, quietly awarded Schwable the Legion of Merit on April twenty-seventh, 1954. Promoted one rank and booted upstairs, Schwable took up a new post in the Pentagon as the Marine Corps' representative on the Navy's Flight Safety Board.[118]

*

In June 1953, Powell announced that the *China Monthly Review* would close after the July issue, due to financial difficulties engendered by the U.S. trade embargo, falling international circulation, and foreign exchange restrictions. By closing after the July issue, the *Review* could "Do so in an orderly and business-like manner" and avoid outright collapse. During a time when most of the Western press was "pursuing a policy of distortion and invention designed to heighten international tensions and whip up a world-wide anti-China hysteria," Powell believed that the *Review* had "made a worthwhile contribution in presenting the *facts* about new China, in telling the exciting and important story of the new civilization abuilding in this ancient land."[119]

In the last issue, Powell expressed his thanks to all the writers, readers and contributors who had helped the *Review* to continue as long as it had. His farewell statement echoed the main thrust of his journal, which had been, after all, to inform the American public of the positive changes being made by the Revolution:

> We are especially glad that we managed to stay around long enough to see the Chinese people put an end to the old state of disorder and start building a new life for themselves. It has been one of the great periods of history and we were particularly fortunate to have been able to witness it at such close range. . .
>
> We shall be returning to our own country, but we shall always remember these years in China, the long struggle of the Chinese people for a better life and their ultimate success.[120]

Powell's return to America was not neglected by the U.S. press. In the Spring of 1953, Victor Riesel, who had a regular column in the *New York Daily Mirror* and often contributed to the digest, *American Mercury*, accused him of participating in the "brainwashing" of captured American soldiers: "The first mental assault on our captured troops is made by members of the American Communist Party now in China. They are aided by 'Americans' such as John Powell, now a Shanghai editor."[121]

In June, the *New York Times* reported that "John W. Powell, editor of Shanghai's famed *China Monthly Review* says he is closing down the now pro-Communist magazine and returning to the United States."[122] The *Times* observed that the *Review* ". . . had difficulty making ends meet despite its Pro-Peking sympathies," and noted that the *Review* ". . . was the last Western-operated publication in China."[123]

Newsweek published a vociferous editorial on the occasion of the *Review*'s closing:

> When Communist forces took Shanghai in 1949, John William Powell's English-language *China Review* was there to welcome them. Shanghai's foreign colony, sickened by the *Review*'s toeing of the party line, boycotted Powell and his magazine. The Communists with a firm leash on the paper, attached an even firmer one to Powell. He was refused permission to leave the city, accept to attend a Red 'peace' rally in Peking last year.
>
> The *Review* itself fared no better. . . Powell, his vociferously pro-Communist wife, and their two children were forced to live in a shabby apartment. Still, the *Review* praised the Reds and damned the free world Powell had chosen to renounce.[124]

Time magazine charged that Powell had turned his father's magazine ". . . into a mouthpiece for the Chinese Reds." *Time* recounted in disgust that Powell had criticized the Rosenberg trial and had supported Communist germ warfare charges in Korea.

> Newsmen who asked Powell last week why he had never criticized any Red action were rewarded with Powell's own version of Orwellian doublespeak: "You just don't understand. In China, there's a new appreciation of the role of the press."[125]

Within a year of Powell's return the situation became much uglier after the former editor appeared before the Senate Judiciary Sub-Committee on Interlocking Subversion in Government. Former American POW's by that time had testified that the *Review* had been used for thought reform activities in the Chinese camps. *Time,* and the *New York Times* had both run articles charging Powell with indirect responsibility for the suffering and even death of POW's who had resisted.[126]

U.S. News and World Report ran a seven-page article on Powell's alleged connection to the "brainwashing" of American prisoners.[127] It too repeated the sensational accusation by a former POW which branded Powell a murderer. In this political climate, it was only a matter of time before Powell, his wife Sylvia, and his former assistant editor Julian Schuman, would all be indicted on charges of sedition.

In the beginning, Powell had hoped for non-confrontational working relations, if not friendship, between the United States and Communist China. He had tried to influence public opinion at home in favor of recognition, and to counter the demonization of the PRC by supporters of Chiang Kai-shek in America. But war between China and the United States in Korea put an end to any hope of improved Sino-American relations. Incorporated by the Press Administration of the PRC into Communist propaganda campaigns, the *Review* played an important role in efforts to discredit U.S. goals and conduct during that conflict to English-speaking readers. With his countrymen dying on Korean hillsides, Powell's pro-communist coverage smacked of sedition back home.

CHAPTER NOTES

1. C.Y.W. Meng, "Why I Signed the World Peace Appeal", *CWR*, 5 August 1950,p.166–7.

2. *Ibid.*

3. Powell, ed. "Peace Can Still Be Won", *CWR*, 29 July 1950,p.146–7.

4. *Ibid.*

5. Bruce Cumings, *The Origins of the Korean War, Volume II, The Roaring of the Cataract, 1947–1950*. (Princeton: Princeton University Press, 1990) p.747–756.

6. Cumings, *The Origins of the Korean War*, p.748.

7. "American POW's Broadcast", (*Hsinhua*, 17 July 1950), *CWR*, 29 July 1950,p.158.

8. *Ibid.*

9. "Wanton U.S. Bombing of Korean Civilians", *CWR*, 5 August 1950, p.167.

10. "Atomic Bomb Suggested", *CWR*, 15 July 1950, p.122; "Atomic Warning", *CWR*, 22 July 1950, p.139; Bruce Cummings, *The Origins of the Korean War, Volume II, The Roaring of the Cataract 1947–1950*. (Princeton: Princeton University Press, 1990) p.745–751. Cummings showed that in December, 1950, General MacArthur asked for 34 atomic bombs for use in Korea. General Ridgway, who replaced MacArthur, asked in May, 1951, for 38 atomic bombs for use in Korea. The bombs were carried to Kaneda Air Force base in Japan, and the Joint Chiefs of Staff on April 5, 1951, ". . . ordered immediate atomic retaliation against Manchurian bases if large numbers of new troops came into the fighting, or, it appears, if bombers were launched against American forces from there." After removing MacArthur from command, President Truman gave the military custody of the fissionable cores necessary to arm those bombs. (Cores in 1951 were stored at the Atomic Energy Commission under presidential control.)

11. Cummings, *Ibid.* p.750–751.

12. "U.S. Adventure in Korea Backfires - Militarily and Psychologically", *CWR*, September 1950,p.10–11.

13. "America's War in Korea", *CWR*, October 1950,p.28.

14. "US Planes Raid China's Northeast", *CMR*, October 1950, p.55.

15. Telegram, Zhou Enlai to Yakov Malik, President of the Security Council and Trygve Lie, Secretary-General of the United Nations, 20 August 1950 in "China's Foreign Relations During the Past Year", Supplement, *China Monthly Review*, 1950,p.63.

16. "US Press Prepares for War", *CMR*, December 1950,p.131–2; *Collier's*, 23 September 1950.

17. *Ibid.*

18. K'e Chia-lung, "The Strafing of Kooloutzu by American Planes", *CMR*, December 1950,p.140; "List of Border Violations by U.S. Planes", *CMR*, December 1950, p.141.The *Review* published an incomplete list of violations of the Chinese border from August 27 to November 14, 1950. The editor referred readers to the more detailed, complete list compiled by *Hsinhua* News Agency for the same period; "Targets of American Planes",(pictorial spread), *CMR*, December 1950,p.142.

19. "Who Commits the Atrocities?", *CMR*, January 1951,p.18. After recapturing Seoul, American authorities exhibited mass graves as evidence of North Korean atrocities. The article replies by drawing attention to South Korean reprisals. There

is ample evidence that both sides carried out mass executions of potential civilian opponents as territory traded hands. For ROK atrocities, see Cumings, *The Origins of the Korean War, Volume II, The Roaring of the Cataract 1947–1950*.p.720.

20. "Never Call Retreat", *CMW*, February 1951, p.70–71.

21. *Ibid*.p.70.

22. "The War in Korea", *CMR*, February 1951, p.77.

23. *Ibid*.p.80–81.

24. Ibid. p.81; Cumings, *The Origins of the Korean War, Volume II*, p.721. As many as 150,000 may have been executed by the Rhee regime during the time the North was occupied. North Korean authorities claimed 15,000 persons had been massacred in Pyongyang.

25. "The Voice of American POW's: POW's Hit by US Airforce",(*Hsinhua*, 15 March 1951), *CMR*, May 1951,p.223.

26. *Ibid*.p.224.

27. "Atrocities in Korea", *CMR*, May 1951, p.226–7.

28. "US Tactics Backfire", *CMR*, June 1951,p.294.

29. "US Tactics Backfire", *CMR*, June 1951,p.294–5.

30. Albert E. Cowdrey, *United States Army in the Korean War, The Medics' War*.(Washington D.C.: Center for Military History, 1987)p.220.

31. Bak Hun Yung, Minister of Foreign Affairs, Korean People's Democratic Republic, to President, United Nations Security Council, 8 May 1951, United Nations Document S / 2142.

32. Endicott and Hagerman, *The United States and Biological Warfare*, p.82–4.

33. Albert E. Cowdrey, *United States Army in the Korean War, The Medics' War*. (Washington D.C.:Center of Military History, United States Army, 1987), p.220; Stephen Endicott and Edward Hagerman, *The United States and Biological Warfare, Secrets from the Early Cold War and Korea*. (Bloomington: Indiana University Press, 1998), p.150–1. Endicott and Engerman obtained a copy of the 'Sams Report'("Report by Brigadier General Crawford F.Sams, MC, Chief, Public Health and Welfare Section, SCAP to Chief of Staff, Far Eastern Command," Subject: "Special Operations in North Korea," 17 March 1951) from John W. Powell, who got it through the freedom of information act from the National Archives; *Newsweek*, 9 April 1951.

34. Albert E. Cowdrey, *The Medics' War* (Washington D.C.: 1987) p. 175

35. "Bubonic Plague Ship", *Newsweek*, 9 April 1951, p.13.

36. *Ibid*. On the other hand, if the United States *had* been testing bacteriological weapons, it would have been necessary to determine if they had produced any effect. General Sams' mission could just as easily have been for that purpose.

37. *North China Daily News*, 11 January 1951, p.1.

38. United Nations Document. S/2684.

39. "MacArthur Stalemated", *CMR,* April 1951, p.190.

40. "Casualty of US Raids",(photograph), *CMR*, June 1951,p.304.

41. "Protests Germ War", *CMR*, June 1951, p.303–4.

42. "Protests U.S. Germ War", *CMR*, June 1951, p.303–4; *Hsinhua*, 4 May 1951.

43. *Ibid*, p.304; *Hsinhua*, 4 May 1951. The Chinese did not hesitate to bring their case to the attention of the Red Cross in 1951. Yet, a year later, following the Soviet lead in 1952, they ironically refused to accept that organization as sufficiently neutral to put together an investigative body.

44. "Report of the Scientific Commission for the Investigation of the Facts Concerning Bacterial Warfare in Korea and China", Supplement, *People's China*, 17 September 1952, p.1–28; Albert E. Cowdrey, *United States Army in the Korean War, The Medic's War.* (Washington, D.C.: Center for Military History, United States Army, 1987), p.221–222; Major General W.F. Dean, *General Dean's Story.* (New York: Viking, 1954), p.264–77.

45. United Nations Document. S/2684; Powell, ed. "The Month in Review, Crime Against Humanity", *CMR*, March 1952, p.225–230.

46. United Nations Document. S/2684/Addendum 1.

47. Ironically, although China had protested alleged U.S. germ warfare activities through the Red Cross a year earlier, it now followed the lead of the Soviet Union in rejecting an investigation organized by the ICRC.

48. "'Germ Warfare' Charges Called Fabrication, Statement by Secretary of State Acheson, 4 March 1952," *Department of State Bulletin*, 17 March 1952, p.427–8.

49. "The United States in the United Nations", (Security Council, 26 March 1952), *Department of State Bulletin*, 31 March 1952, p.516.

50. Endicott and Hagerman, *The United States and Biological Warfare*, p.192; Jozef Goldblat, *The Problem of Chemical and Biological Warfare, Volume IV, CB Disarmament Negotiations, 1920-1970.*(Stockholm: Stockholm International Peace Research Institute, 1971) p.198–9; Earnest A. Gross, Deputy U.S. Representative to the United Nations, "Soviet Germ Warfare Campaign: The Strategy of the Big Lie", *Department of State Bulletin*, 7 July 1952, pp.154,155,156.

51. Endicott and Hagerman, *The United States and Biological Warfare*, p.8.

52. World Peace Council, "An Appeal of the World Peace Council Against Bacteriological Warfare", (Oslo, 29 March-1 April 1952) Supplement, *People's China*, 16 April 1952, p.1.

53. Commission of the International Association of Democratic Lawyers, "Report on the Use of Bacteriological Weapons on Chinese Territory by the Armed Forces of the United States", Supplement, *People's China*, 16 April 1952, p.7–10; Robert Neild, Anders Boserup and Julian Perry Robinson, *The Problem of Chemical and Biological Warfare, Volume V, The Prevention of CBW.* (Stockholm: Stockholm International Peace Research Institute, 1971) p.241–2.

54. "For World Unity Against Germ War", *People's China*, 16 April 1952, p.3.

55. "The Day of Judgment of the American War Criminals Is Near", Supplement, *People's China*, 16 May 1952, p.16; *People's Daily*, 6 May 1952; "Report of the International Scientific Commission for the Investigation of the Facts Concerning Bacterial Warfare in Korea and China", Supplement, *People's China*, 17 September 1952,p. 4–5. The Members of the International Scientific Commission for the Investigation of the Facts Concerning Bacterial Warfare in Korea and China included: Dr. Andrea Andreen, Director of the Central Clinical Laboratory of the Hospital Board of the City of Stockholm, Sweden; Mr.Jean Malterre, Director of the Laboratory of Animal Physiology, National College of Agriculture, Grignon, France; Dr. Joseph Needham, Sir William Dunn Reader in Biochemistry, University of Cambridge, U.K.; Dr. Oliviero Olivo, Professor of Human Anatomy in the Faculty of Medicine of the University of Bolognia, Italy; Dr. Samuel B. Pessoa, Professor of Parasitology at the University of Sao Paulo, Brazil; Dr. N.N. Zhukov-Verezhnikov, Professor of Bacteriology at the Soviet Academy of Medicine, (Zhukov-Verezhnikov had been the Chief Medical Expert at the Khabarovsk Trial

of twelve Japanese bacteriological warfare practitioners.); Dr. Franco Graziosi, Assistant in the Institute of Microbiology, University of Rome participated as observer and consultant.

The Commission's liaison with six Chinese scientists and four members of the World Peace Council who accompanied the ISC to Northeast China and Korea, was Dr. Tsien San-tsiang, Director of the Institute of Modern Physics of Academia Sinica.

The six Chinese scientists were: Dr. Chung Hui-lan, Director People's Hospital, Beijing, Professor of Clinical Medicine, China Union Medical College; Dr. Wu Tsai-tung, Professor of Pathology, Nanking University Medical College; Dr. Fang Kang, Associate Research Member, National Central Institute of Health, Beijing; Dr. Chu Hung-fu, Assistant Director Laboratory of Entomology, Academia Sinica; Dr. Yang Shih-ta, Professor of Public Health, Aurora University, Shanghai; and Dr. Yen Jen-ying, Associate Professor of Obstetrics and Gynecology, Beijing University Medical College.

The political and organizational personnel were: Liao Cheng-chih, Vice-Chairman of the Committee of Reception, World Peace Council; Kung Nai-chuan, Secretary-General of the Committee of Reception, World Peace Council, Director of Shanghai Medical College; Dr. Chi Su-hua, Assistant Secretary-General of the Committee of Reception, World Peace Council, Secretary of the Chinese Medical Association; Li Te-chuan, World Peace Council and member of the Chinese Red Cross Society. See also: Powell, ed. "U.S. Germ Warfare, Report of International Scientists' Commission", *CMR*, November-December 1952, p.439–441.

56. "Report of the International Scientific Commission for the Investigation of the Facts Concerning Bacterial Warfare in Korea and China", Supplement, *People's China*, 17 September 1952, p.7; Neild, Boserup, and Robinson, *The Problem of Chemical and Biological Warfare, Volume V*, pp.244–58; Goldblat, *The Problem of Chemical and Biological Warfare, Volume IV*,p.215.

57. Powell, ed. "The Month in Review, Crime Against Humanity", *CMR*, March 1952, p.226.

58. *Ibid.*

59. *Ibid.*p.229. Since that time, Powell, under the Freedom of Information Act, was able to prove in 1980 from U.S. military documents, that the U.S. War Department knew about the Japanese BW program in Manchuria, and that some of its victims had been American G.I.'s. Powell's documents show that in order to gain access to the data and the expertise of Japanese BW researchers, and to expand the American BW program, U.S. military authorities covered up the war crimes of General Ishii and his followers, granting them immunity from prosecution in return for their cooperation. See: John W. Powell, "A Hidden Chapter in History", *The Bulletin of the Atomic Scientists*, October 1981, p.44–53; John W. Powell, "Japan's Germ Warfare: The U.S. Cover-up of a War Crime", *Bulletin of Concerned Asian Scholars*, October-December, 1980, p.2–15; Sheldon H. Harris, *Factories of Death, Japanese Biological Warfare 1932–45 and the American Cover-up*. (London: Routledge, 1994),p.161–223.

60. "Germ Warfare: A Sign of Desperation in Korea", *CMR*, April 1952, p.327; *New York Times*, 13 April 1951.

61. Peter Williams and David Wallace, *Unit 731, The Japanese Army's Secret of Secrets*. (London: Hodder and Stoughton, 1989), p.16, 73–74. Unit 100 was formed at the same time as Unit 731, in 1936. It was commanded by Lt. General

Yujiro Wakamatsu, a veterinarian. It studied anthrax, glanders, and sheep and cattle plagues. See also: Hal Gold, *Unit 731 Testimony*.(Tokyo: Yenbooks, 1996), p.49.

62. Williams and Wallace, *Unit 731, The Japanese Army's Secret of Secrets*, p.78–80. Orders for the creation of Unit 731 were stamped with the Emperor's personal seal, *but this does not prove that the Emperor knew*, since his seal was routinely affixed to hundreds of documents by military leaders during the war; *Materials on the Trial of Former Servicemen of the Japanese Army Charged with Manufacturing and Employing Bacteriological Weapons*. (Moscow: Foreign Languages Publishing House, 1950),p.104, 112, 113.

63. "Germ Warfare: A Sign of Desperation in Korea", *CMR*, April 1952, p.324–5.

64. *Ibid.* p.325–6.

65. *Ibid.* p.326.

66. "Germ Warfare", *CMR*, April 1952, p.327.

67. *Ibid.* 326; Endicott and Hagerman, *The United States and Biological Warfare*, p.29–30. George W. Merck, head of the pharmaceutical corporation Merck and Company, had been the wartime head of the War Research Service Committee, which sponsored germ weapons research, and a special consultant to the Secretary of War on biological warfare.

68. *Life*, 18 November 1946.

69. "Germ Warfare: A Sign of Desperation in Korea", *CMR*, April 1952, p.326. All nations with BW research programs sought to increase the effectiveness of deadly pathogens, not just the United States.

70. *Ibid.* P.324; *New York Journal-American*, 31 October 1951.

71. *Ibid*, p.328.

72. "Crime Against Humanity", *CMR*, April 1952, p.317–322.

73. "Fantastic New Weapons", *CMR*, June 1952, p.561; *Life*, 18 November 1946; *Saturday Evening Post*, 6 September 1947; "Ounce of New Superpoison Held Able to Wipe Out U.S., Canada", *New York Times*, 19 December 1946.

74. Powell, ed. "The Month in Review, U.S. Germ War Fully Proved", *CMR*, May 1952, p.424; Commission of the International Association of Democratic Lawyers, "Report on the Use of Bacteriological Weapons on Chinese Territory by the Armed Forces of the United States", Supplement, *People's China*, 16 April 1952, p.7–10; "U.S. Germ Warfare in Northeast", *CMR*, May 1952, p.476.

75. Commission of the International Association of Democratic Lawyers, "Report on the Use of Bacteriological Weapons on Chinese Territory by the Armed Forces of the United States",p.7.

76. Dean Acheson, United States Secretary of State, 4 March 1952, "'Germ Warfare' Charges Called Fabrication", *United States Department of State Bulletin*, 17 March 1952, p.427–8. "The inability of the Communists to care for the health of the people under their control seems to have resulted in a serious epidemic of plague. The Communists, not willing to admit and bear the responsibility that is theirs, are trying to pin the blame on some fantastic plot by U.N. Forces."

77. Powell, ed. "U.S. Germ War Fully Proven", *CMR*, May 1952, p.424–5.

78. Powell, ed. "Public Health Drive", *CWR*, 15 July 1950,p.111–112; William Paget, "China's New Medical Program", *CMR*, September 1950, p.23–26; "Spring Anti-Smallpox Drive", *North China Daily News*, 15 February 1951,p.1; Euchinic

Huang, "Anti-Smallpox Drive", *CMR*, April 1951,p.207; "No Major Epidemics", *CMR*, December 1951, p.304.

79. "Germ Warfare: A Sign of Desperation in Korea", *CMR*, April 1952, p.330; Major General W.F. Dean, *General Dean's Story*.(New York: Viking, 1954), p.264–77; Philip Deane, *I Was a Captive in Korea*. (New York: Norton, 1953) p.170–1; *New York Times*, 2 March 1952.

80. Dean, *General Dean's Story*, p.276–7.

81. Powell, ed. "Most Health Conscious Nation", *CMR*, September 1952, p.211.

82. Cowdrey, *United States Army in the Korean War, the Medic's War*, p.225–6.

83. "These Are Napalm Victims", *CMR*, September 1952, p.248.

84. *Letters*, Lieutenants John Quinn, Paul Kniss, and Floyd O'Neal, to United States Delegates at Asian and Pacific Regions Peace Conference, (2–13 October 1952),Beijing, in "American POW's Write to U.S. Delegates at Peace Conference", *CMR*, February 1953,p.178–186.

85. Powell, ed."Report to Readers", *CMR*, March 1953, p.331.

86. H.C.Huang, "A White Christmas in a POW Camp", *CMR*, February 1952,p.182–7.

87. H.C. Huang, "Notes from a POW Hospital in Korea", *CMR*, March 1952, p.256–8; H.C. Huang, "They Want Peace", *CMR*, June 1952, p.575–9.

88. H.C. Huang, "They Want Peace", *CMR*, June 1952,p.578–9.

89. Frank Noel, "U.S. War Correspondent Describes POW Camp Life", *CMR*, August 1952,p.117–121.

90. "POW Camps in Korea: Two Worlds", *CMR*, September 1952,p.235–239.

91. Major William Raymond Shadish, Testimony, United States Senate, Subcommittee to Investigate the Administration of the Internal Security Act and Other Internal Security Laws of the Committee of the Judiciary, *Hearings: Interlocking Subversion in Government Departments*, 27 September 1954, Washington D.C. p.1836.

92. "Another U.S. Lie Debunked", *People's China*, 1 December 1951, p.22–23.

93. "POW Olympics in Korea", *CMR*, June 1953, p.56–9.

94. *Ibid.*

95. "Statements by Two American Air Force Officers, Kenneth Loyd Enoch and John Quinn, Admitting Their Participation in Germ Warfare in Korea and Other Documents", Supplement, *People's China,* 16 May 1952, p.1–15.

96. "Depositions of Nineteen Captured U.S. Airmen on Their Participation in Germ Warfare in Korea", Supplement, *People's China*, 1 December 1953, p.1–66.

97. "U.S. POW's Admit Germ Warfare", *CMR*, June 1952, p.600.

98. "Asia and Pacific Peace Conference Scheduled", *CMR*, August 1952, p.122–5; Rewi Alley, "Peace Conference", *CMR*, August 1952, p.126–130.

99. "Crowd in Tokyo Hears Peiping Session Is Off for Week", *New York Times*, 28 September 1952, p.3.

100. "Acheson Brands Parley as Fake", *New York Times*, 2 October 1952, p.3.

101. "U.S. Germ Warfare, Report of International Scientists' Commission", *CMR*, November-December 1952, p.437–442.

102. "Report of the Scientific Commission for the Investigation of the Facts Concerning Bacterial Warfare in Korea and China", Supplement, *People's China*, 17 September 1952, p.1–28.

103. "U.S. Germ Warfare, Report of International Scientists' Commission", *CMR*, November-December 1952, p.441-2.

104. "Report of the International Scientific Commission", Supplement, *People's China*, 17 September 1952, p.8-10.

105. John Quinn to Delegates, Asia and Pacific Regions Peace Conference, Beijing, in "American POW's Write to U.S. Delegates at Peace Conference", *CMR*, February 1953,p.178-182.

106. Floyd B. O'Neal to Delegates Asian and Pacific Regions Peace Conference, Beijing, in "American POW's Write to U.S. Delegates at Peace Conference", *CMR*, February 1953,p.184-6.

107. "Why U.S. POW's Admit Using Germ Warfare", *CMR*, November-December 1952, p.443-448.

108. Wilfred Burchett to Powell, Interview, "Why U.S. POW's Admit Using Germ Warfare", *CMR*, November-December, 1952, p.447.

109. *Ibid.* p.448.

110. "Why U.S. POW's Admit Using Germ Warfare", p.443-4.

111. Colonel Frank H. Schwable, Deposition, in "Proof Of Germ Warfare, Statements of Captured U.S. Marine Corps Officers", *CMR*, May 1953, p.92-99; Major Roy H. Bley, Deposition in "Proof of Germ Warfare, Major Bley's Statement", *CMR*, May 1953, p.99-103.

112. Schwable, Deposition, *CMR*, May 1953, p.98-9; Colonel Frank H. Schwable, "Statements of Colonel Frank H. Schwable, U.S. Marine Corps," Supplement, *New Times*, 4 March 1953, p.5-6.

113. "'Thoughts' of Returned POW's Worry U.S. Army", *CMR*, July 1953,p.66-7.

114. Endicott and Hagerman, *The United States and Biological Warfare*, p.166-7; *New York Times*, 6 September 1953.

115. Herbert Brownell, the U.S. Attorney General, called for treason indictments (a capital crime) against POW collaborators. Secretary of Defense Charles Willson and Senator Richard Russell, a senior member of Senate Armed Services Committee, also called for the punishment of POW's who had collaborated. See: Endicott and Hagerman, *The United States and Biological Warfare*, p.166-7.

116. "Marines Award Schwable Medal", *New York Times*, 8 July 1953, p.8.

117. United Nations Documents.A / 2231, and A / C.1 / SR.648, and A / C.1 / L.66. Schwable explained the Chinese told him that he could be tried and shot as a war criminal, and said that inadequate food, shelter, and solitary confinement also added to the mental torment preceding his confession.

118. "Marine Colonel Returned", *New York Times*, 6 September 1953, p.1; "Schwable Assigned to Air Saftey Post", *New York Times*, 12 May 1954,p.3; "Marines Award Schwable Medal", *New York Times*, 8 July 1954, p.8.

119. Powell, ed. "*Review* to Close After Next Issue", *CMR*, June 1953, p.2-3.

120. Powell, ed. "Report to Readers", *CMR*, July 1953, p.132.

121. Powell, ed. "Report to Readers", *CMR*, April 1953, p.94-5.

122. "Shanghai Monthly to Suspend", *New York Times*, 20 June 1953,p.5.

123. "Red Ex-Editor Quits China", *New York Times*, 5 August 1953, p.3.

124. "End of the Line", *Newsweek*, 18 May 1953, p.99.

125. "Two Came Home", *Time*, 17 August 1953, p.71.

126. "The Wayward Editor", *Time*, 11 October 1954, p.86; "Ex-Editor in China Called 'Murderer'", *New York Times*, 28 September, 1954, p.12; "Ex-G.I. Calls Writer Red Trade Promoter", *New York Times*, 29 September 1954, p.16.

127. "The Way Reds Used One American: Strange Case of John W. Powell", *U.S. News and World Report*, 15 October 1954, pp.68–76.

CHAPTER ELEVEN

HOMECOMING AND EXECRATION

Allyn and Adele Rickett, two American doctoral students on Fullbright scholarships, spent four years in Chinese prisons undergoing thought reform for the "crime" of delivering periodic written observations on life in China to the U.S. Consulate. When the Ricketts crossed from the Communist side of the border into the British colony of Hong Kong after their release in 1954, they were taken aback by the unsympathetic, red-baiting tone of American reporters who crowded around them in search of a story. When Mrs. Rickett affirmed that she did in fact consider the activities they had been engaged in to be spying and that in her view the People's Government had dealt very leniently with them,

> . . . the expressions on the faces of the reporters quickly changed from enthusiastic welcome to disbelief and then to open hostility. . . . One asked sneeringly, "If you like China so much, why didn't you stay there?"[1]

Her husband Rick encountered similar hostility from American reporters as he tried to explain why socialist propaganda was so effective and why the majority of the Chinese people in his estimation, supported the Communist regime. He concluded:

> That I was unable to convince these reporters that this transformation was based on a higher concept of social morality surprised me little. After all it had taken me four years in prison to understand that the personal happiness of the individual could be assured only when he was willing to identify himself with the happiness of society as a whole.[2]

The reception which Powell, his wife Sylvia and their two sons received at the border as they left China for home in August 1953, was no less charged. Like the Ricketts, Powell and his wife, though more sympathetic to the Revolution from the start, had internalized the basic moral values and assumptions of the New China. And as with the Ricketts, any attempt to explain the Chinese rationale elicited the same hostility from reporters. *Time* magazine described the scene:

> The 5:50pm train that crosses over from Lo Wu, it's last stop in Red China, disgorged harried, sweating John William ("Bill") Powell, his wife and two children. . . . Newsmen who asked Powell last week why he had never criticized any Red action were rewarded with Powell's own version of Orwellian doublespeak: "You just don't understand. In China, there's a new appreciation of the role of the press." [3]

Under Powell's direction, *Time* asserted, the *Review* became little more than "a mouthpiece for the Chinese Reds."[4] *Newsweek* stated that the foreign community in Shanghai had been "sickened" by the *Review*'s conformity to "party line" and labeled Sylvia Powell "vociferously pro-Communist".[5]

Once home, the Powells settled in San Francisco, where Sylvia began working for the National Infantile Paralysis Foundation.[6] John Powell started working as a free-lance writer for various journals and did sporadic lecturing on his experiences in China.[7] In his lectures he called for the repeal of the U.S. trade embargo against China, urged better relations, resumption of business, and diplomatic recognition of the People's Republic of China. By 1956 he was also working as a salesman for a school supplies manufacturer. Julian Schuman, an associate editor who had collaborated with Powell and Sylvia during the last years of the *Review*, did not return until December 1953. Ultimately, the use of Powell's *China Monthly Review* by Chinese captors to indoctrinate American prisoners of war led to the editor's denunciation by a Senate Judiciary Subcommittee, and to the prosecution of the *Review*'s editorial staff for sedition.

*

American prisoners of war were repatriated throughout the summer and early fall of 1953. American reporters in September paid particular attention to former POW's who had made statements concerning germ warfare and other allegations. Why had some prisoners confessed to "crimes" which the American public did not believe and which the U.S. government flatly denied?

A few former POW collaborators, like Colonel Walker M. Mahurin, in part to protect themselves and others, and to deflect the locus of responsibility onto their former Communist captors, rushed forward with stories of coercion and torture. According to Mahurin, their captors were ". . . just about as cruel as they could be," that it ". . . depend[ed] on the individual how long he could fight the problem," and that ". . . the boys who did not write confessions should get the medal of honor."[8]

Only hours after the release by the Communists of American fliers who had confessed to taking part in germ warfare, the Associated Press published reports of torture being used to elicit testimony.

Freed American airmen began unfolding Sunday the gruesome inside story of how Chinese Reds perpetrated the Korean War's biggest hoax-germ warfare "confessions"- by tortures carried on long after the truce was signed.

The article reported that fliers had been ". . . abused and threatened for day on day beyond all physical endurance," and promised that what it was reporting was ". . . only a fragmentary beginning of the horror-etched full account."[9]

Returned fliers who had collaborated were divided into two groups by military authorities. Those eager to relate torture or mistreatment stories were made available to the press. The second group, which was not as eager to recant and required more pressure, included Marine Lt. Colonel Frank H. Schwable, Major Roy H. Bley, Lt. John Quinn, Lt. Kenneth Enoch, Lt. Floyd B. O'Neal and Lt. Paul Kniss. It was declared off limits to reporters and sequestered in a hospital isolation ward.[10]

Airmen from the first group told of death threats, medical mal-treatment, and extreme mental torture being used by their Communist captors to coerce confessions. Colonel Walker M. Mahurin said he was forced to stand at attention for days at a time and threatened with death if he did not confess; 2nd Lt. Richard G. Voss said he had confessed ". . . only after red doctors stood by while maggots crawled over his untreated wounds."[11]

During the ocean voyage home, hostility surfaced between ordinary POW's and the "progressive" ones, who had made broadcasts or statements in captivity. Officers reportedly had to intervene to prevent some of the collaborators from being thrown overboard on the high seas, and the "progressives" had to be separated from the other POW's to safeguard them from attack.[12]

Concern at home over apparent collaboration by U.S. POW's generated several official and unofficial studies. The Department of Defense instituted an inquiry by the "Advisory Committee to the Secretary of Defense" which drew up a code of conduct for future prisoners of war. The U.S. Senate Committee on Government Operations opened extensive hearings on the POW collaboration issue. There was a flurry of interest in both psychiatric and popular journals on the subject of POW collaboration. Army psychiatrist Major William Mayer published an article in *U.S. News and World Report* entitled "Why Did So Many GI Captives Cave In?" An influential interpretation done by Eugene Kinkead, a well-known journalist and author, encouraged the perception that widespread breakdown in morale among American POW's was responsible for wholesale collaboration. It was first published in *The New Yorker* magazine before being released in book form.[13]

Eventually, the story which emerged was one not of torture, but of steady indoctrination coupled with gradually improving living conditions for those who did not actively resist. Prisoners who made a point of resisting however, were dealt with in a more severe manner which some-times led to death. Ninety-one percent of the 4000 returned POW's had written autobiographies as ordered by their captors. Thirty-eight percent of the POW's had signed "peace" petitions or other similar propaganda statements.[14] Yet, almost all POW's practiced some sort of passive resis-tance against Chinese attempts at thought reform carried out through the familiar pattern of small group study, criticism and self-criticism.[15]

Since Powell's *China Monthly Review* had been one of the journals sup-plied by the Chinese for group study, and particularly because it was an American-edited and owned journal, its former staff soon came under po-litical attack. Powell (as editor and publisher), his wife Sylvia Campbell (a contributing editor), and Julian Schuman (an associate editor), were called to testify before the Senate Judiciary Committee's Subcommittee on Inter-nal Security, which was searching for a way to indict them.

*

On September 27, 1954, John Powell appeared before the Senate Judi-ciary Subcommittee, chaired by Senator William E. Jenner (Republican, In-diana). The Chairman opened the session by outlining a theory developed by the Committee and later shown to be baseless, that American Foreign Service Personnel and Office of War Information employees were all part of a large "Communist cell" which had plotted to turn China over to the Communists. Among the named were well known academics who unques-tionably had never been disloyal and Foreign Service officers indisputably devoted to the United States.

According to Senator Jenner, members of the Communist cell included Harvard professor John King Fairbank (whom Jenner claimed was a Com-munist), Johns Hopkins professor Owen Lattimore ("a conscious, articu-late instrument of the Soviet conspiracy"), and State Department officers John Stewart Service, John Patton Davies, John K. Emmerson and John Carter Vincent, among others. Quoting General Claire Chennault, former commander of the Flying Tigers and the U.S. Fourteenth Air Force, Jenner asserted these individuals ". . . functioned as a public relations bureau for the Yanan Communists," and implied that the State Department itself was part of the conspiracy.[16]

After Jenner had given a ". . . picture of the original American group in Chongqing, which had cleared the path for ultimate Communist victory," he asserted that Powell, Sylvia Campbell, and Schuman had been part of a second secret Communist cell which had taken over the work of Soviet subversion in China after the first group had returned home.[17] Indeed, a considerable part of Powell's questioning was designed to establish the links in the alleged conspiracy ("Did you know Owen Lattimore while em-ployed by the OWI?"[18]), to implicate others through his testimony, and to force Powell into perjuring himself if at all possible.

Throughout his Subcommittee testimony, Powell scrupulously avoided naming any persons, relatives, or friends who may have helped him or with whom he had any business after his return to the United States. He refused to comment one way or the other as to whether he was a member of the Communist Party. "I do not think I am called upon to tell you whether I am a Republican or a Democrat or a Communist or anything else."[19] (At a press conference at the National Press Club following his testimony, he stated that he was not and never had been a member of the Communist party[20]).

Powell refused to acknowledge any Chinese government restriction of his editorial control over the *China Weekly/ Monthly Review* and accused the Committee of attempting to entrap him. While silent about any financial support the *Review* may have received from the government of the People's Republic, Powell was quite open about other aspects of his journal's finances. Declaring himself a supporter of the U.S. Constitution, he accused the Committee of not recognizing the First Amendment Rights of that document, and he repeatedly tried to plead the First Amendment rather than the Fifth Amendment when refusing to answer questions which he felt were none of the Committee's business.

> *Mr. Sourwine*: Do you think the Communist Party of China is a political and ideological organization? Do you think you as an American have a right, a constitutional right, to belong to the Communist Party of China?. . . .
> *Mr. Powell*: I decline to answer the question.
> *Mr. Sourwine*: Why?
> *Mr. Powell*: Because, as I said before, under the first amendment I believe that my associations and beliefs and freedoms of thought and speech are protected from investigation by you in this place.
> *Mr. Sourwine*: The question was not about your associations; the question was about whether you had an opinion on your constitutional right.
> *Mr. Powell*: Yes; I have an opinion. My opinion is that I have a constitutional right not to answer under the provisions of the first amendment.[21]

When the Committee demanded to know where his wife worked, Powell asked the purpose of the question. the Chairman cut him off: "Just answer the question. It is not your right to know what the purpose is." Refusing to answer, Powell replied:

> I think questions about my wife are an invasion of my privacy. My Wife is available. If you gentlemen have questions about my wife, she will be more than pleased to come here and give you her views on any variety of subjects. I think that if you gentlemen are married men you certainly know better than to ask a husband to say what his wife thinks.[22]

If these were the only themes the Committee had pursued, it would have produced little of political value. But it also heard the testimony of several former prisoners of war who focused on the use of the *China Monthly Review* as a propaganda tool in the process of thought reform in POW camps. Testimony on cruel treatment of prisoners by North Korean and Chinese Captors, along with lots of material on the conditions of POW camps, was employed by the Committee to discredit numerous articles in the *Review* which purported to show the opposite. Sedition in wartime involves the intentional dissemination of untruths: the Committee intended to provide a basis for this charge.

Early in the hearings, Mrs. Dolores Gill, the wife of a deceased POW, gave testimony that Powell sent her a letter and clippings from the *Review*, (January, 1951) giving assurance that her husband was well treated and comfortable.[23] Mrs.Gill then tearfully[24] informed the Committee that her husband, Second Lieutenant Charles L. Gill, had died of malnutrition and dysentery while in the POW camp. In January, 1951 Powell had claimed Gill was in good health and expected to be returning home soon.[25] Subsequent testimony established that by the end of May, 1951, Lt.Gill was already suffering from dysentery and malnutrition which would lead to his death in early July.[26] Although Gill's death occurred six months after Powell wrote his letter of reassurance, Senator Jenner singled out the letter as evidence of duplicity on Powell's part.

The Committee asked Powell why the *Review* published the names of Americans being held as Prisoners of War and where they got the information? He answered that the data came from Chinese newspapers. He published the lists because there had been no official exchange of information between the American and Chinese governments at that time and "We thought it was information which people would like to have."[27] As Powell noted, these were generally POW's who had signed petitions, made statements, or otherwise cooperated with their captors.

The Committee intended to show that Powell had misrepresented the treatment of American soldiers in North Korean prisoner of war camps, that his journal had been an important element of Communist indoctrination in the camps, and that he should share some of the blame for POW's who were punished by Communist captors for resisting the thought reform process. The letter Powell sent to Mrs.Charles L. Gill, reassuring her that her husband was probably being well treated was intended as part of the evidence. That evidence however clearly delineated the limits of Powell's knowledge. It explained that he was extrapolating from what he had observed of the PLA's treatment of Guomindang soldiers during the Chinese Civil War.

> From our own personal observation of the actions of the Chinese People's Government here in Shanghai, we know it is the policy to treat all prisoners captured, Kuomintang soldiers, as well as criminals, with the greatest leniency and fairness in order to win over their support. We are sure this is

the same policy being carried out by the People's Volunteers in Korea. This accounts for the numerous statements of gratitude and good will of American POW's which appear in our local papers almost daily.[28]

Major William Raymond Shadish, an Army physician from Walter Reed Hospital who had been a prisoner of war in Korea for almost three years, gave a vivid description of forced indoctrination sessions at the camps. On average, POW's were required to study, listen to lectures, read articles and comment on them, for about six hours daily. The *China Monthly Review* was one of the more frequently used publications for this purpose, and according to Shadish, was widely disliked by the men.

> The ordinary program of study was divided up among various types of approaches. There would be lectures by English-speaking Chinese, there would be discussion periods in which we were supposed to discuss various articles. Before these discussion periods, various publications were distributed to each squad of men to read, and in these publications there would be articles marked with red crayon as required reading. Among the publications most commonly received was this *China Monthly Review*.
>   . . . I would like to say there was no middle of the road affair. The Communists did not practice that. We were told that you had one opinion. If you did not comment for the article, you were against the article. Consequently, a large number of prisoners got into a great deal of trouble and a large number of deaths were indirectly or directly responsible or occurred, rather, because of the difficulties starting over these articles.[29]

Shadish gave testimony contradicting assertions in *Review* articles about adequate medical attention, heated lodgings, and sufficient food. However his remarks supported *Review* claims about baseball and other sports activities for the POW's and swimming or bathing (for the officers). According to Shadish, quilted clothing was not issued until spring, 1951, and conditions gradually improved after the peace negotiations began.[30]

Food was used to reinforce a moderate level of cooperation among the prisoners. "As long as the prisoners cooperated without resisting too strongly, the food would stay at a level where all the men or practically all the men could live. As soon as resistance came up, conditions became worse."[31] *Review* articles by H.C. Huang covering Christmas and Thanksgiving celebrations and feasts by the POW's were verified by Shadish's testimony.[32]

> *Mr.Carpenter*: In the issue of January 1952 of the *China Monthly Review*, pages 70 and 72, it describes Thanksgiving in a POW camp. Do you have any recollection of that?
> *Major Shadish*: That was describing, I imagine, the Thanksgiving of 1951. This was at the time the negotiations were beginning to look fairly good. We were told by the Chinese things were going well and we may be home within several months. This time they brought a large amount of food, of meats, breads, candies, cigarettes, some sake- all kinds of things. They

gave us a thanksgiving party. It was fabulous to us at that time because we had not seen anything like it.[33]

According to Shadish, celebrations like this were given on three occasions: twice on Christmas and once on Thanksgiving, but rations were cut for some time afterward to cover the expense of the feasts. A short article which Shadish and four other surviving POW physicians wrote for the *Journal of the American Medical Association* recounting captivity, medical care and indoctrination in Communist prisoner of war camps was reproduced in the Committee's records.[34]

Mr.Carroll Wright,Jr. of Arlington, Virginia, also described how the *Review* was utilized to indoctrinate American POW's in North Korea.

> *Mr.Carpenter:* During your imprisonment in the Communist prison camps in Korea, did you ever see the *China Weekly Review* and later the *China Monthly Review?*
> *Mr.Wright:* Yes, sir; I did.
> *Mr.Carpenter:* Would you tell us under what circumstances you saw that?
> *Mr.Wright:* Yes, sir. This periodical was at first distributed to us through this monitor system in our squads. The political commissars in the camp, the English-speaking Chinese that controlled the study program, would issue this magazine to the squad monitors, giving them instructions as to what articles were to be read, and have them conduct or request them to conduct, and where possible to see that it was done, that they were discussed. Normally, they require that each member of the squad write some sort of article or comment relative to the article.[35]

Those who refused to take part in indoctrination were punished, often with prolonged solitary confinement.

Corporal Page Thomas Baylor, Jr. testified to being held in solitary confinement twice, for fifteen and thirty-three days. The two incidents were punishment for refusal to comment and having criticized *China Monthly Review* articles which had been marked for study and comment by the POW's in his squad. He had received beatings and been deprived of food while in solitary confinement. Baylor said the *Review* and other magazines were brought into the POW camps about once a week.[36]

Carroll Wright, Jr. testified that the *Review* and other magazines and papers were sent to the camps in large quantities, taking up considerable space on supply trucks or wagons that might have otherwise been devoted to food or medical supplies.

> I would certainly feel without any question in my mind that had the space that those magazines occupied on transportation, and also the expense, if you want to get down to that, had been devoted to medical supplies, that a great deal more of our boys would have come home, and the approximately 55 percent of them that were captured earlier that did die would have made it back home.[37]

Wright expressed outrage that Powell was free, enjoying the rights of a citizen, and called for the former editor's punishment.

> I can't help but wonder how many of our boys would have come home if they had something like that. I really feel that in my opinion this man is responsible for physical injury and also I think directly through his magazine or indirectly, whichever you want to call it, must bear some of the stains of the blood of the boys that did die there, and who did receive punishment.
> In my opinion I would classify him as a murderer.[38]

To make certain no one missed the point, the Committee asked Wright to clarify who he was accusing of murder:

Mr. Carpenter: "Whom do you mean when you say 'this Man'?"

Mr. Wright: "I am referring to the gentleman who was here on the stand a short while ago, known as Mr. Powell."[39]

The Chairman ended the day's session by assuring Carroll Wright that the Committee meant to prosecute Powell. "This entire record is going to be sent to the Department of Justice to see that justice is done", he announced. The following day, Senator Jenner asked U.S. Attorney General William P. Rogers to press for a treason charge against Powell, and submitted the previous two days' testimony to the Department of Justice.[40]

*

In his September twenty-eighth press conference at the National Press Club, Powell denied ever having been a member of the Communist Party. He explained that he refused to give the same answer under oath during the hearings because questions about his politics invaded his privacy.[41] Powell read a statement which he had been barred from reading the previous day at the Senate Judiciary Subcommittee Hearings.

In his statement, Powell said that China's program of rapid industrialization offered a potentially growing market for American industrial products. However the U.S. trade embargo had forced American businessmen out of the China market. He traced American trade with China back to the days of the clipper ships and affirmed that trade could be a way for the United States to resolve its differences with the mainland government. It would be difficult for the two governments to remain hostile toward each other once they began a brisk trade, he opined. China's development projects would continue whether the U.S. government liked it or not, so why not take advantage of the opportunity, he asked?[42]

Powell's testimony before the Judiciary Subcommittee was widely reported in the mainstream print media. Articles in *Newsweek, Time, U.S. News and World Report*, and the *New York Times* all reported the use of Powell's magazine for forced political indoctrination of American POW's and repeated the sensational accusation that Powell, as editor, was guilty of murder.[43] Most quoted ex-POW Carroll Wright, Jr.'s statement: "In my opinion, I would classify him as a murderer."[44] *Newsweek* reported: "One witness told of a U.S. officer whose death resulted from abuses inflicted after he declared the *Review* 'Wasn't worth the paper it was printed on.'"[45]

U.S. News and World Report published a seven-page article comprised of extensive quotations from the hearings which told the story of how the *Review* was used to indoctrinate American Prisoners. It included a shot of Mrs. Gill wiping a tear from her eye and a worried-looking photograph of Powell.[46] The *New York Times* reported that Powell had refused to tell the Judiciary Subcommittee that he had never been a Communist because "the whole hearing was an entrapment procedure."[47] By October 1954, both the press and the subcommittee hearings had execrated Powell before the American public as one who had helped the Chinese Communists "brainwash" captive American servicemen and who hence shared a measure of responsibility for the blood of Americans who had died resisting.

Although the Committee turned over the testimony with a request for prosecution to the Justice Department, there were problems proceeding either with a charge of treason or of sedition which led to initial inaction. To prosecute a charge of treason, there had to be a particular treasonable act with at least two witnesses; both the act and the two witnesses were lacking in the evidence. For a charge of sedition to be appropriate, the act of spreading falsehoods giving aid or comfort to the enemy had to take place within the United States or within its maritime jurisdiction. But Powell's journal was printed in Shanghai, and had been used to indoctrinate POW's in North Korea.

Since the requisite conditions for either charge were lacking, the Justice Department at first took no action.[48] By December, an angry Senator Herman Welker (Republican, Idaho) on behalf of the Subcommittee called for ". . . corrective legislation if the Justice Department found itself unable to deal adequately with John W. Powell, editor of the now-defunct *China Monthly Review*."[49]

After prodding by the FBI, the Justice Department convened a Federal Grand Jury which charged Powell, his wife Slyia, and Julian Schuman with seditious activities affecting the armed forces of the United States. On April 25, 1956, the government filed an indictment for thirteen counts of sedition against former editor John W. Powell, and one count of sedition against both Sylvia Campbell Powell and Julian Schuman, who had been associate editors.[50] Warrants were issued for their arrest and bail was set at $5000 each for John and Sylvia and $3000 for Schuman. Curiously, the judge must have recognized the inappropriateness of the sedition charges based on activities undertaken outside the United States from the start, but let the Powells wrestle with years of legal problems before finally pointing out the fact to the prosecution in January, 1959.[51]

The essence of the first count was that the defendants, through the *China Monthly Review*, had circulated false statements and reports with the intention of creating insubordination and disloyalty among American soldiers. Counts two through eleven charged Powell with trying to interfere with the success of U.S. Armed Forces through circulating false statements in the *Review*. The twelfth and thirteenth counts similarly allege that Powell published derogatory statements in the *Review* to cause disloyalty and insubordination among U.S. forces.[52]

The charges could be divided into four main groupings: first, that Powell had said that the United States (not North Korea) was the aggressor in Korea; second, that he had stated that the U.S. had used bacteriological weapons in Korea and China; third, that he had charged the U.S. with stalling and disrupting the peace negotiations; and fourth, that he had overstated the number of American casualties in the war.[53] Rather than contest the intention of inciting insubordination, or the alleged tendency of the *Review* to interfere with or undermine military activities, the Powells, Schuman, and their defense lawyers (A.L. Wirin, Doris Brin Walker, Charles R. Garry and Stanley Faulkner[54]) decided to concentrate on proving the truth or at least plausibility of statements in the *Review*.

The court proceedings can be divided into two parts. The first extended for more than two years, from late Spring, 1956 through March, 1958, and centered around Powell's attempts to produce witnesses and testimony that would prove the veracity of his reporting in the *Review*. Since most of the witnesses lived in China and North Korea, with which the U.S. had no diplomatic relations, an impasse developed over Powell's right to have witnesses testify on his behalf. The U.S. State Department, which was enforcing a blackout on news gathering in China, at first refused to issue travel visas to Powell's lawyers to take depositions in China and North Korea.

This paralleled a confrontation that same year over the State Department's refusal to allow American journalists to visit the People's Republic of China at the invitation of Foreign Minister Zhou Enlai issued in the summer of 1956.[55] Three journalists: William Worthy, correspondent of the *Afro-American*, *Look* Magazine correspondent Edmund Stevens, and his photographer, Philip Harrington all defied the State Department ban by traveling to China. CBS then broadcast reports by Worthy on China, editorial comments by Edward R. Murrow which were critical of the ban, and aired an interview of Worthy conducted by Eric Sevareid on 10 February 1957.[56]

This violation of the government's travel ban sparked a campaign in the liberal press, especially the *New Republic*, calling for a reappraisal of America's foreign policy of isolation in regard to China. Throughout the spring and early summer, 1957, editorials and articles in the *New Republic* by Harold R.Isaacs (adapted from his book *Scratches On Our Minds)*, Howard L. Boorman of Columbia University, John King Fairbank of Harvard University, Richard Hughes (of the London *Sunday Times*, the *Economist* and the *Financial Times)*, Zhao Guozhun of Harvard, Dr.Robert J. Lifton, psychiatrist at the Harvard Medical School, Alexander Eckstein, a Harvard economist, Robert Guillain of *Le Mond*, Peter Schmid of *Die*

Weltwoche, Richard L. Walker of Yale University, and Robert C. North of Stanford University, all called for an end to the U.S. travel ban and a practical re-assessment of America's diplomatic position on China.[57]

Powell's lawyers were pressing for State Department permission to visit China and North Korea at the same time that American newsmen and academics were calling for an end to Secretary of State John Foster Dulles's black-out on China news gathering. In China, this all coincided with a brief period of relative press freedom due to Mao Zedong's "Hundred Flowers" campaign.[58]

After extensive hearings in the U.S. District Court, the tactics of Powell's attorneys came to fruition when the court ordered the State Department to either validate defense attorney A.L.Wirin's passport for travel to China and North Korea within thirty days, or face dismissal of all the charges.[59] Faced with this choice, the State Department relented and granted Wirin the visas he needed.

Although the *New Republic* called for an end to the travel ban, a resumption of trade, and recognition of China (all issues which Powell actively supported)- it did not speak out in defense of Powell, or mention his sedition trial.[60] The well-known liberal journal, *The Nation*, however, did. In an article called "Sedition or Press Freedom?," *The Nation* rebutted the elements of Powell's indictments one by one. It was the first journal to recognize the inappropriateness of the sedition charge based on the jurisdictional restrictions of the statute, an oversight that would eventually lead to the dismissal of the most important part of the State's evidence early in the trial.

> Its [the *Review*'s] circulation, of course, is almost entirely in the Far East. Farreaching as is the Sedition Act, it doesn't cover publication in Asia. Therefore, the Powell case rests on the fact that a few copies were circulated in the United States.[61]

The Nation pointed out that Powell had not called for the overthrow of the U.S. government, he had not called on military personnel to desert, nor had he made any remarks which might tend to interfere with the draft or with military recruitment in the United States. In *The Nation*'s view, Powell was indicted mainly because he had expressed an unpopular editorial opinion:

> In effect, then, Powell's statements (taking germ warfare as an example) took this form:(a) charges of germ warfare have been made against the United States;(b) I have examined published evidence which is said to prove the truth of these charges as well as evidence said to demonstrate their falsity;(c) *In my opinion*, the evidence is sufficient to prove the charges true.[62]

The Nation noted that the charges in the *Review* did not originate with Powell. Many mainstream journals had published the same information.

The difference was that Powell had published the charges as true, without printing a rebuttal from the U.S, side. *The Nation* doubted that Powell would receive a fair trial because of the strength of anti-communist sentiment and the particular way the charges were framed:

> Finally, the emotionalism surrounding the case makes a fair trial almost impossible. The matters dealt with include the Korean War, Nationalist vs. Communist China and the unspoken implication that Powell is the darkest of villains, a Communist. But most of all, they involve the germ warfare charge. Universally, press reports have tended to reduce the complex indictment to the simple charge that the Powells and Schuman are accused of falsely publishing the germ warfare allegations. Consequently there is danger that any jury will feel that if it acquits Powell, it will by implication convict America of using germ warfare.
>
> . . . the form of the indictment is such that the jury is asked to pass, not on Powell's right to his opinion, or his right to express that opinion editorially, but on the truth or falsity of the germ warfare charges against the United States.[63]

The second part of the court proceedings is comprised of the sedition trial itself, which began January 29, 1959. As these proceedings opened, the prosecution tried to introduce the same American prisoner of war testimony that had been featured in the Senate Judiciary Subcommittee hearings. As soon as the prosecution introduced the first former POW witness, U.S. Army Corporal Page Thomas Baylor, Jr., Powell's lawyers objected.[64] Because of the limitation of the sedition statute to the United States or its admiralty and maritime jurisdiction, the testimony of former prisoners about their experiences in North Korea was immaterial and inadmissible. Judge Goodman upheld the objection and consequently threw out most of the emotional and motive basis for the case which the prosecution had hoped to make.

With the jury out of the courtroom, Judge Goodman explained the difficulties of the sedition charge, and suggested to the prosecuting attorneys that a charge of treason would have been more appropriate, since the parameters for treason were broader. The press, which had been present during this discussion, published prejudicial headlines claiming the judge had declared the Powells guilty of treason. The prejudicial press reports led to the granting of a mistrial.

The prosecuting attorneys, barred from presenting their most damaging evidence because the sedition statute applied only to the United States or its maritime jurisdictions, filed a new complaint for treason the same day the mistrial was declared, since treason could be committed "within the United States or elsewhere." Yet no indictment followed, and the case was ultimately dismissed May 2, 1961, on the grounds that the lack of diplomatic relations with the People's Republic prevented the prosecution from finding the prerequisite two witnesses to an overt act of treason.[65]

*

From the start, most of the efforts to secure witnesses by Powell's defense attorneys focused on those connected to the germ warfare allegations. This was the case simply because the witnesses in this area were the best known and documented by Powell, and consequently the first he sought out. The *China Monthly Review* had published the names, biographies, and some of the findings of several foreign and Chinese scientists who had participated in the International Scientific Commission for the Investigation of the Facts Concerning Bacterial Warfare in Korea and China. *People's China* had published the Commission's report in its entirety.

As Powell and his lawyers increasingly secured promises of depositions by many of the scientists and peasants who had testified before the Scientific Commission, they were able to focus their defense, and hence the trial, more narrowly on the bacteriological warfare issue. Powell was seeking to introduce into the U.S. District Court as evidence for his defense the same basis for bacteriological warfare allegations which China had leveled at the United States in 1952–53. In so doing, his attorneys were tying to shift the burden of guilt from the defendants to the government which was prosecuting them, in effect, putting the government on trial in the process.

The prosecution facilitated this strategy. After initially trying to block the defense's access to witnesses in China and North Korea, prosecutors ultimately decided to focus on the germ warfare allegations in Powell's journal at the expense of the other three categories of alleged "false charges." By so doing, they allowed the defense to manipulate the proceedings and to pick their own ground in making their case.

*

Pre-Trial Maneuvers

Before the trial, a complicated series of motions, counter-motions and hearings stretching over a three year period (April 1956 to January 1959) saw both sides maneuvering for advantages. The defendants' lawyers tried to force the government into a position where it would either have to reverse foreign policy in regard to China and North Korea, or dismiss the charges against the accused. The prosecution tried to limit the scope of the defendants' access to witnesses and documents.

After initial legal exploration of the charges, Powell's attorneys throughout the month of September, 1956, filed numerous motions asking the court to facilitate travel to China and North Korea to gather evidence supporting the truth of Powell's statements in the *Review*.[66] The Powells asserted that (among others) Dr. Joseph Needham of Cambridge, England, Professor Samuel B. Pessoa of Sao Paulo, Brazil, and Dr. Andrea Andreen of Stockholm, Sweden, who had all been members of the International Scientific Commission for the Investigation of the Facts Concerning Bacterial

Warfare in Korea and China, could testify to the truth of *Review* articles on germ warfare.

They requested the court to order the United States to pay the cost of traveling to China and Korea to take depositions from over 200 persons listed in the Report of the Scientific Commission for the Investigation of the Facts Concerning Bacterial Warfare in Korea and China.[67] These witnesses, th defense asserted, would provide firsthand observations of bacteriological attacks, of the vectors, or of tests performed to determine the pathogens. As for witnesses to uphold the *Review*'s statements on casualty figures or U.S. stalling on peace negotiations and violations of the Armistice agreement, no specific persons were named.[68]

The Powells wrote to Dang Mingzhao, of the Chinese People's Committee for World Peace which had helped coordinate the efforts of the International Scientific Commission for the Investigation of the Facts Concerning Bacterial Warfare in Korea and China. They asked Dang to determine for the court the availability of witnesses who would be willing to testify, and to provide the substance of the evidence they would offer. By late September, Dang promised that fifty witnesses would be available and willing to testify on the germ warfare accusations, and specified the general nature of their assertions. However, the witnesses would not be able to travel to the United States and depositions would have to be taken in China.[69]

On October fifth, 1956, the Powells filed a list narrowed down to fifteen of the fifty names Dang Mingzhou had first put forward, along with the nature of the testimony each would give.[70] Judge Goodman then issued a court order stating that if the defense could show by November 19, 1956 that specific defense witnesses would be available at a certain place and time to testify on Powell's behalf, then the Court would authorize counsel to travel to China and North Korea to take the depositions.[71] The depositions were to be taken at the British Embassy in Beijing and the U.S. government was directed to pay the cost of travel involved since the defendants could not afford to do so.

The Fifth and Sixth Amendments to the Constitution guarantee the right of defendants to summon witnesses, their right to counsel, and to due process. Judge Goodman granted the Powell's motion to have their lawyer take depositions abroad because he feared that not to do so would deny the defendants' constitutional right to summon witnesses on their behalf, and amount to a denial of due process.[72] The prosecution, for its part, met the defendants' motions for gathering depositions abroad with countermotions to block the same.[73] Although Judge Goodman sided with the paramount need of the defendants to present witnesses who might prove their innocence, or at least to show plausible evidence in support of their assertions, he imposed qualifications designed to prevent a vague, open-ended search for depositions.

While accepting the proposed depositions of fifteen witnesses who would verify allegations of bacteriological warfare, the judge imposed the further condition that testimony of nine of these who had done diagnosis and laboratory tests only, would not be considered unless six others, who were eye witnesses to bacteriological attacks, also testified. He required that specific places and times be indicated in advance for the taking of testimony before the court would grant the defendants' request that the U.S. government bear the cost of taking the depositions.[74]

Assurances were received from Dang Mingzhao on the seventh of November that all fifteen persons requested by the court had agreed to give depositions. The six eyewitnesses, he said, had agreed to testify in Beijing during the first half of March, 1957.[75] When the Powells, having fulfilled the court's stipulations, requested an order directing their attorney to visit Beijing during the first half of March at government expense to take the depositions, the prosecution objected. Since the U.S. government did not recognize the People's Republic of China, prosecutors pointed out, no representative of the government would be present at the depositions. Consequently, Judge Goodman, at a November sixteenth hearing, ordered the depositions to be taken in the British Crown Colony of Hong Kong before February 1, 1957.[76] This change of venue was no simple matter, however, as it involved crossing national boundaries between the communist and capitalist worlds.

The Chinese witnesses were unable to go to Hong Kong to make the depositions, Dang Mingzhou informed the defense lawyers on December 3. But the People's government would be happy to issue a visa for the entry of Powell's attorney into China, he asserted.[77] Dang also affirmed that a validated U.S. passport would be necessary to enter China.[78]

Anticipating this necessity, Powell attorney A.L. Wirin applied to get his passport validated for China, only to be informed by the State Department that his request was denied. No passports were currently being issued for travel to China, the State Department informed him, because of the lack of diplomatic relations between the two countries.[79] Powell's attorneys responded (February 1, 1957) by asking the court to either order the State Department to validate Wirin's passport for travel to China, or else dismiss all charges against the defendants.[80]

Caught in a dilemma, Judge Goodman believed that on the one hand, the court did not have the constitutional power to interfere with the formulation of foreign policy by the State Department and the executive branch of the government. Therefore, he did not order the former to validate Wirin's passport. But on the other hand, he recognized that to withhold validation effectively denied the defendants their constitutional right to present witnesses in their own defense. Judge Goodman therefore gave the United States government a choice: it could either stick to its policy of refusing to issue passport validations for travel to China and drop the charges against the defendants; or if the case was important enough, it could issue Wirin a passport validation and continue pursuing the case. Goodman put off the trial date pending the government's decision.

> Ordered: Unless the United States validates the passport of attorney Wirin for travel to and in China and North Korea within thirty days from date, the indictment will be dismissed. The order setting the case for trial on December 2, 1957 is vacated. In the event the United States elects to validate Mr. Wirin's passport, the cause, on appropriate motion and notice may be re-set for trial. Dated October 31, 1957. (J.Goodman).[81]

The Powells, meanwhile, filed a supplementary affidavit expanding the list of would-be witnesses to include China's Foreign Minister Zhou Enlai, North Korean President Kim Il Sung, and a wish-list of other less prominent non-governmental Chinese leaders.[82] Depositions by hundreds of new witnesses in China and North Korea, many unnamed, were now said to be necessary by the defense to prepare its case.[83]

Judge Goodman was not impressed. He had asked for written commitments by the witnesses themselves to give depositions at a set time and place. Instead he had only the indirect promise of Dang Mingzhou, who was not a member of the People's Government, that six witnesses would show up in Beijing sometime in early March and that the date and place for depositions by forty-four other witnesses was as yet unknown. He had been willing to accept this as sufficient to justify taking depositions by fourteen selected witnesses at government expense. But he refused to accede to defense requests that many new witnesses be included without direct written commitments by the witnesses themselves stating the time, place, and nature of their testimony.[84]

Faced with the choice of either violating its travel ban on China or abandoning the prosecution of Powell, the State Department reluctantly agreed to validate Wirin's passport. Judge Goodman then granted Wirin more time to collect his depositions in China and Korea.[85] The trial was accordingly rescheduled, originally to July 14, 1958, then to September 22, 1958. It would not finally begin until January 23, 1959.[86]

For two months (January - February, 1958) Wirin gathered depositions from fifty persons in China and North Korea. Some were witnesses who had seen canisters of insects being dropped by American aircraft, and others had performed laboratory tests which determined that the vectors were carrying fatal diseases. On March 19, he reported his findings to Judge Goodman.[87]

But Wirin had not had enough time to gather all of the depositions the defense believed were necessary. Because *all* the depositions were not yet completed and because the Chinese and North Korean witnesses would be unable to travel to the United States to testify in person at the trial since the U.S. and China had no Judicial Assistance Treaty,[88] Powell's attorneys now petitioned the United States Court of Appeals for a writ of mandamus or prohibition directing Judge Goodman and the District Court to dismiss their case. The justification put forward was that, through no fault of their own, they had been unable to produce foreign witnesses to testify at the trial, and had been unable to complete the gathering of depositions. The

Court of Appeals however denied their motion to dismiss or abate the criminal proceedings.[89] This amounted to a vote of confidence by the higher court in Judge Goodman and the proceedings thus far in Circuit Court.

To date, the difficulties faced by the defense in gaining access to witnesses outside the country had not proven grave enough to merit dismissal by Judge Goodman or by the Court of Appeals. But the same principle which had led Judge Goodman to threaten dismissal of the indictments over the government's attempts to block the defendants' access to witnesses in China might also work in regard to restricted U.S. government documents of a sensitive nature. For this reason as well as to prove the veracity of articles in the *Review*, Powell's attorneys began to subpoena classified government documents which they hoped would lend credibility to Powell's allegations of bacteriological warfare, U.S. culpability for starting the Korean War, stalling the peace negotiations, and violating the truce. Numerous subpoenas demanding a multitude of documents from the Department of Defense, the State Department, the CIA, the National Security Agency, and other sources were served. [90]

On June 12, Judge Goodman denied the defense motions to produce all the subpoenaed items. He complained that the subpoenas would produce huge quantities of documents, most of which would not be relevant. To find the few which did pertain to the case, the court would have to sort through "boxcars" full of paper. Powell's attorneys again filed a motion to dismiss the indictments, which was again denied, and then upped the ante by sending subpoenas to several retired U.S. generals, including Omar Bradley, Mathew Ridgeway, and Mark Clark, to appear as witnesses for the defense.[91] Powell's attorneys continued to subpoena documents on the U.S. biological warfare program right up to the start of the trial.[92]

According to Stanley I. Kutler, who devoted a chapter to Powell's trial in his book, *The American Inquisition*, the Defense Department was worried that once the trial started, subpoenaed documents and testimony by officers in the military would compromise the American biological warfare capability. They were particularly worried Powell's attorneys would subpoena the report of Brigadier General Crawford Sams (the "Sams Report"), which revealed planned actions which clearly violated the Geneva Rules on Land Warfare.[93] Sams had led a Navy epidemic control laboratory ship into North Korean waters in March 1951 to determine whether bubonic plague had broken out in North Korea. This event had launched Communist allegations that the U.S. was using bacteriological weapons in North Korea.

Moreover, the Army informed the Justice Department that the U.S. Commander in Chief in Korea had requested bacteriological weapons, although these were only to be used in retaliation for any enemy bacteriological attack.[94] General Bradley, if called to the witness stand, would have to reveal this fact. According to Kutler, the Department of Defense favored dropping the Powell case rather than to risk compromising the U.S. bacteriological weapons program, while the State Department believed it was important to continue prosecuting the case.[95]

The prosecution vigorously filed to quash these subpoenas throughout the proceedings. Ultimately, it decided to drop or quash all other parts of the indictment except the segment focusing on biological warfare. The prosecution believed that the germ warfare allegations, because of their specific content, provided the best opportunity for proving Powell's statements in the *Review* to be false. Judge Goodman granted most of the plaintiff's motions while warning that he would uphold Powell's right to subpoena specific documents. He refused to grant the prosecuting attorney's motion to limit the scope of the issues discussed; the Powells would remain free to call for the production of specific documents throughout the trial.[96]

*

TRIAL AND MISTRIAL

Powell's trial had the potential to re-open the whole bacteriological warfare issue once again in a very public way, in part because both sides believed that, in the process, they would be exonerated. Yet, it ended in a mistrial only a few days after it began. The actual trial opened with Powell's attorneys continuing their efforts to force the government to produce documents which might put the lie to U.S. denials of using germ weapons in Korea, and filing alternative motions to dismiss the case.[97]

On the second day of the proceedings, the Prosecution began introducing the same prisoner of war testimony and evidence which had been gathered and aired at the Senate Judiciary Subcommittee hearings during the fall of 1954. Although the technical substance of the sedition charge revolved around proving Powell's statements false, the real substance and emotional basis for Powell's indictment in the first place was moral outrage over the use of his journal for indoctrinating American POW's. Nor could Powell plead ignorance in this regard. Although it was true that the sales and circulation of the *Review* in China were in the hands of the Chinese postal service, the articles of contributing editor H.C. Huang, who was in the POW camps to help organize the prisoners, had to have apprised Powell of his journal's role. If a jury convicted the *Review*'s editors, this would remain the heart of the matter.

So it was that as the trial got underway, the prosecution called former POW Corporal Page Thomas Baylor, Jr. (whose testimony we have seen earlier) to the witness stand. Baylor had been held in solitary confinement for long periods of time because of his opposition to *Review* articles. He was used by the prosecution both to show the *Review*'s distribution in the POW camp, and to demonstrate the journal's tendency to be "dangerous" to the interests of the United States.[98] With Baylor still on the stand, the U.S. Attorney announced to the jury that the government had many more witnesses like Baylor, who were waiting to be called to the stand to testify.

Immediately, Powell's attorneys objected that the testimony of Baylor and the other POW's was "immaterial and inadmissible" because the sedition statute only applied within the United States or its admiralty or maritime jurisdictions.[99] The defense attorneys also argued that the POW testimony was "prejudicial and inflammatory." Before discussing the matter, Judge Goodman excused the jury from the courtroom, and ultimately threw out all of the POW testimony because the events described therein had all taken place in China and North Korea.[100]

In the course of the deliberations, Judge Goodman told the prosecuting attorneys that he believed they had already presented prima facie evidence that could sustain a conviction on the charge of treason, and he noted that treason had a much broader jurisdictional focus.[101] Although the jury was not present, newspaper reporters were, and the headlines in the local San Francisco papers which came out the following day, January 13, announced that Judge Goodman had declared the Powells guilty of treason.[102] This led Powell's attorney Doris Brin Walker to file a motion for a mistrial on the grounds that the newspaper headlines were "inflammatory" and could effect the jurors.[103]

Judge Goodman did not canvass the jury first to see if any harm had actually been done by the newspaper headlines before granting the mistrial motion. United States Prosecuting Attorney Robert H. Schnacke announced that the government would not oppose the motion. But on the same day that the mistrial was declared, the prosecution filed a complaint for treason (a potential capital crime) against the three defendants.[104] The prosecution intended to combine the sedition and treason charges in a new trial. Because treason is a graver charge than sedition, Schnacke asked that the Powells and Schuman be held in jail without bond, but Judge Goodman refused, allowing the same bail arrangements to remain in effect.[105]

Although the government continued to develop its treason case for a time and the defense attorneys continued for several more months to subpoena documents and to collect depositions,[106] the indictment against John and Sylvia Powell and Julian Schuman was ultimately dismissed on May 2, 1961, after almost six years of expensive legal maneuvers.[107] Attorney General Robert Kennedy noted the case was dropped because the lack of diplomatic relations with the People's Republic made it impossible to find the two requisite witnesses for treason, and the jurisdictional restrictions of the sedition statute prevented the use of POW testimony.[108]

Meanwhile, the Powell case entered U.S. criminal law as one of the earliest precedents for declaring a mistrial because of prejudicial publicity.[109] The same difficulties foreseen by *The Nation*, difficulties which had caused the U.S. Department of Justice to hesitate before calling a Federal Grand Jury in the first place, had been the downfall of the government's case.

CHAPTER NOTES

1. Allyn and Adele Rickett, *Prisoners of Liberation*. (New York:Cameron Associates,1957) p.266–8, 280.

2. *Ibid*, p.284.

3. "Two Came Home", *Time*, 17 August 1953, p.71.

4. *Ibid*.

5. "End of the Line", *Newsweek*, 18 May 1953, p.99.

6. Jim Weed, "Germ Warfare Charges: They Called It Sedition", *San Francisco Sunday Examiner and Chronicle*, 13 March 1977; "San Francisco Writer and Wife Indicted for Sedition", *San Francisco Chronicle*, 26 April 1956.

7. Powell, Testimony, United States Senate, Subcommittee To Investigate the Administration of the Internal Security Act and Other Internal Security Laws of the Committee on the Judiciary, *Hearings: Interlocking Subversion in Government Departments*, 27 September 1954, Washington D.C. p.1848, 1881.

8. "POW's Bare Tortures Behind Germ-War Confessions", *The Oregonian*, 7 September 1953.

9. *Ibid*.

10. "Freed Fliers Say Torture Forced Germ Confession", *The Oregonian*, 6 September 1953; "POW's Bare Tortures Behind Germ-War Confessions", *The Oregonian*, 7 September 1953.

11. *Ibid*.

12. "Political Rows Upset Repatriated Prisoners' Trip Home", *The Oregonian*, 10 September 1953.

13. U.S. Department of Defense, August, 1955, *POW: The Fight Continues After the Battle. The Report of the Secretary of Defense's Advisory Committee on Prisoners of War*,(Washington, D.C.: U.S. Government Printing Office, 1955.); W.E. Mayer, "Why Did So Many GI Captives Cave In?", *U.S. News and World Report*, 24 February 1956,p.56–62; Eugene Kinkead, "A Reporter at Large: The Study of Something New in History", *The New Yorker*, 26 October 1957, p.102–153; Eugene Kinkead, *In Every War But One*.(New York: Norton, 1959).

14. Eugene Kinkead, *In Every War But One*. (New York: Norton, 1959) p.136,190–200; Albert D. Biderman, *March to Calumny, the Story of American POW's in the Korean War*.(New York: MacMillan,1963)p.38–9.

15. Bidderman, *March to Calumny*. p.43

16. United States Senate, Subcommittee to Investigate the Administration of the Internal Security Act and Other Internal Security Laws of the Committee of the Judiciary, *Hearings: Interlocking Subversion in Government Departments*, Washington D.C., 27 September 1954, p.1820–21.

17. *Ibid*, p.1821–22.

18. *Ibid*. p.1868.

19. Powell, Testimony, United States Senate, Subcommittee to Investigate the Administration of the Internal Security Act and Other Internal Security Laws of the Committee of the on the Judiciary, *Hearings: Interlocking Subversion in Government Departments*, Washington D.C., 27 September 1954, p.1863.

20. Kumar Goshal, "A Tale of Two Americans Home from China", *National Guardian*, 18 October 1954.

21. Powell, Testimony, United States Senate, Subcommittee to Investigate the Administration of the Internal Security Act, p. 1863–1866, 1869, 1880–1890.

22. Powell, Testimony, United States Senate, Subcommittee to Investigate the Administration of the Internal Security Act, Washington, D.C., 27 September 1954, p.1881.

23. Letter, John W. Powell to Dolores Gill, Shanghai, 10 January 1951, in Testimony, U.S. Senate, Subcommittee to Investigate the Administration of the Internal Security Act, Washington D.C., 27 September 1954, p.1823; *National Guardian*, 7 March 1951.

24. "The Way Reds Used One American: Strange Case of John W. Powell", *U.S. News and World Report*, 15 October 1954, photograph of Mrs. Gill wiping away a tear with her handkerchief as she gives testimony, p.70.

25. Mrs.Dolores Holmes Gill, Testimony, U.S. Senate, Subcommittee to Investigate the Administration of the Internal Security Act, Washington D.C., 27 September 1954, p.1829–30.

26. Major William Raymond Shadish, M.D., Testimony, U.S. Senate, Subcommittee to Investigate the Administration of the Internal Security Act, Washington D.C., 27 September 1954, p.1834–5.

27. Powell, Testimony, U.S. Senate, Subcommittee to Investigate the Administration of the Internal Security Act, Washington D.C., 27 September 1954, p.1901.

28. Powell, Testimony, U.S. Senate, Subcommittee to Investigate the Administration of the Internal Security Act, *Hearings: Interlocking Subversion in Government Departments*, 27 September 1954, p.1903; *Letter*, John W. Powell to Mrs. Charles L. Gill, Shanghai, 10 January, 1951, Exhibit No.459, *Ibid.* p.1829; *Letter*, John W. Powell to Mrs. Charles L. Gill, Shanghai, 15 January 1951, Exhibit No.459-A, *Ibid.* p.1829.

29. *Ibid.* p.1832.

30. *Ibid*, 1835.

31. *Ibid*, p.1837.

32. *Ibid*. 1836–1841.

33. *Ibid*, p.1840–1.

34. Major Clarence L. Anderson, et al. "Medical Experiences in Communist POW Camps in Korea", *Journal of the American Medical Association*, 11 September 1954.

35. Powell, Testimony, U.S. Senate, Subcommittee to Investigate the Administration of the Internal Security Act, 27 September 1954, p.1908–9.

36. Page Thomas Baylor, Testimony, U.S, Senate, Subcommittee to Investigate the Administration of the Internal Security Act, 27 September 1954, p.1904–5.

37. Carroll Wright, Jr., Testimony, U.S. Senate, Subcommittee to Investigate the Administration of the Internal Security Act, 27 September 1954, p.1909.

38. *Ibid*.p.1909.

39. *Ibid*.p.1910.

40. "Senator Jenner: 'I Was Shocked'", *U.S. News and World Report*, 15 October 1954, p.69.

41. Kumar Goshal, "Jenner Rides the Headlines, A Tale of Two Americans Come Home From China", *National Guardian*, 18 October 1954, p.6; "Senator Jenner: 'I Was Shocked'", *U.S. News and World Report*, 15 October 1954, p.69. Jenner also mentioned Powell's press conference at the National Press Club: "I was shocked beyond words to learn that this renegade American was permitted to hold a press conference yesterday in the National Press Club of Washington."

42. Kumar Goshal, "A Tale of Two Americans", *National Guardian*, 18 October 1954,p.6.

43. "The Wayward Editor", *Time*, 11 October 1954,p.86; "Red China Boy", *Newsweek*, 11 October 1954, p.71; "The Way Reds Used One American:The

Strange Case of John W.Powell", *U.S.News and World Report*, 15 October 1954, p.68–76; "Ex-Editor in China Called 'Murderer'", *New York Times*, 28 September 1954, p.12; "Ex-G.I. Calls Writer Red Trade Promoter", *New York Times*, 29 September 1954, p.16; "Jenner Asks Treason Action", *New York Times*, 30 September 1954, p.16.

44. The *New York Times*, *U.S. News and World Report*, and *Time* all quoted Wright directly.

45. "Red China Boy", *Newsweek*, 11 October 1954, p.70.

46. "The Way Reds Used One American: Strange Case of John W. Powell", *U.S. News and World Report*, 15 October 1954, p.68–76.

47. "Ex-G.I. Calls Writer Red Trade Promoter", *New York Times*, 29 September 1954, p.16.

48. *United States of America, Plaintiff, v. John William Powell, et al., Defendants, No. 35065*, United States District Court, N.D. California, S.D. February 3, 1959, *Federal Supplement, Volume 171, Cases Argued and Determined in the United States District Courts, United States Courts of Claims and the United States Customs Court*. (St.Paul: West Publishing Company, 1959) p.203; Stanley I. Kutler, *The American Inquisition, Justice and Injustice in the Cold War*. (New York: Hill and Wang, 1982) p.228.

49. Lawrence E. Davies, "Welker Assails Accused Editor", *New York Times*, 14 December 1954, p.25.

50. United States District Court, Northern District of California, Criminal Docket 35065, Proceedings, *The United States vs. John William Powell, Sylvia Campbell Powell and Julian Schuman, Title 18, United States Criminal Code 2388 - Seditious Activities Affecting Armed Forces During War*.

51. *United States of America v. John William Powell, et al., Federal Supplement* Volume 171, p.203–4.

52. *United States of America, Plaintiff, V. John William Powell, Sylvia Campbell Powell, and Julian Schuman, Defendants. Docket 35065*. The United States District Court, Northern District, California, Southern District, 1 November 1957, *Federal Supplement Volume 156, Cases Argued and Determined in the United States District Courts, United States Court of Claims and the United States Customs Court*.(St.Paul, Minnesota: West Publishing Company, 1958)p.527.

53. *Ibid.*

54. Abraham Lincoln Wirin of Los Angeles, Doris Brin Walker of San Francisco, and Stanley Faulkner of New York were all members of the National Lawyers Guild who had rallied to Powell's defense. Charles Garry of San Francisco, who joined the defense team in 1959, achieved fame in the late 1960's for his defense of Black Panther Party leaders Huey P. Newton, Edridge Cleaver, David Hilliard, and Bobby Seale. In 1969 he was also involved as defense council in the high profile trial of the "Chicago Seven", peace activists accused of planning to disrupt the 1968 Democratic National Convention. Wallace Turner, "Panther Lawyer Finds Job Fulfilling", *New York Times*, 16 December 1969, p.22; *United States of America, Plaintiff, v John William Powell et al., Defendants. No.35065. Federal Supplement Volume 171*, p.203; Stephen Endicott and Edward Hagerman, *The United States and Biological Warfare, Secrets from the Early Cold War*. (Bloomington: Indiana University Press, 1998), p.39.

55. "'Recognizing' China", *The New Republic*, 13 May 1957, p.5.

56. "Blackmail?" *The New Republic*, 18 February 1957, p.3–4.

57. Harold R. Isaacs, "How We 'See' the Communists", *The New Republic*, 25 February 1957, p. 7–13; "C-H-I-N-A",(editorial), *The New Republic*, 18 March 1957, p.1–2; "'Recognizing' China", (editorial), *The New Republic*, 13 May 1957, p.3–4; Howard L Boorman, "How Has China Changed?", *The New Republic*, 13 May 1957, p.6–10; John King Fairbank, "Past and Present", *Ibid.*, p.11–14; "Richard Hughes, "Rule by Brute Reason", *Ibid.*, p.15–18; Zhao Guozhun, "How Beijing Reaches So Many", *Ibid.*,p.19–20; Dr.Robert J.Lifton, "Brainwashing in Perspective", *Ibid.*, p.21–25; Alexander Eckstein, "Industrializing in a Hurry- Plans and Problems", *Ibid.*,p.26–29; Robert Guillain, "Taking Away the 'Good Earth'", *Ibid.*,p.30–34; Peter Schmid, "God in China", *Ibid.*,p.35–38; Richard L. Walker, "The Chinese Red Army", *Ibid.*,p.39–42;Robert C.North, "Mao and the Succession", *Ibid.*,43–47.

58. In 1956–7, Mao called on the professional and academic intellectuals, whom he believed had been transformed through thought reform, to publicly criticize CCP cadres in a Yan'an-style rectification campaign. When intellectuals began criticizing the authoritarian Communist system itself, rather than just corruption within the Party, the government harshly suppressed the movement.

59. "Opinion and Order on Motion to Dismiss", 1 November 1958, Proceedings, *The United States vs. John William Powell, Sylvia Campbell Powell and Julian Schuman, Title 18 U.S.C. 2388 - Seditious Activities Affecting Armed Forces During War*, Criminal Docket 35065, United States District Court, Northern District of California, District Judge Lewis E.Goodman. Cited hereafter as: Proceedings, *The United States vs. John William Powell et al.*

60. Interestingly, the U.S. Communist Party's organ, the *Daily Worker* didn't give Powell any public support either, perhaps because they realized that it would only have hurt Powell's case.

61. Gene Marine, "Sedition or Press Freedom?", *The Nation*, 16 February 1957,p.136–8.

62. *Ibid.*

63. *Ibid.*

64. *United States of America, Plaintiff, v John William Powell et al., Defendants. No.35065. Federal Supplement Volume 171*, p.203–4.

65. *Ibid.*p.204–5, n.2. United States Code, 2381 Treason "Whoever, owing allegiance to the United States, levies war against them or adheres to their enemies, giving them aid and comfort within the United States or elsewhere, is guilty of treason and shall suffer death . . ." In addition, the treason statute requires two witnesses to an actual treasonous act.; "Motion to Dismiss Indictment and Order Dismissing Indictment", 2 May 1961, Proceedings, *The United States vs. John William Powell et al.*; Elmot Waite, "Sedition Trail Off, Powells Now Face Treason Charge", *San Francisco Chronicle*, 32 January 1959, p.1,8.

66. "Motion for Order Authorizing Taking Depositions from Witnesses Abroad-with Affidavit and Exhibit", 5 September 1956, Proceedings, *The United States vs. John William Powell et al.*; "Notice of Motion for Taking of Depositions Abroad",17 September 1956, Proceedings, *Ibid*; "Motion for Authority to Take Depositions Abroad", 19 September 1956, Proceedings, *Ibid*; "Supplemental Affidavit in Support of Motion for Order Authorizing the Taking of Depositions of Witnesses Abroad", 20 September 1956, Proceedings, *Ibid*; "Affidavit of Doris Brin Walker,(Radiogram for Taking of Depositions Abroad)", 2 October 1956, Proceedings, *Ibid*; "List of Witnesses Resident in China Who Are Willing to Testify

by Deposition", 5 October 1956, Proceedings, *Ibid.*; *The United States of America, Plaintiff, v. John William Powell et al., Defendants, Federal Supplement, Volume 156*, p.527.

67. *Ibid*; *The United States of America, Plaintiff, v. John William Powel et al., Defendants, Federal Supplement, Volume 156*, p.531; "Report of the Scientific Commission for the Investigation of the Facts Concerning Bacterial Warfare in Korea and China", Supplement, *People's China*, 17 September 1952, p.1–28; "U.S. Germ Warfare, Report of International Scientists' Commission", *China Monthly Review*, November-December 1952, p.437–442.

68. *The United States of America, Plaintiff, v. John William Powell et al, Defendants, Federal Supplement, Volume 156*, p.531–2.

69. "Supplemental Affidavit in Support of Motion for Order Authorizing the Taking of Depositions of Witnesses Abroad", 20 September 1956, Proceedings, *The United States vs. John William Powell, et al.*; "Affidavit of Doris Brin Walker (Radiogram for Taking of Depositions Abroad), 2 October 1956, Proceedings, *Ibid.*; List of Witnesses Resident in China Who Are Willing to Testify by Deposition", 5 October 1956, Proceedings, *Ibid.*; *The United States of America, Plaintiff, v. John William Powell, et al., Federal Supplement, Volume 156*. p.532.

70. "List of Witnesses Resident in China Who Are Ready, Willing, and Able to Testify by Deposition", 5 October 1956, Proceedings, *The United States vs. John William Powell et al.*

71. "Order Directing Taking Depositions of Witnesses", 5 October, 1956, Proceedings, *The United States vs. John William Powell, et al.*; "Order Motion to Take Depositions Granted", 5 October 1956, Proceedings, *Ibid.*

72. *The United States of America, Plaintiff, v. John William Powell et al., Defendants, Federal Supplement, Volume 156*, p.530–1.

73. "Memorandum in Opposition to Defendant's Motion to Take Depositions of Witnesses Abroad", 17 September 1956, Proceedings, *The United States vs. John William Powell et al.*; "Memorandum in Opposition to Defendant Julian Schuman's Motion for Authority to Take Depositions Abroad", 19 September 1956, Proceedings, *Ibid.*

74. "Order Directing Taking Depositions Outside of the United States at Government Expanse", 9 January 1957, Proceedings, *The United States vs. John William Powell et al*; *The United States of America, Plaintiff, v. John William Powell et al. Defendants, Federal Supplement, Volume 156*, p.533.

75. "Supplement Affidavit in Support of Motion for Taking Depositions in China", 9 November 1957, Proceedings, *The United States vs. John William Powell et al.* This contains the information from Dang Mingzhao's November seventh cable.

76. "Order that Depositions Be Taken in Hong Kong before February 1, 1957", 16 November 1956, Proceedings, *Ibid.* The time limit was later extended to February 15.; *The United States of America, Plaintiff, v. John William Powell et al, Defendants, Federal Supplement, Volume 156*, p.533.

77. "Motion for Order Modifying Order Filed November 27, 1956", 27 December 1956, Proceedings, *United States vs. John William Powell et al.*; *The United States of America, Plaintiff, v. John William Powell et al, Defendants, Federal Supplement, Volume 156*, p.534.

78. "Supplementary Affidavit in Support of Motion for Further Assistance of the Court", 25 January 1957, Proceedings, *United States vs. John William Powell,*

et al. This affidavit filed by Doris Walker recounted the contents of Dang Mingzhou's cable of 15 January 1957 (that Wirin would need a validated passport to enter China.)

79. *Ibid.*

80. "Motion for Further Assistance of the Court with Respect to Order Directing Taking Depositions Outside of the U.S.", 24 January 1957, Proceedings, *United States vs. John William Powell et al.* (a request that the court direct the State Department to validate Wirin's Passport).; "Counter Affidavit of Doris Walker", 1 February 1957, Proceedings, *Ibid.* (an alternative motion asking the court to dismiss the indictment if the State Department still refused to validate Wirin's passport).

81. "Ordered Setting Case for December 2nd Vacated", 1 November 1957, Proceedings, *Ibid.*; "Opinion and Motion on Order to Dismiss", 1 November 1957, Proceedings, *Ibid.*

82. "Supplemental Affidavit in Support of Pending Motion and Counter Affidavit of Assistant U.S. Attorney Robert H. Schnacke", 20 February 1957, Proceedings, *Ibid.*

83. *The United States of America, Plaintiff, v. John William Powell et al, Defendants, Federal Supplement, Volume 156,* p.535.

84. *Ibid.* p.534.

85. "Order Extending Time of Mr. Wiring to Travel to China", 6 February 1957, Proceedings, *The United States vs. John William Powell et al.*

86. "Order Case Set for Trial July 14, Jury", 24 March 1958, Proceedings, *The United States vs. John William Powell et al.*; "Order Continued from July 14th to September 22nd, 1958 for Trial", 19 June 1958, Proceedings, *Ibid.*; "Trial Begun, Jury Impaneled, Motion to Dismiss by Defendants", 23 January 1959, Proceedings, *Ibid.*

87. "Report of A.L. Wirin Regarding Trip to China", 19 March 1958, Proceedings, *The United States vs. John William Powell et al.*

88. *The United States vs. John William Powell et al. Federal Supplement Volume 156,* p.528 n.2

89. "In the Matter of the Petition of John William Powell, Sylvia Campbell Powell, and Julian Schuman, for Writ of Mandamus or Prohibition. No. 16068.", United States Court of Appeals, Ninth Circuit. 14 July 1958. *Federal Reporter Second Series Volume 260 F.2d, Cases Argued and Determined in the United States Courts of Appeals, United States Court of Customs And Patent Appeals and United Sates Emergency Court of Appeals.* (St.Paul, Minnesota: West Publishing Company, 1959) p.159–160.

90. "Affidavit in Support Duces Tecum, Issued Subpoena", 21 March 1958, Proceedings, *The United States vs. John William Powell et al.*; "Subpoena Duces Tecum to U.S. Attorney, Unexecuted",24 April 1958, *Ibid.*; "Defendants' Motion for Order Amending Duces Tecum and for Directing Plaintiff and the United States Attorney to Produce Certain Documents Prior to Trial", 28 April 1958, Proceedings, *Ibid.*; "Defendants' Memorandum on Production of Documents Prior to Trial", 19 May 1958, Proceedings, *Ibid.*; "Oral Motion for Production of Documents Made",22 May 1958, Proceedings, *Ibid.*; "Motion for Production of Subpoenaed Documents",2 June 1958, Proceedings, *Ibid.*; "Affidavit in Support of Motion", 2 June 1958, Proceedings, *Ibid.*; "Order Motion to Produce Documents

Submitted", 6 June 1958, Proceedings, *Ibid.*; "Execute Subpoena to Produce Documents, Custodian of Department of Defense", 20 October 1958, Proceedings, *Ibid.*

91. "Notice of Hearing on Defendants' Motion to Produce Documents Prior to Trial", 2 June, Proceedings, *Ibid.*; "Order Denying Production of Documents", 12 June 1958, Proceedings, *Ibid.*; "Motion to Dismiss with Copy of Indictment Attached", 11 September 1958, Proceedings, *Ibid.*; "Filed Seven Subpoenas on Retired U.S. Generals", 15 September 1958, Proceedings, *Ibid.*; "Execute Subpoena to Produce Documents, Custodian of Department of Defense", 20 October 1958, Proceedings, *Ibid.*

92. "Executed Subpoena to Produce Documents", 23 January 1959, Proceedings, *Ibid.*; "Executed Subpoenas to Produce Documents", 29 January 1959, *Ibid.* "Subpoenas to Testify",29 January 1959, Proceedings, *Ibid.*; "Executed Subpoenas to Produce Documents", 3 February 1959, Proceedings, *Ibid.*; "Executed Subpoenas to Testify", 3 February 1959, *Ibid.*

93. Stanley I. Kutler, *The American Inquisition, Justice and Injustice in the Cold War.* (New York: Hill and Wang, 1982) p.234; Stephen Endicott and Edward Hagerman, *The United States and Biological Warfare, Secrets from the Early Cold War and Korea.* (Bloomington: Indiana University Press, 1998), p.150–1. "Report by Brigadier General Crawford F. Sams, MC, Chief, Public Health and Welfare Section, SCAP to Chief of Staff, Far Eastern Command," Subject: "Special Operations in North Korea," 17 March 1951.

94. Kutler, *The American Inquisition*, p. 235,236.

95. *Ibid.* p.235–6.

96. Kutler, *The American Inquisition*, p.237; "Notice of Motions to Dismiss Count Four, for Order Limiting Issues and to Modify and Quash Subpoenas", 9 January 1959, Proceedings, *The United States vs. John William Powell et al.*; "Ordered Count Four of Indictment Dismissed", 9 January 1959, Proceedings, *Ibid.*; "Ordered Motion to Limit Issues, Denied", 9 January 1959, Proceedings, *Ibid.*; "Ordered Motion to Quash Granted as Specified by the Court without Prejudice to Right of Defendants to Demand Production of the Documents Referred to in the Subpoena", 9 January 1959, Proceedings, *Ibid.*

97. "Filed Exc. Subpoenas to Produce Documents", 23 January 1959, Proceedings, *Ibid.*; "Motion to Dismiss by Defendants, Denied", 23 January 1959, Proceedings, *Ibid.* ; *The United States of America, Plaintiff, v. John William Powell et al, Defendants, Federal Supplement, Volume 171*, p.202–5.

98. "*United States of America, Plaintiff, v. John William Powell et al., Federal Supplement, Volume 171*,p.203—4.

99. *Ibid.* p.203–4.

100. *Ibid.*

101. *Ibid.*p.204.

102. "Judge Says Powells, Aid Guilty of Treason", *Oakland Tribune*, 30 January 1959; "Powell Flayed By Trial Judge", *San Francisco Chronicle*, 30 January 1959; *United States v. John William Powell et al. Federal Supplement, Volume 171*, p.205.

103. "Motion for Mistrial Granted", 30 January 1959, Proceedings, *The United States vs. John William Powell et al.*; *United States v. John William Powell et al. Federal Supplement, Volume 171*, p.205.

104. *United States v. John William Powell et al. Federal Supplement, Volume 171*, p.204–5.; "United States Attorney Filed Complaint for Violation Title 18

United States Criminal Code section 2381 Treason", 30 January 1959, Proceedings, *The United States vs. John William Powell et al.*

105. Elmont Waite, "Sedition Trial Off, Powells Now Face Treason Charge", *San Francisco Chronicle*, 31 January 1959, p.1,8.

106. "Order Granting Additional Time to A.L. Wirin to Complete Taking of Depositions", 6 March 1959, Proceedings, *The United States vs. John William Powell et al.*

107. "Motion to Dismiss Indictment and Order Dismissing Indictment", 2 May 1961, Proceedings, *Ibid.*; "Motion by Charles R. Renda, AUSA, to Dismiss Indictment, Granted: Ordered Indictment Dismissed and the Bonds Exonerated", 2 May 1961, Proceedings, *Ibid.*

108. Kutler, *The American Inquisition*, p.240.

109. Federal Cases, Criminal Law: Mistrial for Prejudicial Publicity, *The Hastings Law Journal*, Volume 11, 1959–1960. (San Francisco: Hastings College of Law, 1960) p. .

CHAPTER TWELVE

CONCLUSION

Powell had revived his father's China Weekly Review in December, 1945 with the intention of supporting U.S. China policy and the desire to further American interests in China. After the U.S. attempt to promote a coalition government and to prevent renewed fighting between the Guomindang and the Chinese Communist Party broke down in late 1946, Powell and the Review supported student and faculty demonstrations for peace and hoped for a return to the bargaining table.

As the Truman Administration readjusted its policy to containment of Communism abroad, and Chiang's government crushed the 1947 Taiwan revolt and increased its repression of student demonstrators in China, Powell opened the pages of the Review to the voices of the discontented and oppressed, exposed the crimes of the GMD military in Taiwan, and questioned the justice meted out by China's courts. He called on the United States to use its economic power to force France, the Netherlands, and Britain to end their colonialism in Southeast Asia and worried that the Truman Doctrine would transform the United States into a bastion of reaction.

Disillusioned by the Nationalist government's mismanagement of the economy, of the student Anti-War, Anti-Hunger Movement, and its failure to democratize the one-party state, Powell and numerous Western business interests began to explore the possibility of continuing operations under Communist rule, especially after it became obvious that the Nationalists were losing the civil war. Determined to stay put as the Communists entered Shanghai in 1949, Powell and the Review adapted to the demands of the new regime, committed themselves to reporting the positive changes brought about by the Revolution to an American audience, and campaigning for U.S. recognition of China's new government and improved Sino-American relations.

When the CCP coordinated all of the media in China under government direction, the Review conformed. As the Korean War broke out, Powell hesitated, but ultimately continued publishing his journal. As the war intensified, the Review covered the destruction and suffering which U.S. bombing raids visited on North Korea and parts of China and viewed U.S. intervention as unwarranted intrusion in the internal affairs of the Korean people. When North Korea and China made atrocity and bacteriological warfare accusations against the United States, the Review echoed the charges and became the foremost American-owned journal purveying the allegations throughout 1952–1953. The Bacteriological warfare charges became the focus of a world-wide controversy echoing through the world press and United Nations debates in spite of repeated denials by Secretary of State Dean Acheson and the U.N. Korean Command.

After China's entry into the Korean War in the late fall of 1950, the Review was used, along with other publications, to indoctrinate American prisoners of war. Frequent articles in the Review portrayed conditions within Chinese prisoner of war camps in positive terms, and gave scope to Communist-sponsored anti-war activities by the POW's. After the Korean Armistice went into effect, with his two sons approaching primary school age and the Review no longer able to continue for economic reasons, Powell and his family returned to the United States to face a hostile U.S. Senate Subcommittee and prosecution for sedition.

In their defense strategy, Powell's lawyers attempted to shift the focus of the trial from the defendants to the government that was charging them. Perhaps the strongest indication of Powell's belief in the veracity of bacteriological warfare charges and other accusations published in the Review, was his willingness to stake his entire defense upon it. Yet, as a recent study by Stephen Endicott and Edward Hagerman inadvertently demonstrated, a reworking of the evidence presented by the Communists in 1952 and 1953 would not have been sufficient either to prove or disprove the charges.[1]

Nevertheless, the possible admission by General Omar Bradely that he had called for delivery of bacteriological weapons, albeit for defensive purposes, and the forced production of the "Sams Report" by the prosecution would have been embarrassing to the government. In the eyes of a jury, it would undermine the prosecution's case which already rested on shaky jurisdictional grounds, by lending plausibility to the Review's bacteriological accusations, while raising ethical questions about the judgement of U.S. military authorities in the Sams affair.

Was the Review guilty of giving aid and comfort to the enemy? Certainly it was part of the general Chinese propaganda effort, but it did not have much influence within the United States, except when Review exposes were picked up by the mainstream media, as was the case with Powell's coverage of the Taiwan Rebellion. The Review had not called for the overthrow of the U.S. government or Constitution, nor had it tried to interfere with the American war effort or the recruitment of troops within the United States. Powell had come to opposition only gradually, as events in China and changes in U.S. policy pushed him toward it. Once the Chinese

Communist government had instituted its policy of national press coordination, Powell's choices were limited to how he would participate in press campaigns, not if he chose to.

There was nothing inherently wrong in Powell's enthusiasm in presenting the early changes of the Revolution in a positive light. Compared to the last years of Guomindang rule, the weight of historical evidence is that the new government really was trying hard to improve the general welfare of the people. Similarly, Powell's anti-imperialist stand proceeded from a positive vision of what the United States might have represented to peoples struggling against resurgent European colonialism just after World War II. Without the Korean War, without the Cold War, without the anti-communist crusade within the U.S., recognition and normal relations between the United States and the new government of China might have developed as Powell had hoped. There was nothing subversive in what the Review had wanted. Diplomatic recognition and normal trade relations could reasonably be expected. Subsequent normalization of trade and diplomatic relations in the changed environment of the 1970's raises the question "could this have happened earlier," a question historians continue to struggle with.

CHAPTER NOTES

1. Stephen Endicott and Edward Hagerman, *The United States and Biological Warfare, Secrets from the Early Cold War and Korea.*(Bloomington: Indiana University Press, 1998).

Bibliography

Primary Sources

Books and Articles:

Acheson, Dean. Statement by United States Secretary of State, 4 March 1952. "'Germ Warfare' Charges Called Fabrication." *United States Department of State Bulletin*. 17 March 1952. 427-428.

Barnett, A. Doak. *China on the Eye of Communist Takeover*. New York: Frederick A. Praeger Publishers, 1968.

Barret, Mary. "The Liberation of Shanghai." *China Weekly Review*, 4 June 1949.

_____. "People's Conferences in China." *China Weekly Review*, 1 April 1950. 73-76.

_____. "The Ward Case." *China Weekly Review*, 14 January 1950. 104-106.

Barret, Mary and Kiang, Chun-chang. "What's Happening at Christian Colleges." *China Weekly Review*, 29 October 1949. 131-133.

Barrett, David, D. *Dixie Mission: The United States Army Observer Group in Yenan, 1944*. Berkeley: University of California Press, 1970.

Belden, Jack. *China Shakes the World*. New York: Harper and Brothers, 1949.

Bently, Eric, ed. *Thirty Years of Treason, Excerpts from Hearings before the House Committee on Un-American Activities, 1938-1968*. New York: The Viking Press, 1978.

Biggerstaff, Knight. *Nanking Letters, 1949*. Ithaca, N. Y.: Cornell University East Asia Papers, 1979.

Bley, Major Roy H. Deposition. In: "Proof of Germ Warfare, Major Bley's Statement." *China Monthly Review*, May 1953. 99-103.

Canning, Charles J. "The Question of Recognition." *China Weekly Review*, 11 June 1949. 34-35.

_____. "Notes on China's Domestic and Foreign Policy." *China Weekly Review*, 16 July 1949. 143-145.

_____. "New Democracy-Theory and Practice." *China Monthly Review*, 25 June 1949. 76.

_____. "Settlement of Kunming Student Strike Does Not End Struggle." *China Weekly Review*, 23 February 1946. 215.

Chang, T'ien-fu. Translator. "The Shanghai Court's Reply," A Translation of "A Review of 'China's Courts' - An Editorial of the *China Weekly Review*, By the Secretariat of the Shanghai High Court." *China Weekly Review*, 7 June 1947. 24-26.

Chao, Arnold. "Democratic League Mirrors Views of Middle Classes." *China Weekly Review*, 19 October 1946. 202.

Chen, Walter K.C. "China's Habeas Corpus Law on Trial: Government by Law or by Terror?" *China Weekly Review*, 3 May 1947. 268.

Ch'en Yi. "Text of a Report on the Work of the Shanghai Military Control Commission and the Shanghai People's Government for June and July Submitted by General Ch'en Yi, Mayor of Shanghai, to the Shanghai People's Conference, August 3, 1949." *China Weekly Review*, 20 August 1949, 219-221.

Ch'en Yi. "Inaugural Address at the Opening Session of the Second Shanghai Conference of People's Representatives." 5 December 1949, U.S. Consulate General, Press Translation Service, Shanghai, China, *Chinese Press Review*. 15 December 1949.

Clubb, Edward O. *Communism in China as Reported from Hankow in 1932*. New York: Columbia University Press, 1972.

_____. *The Witness and I*. New York: Columbia University Press, 1974.

Commission of the International Association of Democratic Lawyers. "Report on the Use of Bacteriological Weapons on Chinese Territory by Armed Forces of the United States." Supplement. *People's China*, 16 May 1952. 7-10.

Cooley, Caroline. "Peace Far Away in Indochina." *China Weekly Review*, 21 June 1947. 75-77.

"Court Flays *China Weekly Review*." *North China Daily News*, 17 May 1947. 3.

Davis, John P. Jr. "Memoranda by Foreign Service Officers in China, 1943-1945," *China White Paper*, Washington: United States Government Printing Office, 1949. 564-575.

Dean, Major General W. F. *General Dean's Story*. New York: Viking, 1954.

Degrass, Jane. *The Communist International 1919-1943: Documents. Volume 3*. London: Oxford University Press for Royal Institute of International Affairs, 1965.

————."Depositions of Nineteen Captured U.S. Airmen on Their Participation in Germ Warfare in Korea." Supplement. *People's China*, 1
December 1953. 1-66.

Douglas, Fred T. "Statement by Fred T. Douglas." *China Weekly Review*,
23 July 1949, 165.

Esherick, Joseph W. ed. *Lost chance in China, the World War II Dispatches of John S Service*. New York: Random House, 1974.

Essoyan, Roy. "China Editor's Son Has Own Rapier Pen." *Washington
Post*, 6 July 1947. B3.

Fairbank, John King. *Chinabound: A Fifty-Year Memoir*. New York:
Harper and Row, Publisher, 1982.

Falconer, Alun. "Changes in Shanghai's Press." *China Weekly Review*, 11
March 1950. 26-28.

Fei, Hsiao-tung. "My Search For Democracy." (translated from *Sin Wen
Jih Pao*) *China Weekly Review*, 1 October 1949. 65-66.

————. "Report on the National Higher Education Conference." *Hsin
Kwan Cha* (The *New Observer*), 1 July 1950, summarized in "Educating the Educators." *China Weekly Review*, 29 July 1950.
157.

————."Full Text of Organic Law of Central People's Government." (Organic Law of The Central People's Government of the People's
Republic of China passed by the first session of the People's Political Consultative Conference on September 27, 1949) *China
Weekly Review*, 15 October 1949. 104-105.

Gould, Randal. "Statement by Randal Gould, former Editor, *Shanghai
Evening Post and Mercury*." *China Weekly Review*, 23 July 1949,
164-165.

Gould, Randal. "Shanghai During the Takeover, 1949." *The Annals of
the American Academy of Political and Social Science*. 277: 182.
(September, 1951).

Hendrick, J. "The Story of Vietnam Verses French Propaganda." *China
Weekly Review*, 17 January 1948. 198.

Hollander, Paul. ed. *Political Pilgrims: Travel of Western Intellectuals to
the Soviet Union, China, and Cuba, 1928-1978*. New York: Oxford University Press, 1981.

Hsia, Li. "Art Education in New China." *China Weekly Review*, 3 June
1950. 7-8.

Hsia, Yen. Director of the Bureau of Cultural Affairs of Shanghai, "Report on Cultural and Educational Work in Shanghai." Delivered
on Behalf of the Bureau of Education, Bureau of Cultural Affairs,
and the Press and Publications Office of the Shanghai Municipal
People's Government at the First Session of the Second Conference of People's Representatives of All Circles in Shanghai. *China
Monthly Review*, December 1950. 6-9.

Huang, H.C. "Life in a Communist Training Camp." *China Weekly Re-*

view, 23 July 1949. 168.

_____. "Peasants Accuse Local Despots." *China Weekly Review*, 18 March 1950. 37-38.

_____. "Letter From the Front." *China Weekly Review*, 18 March 1950. 78.

_____. "A White Christmas in a POW Camp." *China Monthly Review*, February 1952. 182-187.

_____. "Notes From a POW Hospital in Korea." *China Monthly Review*, March 1952. 256-258.

_____. "They Want Peace." *China Monthly Review*, June 1952. 575-579.

Huang, Hua. "My Contact With Stuart After Nanking Liberation." trans. Li Xiaobing, *Chinese Historians*. 5: 47-56 (Spring 1992).

Irie, Akira. ed. *U. S. Policy Toward China, Testimony of the Times: Selections from Congressional Hearings*. Boston: Little, Brown and Company, 1968.

Johnson, William. "Vietnam's Three Year War." *China Weekly Review*, 16 October 1948. 178-179.

_____. "Vietnam Fights for Freedom." *China Weekly Review*, 4 December 1948. 15-17.

_____. "Vietnam's Fight for Freedom." *China Weekly Review*, 1 January 1949. 109-111.

Khrushchev, Nikita. *Khrushchev Remembers*. Translated and edited by Stone Talbot. London: Deutsch, 1971.

Kuo, Mo-jo. "Cultural and Educational Work in China." Report Delivered to the Second Meeting of the National Committee of the Chinese People's Political Consultative Conference, Peking, 14-23 June 1950. *China Weekly Review*, 8 July 1950. 106-107.

Kwei, Arthur C. P. "Liberals Form League to Protect Basic Human Rights, Freedoms." *China Weekly Review*, 18 January 1947. 195.

Lattimore, Owen. *Ordeal by Slander*. Boston: Little, Brown and Company, 1950.

_____. *The Situation in Asia*. Boston: Little, Brown and Company, 1949.

Lee, Duncan C. "Changeover in the Post Office." *China Weekly Review*, 16 July 1949. 146.

_____. "China's Changing Countryside." *China Weekly Review*, 13 May 1950. 186.

_____. " Peking Panorama." *China Weekly Review*, 10 June 1950. 29.

Lee, Tsung-ying. "The New Village Democracy." *China Weekly Review*, 1 October 1949. 61-63.

Lewis, John Wilson. ed. *Major Documents of Communist China*. New York: W. W. Norton and Company, Inc., 1964.

Lindsay, Michael. *The Unknown War, North China 1937-1945*. London: Bergstrom and Boyle Books Limited, 1973.

Lin, Wo-chiang. "Arbitration Said Best For Indonesia." *China Weekly Review*, 30 August 1947. 381-382.

Liu, Grace D. "Education in New China." *China Weekly Review*, 10 December 1949. 25-26.

Liu, Tsun-chi. "The Press in New China." *People's China*, 16 December 1950. 8.

MacKinnon, Stephen R. and Friesen, Oris. *China Reporting: An Oral History of American Journalism in the 1930s and 1940s.* Berkeley: University California Press, 1987.

Mao, Tse-tung. "Mao Tse-tung on China's Future Government." (Text of Address to the Preparatory Meeting of the New Political Consultative Conference, 15 June 1949) *China Weekly Review*, 25 June 1949. 82.

_____. "The People's Democratic Dictatorship." *China Monthly Review*, 9 July 1949. 131-134.

_____. "Closing Address to the Second Meeting of the National Committee of the Chinese People's Political Consultative Conference." Peking, 14 June 1950. *China Weekly Review*, 8 July 1950. 105-106.

_____. *Selected Readings from the Works of Mao Tsetung.* Peking: Foreign language Press, 1971.

_____. *Selected Works of Mao Tse-tung.* Volume 4. Peking: Foreign Language Press, 1969.

_____. *Selected Writings.* Volume 5, 1945-1949. New York: International Publishers, 1977.

Mayo, C. W. "The Question of Impartial Investigation of Charges of Use by United Nation Forces of Bacteriological Warfare: Statements to the Political Committee, United State General Assembly," *United States Delegation to the General Assembly Press Release no. 1786*, Oct. 26, 1953.

_____ . "The Role of Forced Confessions in the Communist Germ Warfare Propaganda Campaign," U.S. Department of State, *Bulletin*, Volume 29, 641-647. Washington D.C.: Government Printing Office, 1953.

Melby, John F. *The Mandate of Heaven, Record of a Civil War, China 1945-1949.* Toronto: University of Toronto Press, 1968.

Meng, C.Y.W. "Chinese Democratic League Works for Unity and Peace." *China Weekly Review*, 5 January 1946. 92-93.

_____."Constructive Efforts, Government Needed to Put China's House in Order at Once." *China Weekly Review*, 25 May 1946. 272-273.

_____. "China's Hyper Inflation: How to Stop It." *China Weekly Review*, 10 May 1947. 288-289.

_____. "A Chinese View of American Aid." *China Weekly Review*, 19 March 1949. 59-60.

————."Popular Magazines Vanish." *China Weekly Review*, 29 January 1949. 214-215.

————."Sino-Soviet Relations." *China Weekly Review*, 11 March 1950. 22-24.

————."New Direction for Shanghai's Business." *China Weekly Review*, 27 May 1950. 223-226.

Noel, Frank. "U.S. War Corespondent Describes POW Camp Life." *China Monthly Review*, August 1952. 117-121.

Paget, William. "China's New Medical Program." *China Monthly Review*, September 1950. 23-26.

Parker, Peggy. "World Impressions of Saigon." *China Weekly Review*, 17 May 1948. 324-325.

Powell, John B. *My Twenty-Five Years in China*. New York: Da Capo Press, 1976.

————. "I Was a Prisoner of the Japanese", *Readers' Digest* (November 1942) 4: 63-66.

Powell, John B. and Eastman, Max. "The Fate of the World Is at Stake in China", *Readers' Digest* (June 1945), 46: 13-22.

Powell, John William. "A Hidden Chapter in History", *The Bulletin of the Atomic Scientists*. Volume 37, no.8. (October, 1981)

————. "Japan's Germ Warfare: The U.S. Cover-Up of a War Crime", *Bulletin of Concerned Asian Scholars, Volume 12*, no.4 (October-December 1980): 2-17.

————. "An Exclusive Account of the Taiwan Bloodbath as Detailed by Eyewittnesses." *China Weekly Review*, 29 March 1947. 115-117.

————. "An Open Letter to Passengers on the 'General Gordon.'" *China Weekly Review*, 24 September 1949. 46.

————. "The American Scene." *China Weekly Review*, 3 December 1949. 11-14.

————. "Good Government, Common Sense Needed in Administering Taiwan." *China Weekly Review*, 5 April 1947. 142-144.

————. "Reply to an Attack on the *China Weekly Review*." *China Weekly Review*, 25 March 1950. 54-55.

————. "China Cleans House." *China Monthly Review*, May 1952. 456-464.

Powell, John William. Editor. "Teachers' Salaries." *China Weekly Review*, 12 April 1947. 78-79.

————. "Student Demonstrators." *China Weekly Review*, 19 January 1946. 129.

————. "Students' Detractors." *China Weekly Review*, 26 January 1946. 145.

————. "Democratic Elections?" *China Weekly Review*, 16 March 1946. 48-49.

————. "China's Universities." *China Weekly Review*, 13 April 1946. 138-139.

_____. "Voice of Reaction Again." *China Weekly Review*, 4 May 1946.

_____. "The Death of a Journalist." *China Weekly Review*, 19 January 1946. 129.

_____. "Democratic League's Protest." *China Weekly Review*, 2 February 1946. 164-165.

_____. "Taiwan Travesty." *China Weekly Review*, 6 April 1946. 113.

_____. "Educational Reform." *China Weekly Review*, 18 May 1946. 247-248.

_____. "Political Assassination." *China Weekly Review*, 27 July 1946. 191-192.

_____. "The Legacy of Dr. Sun." *China Weekly Review*, 12 October 1946. 155.

_____. "China's New Constitution." *China Weekly Review*, 30 November 1946. 383.

_____. "The Kuomintang's Future." *China Weekly Review*, 18 January 1947. 187-188.

_____. "American 'Atrocities'." *China Weekly Review*, 25 January 1947. 213.

_____."Common Front or Eclipse?" *China Weekly Review*, 1 February 1947. 240-241.

_____."J. B. Powell Passes." *China Weekly Review*, 8 March 1947. 33-34.

_____. "Rioting in Taiwan." *China Weekly Review*, 8 March 1947. 34-35.

_____. "Armed Riots Spread." *China Weekly Review*, 5 April 1947. 138-139.

_____."Nanking Should Act." *China Weekly Review*, 12 April 1947. 165-166.

_____. "Taiwan's New Deal." *China Weekly Review*, 26 April 1947. 233.

_____. "Censorship in Taiwan." *China Weekly Review*, 10 May 1947. 285-286.

_____. "Taiwan in Trouble." *China Weekly Review*, 13 December 1947. 44-45.

_____. "An Independent Taiwan?" *China Weekly Review*, 18 September 1948. 56-57.

_____. "Dust in the Eyes." *China Weekly Review*, 9 October 1948. 133-134.

_____. "Taiwan Travel Restrictions." *China Weekly Review*, 23 October 1948. 200.

_____. "Crying for Peace." *China Weekly Review*, 24 May 1947. 340.

_____. "The Student Crisis." *China Weekly Review*, 24 May 1947. 41-343.

_____. "Freedoms Restricted." *China Weekly Review*, 31 May 194.

371.

———. "Crisis In China." *China Weekly Review*, 7 June 1947. 12.

———."China's Treaties and Laws." *China Weekly Review*, 5 April 1947. 137-138.

———."Court Behavior." *China Weekly Review*, 12 April 1947. 167.

———. "China's Courts." *China Weekly Review*, 3 May 1947. 257-259.

———."Perpetual Martial Law." *China Weekly Review*, 26 July 1947. 222.

———."Who's Kidding Who." *China Weekly Review*, 19 July 1947. 198.

———. "Dead Man's Tale." *China Weekly Review*, 29 November 1947. 403-404.

———. "Efforts of Thirty-Six Years." *China Weekly Review*, 11 October 1947. 163-165.

———. "Showdown in Indonesia." *China Weekly Review*, 29 March 1947. 113.

———. "Reforms in Taiwan." *China Weekly Review*, 15 March 1947. 59-60.

———. "War in Indonesia." *China Weekly Review*, 21 June 1947. 70-71.

———. "Blood on the Flag." *China Weekly Review*, 2 August 1947. 250-251.

———. "Independence Day." *China Weekly Review*, 28 June 1947. 99.

———. "'Rioting' Students." *China Weekly Review*, 7 February 1948. 279-280.

———. "Blessings of Colonialism." *China Weekly Review*, 26 June 1948. 100-101.

———. "Bullitt Fires Again." *China Weekly Review*, 17 January 1948. 194-195.

———. "Doubtful Logic." *China Weekly Review*, 13 November 1948. 227-228.

———. "Dutch at It Again." *China Weekly Review*, 25 December 1948. 83-84.

———. "American Dilemma." *China Weekly Review*, 4 December 1948. 7-10.

———. "America's China Policy." *China Weekly Review*, 6 November 1948. 249-251.

———. "Coalition Government." *China Weekly Review*, 18 December 1948. 69.

———. "Information Agencies." *China Weekly Review*, 2 February 1946. 163-164.

———. "Death of Tai Li." *China Weekly Review*, 30 March 1946. 91-92.

———. "The State Department's Unburied Dead." *China Weekly Re-*

view, 11 May 1946. 228.

————. "Diplomatic Pay." *China Weekly Review*, 13 April 1946. 138-139.

————. "U.S. Propaganda." *China Weekly Review*, 8 February 1947. 265.

————. "A Short Sighted Policy." *China Weekly Review*, 9 August 1947. 280-281.

————. "Who's Slanting What?" *China Weekly Review*, 31 January 1948. 254-255.

————. "Modern Espionage." *China Weekly Review*, 20 November 1948. 299-300.

————. "Fullbright Scholarships." *China Weekly Review*, 18 December 1948. 52-53.

————. "The Scorched Earth Policy." *China Weekly Review*, 11 December 1948. 85-86.

————. "What About Shanghai?" *China Weekly Review*, 11 December 1948. 30-31.

————. "After the Interim Period." *China Weekly Review*, 25 December 1948. 81-82.

————. "The War Will Go On." *China Weekly Review*, 29 January 1949. 208.

————. "Where Will Nanking Go?" *China Weekly Review*, 15 January 1949. 161.

————. "Day of Reckoning." *China Weekly Review*, 1 January 1949. 105-106.

————. "Irresponsible Behavior." *China Weekly Review*, 9 April 1949. 125.

————. "Abundance for All." *China Weekly Review*, 9 April 1949. 123.

————. "Postwar Development." *China Weekly Review*, 5 February 1949. 237-238.

————. "China's Untapped Power." *China Weekly Review*, 12 February 1949. 263-264.

————. "Ten Million Houses." *China Weekly Review*, 12 March 1949. 30-31.

————. "What Is Communist Policy?" *China Weekly Review*, 26 February 1949. 308.

————. "Misplaced Emphasis." *China Weekly Review*, 4 June 1949. 9-10.

————. "Shanghai's Foreign Press." *China Weekly Review*, 25 June 1949. 70.

————. "The Same Old Pattern." *China Weekly Review*, 18 June 1949. 50.

————. "Realistic Approach." *China Weekly Review*, 25 June 1949. 72-73.

_____. "The Fourth of July." *China Weekly Review*, 2 July 1949. 93-94.

_____. "The Evacuation Ship." *China Weekly Review*, 27 August 1949. 228.

_____. "Two Policies." *China Weekly Review*, 3 September 1949. 2.

_____. "World's Richest Refugees." *China Weekly Review*, 24 September 1949. 44.

_____. "What Will America Do?" *China Weekly Review*, 15 October 1949. 92.

_____. "Definition of Government." *China Weekly Review*, 29 October 1949. 128-129.

_____. "Another Hole in Blockade." *China Weekly Review*, 22 October 1949. 110.

_____. "Are We Objective?" *China Weekly Review*, 29 October 1949. 124.

_____. "U.S. Trade Ban Hits China." *China Weekly Review*, 19 November 1949. 180-181.

_____. "U.S. Trade Ban Will Not Cripple China." *China Weekly Review*, 10 December 1949. 23-24.

_____. "America's Best Interests." *China Weekly Review*, 31 December 1949. 66-67.

_____. "How Much Longer?" *China Weekly Review*, 14 January 1950. 102-103.

_____. "U.S. Diplomatic Dispute." *China Weekly Review*, 28 January 1950. 134-135.

_____. "The Last Act on Taiwan." *China Weekly Review*, 17 June 1950. 38-39.

_____. "Practical Politics." *China Weekly Review*, 1 July 1950. 74-75.

_____. "Anti-Communist Laws." *China Weekly Review*, 24 June 1950. 56-57.

_____. "People Must Fight for Peace." *China Weekly Review*, 8 July 1950. 92-93.

_____. "The Lesson of Korea." *China Weekly Review*, 15 July 1950. 110.

_____. "*Review* to Close." *China Weekly Review*, 15 July 1950. 110.

_____. "Public Health Drive." *China Weekly Review*, 15 July 1950. 111-112.

_____. "Peace Can Still Be Won." *China Weekly Review*, 29 July 1950. 146-147.

_____. "*Review* to Continue." *China Weekly Review*, 5 August 1950. 164.

_____. "The Month in Review, Thought Reform." *China Monthly Review*, February 1952. 120-122.

_____. "The Month in Review, Crime Against Humanity." *China Monthly Review*, March 1952. 226-227.

_____. "Germ Warfare, A Sign of Desperation." *China Monthly Review*, April 1952. 324-331.

_____. "The Month in Review, U.S. Germ War Fully Proven." *China Monthly Review*, May 1952. 424-425.

_____. "Most Health Conscious Nation on Earth." *China Monthly Review*, September 1952. 211.

_____. Interview with Wilfred Burchett "Why U.S. POW's Admit Using Germ Warfare." *China Monthly Review*, November-December 1952. 443-448.

_____. "Review to Close After Next Issue." *China Monthly Review*, June 1953. 2-3.

_____. "Report to Readers." *China Monthly Review*, July 1953. 132. "Renovation of N.Chekiang Road Gaol." *North China Daily News*, 17 May 1947. 3. "Report of the International Scientific Commission for the Investigation of the Facts Concerning Bacteriological Warfare in Korea and China," Supplement, *People's China*, 17 September 1952.

Roth, Andrew. "The French Aren't French in Indochina." *China Weekly Review* 7 February 1948. 290-291.

_____. "Indochina's Puppet Politics." *China Weekly Review* 21 February 1948. 349-350.

_____. "The French Are Fighting Maquis." *China Weekly Review* 28 February 1948. 376-377.

Schuman, Julian. "The Last Act on Taiwan." *China Weekly Review*, 25 February 1950. 189-191.

_____. "The Voice of America." *China Weekly Review*, 27 May 1950. 222.

Schwable, Colonel Frank H. Deposition. In: "Proof of Germ Warfare, Statements of Captured U.S. Marine Corps Officers." *China Monthly Review*, May 1953. 92-99.

Service, John S. *Lost Chance in China: The World War II Dispatches of John S. Service*. Ed. Joseph W. Esherick. New York: Random House, 1974.

_____. *The Amerasia Papers: Some Problems in History of U.S.-China Relations*. Berkley: University of California Press, 1971.

Service, John S. ed. *Golden Inches, The China Memoir of Grace Service*. Berkley: University of California Press, 1989.

Shih, H.Y. "Learning from the Peasants." *China Weekly Review*, 27 May 1950. 220-221.

Snow, Edgar. *Journey to the Beginning*. New York: Random House, 1958.

Snow, Helen Foster. *My China Years: A Memoir*. New York: William Morrow and company, Inc., 1984.

Song, Datu. translator, "Communication Between Mao and Stalin: Seven Telegrams, January, 1949." *Chinese Historians, Volume 7* (Spring 1994): 163-172.

———."Statements by Two American Air Force Officers, Kenneth Loyd
Enoch and John Quinn, Admitting Their Participation in Germ
Warfare in Korea and Other Documents." Supplement. *People's
China*, 16 May 1952. 1-15
Stuart, John Leighton. *Fifty Years in China*. New York: Random House,
1954.
Tao, Wei-lien. "Land Reform Begins in the Liberated Areas." *China
Weekly Review*, 22 October 1950. 111-113.
———. "U.S. Trade Ban Will Not Cripple China." *China Weekly Re-
view*, 10 December 1950. 23-25.
———. "Foreign Relief and China's Famine." *China Weekly Review*,
22 April 1950. 126-128.
———. "Western Press Distorts China News." *China Weekly Review*,
17 June 1950. 44-46.
Wang, Peter S. "Kunming Killings May Herald Reign of Terror in China."
China Weekly Review, 27 July 1946. 200.
Willmott, Earl. "New Deal at Christian University." *China Weekly Re-
view*, 8 April 1950. 91-92.
———. "New Democracy on the Campus." *China Weekly Review*, 1
July 1950. 77.
———. "A Chengtu Diary." *China Weekly Review*, 4 March 1950. 8-
12.
Zhe, Shi. "With Mao and Stalin: The Reminiscences of a Chinese Inter-
preter," Translated by Chen Jian, *Chinese Historians, Volume 5*
(Spring 1992): 35-46
Zhang, Shuguang and Chen, Jian. eds. *Chinese Communist Foreign Policy
and the Cold War in Asia, New Documentary Evidence, 1944-
1950*. Chicago: Imprint Publications, 1996.

Government and United Nations Documents

Congressional Quarterly Service, *China and U.S. Far East Policy, 1945-
1967*. Washington: United States Government Printing Office,
1969.
*Materials on the Trial of Former Servicemen of the Japanese Army
Charged with Manufacturing and Employing Bacteriological
Weapons*. Moscow: Foreign Languages Publishing House, 1950.
United Nations, General Assembly, *Official Records*.
———. Security Council, Official Records.
United Stated of America, Plaintiff, V John William Powell, Sylvia Camp-
bell Powell, and Julian Schuman, defendants. No. 35065. United
States District Court, N.D. California, S. D. February 3, 1959.
Federal Supplement, Volume 171, *Cases Argued Determined in
the United States District Courts, United States Court of Claims
and the United States Customs Court*. ST. Paul: West Publishing

Co., 1961.

United Stated of America, Plaintiff, V John William Powell, Sylvia Campbell Powell, and Julian Schuman, Defendants. No. 35065. United
States District Court, N.D. California, S. D. 1961. *Federal Supplement, Volume 260, Cases Argued and Determined in the United
States District Courts, United States Court of Claims and the
United States Customs Court*. St. Paul: West Publishing Co.,
1961.

United States Congress, House of Representatives, Committee on Foreign
Affairs, 81st Congress, 2nd Session, *Report, Foreign Policy of the
United States on the Far East*. Washington: United States Govern-
ment Printing Office, 1950.

United States Congress, House of Representatives, Committee on Foreign
Affairs, 80th Congress 2nd Session, February, 1948, *Hearings on
United States Foreign Policy for a Postwar Recovery Program*,
2076-92.

United States Congress, House of Representatives, Committee on Foreign
Affairs, Subcommittee No. 5, *Report, The Strategy and Tactics of
World Communism*, Supplement III. Washington D.C.: United
States Government Printing Office, 1948.

United States Congress, Senate, The Committee on Armed Services and
the Committee on Foreign Relations, 82nd Congress, 1st Session,
Joint Hearings on the Military Situation in the Far East. Washington: United States Government Printing Office, 1951.

United States Congress, Senate, Committee on Foreign Relations, *Hear-
ings on State Department Employee Loyalty Investigation*, 81st
Congress, 2nd Session. Washington: United States Government
Printing Office, 1950.

United States Congress, Senate, Committee on the Judiciary, 82nd congress, 2nd Session, *Hearings on the Institute of Pacific Relations*,
Parts 1-14 and *Report No. 2050*. Washington: United States Government Printing Office, 1952.

United States Congress, Senate, Committee on the Judiciary, 83rd Con-
gress, 2nd Session, Subcommittee to Investigate the Administra-
tion of the Internal Security Act and Other Internal Security Laws,
Hearings, Interlocking Subversion in Government Departments.
Testimony of John William Powell. Washington: United States
Government Printing Office, 1954. (September, 1954) 1819-2018.

United States Congress, Senate, Committee on the Judiciary, 83rd Con-
gress, 2nd Session, Subcommittee to Investigate the Administra-
tion of the Internal Security Act and Other Internal Security Laws,
Hearings, Interlocking Subversion in Government Departments.
Testimony of Sylvia Campbell Powell. Washington: United States
Government Printing Office, 1954. (December, 1954)

United States Congress, Senate, Committee on the Judiciary, 84th Con-

gress, 2nd Session, Subcommittee to Investigate the Administration of the Internal Security Act and Other Internal Security Laws,
Hearings, Scope of Soviet Activity in the United States, Testimony
of Julian Schuman. Washington: United States Government Printing Office, 1956. (March, 1956) 515-550.

United States Consulate General, *Survey of China Mainland Press*. Hong
Kong: U.S. Consulate General, 1950-1977.

United States Consulate General, *Survey of China Mainland Press, Supplements*. Hong Kong: U. S. Consulate General, 1950-1977.

Unites States Department of State, *Bulletin*. Washington: United State
Government Printing Office.

United States Department of State, *Foreign Relations of the Unites States,
Diplomatic Papers, 1948, Volume 7, The Far East: China*. Washington: United States Government Printing Office, 1973.

United States Department of State, *Foreign Relations of the Unites States,
Diplomatic Papers, 1948, Volume 8, The Far East: China*. Washington: United States Government Printing Office, 1973.

United States Department of State, *Foreign Relations of the Unites States,
Diplomatic Papers, 1949, Volume 8, The Far East: China*. Washington: United States Government Printing Office, 1978.

United States Department of State, *Foreign Relations of the Unites States,
Diplomatic Papers, 1949, Volume 9, The Far East: China*. Washington: United States Government Printing Office, 1974.

United States Department of State, *Foreign Relations of the Unites States,
Diplomatic Papers, 1952-1954, Volume 15, Korea, Part 1*. Washington: United States Government Printing Office, 1984.

United States Department of State, *Foreign Relations of the Unites States,
Diplomatic Papers, 1952-1954, Volume 15, Korea, Part 2*. Washington: United States Government Printing Office, 1984.

United States Department of State, *Foreign Relations of the Unites States,
Diplomatic Papers, 1952-1954, Volume 15, Korea, Part 2*. Washington: United States Government Printing Office, 1984.

United States Department of States, *Transcript of Round Table Discussion
on America Policy Toward China*. Washington: United States
Government Printing Office, 1949.

Unites States Department of State, *United States Relations With China
With Special Reference to the Period 1944-1949*. Washington:
United States Government Printing Office, 1949.

United States v. John William Powell, Sylvia Powell, and Julian Schuman,
Title 18 U.S. Code 2388-Seditious Activities Affecting Armed
Forces During War, *Criminal Docket and Proceedings* (April 25,
1956 to May 2, 1961, Comprising 178 Filed Motions, Subpoenas,
Orders, etc.), United States District Court, Northern District of
California.

Van Slyke, Lyman P. ed. *The Chinese Communist Movement: A Report of* the Unites States War Department, July 1945. Stanford: Stanford University Press, 1968.

_____. *Marshall's Mission to China, December 1945-January 1947: The Report and Appended Documents*. Two Volumes. Arlington, Va.: University Publications of America, 1976.

White, Theodore. *In Search of History: A Personal Adventure*. New York: Warner Books, 1978.

_____. *Thunder Out of China*. New York: William Sloan Associates, Inc., 1946.

Newspapers and Periodicals

Amerasia
China Digest (Hong Kong)
China Monthly Review (Shanghai)
China Press (Shanghai)
China Weekly Review (Shanghai)
Collier's
Life
London Times
Nation
New Republic
New York Times
North China Daily News (Shanghai)
Pacific Affairs
People's China (Peking)
San Francisco Chronicle
Shanghai Evening Post and Mercury
Unites States Department of State Bulletin
Washington Post

Secondary Sources

Books

Alley, Rewi. *Six American in China*. Beijing: International Cultural Publishing Corporation, 1985.

Bailey, P.J. *China in the Twentieth Century*. New York: Basil Blackwell, 1988.

Barnett, A. Doak. *Communist China and Asia*. New York: Harper: For the Council on Foreign Relations, 1960.

Kim, Chull Baum and Matray, James I. eds. *Korea and the Cold War, Division, Destruction, and Disarmament*. Claremont: Regina Books, 1963.

Biderman, Albert D. *March to Calumney, the Story of America POWs in the Korean War*. New York: The Macmillan Company, 1963.

Borg, Dorothy and Heinricks, Waldo. eds. *Uncertain Years, Chinese-American Relations, 1947-1950*. New York: Columbia University Press, 1980.

Chang, Tsan-Kuo. *The Press and China Policy: The Illusion of Sino-American Relations, 1950-1984*. Norwood, N.J.: Ablex Publishing Corporation, 1993.

Chan, Theodore Hsi-en. *Thought Reform of the Chinese Intellectuals*. London: Oxford University Press, 1960.

Chiu, Hungdah. ed. *China and the Taiwan Issue*. New York: Praeger, 1979.

_____. *China and the Question of Taiwan, Documents and Analysis*. New York: Praeger, 1973.

Cohen, Warren. *America's Response to China*. New York: John Wiley and Sons, 1971.

Cotton, James and Neary, Ian. eds. *The Korean War in History*. Manchester: Manchester University Press, 1989.

Cowdrey, Albert E. *The United States Army in the Korean War, The Medics' War*. Washington: United States Army Center for Military History, 1987.

Cumings, Bruce. *The Origins of the Korean War, Volume II, The Roaring of the Ctaract, 1947-1950*. Princeton: Princeton University Press, 1990.

Clubb, Edmund O. *China and Russia, The "Great Game"*. New York: Columbia University Press, 1971.

_____. *The International Position of Communist China, Background Papers and Proceedings of the Fifth Hammarskjold Forum*. Dobbs Ferry, N.Y.: Oceana Publication, Inc., 1965.

_____. *Twentieth Century China*. New York: Columbia University Press, 1972.

Dulles, Foster Rhea. *American Policy Toward Communist China, 1949-1969*. New York: Thomas Y. Crowell Company, 1972.

Eastman, Lloyd E. *Seeds of Destruction: Nationalist China in War and Revolution, 1937-1949*. Stanford: Stanford University Press, 1984.

_____. *The Abortive Revolution, China Under Nationalist Rule, 1927-1937*. Cambridge: council on East Asian Studies, Harvard University Press, 1990.

Endicott, Stephen and Hagerman, Edward. *The United States and Biological Warfare, Secrets from the Early Cold War and Korea*. Bloomington: Indiana University Press, 1998.

Evans, Paul M. *John Fairbank and the American Understanding of Modern China*. New York: Basil Blackwell Ltd., 1988.

Fairbank, John King. *China Perceived, Images and Policies in China-American Relations*. New York: Alfred A. Knopf, 1974.

_____. *China Watch*. Cambridge: Harvard University Press, 1987.

_____. *China, The People's Middle Kingdom and the U.S.A.* Cambridge: The Belknap Press of the Harvard University Press, 1967.

_____. *The United States and China*. Cambridge: Harvard University Press, 1983.

Fairbank, John K. ed. *The Cambridge History of China, Volume 12, Republican China 1912-1949, Part 1*. Cambridge, G.B.: Cambridge University Press, 1983.

Fairbanks, John K. and Feuerwerker, Albert. eds. *The Cambridge History of China, Volume 13, Republican China 1912-1949, Part 2*. Cambridge, G.B.: Cambridge University Press, 1983.

Fairbank John K. and MacFarquhar, Roderick. eds. *The Cambridge History of China, Volume 14, The People's Republic, Part 1: The Emergence of Revolutionary China 1949-1965*. G.B.: Cambridge University Press, 1987.

Garson, Robert. *The United States and China Since 1949, A Trouble Affair*. Madison: Fairleigh Dickson University Press, 1994.

Gold, Hal. *Unit 731 Testimony*. Tokyo: Yenbooks, 1996.

Goldman, Merle. *Literary Dissent in Communist China*. Cambridge: Harvard University Press, 1967.

Goldstein, Jonathan; Israel, Jerry; and Conroy, Hilary. eds. *America views China, American Images of China Then and Now*. London: Lehigh University Press, 1991.

Goodman, Walter. *The Committee, The Extraordinary Career of the House Committee on Un-American Activities*. New York: Farrar Straus and Giroux, 1968.

Grass, June M. *Truman's Two-China Policy, 1948-1950*. New York: M.E. Sharpe, Inc., 1987.

Gregor, A. James. *The China Connection, U.S. Policy and the People's Republic of China*. Stanford: Hoover Institution Press, 1986.

Gupta, D. C. *United States' Attitude Towards China*. New Delhi: S. Chand and Company, 1969.

Hamilton, John M. *Edgar Snow: A Biography*. Bloomington: Indiana University Press, 1989.

Harding, Harry and Ming, Yuan. eds. *Sino-American Relations, 1945-1955, A Joint Reassessment of a Critical Decade*. Wilmington: Scholarly Resources Books, 1989.

Harris, Sheldon H. *Factories of Death, Japanese Biological Warfare 1932-1945 And the American Cover-up*. New York: Routledge, 1994.

Howe, C. ed. Shanghai: *Revolution and Development in an Asian Metropolis*. Cambridge, G.B.: Cambridge University Press, 1981.

Iriye, Akira. *The Cold War in Asia: A Historical Introduction*. Englewood Cliffs, N.J.: Prentice-Hall, 1974.

Jaffee, Phillip J. *New Frontiers in Asia: A Challenge to the West*. New York: Alfred A. Knopf, 1945.

_____. *The Rise and Fall of American Communism*. New York: Horizen Press, 1975.

_____. *The American Case, 1945 to the Present*. New York: Jaffee, 1979.

Johnson, Chalmeers. *Communist Policies Toward the Intellectual Class*. Hong Kong: Union Research Institute, 1959.

Kahn, E. J. Jr. *The China Hands, American's Foreign Service Officers and What Befell Them*. New York: Penguin Books, 1975.

Kinkead, E. *In Every War But One*. New York: Norton, 1959.

Klein, Donald W. and Clark, Anne B. *Biographic Dictionary of Chinese Communism 1921-1965*. 2 Volumes. Cambridge: Harvard University Press, 1971.

Koen, Ross Y. *The China Lobby in American Politics*. New York: Octagon Books, 1974.

Kutler, Statley I. *The American Inquisition, Justice and Injustice in the Cold War*. New York; Hill and Wang, 1982.

Lai, Tse-Han; Myers, Ramon H.; and Wei Wou, *A Tragic Beginning, The Taiwan Upraising of February 28, 1947*. Stanford: Stanford University Press, 1991.

Leitenberg, Milton. *The Korean War: Biological Warfare Resolved*. Stockholm: Stockholm International Peace Research Institute, 1998.

Levine, Steven I. *Anvil of Victory, The Communist Revolution in Manchuria, 1945-1948*. New York: Thomas Y. Crowell Company, 1972.

Lifton, Robert Jay. *Thought Reform and the Psychology of Totalism: A Study of "Brainwashing" in China*. New York: Norton, 1950.

Lindsay, Michael. *China and the Cold War*. Melbourne University Press. 1955.

_____. *Educational Problems in Communist China*, New York: Institute of Pacific Relations, 1950.

_____. *Is Peaceful Coexistence Possible?* Anarbor: Michigan State University Press, 1960.

_____. *The New China: Three Views with Otto Van der Sprenkel and Robert Guillaine*. London: Turnstile Press, 1950.

Liu, Alan P.L. ed. *The Press and Journals in Communist China*. Cambridge: Center For International Studies, Massachusetts Institute of Technology, 1966.

Loh, Pichon P. Y. ed. *The Koumintang Debacle of 1949, Conquest or Collapse?* Boston: Heath and Company, 1965.

Martin, Edwin A. *Divided Councel, the Anglo-American Response to Communist Victory in China*. Lexington: The University Press of Kentucky, 1986.

MacCarthy, Joseph R. *America's Retreat from Victory*. New York: the Devin-Adair Co., 1951.

Middleton, Harry J. *The Compact History of the Korean War*. New York:

Hawthorne Books, Inc., 1965.

Newman, Robert P. *Recognition of Communist China? A Study in Argument*. New York: The Macmillan Company, 1961.

Parker, Elliot S. and Parker, Emelia M. *Asian Journalism: A Selected Bibliography of Sources on Journalism in China and Southeast Asia*. Metuchen: Scarecrow Press, 1979.

Pepper, Suzanne. *Civil War in China: The Political Struggle, 1945-1949*. Berkeley: University of California Press, 1978.

Ress, David. *A Short History of Modern Korea*. New York: Hippocrene Books, 1988.

Simmons, Robert R. *The Strained Alliance: Peking, P'yongyang, Moscow and the Policies of the Korean War*. New York: The Free Press, 1975.

Shewmaker, Kenneth E. *American and Chinese Communists, 1927-1945: A Persuading Encounter*. Itaica: Cornell University Press, 1971.

Steele, A. T. *The American People and China*. New York: McGraw-Hill Book Co., 1966.

Tang, Tsou. *America's Failure in China, 1941-1950*. Chicago: University of Chicago Press, 1963.

Tucker, Nancy Bernkopf. *Patterns in the dust: Chinese-American Relations and the Recognition Controversy, 1949-1950*. New York: Columbia University Press, 1983.

Vogel, Ezra F. *Canton Under Communism: Programs and Policies in a Provincial Capital, 1949-1968*. Cambridge: Harvard University press, 1969.

Varg, Paul A. *Missionaries, Chinese, and Diplomats, The American Protestant Missionary Movement in China, 1890-1952*. Princeton: Princeton University Press, 1958.

Whiting, Allen S. *China Crosses the Yalu: The Decision to Enter the Korean War*. Stanford: Stanford University Press, 1968.

Williams, Peter and Wallace, David. *Unit 731, The Japanese Army's Secret of Secrets*. London: Hodder and Stroughton, 1989.

Articles

Ballou, Earl H. "China Since 1949." *Social Action*, Vol. 26 (March, 1960).

Chen, Jian. "The Myth of America's 'Lost Chance' in China: A Chinese Perspective in Light of New Evidence." *Diplomatic History*, Volume 21, no. 1 (winter, 1997).

Cheng, J. Chester. "The Korean War Through Chinese Eyes: China Crosses the Rubicon." *Journal of Oriental Studies*, Volume 31, no.1 (1993).

Chiu, Hunduh. "Constitutional Development in the Republic of China in Taiwan." *In the Shadow of China, Political developments in Tai-*

wan since 1949. Steve Tsang ed. Honolulu: University of Hawaii
    Press, 1993.
Cohen, Warren I. "Symposium: Rethinking and Ideologies." *Diplomatic
    History*, Volume 21, no. 1 (Winter 1997).
Garver, John W. "Little Chance, Revolutions and Ideologies." *Diplomatic
    History*, Volume 21, no. 1 (Winter 1997).
Lindsay, Michael. "Post Mortem on American Mediation in China." *In-
    ternational Journal*, Volume 2, (Summer, 1997).
Moon, John Ellis van Courtland. "Dubious Allegations, The United States
    and Biological Warfare: Secrets from the Early Cold War and
    Korea," *The Bulletin of the Atomic Scientists*, May-June, 1999.
    70-72.
Schein, Edger H. "The Chinese Indoctrination Program for Prisoners of
    War." *Psychiatry*, Volume 19, no 2, (May, 1956).
Tozer, Warren W. "The Last Bridge to China: The Shanghai Power Com-
    pany, the Truman Administration, and the Chinese Communists."
    Diplomatic History, Volume 1, no. 1 (Winter 1977).
Tucker, Nancy Bernkopf. "An Unlikely Peace: American Missionaries and
    the Chinese Communists, 1948-1950." *Pacific Historical Review*,
    Volume 45 (February, 1976).
Westad, Odd Anne. "Losses, Chances and Myths: The United States and
    the Creation of the Sino-Soviet Alliance, 1945-1950." *Diplomatic
    History*, Volume 21 no.1 (Winter, 1997).

Dissertations and Masters Theses

Chang, Su-ya. "Pragmatism and Opportunism: Truman's Policy Toward
    Taiwan, 1949-1952". Ph.D. dissertation, Pennsylvania State Uni-
    versity, 1989.
Chao, Ena. "The China Bloc: Congress and the Making of Foreign Policy,
    1947-1952." Ph.D. dissertation, 1991.
Chen, Jian. "China's Road to the Korean War: A Critical Study of the Ori-
    gins of Sino-American confrontation, 1949-1950." Ph.D. disserta-
    tion, Southern Illinois University at Carbondale, 1990.
Chiba, Hiromi. "From Enemy to Ally: American Public Opinion and Per-
    ception about Japan, 1945-1950." Ph.D. dissertation, University
    of Hawaii, 1992.
Deng, Peng. "China's Crisis and Revolution Through American Lenses,
    1945-1949." Ph.D. dissertation, Washington State University,
    1990.
Exon, Karen Hunt. "Fortress America: The U.S. Senate and the Great De-
    bate of 1950-1951." Ph.D. dissertation, University of Kansas,
    1990.
Huo, Hwei-Ling. "A Study of the Chinese Decision to Intervene in the Ko-
    rean War." Ph.D. dissertation, Columbia University, 1989.

Kennedy, Thomas L. "The Treatment of Americans in Red China Prior to the Korean War: A Study of Selected Cases." M.A. thesis, Georgetown University, 1961.

Kim, Gye-dong. "Western Intervention in Korea, 1950-1954." Ph.D. dissertation, University of Oxford (U.K.), 1989.

Kim, Myung Jun. "Coverage of the Korean War by the *New York Times* and *Asahi Shinbun*: Foreign Policy as the Key Constraint on the War Reporting." Ph.D. dissertation, Temple University, 1992.

Kozlowski, Francis Xaviar. "Defiant Issue: Cold War Influence on United States Taiwan Policy, 1945-1952." Ph.D. dissertation, State University of New York at Binghamton, 1990.

Mann, William Alexander. "United States Policy Towards Asia, 1949-1950 and the Development of NSC 68." M.A. thesis, Michigan State University, 1990.

Marolda, Edward John. "The U.S. Navy and the Chinese Civil War, 1945-1952." Ph.D. dissertation, George Washington University, 1990.

Rosenberg, Victor Robert. "When the Weather Clears: Soviet-America Relations, 1953-1955." Ph.D. dissertation, Kent State University, 1990.

Weathersby, Kathryn. "Soviet Policy Toward Korea; 1944-1946." Ph.D. dissertation, Indiana University, 1990.

Index